RELIGION AND POLITICS IN JAMMU AND KASHMIR

This book examines the shifting, non-linear relationship between religion, nationalism and politics in the state of Jammu and Kashmir, India. In the wake of the revocation of Article 370, the state's plural and relatively harmonious society has come under multiple strains, with religion often informing day-to-day politics.

The chapters in this volume:

- Trace the formation of the political entity of Jammu and Kashmir and the seemingly secular politics of its three regions
- Discuss the rise of militancy and resistance movements in the Kashmir Valley
- Highlight the intersection between everyday life, nationalism and resistance through a study of the literary traditions of Kashmir, contemporary resistance photography and everyday communalism located in the changing food practices of Hindu and Muslim communities

Religion and Politics in Jammu and Kashmir will be an indispensable read for students and researchers of religion and politics, democratization and democracy, secularism, sociology, cultural studies and South Asian studies.

Reeta Chowdhari Tremblay is Professor of Comparative Politics and former Provost/ Vice-President Academic at the University of Victoria, Canada. Her research interests include identity-based politics, secessionist movements (Kashmir) in South Asia and the politics of subaltern resistance and accommodation in post-colonial societies. Her recent publications include *Kashmir Elections: A Precursor to 'No More Two Flags, Two Constitutions'* (2020); *Contested Governance, Competing Nationalisms, and Disenchanted Publics: Kashmir beyond Intractability?* (2018) and *Modi's Foreign Policy* (2017).

Mohita Bhatia is a postdoctoral fellow at the Centre for South Asia, Stanford University, California, USA. She was formerly Assistant Professor at the Centre for the Study of Discrimination and Exclusion, Jawaharlal Nehru University, Delhi, India. Her research interests include the ethnography of ethno-national conflicts, migration, refugees and border making. She is the author of *Retelling Conflict in Jammu and Kashmir: Marginal Hindu Communities and Politics in Jammu* (2020). She has published in journals such as *Asian Survey* and *Economic and Political Weekly*.

"Religion and Politics in Jammu and Kashmir is a collection of eleven essays written by thirteen scholars whose research on the area have been recognized internationally. The two editors, Reeta Chowdhari Tremblay and Mohita Bhatia have ensured consistency and a high level of academic standard. As the title suggests, religion is here at the heart of the discussion. The innovative and enlightening perspective, however, is that, with regard to the protracted Kashmir issue, religion is treated as a multifaceted and intersectional paradigm that is inherently articulated with politics, gender, class and region. This particular perspective sheds new light on the complex political history (histories) of this region. Religion and Politics in Jammu and Kashmir is indispensable for understanding the complex and dynamic identities presently at work in this contested region."

—**Mathieu Boisvert**, *Director, Centre d'études et de recherches sur l'Inde, l'Asie du Sud et sa diaspora, Université du Québec à Montréal (UQAM), Canada.*

"In this insightful and thought provoking discussion of the pluralistic Jammu and Kashmir society, the strict religion and secular/politics polarity is abandoned. Instead, in a nuanced manner, the volume points out that religion cannot be understood as a stand-alone analytical category but as one that is intertwined with other social categories. And the discussion of religion cannot be considered without taking into account how it is lived out in the daily lives of the people. The contributors explore local configuration in the state, and look at the manifold social, religious, regional, caste, and political factors and their complex interactions to analyze the processes of secularization, conflict resolution and peace."

—**Priyankar Upadhyaya**, *UNESCO Chair for Peace, Banaras Hindu University, India.*

"The significance of Tremblay and Bhatia's volume is that, from diverse conceptual points of entry, each chapter critically challenges the Enlightenment dogma of a religion-politics divide by applying intersectional methodologies to new, lived understandings of the Kashmir region. The virtue of this book is that in adopting intersectional and even coalitional methods of analysis, these essays avoid and challenge the worn-out discourse of identity politics. What phenomena of everyday life – secular or religious – shape identity? What alliances have been (or can be) forged across historical differences?

The intersections within and between religion, secularism, and politics are revealed by these authors to illuminate hitherto under-recognized alliances, exclusions, and solidarities in Kashmiri civic life and policy-making. Amidst global events of ultranationalism and the political weaponization or cultural insouciance towards religion, this volume reconsiders religion in and as part of identity. Tremblay and Bhatia have produced a fresh take on what religion has to do with identity, what politics has to do with secularity, and how mobilizing the recognition of difference is a constructive form of alliance."

—**Jennifer Dyer**, *Department Chair, Gender Studies and Humanities, Memorial University*

RELIGION AND POLITICS IN JAMMU AND KASHMIR

Edited by
Reeta Chowdhari Tremblay
and Mohita Bhatia

Routledge
Taylor & Francis Group

LONDON AND NEW YORK

First published 2021
by Routledge
2 Park Square, Milton Park, Abingdon, Oxon OX14 4RN

and by Routledge
52 Vanderbilt Avenue, New York, NY 10017

Routledge is an imprint of the Taylor & Francis Group, an informa business

British Library Cataloguing-in-Publication Data
A catalogue record for this book is available from the British Library

Library of Congress Cataloging-in-Publication Data
Names: Bhatia, Mohita, editor. | Tremblay, Reeta Chowdhary, editor.
Title: Religion and politics in Jammu and Kashmir / edited by Mohita
    Bhatia and Reeta Chowdhari Tremblay.
Description: Abingdon, Oxon ; New York, NY : Routledge, 2020. |
    Includes bibliographical references and index. |
Identifiers: LCCN 2020006641 (print) | LCCN 2020006642 (ebook) |
    ISBN 9781138307643 (hardback) | ISBN 9780367510688 (paperback) |
    ISBN 9781003052289 (ebook)
Subjects: LCSH: Religion and politics—India—Jammu and Kashmir. |
    Jammu and Kashmir (India)—Religion. | Jammu and Kashmir (India)—
    Politics and government. | India—Politics and government—1947–
Classification: LCC BL2015.P57 R45 2020 (print) | LCC BL2015.P57
    (ebook) | DDC 201'.7209546—dc23
LC record available at https://lccn.loc.gov/2020006641
LC ebook record available at https://lccn.loc.gov/2020006642

ISBN: 978-1-138-30764-3 (hbk)
ISBN: 978-0-367-51068-8 (pbk)
ISBN: 978-1-003-05228-9 (ebk)

Typeset in Bembo
by Apex CoVantage, LLC

CONTENTS

CONTRIBUTORS

Zehra Abrar is a graduate student at the Faculty of Law at University of Victoria, Canada. Her research focuses on "Human Rights violations committed by private military and security companies towards refugees". She has worked with the Red Cross Society Program, as well as the office of the former Bar President of the Kashmir Bar Association where she dealt with human rights cases in the Kashmir Valley.

Noor Ahmad Baba is Professor at the Central University of Kashmir, India. He has written extensively on South and West Asia. His present focus is Kashmir and South Asia with a peace research perspective. He has been a visiting professor at a number of universities and institutions including Indian Institute of Advance Studies, Simla, India; King Saud University, Riyadh, Saudi Arabia; King Abdul Aziz University, Jeddah, Saudi Arabia. In addition, he was a Fulbright Scholar at University of Massachusetts, USA.

Namitha George is a PhD student in Political Science at University of Victoria, Canada, with a focus in comparative politics. She has worked with research organizations and print media while pursuing her studies in India. Her research interests include nationalism, issues of international migration in South Asia, religion and identity politics.

Shahnawaz Gull is a PhD student at the University of Kashmir, India. His MPhil dissertation was a comparative analysis of Kashmir and Aland Islands autonomies. His doctoral project examines autonomy as a shared sovereignty tool for resolving identity-based conflict.

Nyla Khan is Professor at Rose State College, Midwest City, Oklahoma, USA. She has also been a visiting professor at the University of Oklahoma. Formerly, she was a professor at the University of Nebraska-Kearney, USA. She is the author of several books and essays including *Parchment of Kashmir* (2012), *Islam, Women, and Violence in Kashmir: Between Indian and Pakistan* (2010) and *Fiction of Nationality in an Era of Transnationalism* (2005). She is a member of the Harvard-based Scholars Strategy Network.

Chakraverti Mahajan is Assistant Professor in Anthropology at the University of Delhi, India. His research focuses on the Western Himalayas (especially Jammu and Kashmir and Himachal Pradesh), Delhi, and engages a broad range of ethnographic and theoretical issues including the politics of militarization, state–society relations, communalism and Hindu–Muslim relations, shifting practices of food, Sufism and shared sacred spaces, Islamic Law and property inheritance, visibility/invisibility of Muslims in urban spaces and Devta institutions. He has published in various journals, including *Economic and Political Weekly*, *Contributions to Indian Sociology*, *Sociological Bulletin*, and *Journal of Indian Anthropological Society*.

Sadaf Munshi is Associate Professor and Chair of the Linguistics Department at University of North Texas, USA. She does research in language documentation, historical linguistics, and language contact. Her most recent publication is *Burushaski Language Resource* – a digital collection of documentation materials in the Burushaski language housed at the Digital Collections Library of the University of North Texas.

Aijaz Ashraf Wani is Senior Assistant Professor at the Department of Political Science, University of Kashmir, India. He is the author of *What Happened to Governance in Kashmir?* (2019). His research interests include governance, peace, and conflict studies. In 2013, he was the recipient of the US Government funded fellowship, Study of the US Institute for Scholars. For his projects on Kashmir and governance, he has received funding from ICSSR and CSDS, New Delhi, India.

Andrew M. Wender is Assistant Teaching Professor in the Departments of Political Science and History, University of Victoria, Canada, where he also contributes to teaching in the Religious Studies programme. His teaching and research interests include historical and contemporary intersections among politics, society, law and religion; Middle East politics and history; political theory within historical as well as comparative contexts. His work has appeared in journals, edited volumes, and online venues such as *Implicit Religion; Capitalism, Nature, Socialism; Digest of Middle East Studies; Sociology of Islam; Middle East Conflicts & Reforms; The Middle East: New Order or Disorder; Telosscope;* and *Middle East Media and Book Reviews Online*.

Andrew Whitehead is Honorary Professor at the University of Nottingham, England, UK, and an associate editor of *History Workshop Journal*. He is the author of *A Mission in Kashmir* (2007) and *The Lives of Freda: The Political, Spiritual and Personal Journeys of Freda Bedi* (2019). He established and moderates the site Kashmir-Connected, intended as a resource for historians of Kashmir: kashmirconnected.com

Tabzeer Yaseen is Assistant Professor, Political Science, at Government College for Women, Srinagar, Jammu and Kashmir, India. Her research interests include Muslim feminism, gender studies, and Jammu and Kashmir politics.

ACKNOWLEDGEMENTS

It is Rekha Chowdhary who was responsible for the initial conceptualization of this volume to explore the complex theme of religion and politics in Jammu and Kashmir – a topic generally avoided by the scholarly community due to the different, and often sharp, sensibilities pertaining to nation-building, nationalism and secularism. She actively recruited most of the contributors for this edited book. Unfortunately, she had to withdraw from the project for personal reasons. Thank you, Rekha, for getting us going on this important initiative! Our heartiest and sincere thanks to Mike Tremblay for his careful and thorough text editing. We would like to express our gratitude to Aakash Chakrabarty, Senior Commissioning Editor at Routledge who has waited patiently for us to complete this manuscript. And, finally we extend our thanks to the production team at Routledge. We would like to dedicate this edited volume to Harbans Chowdhari (father to Reeta and Rekha) who passed away on 11 August 2019. He would have loved to read our discussion and appreciate the diversity of approaches with which the authors have treated the theme of religion and politics. Harbans Chowdhari, who was born in Kotli-Mirpur (now part of Pakistan-administered Kashmir) and lived his youth in Poonch, moved to Srinagar and Jammu after 1947. His keen interest in the subaltern history of the Poonch region was a constant reminder to us that we cannot neglect the ordinary, the average, the everyday lives in the new past-colonial geography of Jammu and Kashmir. And that we must read the complex history and politics of Jammu and Kashmir against the grain. We hope this edited volume in some small way captures his commitment to the secular Kashmir project and the processes of secularization.

1

SETTING THE CONTEXT

Religion, secularism and secularization – diversities in Jammu and Kashmir

Reeta Chowdhari Tremblay and Mohita Bhatia

This edited volume invites a conversation among scholars on the dynamic and fluid interaction between religion, secularism, secularization and the social processes which work their way through society within a localized context in the Indian state of Jammu and Kashmir (1947–2019). The Kashmir conflict, stretching across a seven-decade period, is intertwined with Kashmir's political history of a contested relationship with the Indian state and its kin state Pakistan. Competing narratives of nationalism have dominated in its three religious/linguistically divided regions. Religion and region have played significant roles in the varied, often opposed self-perceptions of marginalization among the state's Hindus, Muslims and Buddhists.

While there is an abundance of scholarly studies on the Kashmir conflict, these analyses are generally framed around the issues of identity, the political and structural roots of the conflict and governance and nationalism. Religion is often discussed as if it entailed qualitatively static phenomena and/or, to use Humeira Iqtidar and Tanika Sarkar's term, in a quantitative manner, tracing an increase or a decrease in religiosity. Thus some speak about the Kashmir conflict as a religious conflict, others present it as the communalization of a political dispute and yet others refer to monolithic religious identities – Islamic or Hindu ideologies. However, the deeper, fuzzy, interactive and intersecting relationship between religion and socio-political categories remains virtually unexplored.

In this edited volume, we would like to complicate the Kashmir question by recognizing that the social, political and religious do not operate as distinct domains. Rather than the straightforward thesis of 'increase or decline of religion', a more complicated and entwined relationship is envisioned among religious, secular, public and private spaces. We must pay attention to the non-linear interaction of the religious and political spheres of life. In this regard, we find that the processes associated with secularism and secularization provide us a useful guide in understanding the conflict from three different lenses: exploring the historical roots of socially and politically constructed identity categories; investigating how relative power and subordination attach to different intersecting identities; and relating everyday religiosity and the emergence of nationalism from below. As this volume was written before the August 5th decision, our discussion does not take into account either the rationale of the Modi government's decision and the processes accompanying it or the events following it.

The 2013 special issue of the *Economic and Political Weekly* initiated a fruitful discussion on the issues of religiosity, secularism and secularization. Iqtidar and Sarkar in their insightful edited book, *Tolerance, Secularization and Democratic Politics in South Asia* take this debate further. Their discussion is useful from the point of view of understanding the influences and interaction between religion, the secular and secularization. Nevertheless, it is also helpful in thinking about how to get out of the Kashmir conundrum. We believe that we are most probably going to witness the cycle of repression, violence and the already shrunk democratic spaces in the wake of the August 2019 decision to change the political status of the state. We are interested in exploring how we might advance the political project of democracy in this conflict-driven region of India.

We keep central to our discussion the caution that Iqtidar and Sarkar propose in defining religion. For them, there cannot be a universal definition of religion. Not only because its constituent elements and relationships are historically specific, but also because any definition of religion is itself a product of historical processes. This makes it impossible to demarcate or neatly define the social, political and the religious categories 'without reference to each other'. Historical processes, the socio-political context and local dynamics matter, producing both variation and a non-linear interactive and an intersectional relationship between religion and other social and political categories such as region, class and gender. Not only are the boundaries between secularism (a state and ideological project), secularization (social processes), and religion fuzzy and difficult to capture, but the presence of nationalism further complicates situating the boundaries between religion and secularization. Religion remains neglected in the modernist literature on nationalism, the result of what Brubaker calls 'a secularist bias', obscuring 'interesting connections and affinities between religion and nationalism' (2012, 15). We maintain that religion is intertwined with nationalism. In the case of Jammu and Kashmir, religious and national boundaries often coincide. Moreover, religion as a mode of identification, as a mode of social organization and as a way of framing political aims 'supplies myths, metaphors and symbols that are central to the discursive or iconic representation of the nation' (2012, 8).

The protracted conflict in the state along with the multiplicity of stakeholders complicates both the recognition and understanding of the influences and interaction between religious and secular on the one hand, and secular and secularization on the other. This book project is not about religion but it is an attempt to reflect upon the complexities of identities, including religious identity, and upon their interaction with institutions, both political and social. We also do not view religion as a unitary or universal category, since its constituent elements are historically specific. This *foundational intersectionality*, drilling 'down to the historical roots of socially constructed identity categories',[1] also enables us to investigate how relative power and subordination attach to different intersecting identities (Wordsworth, 2011, 204).

The former state of Jammu and Kashmir, with its three distinct linguistic and religious communities, was a relatively recent political and geographical entity whose origin can be traced to the March 1846 Treaty of Amritsar between the British and the Sikhs. On October 26, 1947, the maharaja of Jammu and Kashmir acceded to India. On August 5, 2019, the state was split into two Union Territories – Jammu and Kashmir (with a legislature) and Ladakh (without a legislature). The Kashmiri speaking Valley has a 97.2 per cent Muslim population and less than 2 per cent Hindus; Jammu's population is predominately Dogri-speaking and consists of 65.2 per cent Hindus and 35.7 per cent Muslims; and Ladakh has a 47.4 per cent Muslim and 46.9 per cent Buddhist population – almost all Ladakhi speakers. Each respective region's unique perceptions and experiences relating to their collective identity issues is accompanied by a pronounced sense of 'minority'/marginalization. However, this perception of marginalization shows a complex intersection of religion and cultural ethnicities with regional and sub-regional identities.

These perceptions of marginalization operate at different levels. For example, if one were to view things from the point of view of religion as a unified category, Muslims of Kashmir, while asserting the 'Muslim-majority character' of the state, see themselves as 'minority' vis-à-vis the Hindu majority in India. The Muslims located in Jammu region perceive their marginalization vis-à-vis the Hindu majority in the region. Although Muslims in Ladakh, particularly in Kargil, outnumber Buddhists, yet they define their marginalization with reference to the domination of the Buddhists in the politics of Ladakh. Hindus of Jammu meanwhile see themselves as a 'minority' in the context of the Muslim majority character of the state (one of the major rationales behind the division of the state into two Union Territories). The Kashmiri Pandits refer to their marginalization vis-à-vis the Kashmiri Muslims. On the other hand, the ethnic identity becomes predominant when a Kashmiri Muslim invokes the 'Kashmiri' identity, based on its distinct historical and cultural traditions. This explains why the autonomy or the secessionist movements do not cross the Valley of the state, leaving Muslims of other parts of the state, whether in Jammu region or in Ladakh out of the picture. Similarly, Jammu's Hindus and Ladakh's Buddhists have seen their discrimination and marginalization as regional and largely the product of state policies which favour the Valley. Moreover, regional identity politics is challenged by other subaltern sub-regional identities from the backward and peripheral areas. While sharing the regional sense of deprivation, these peripheral areas, whose populations consist of marginal tribal communities such as the Gujjars and the Paharis, feel excluded not merely from the larger politics of the state but also from the dominant politics of the region. What is certain is that this complexity cannot be captured or analyzed in terms of a single identity marker.

Religion, secularism and secularization

Both the scholarly community and the policy makers have been hesitant to speak about the multifaceted and the intersectional role of religion, region, politics, class and gender with regard to the protracted Kashmir issue. In particular, the absence of any discussion about religion can be directly related to the post-1947 state-construction of the Kashmiri identity. This has come to define the content of nationalism – whether it be formal nationalism, or that of the nationalist/separatist groups of the Kashmir Valley, or the reactive nationalism of the Hindu majority of Jammu and the Buddhist dominated Ladakh regions of the state. After independence and the partition of India, during the process of nation building and integrating the princely states into the nation-state, the Indian state arrogated to itself the power to name the Kashmir identity. It did so through two specific constitutional and legal measures – Article 370, recognizing a special status for the status, and Section 35 A, creating specific state-subject requirements for employment and ownership of property for the citizens of the Jammu and Kashmir state. In this process of political construction of an identity, the state selectively appropriated certain historical references and symbols, which would satisfy its own need for cultural homogeneity and its own version of nationalism. A product of elite alliances based on ideological grounds and the exigencies of political power, the Indian leaders reaffirmed the nature and boundaries of the Kashmir nation as espoused by the Kashmiri nationalist movement against the Hindu Dogra rule, headed by leader Sheikh Abdullah. Kashmiriyat, a suitably tailored ethnic identity (peaceful co-existence of the Hindu and Muslim communities) was a recent amalgam of a fourteenth-century golden age symbol and of a New Kashmir Manifesto, a political socialist platform; it became the legal and symbolic tool for defining both the Kashmiri identity and the very *raison d'être* for integrating the state within India. In so doing, it not only profoundly affected the process by which collective identities of the ethnically/religiously diverse population of the three regions were constructed, but it also impacted the discourse by which the conflict in the state was to be defined, articulated and rearticulated during the last seven decades (Tremblay, 1996–7). The absence of an incorporation of the religious factor in the Kashmir conflict is a by-product of this state-constructed political identity discourse.

The essays gathered in this book attempt to correct this state-constructed secularist-nationalist bias by exploring, each in its own way, the obscured but interesting connections and affinities between religion and nationalism in the state of Jammu and Kashmir as it existed until August 2019. The contributors to this edited volume ask a number of probing questions. How are competing nationalisms in this region intertwined with social structures and processes? How does religion as a mode of identification intersect with 'the politicisation of culture and the culturalisation of politics' (Brubaker, 2012, 5)? Is religion intertwined with nationalism and, if so, to what extent? What is the relationship between religious nationalism, political claims and violence? How can we capture the vivid, fluid and multifunctional essence of religion as it is practised in society? Moreover, what is the relationship between daily-lived religious practices and nationalism? We also ask ourselves the question, following Bourdieu: how and to what extent does religion, as a mode of identification and as a mode of social organization, generate its own set of positions and practices, as well as its struggles for position as people mobilize their capital to stake claims within a particular social and political domain? Our project does not take a position on religious nationalism but it pushes the point that religion matters. Indeed, our objective is to bring religion back into the study of nationalism, ethnicity and subalternity.

Religion poses a very crucial question not only in this conflict but in the contemporary global situation as well. In presenting Jammu and Kashmir as an existential case study, while analyzing the ongoing complex dynamics of religion, society and politics, this edited volume can be viewed as attempting to extend the project of those scholars and observers who have been questioning the modern view of a dichotomous opposition between the religious and the secular. In examining the Kashmir case, we follow in the footsteps of two historians, Mridu Rai and Chitralekha Zutshi, who in their individual works on the pre-1947 Kashmiri history have tackled head-on the important dynamic interplay between religious and regional identities, and have done so despite a general strong reluctance by analysts of the contemporary Kashmir conflict to bring religion into the discussion. Zutshi, in describing the centrality of religion to the discourse of identities in the late nineteenth and early twentieth centuries and the dialectic interaction of religion and region, points out how, during the turn of the century, religion itself was to emerge 'as the most vociferously contested component of the public discourse on identities'. Moreover, she asserts that,

> the Muslim leadership's focus on religion did not translate easily into a politics of cultural nationalism based on antagonism toward other religious communities. In fact, the descendants of this leadership, educated in British India and imbued with nationalist ideologies, while retaining the use of Islam as a symbol for the unification of the Kashmiri Muslim community, articulated a regional and national vision for the Kashmiri people that transcended religious community and social class. In the process, however, they refused to allow simultaneous allegiance to both religious community and regional homeland, seeing the two as mutually exclusive affiliations. The resultant spectre of 'communalism' would haunt Kashmiri politics in the 1930s and 1940s. Despite their best efforts, or perhaps as a result of them, religion continued to unite as much as divide the Kashmiri Muslims for the remainder of the century.
>
> *(2000, 128)*

Mridu Rai, in narrating how religion has dominated the geopolitics of Kashmir since the emergence in 1846 of a new political entity – the state of Jammu and Kashmir – carefully interrogates Kashmiriyat as a historical entity (2004). Her work suggests that connecting the dots between historical colonial legacies, region, nation and religious community is essential in order to understand the Kashmir conflict as well as an emerging Islamization, particularly of the local Kashmiri youth driven militancy and the subsequent Hindu nationalist response.

However, most of the contemporary analyses on the Kashmir issue suffer from: 1) an understanding 'of nationalism as a distinctively secular phenomenon'; and 2) the dominant cognitive script of the nationalist politics and its practices, even when there is a recognition that the 'idioms of religion and nationalism are intertwined' (Brubaker, 2015). The 'shared public understanding of the nation' in both India and Kashmir continues to be filtered through the lens of state-constructed secular politics. In the Kashmir Valley, the word 'political' has become synonymous with secular. It is the operative phrase to describe the 'legitimate' resistance of the Kashmiri population to the Indian state and the solution to the Kashmir conflict. While appropriately acknowledging extremist forms of both Islam and Hinduism, it, nevertheless, denies the everyday intermingling of religion and politics.

Islam in the Kashmir Valley has always maintained and continues to maintain the status of both a public and a private religion – a 'way of identifying oneself and others – of constructing sameness and difference' (Brubaker, 2015, 4). However, the relationship between these domains, both in the daily lives of the population and in the political realm, is sometimes ambiguous; at other times, these two operate in sync with each other, and sometimes in opposition. Sometimes demands made in the name of religion are formulated alongside those made in the name of nationhood. And other times, political demands made in the name of ethnicity and nationhood have a deep relationship with religion as a 'powerful framework for imagining community and a set of schemas, templates and metaphors for making sense of the social world and, of course, the supra-mundane world as well' (Brubaker, 2012, 4). Similarly, in Jammu and Ladakh, Hinduism and Buddhism are an important part of the intersectional dynamics between religion and politics. While religious identity-based mobilization has been an essential dynamic of the politics there, with a vocal minority of Hindus supporting the Hindutva project, a majority of Hindus in Jammu or Buddhists in Ladakh do not deny their religious identity, and in myriad ways, their secular domain is, in an often-undefined manner, intertwined with their daily religious practices.

Objectives and organization of this edited volume

Our intention in this volume is to move beyond the binaries of mosque/temple and state, and communal versus secular. Instead, we suggest that for a more fruitful understanding of the Kashmir issue (and thus for an eventual solution to the protracted conflict), we must move beyond this imagined 'wall of separation', and explore the complexity and dynamics of the intersection between religion and politics.[2] The underlying argument of this edited book is that, although an important identity marker in the state, religion is intersected by regional, linguistic, cultural, tribal, caste and other affiliations (Bhatia, 2014). Rather than presenting a linear context of religious differences, the authors, in discussing the pre-August 2019 multi-religious state, present the picture of a complex mosaic of multi-layered diversities. This pluralistic state is a prime example of where a religious–secular system of classification was to emerge as an artefact of political dynamics, strategically deployed as an instrument of governing control. Its plural and relatively harmonious society has come under multiple strains, with religion often informing day-to-day politics. With the ongoing conflict, both nationalism and religion have become entangled in varying interpretations and discourses by different constituencies and stakeholders.

Thus, our first objective is to attempt to understand some of the differing ways in which religious nationalism and competing practices of religion within a modern nation state shape national and sub-national identities, without treating the religious and the secular as being essentially in opposition to each other. To use Michael Barr's words, we are not interested in presupposing 'boundaries between the secular and the religious', but rather in the interactive and dialogic relationship between these spheres, including the politicized ways in which they have often been depicted relative to one another (Barr, 2010, 256).

Second, in this volume, we adopt the approach that religion is one of many constitutive forces in identity-based politics and that the Kashmir story is much bigger than what might be perceived as, for instance, Islamic fundamentalism or terrorism – or, more specifically, violence propagated in the name of religion. In order to comprehend both differences and contradictions in Kashmir's past and the present, we must address the intersectionality of religion with other identity-markers such as class, ethnicity and region.

Third, following Barr, we suggest, 'religion should be regarded as an ordinary and routine aspect of ethnic and national identity'. However, 'in some cases, it will have a direct and simple relationship with state-anchored nationalism; in others, it will have a complex and contingent relationship that is intertwined with other elements of ethnic and/or civil identity and with ethnic and/or "secular" politics' (Barr, 2010, 258). In other words, while acknowledging the relevance of the constructivist concept of religious nationalism, one aspect of which is political mobilization by the elites, we underscore the lived experiences and the daily intersectionality between religion and other identity markers. The latter probably give us better conceptual tools with which to analyze and understand the challenges that the state of Jammu and Kashmir has been facing in this most recent period of militancy and separatism. In short, our project is in line with the insight associated with someone like Talal Asad that the 'secular' cannot be viewed separately from the 'religious', as these are mutually constituted, modern domains whose conceptual construction and invocation carry a great deal of cognitive as well as political power (Asad, 1993, 2003). Moreover, through this edited work, we intend to move beyond the representation of religion as primarily an active and politically assertive tool used by the elites, and focus instead on the lived experiences of the citizenry where opposition between the secular and religious is often blurred. Accordingly, the four major themes of the book are: the role of religion, particularly in the daily lived experiences; the multi-faceted identity politics of the state and its relationship to competing nationalisms; the nature of inter-community relations; and the significance of shared religious and cultural spaces. Recognizing the complex social and political reality of the state, the contributors to this volume present a nuanced understanding of the way religion operates in relation with other identity markers, including the ethnic, linguistic, cultural, gender and regional.

This edited volume opens with the Andrew Wender and Mohita Bhatia study (Chapter 2), 'Moving Beyond Secular-Religion Binaries: A Framework for understanding the interaction between Religion and Politics'. Here they briefly introduce the reader to two current debates: 1) contemporary scholarly global debate on the relationship between religion and politics in general; and, 2) the Indian version of this debate which entails a discussion of competing and contradictory dimensions attached to the meaning of secularism and the distinct ways of secularization. Nevertheless, both debates are concerned with the decoupling of religion and politics. Contextualizing the case of Jammu and Kashmir within the global and the South Asian discussions is imperative for the purpose of not only understanding the protracted Kashmir conflict but also making the point that the academic debates frequently have policy outcomes with serious implications for social cohesion. Scholarly discourse often gets strategically employed by the governing elites to control their diverse populations. In short, there are urgent everyday consequences to how the conceptualization of religion in relation to the political is formulated, discussed and adopted within the political arena.

Reeta Chowdhari Tremblay and Shahnawaz Gull (Chapter 3), in tracing the resistance movement in the Kashmir Valley, suggest that a particular version of secular nationalism, first witnessed in the Valley's resistance to the Hindu ruler, and now to the Indian state, has, on the one hand, been consciously separated from religious nationalism, and, on the other hand, has been built upon the inherited and the ongoing dynamic and complex processes of secularization.

This is followed by Mohita Bhatia's critical examination (Chapter 4) of the complicated trajectories of secularism, secularization and desecularization processes in the Jammu region and suggests that Jammu's case points to a process of secularization of society that can take place without secular politics in place.

Noor Baba and Nyla Khan in separate chapters historically contextualize Tremblay and Gull's argument of Kashmiri secular nationalism founded on the processes of secularization. In his chapter on the dynamics of Kashmir identity, Noor Baba (Chapter 5) traces the historical origins of the Kashmiri culture of inclusivity embedded in its *Reshi* mystic traditions and the challenges it has encountered during the past 70 years. In tracing the rise of militancy, the abnormal politics, violence, and state repression, he points out that Kashmir Valley has not seen serious inroads of radical religious extremism because of its ethos.

However, the processes of secularization are being seriously challenged due to the current repressive state policies. Nyla Khan (Chapter 6) discusses the confluence of religious nationalism, secular nationalism and ethnic nationalism in the state's three distinct regions.

On the other hand, Aizaj Wani and Tabzeer Yaseen (Chapter 7), in tracing the formation of the political entity of Jammu and Kashmir and the subsequent politics of its three regions (Kashmir, Jammu and Ladakh), discuss that religion and nationalism have consistently remained analogous phenomena in the state. In each of these regions with their respective religious majorities, religion has performed two sets of functions: it has provided a way for imagining community and served the purpose of creating a social organization; however, it has been used as well by the political elites to frame their claims.

The last four chapters address the relationship between everyday life (religion, language and art), nationalism and resistance. Chakraverti Mahajan's (Chapter 8) insightful study of Doda district (the Muslim majority district of Jammu division with a complex intersectionality of regional, linguistic, cultural and multi-religious affiliations) and everyday food practices following the militancy speaks to the hardening of religious boundaries. In explaining the processes of de-secularization, he points out that through the 'everyday' and food practices people have drawn new boundaries. While food has become a means of not just survival and existence but a marker of religious and political affiliations, however, the complex realities of mixed living keep challenging the orthodox positions and help in blunting the ideology that defies everyday communalism. In other words, the processes of secularization and desecularization co-exist.

Sadaf Munshi (Chapter 9), in tracing the literary traditions of Kashmir, points out that in the ongoing separatist movement, the role of Kashmiri linguistic identity has been minimal in most of the political discourse. Urdu, the language of the Muslim political elite in late nineteenth-century India, not only served as the main language of political expression, it was also the language of solidarity with the neighbouring Pakistan with which the Kashmiri Muslims were emotionally, and to a great extent politically, affiliated. Changes in the social and political scenario of Kashmir were reflected in the use of signs, slogans and terminology symbolic of the Muslim political identity.

Andrew Whitehead (Chapter 10) takes us back to October 27, 1947 when the Baramulla mission was overrun by tribal fighters from Pakistan; the manner in which those events have been memorialized by the church and by others; the reworking of the concept of 'conversion' as envisaged by the woman who remains the Catholic church's only martyr in Kashmir; and the interlocking of clerical and geopolitical narratives.

Zehra Abrar and Namitha George (Chapter 11) look at the art of four photographers from the Valley voicing their everyday resistance. Using the concept of dispersed resistance, they explore 'resistance photography' as a practice of resistance in terms of both its self-reflexivity and its expression of the collective trauma of the repressed society. Photographs, for them, are to be interpreted as a representation of the photographer's 'self' as well as a representation of the collective climate of resistance. In this subtle and clamorous dispersed resistance, it is difficult to separate nationalism and everyday religion.

Background of the Kashmir conflict: competing nationalisms and symbols

In the remaining part of this introduction, we provide a brief history of the state of Jammu and Kashmir, the general contours of the conflict and competing nationalisms in its three regions. Some of the essential points underlined here relate to the colonial arrangement by which a new political and geographical entity was created out of disparate territories, some sovereign and others with shared sovereignty under a single sovereign authority in 1846; the rise of a nationalist movement in the Muslim majority Kashmir Valley where religion and politics interlocked and overlapped; the post-partition arrangements between India and Kashmir, initially granting the latter the promise of a plebiscite and later a constitutional special status within India; and finally the demands for *azadi* in the Valley and counter-demands for full integration of the state within the Indian federation. In this long process, a repertoire of myths and memories has emerged in the state's three distinct regions as symbols and even as weapons in their respective competing narratives of nationalism and identity.

The state, in its present formation as a new political geographical entity, can be traced back to the 1846 Treaty of Amritsar between the British and the Sikhs, transferring the Kashmir region to Jammu's Dogra Hindu ruler Raja Ghulab Singh (who had already acquired the principality of Jammu from the Sikh ruler of Punjab, Maharaja Ranjit Singh) in return for a payment to the British of 7.5 million rupees and annual tributes of one horse, 12 shawl goats of approved breed (six male and six female) and three pairs of Cashmere shawls. Ghulab Singh now was in charge of three distinct regions. He had earlier in 1834 annexed the kingdom of Ladakh. The three regions, with different political arrangements (some small independent kingdoms, some with shared sovereignty) and with three distinct religious and linguistic populations (predominantly Kashmiri-speaking Muslims, majority Dogri-speaking Hindu Jammu and majority Ladhaki-speaking Buddhists) were united into one geographical political identity under one sovereign.

In Kashmiri Muslim nationalist history, the Treaty of Amritsar emerges as one of the first signs of occupation. The sale of Kashmir to the Hindu ruler is often cited as the darkest day of Kashmir's history having inflicted a deep wound upon the Kashmiri mass psyche, which, even after more than one-and-a-half centuries, refuses to heal. Even some of the nineteenth-century European travellers to the Kashmir Valley, seeing the impoverished conditions of the Muslim population along with exploitative labour practices of *begaar* (forced labour) and heavy taxation, were constantly to begrudge the decision of the British government to gift (or sell) the state to the Hindu ruler, instead of directly ruling over it. Until 1947, the state's relationship with British India was guided by this 1846 treaty – whereby the Hindu ruler supposedly maintained his internal autonomy (in practice, the British Resident in Kashmir kept a watchful eye on the state and no legal or political action was taken without his and finally the British government's approval) while the British controlled security and defense.

Largely due to the British trade interests in Central Asia and concerns over Russian expansion, the British were to actively participate in state building, pushing the maharaja to pursue both administrative and political reforms. The standardization of administration saw the formulation and consolidation of criminal and civil laws, a council of ministers with distinct duties for different portfolios, such as justice and revenue, and a partially elected legislative assembly. Concerned with the poverty of the agrarian Muslim population in the Valley, the British government insisted on some types of land reforms. In 1887, under the direction of Sir Walter Lawrence, the Settlement Commissioner, the state government carried out the first land settlement. As a result, the rights of the agriculturists were clearly defined and *begaar* was abolished. These reforms were accompanied by the introduction of English education, the establishment of colleges and the introduction of Western medicine largely due to the efforts of the medical missionaries who had arrived in the Valley in the latter part of the nineteenth century. In addition and more significantly, the Kashmir Valley, which until then could only be accessed over rough mountainous terrain through hiking or by pony and by boat crossing over the river Jhelum, was to be connected with the rest of India through the construction of a set of roads. The remote northern areas of Gilgit and Baltistan were leased from the maharaja by the British government, so that it could through its direct rule over the region protect its trade interests with Central Asia and ensure its supremacy vis-à-vis the Russians.

Two developments stand out during the Dogra regime which would emerge as potent national symbols affecting national identity: first, the Kashmiri citizenship and the property and employment privileges as per the 1927 and 1932 state–subject promulgation by Maharaja Hari Singh and second, the July 13, 1931 killing of 22 Muslims in Srinagar (summer capital of the state) by the police during a protest march against the Dogra government outside the jail where a Kashmiri Muslim provocateur Abdul Qadeer was being tried on the charge of terrorism and inciting the public against the maharaja of Kashmir. While the state–subject regulations were to become an important component of the special status granted by India to the state of Jammu and Kashmir after the 1947 partition, July 13 was concomitantly to be immortalized in the memory of Kashmir Muslims as a symbol of state oppression. Since 1931, this particular day is commemorated in the Valley as Martyrs Day. The intensity of the celebration of Martyrs Day varies from year to year depending upon the Valley's Muslim population's perception of the severity of threat either to their religious or to their political identity (the revocation of the special status) or to both.

Jammu and Kashmir was one of the three princely states, which did not accede to either India or Pakistan and only after the tribal invasion from Pakistan, did Maharaja Hari Singh accede to India on October 27, 1947.[3] In accepting Hari Singh's offer of accession, Indian Prime Minister Nehru and Governor-General Mountbatten categorically stated that the question of accession would be resolved through a referendum, whereby the citizens of the state could freely express their opinion, once law and order had been restored, and the invaders had been pushed out of Kashmir. Prime

Minister Nehru was to confirm the conditional acceptance of Kashmir's accession to India and the necessity for the Kashmiri people to 'ultimately decide' and 'have their say'. In a detailed statement to India's Constituent Assembly on November 2, 1947, he reiterated that the will of the people of Kashmir should be ascertained through an impartial tribunal such as the United Nations (Das Gupta, 1968, 110).

In the event, the Indian armed forces were able to free only two-thirds of the state. Since then the state has been partitioned into two parts – two-thirds, known as the Indian state of Jammu and Kashmir, under Indian control and one-third, known as Azad Kashmir, under Pakistani administration. India's attempts to lodge a complaint of aggression against Pakistan to the United Nations' Security Council backfired severely. The Security Council was to treat both India and Pakistan as equal parties to the dispute of Kashmir and confirm through its 1948 resolution that the state was a disputed territory. It set two conditions for the resolution of the dispute: 1) the withdrawal of Pakistani troops from the occupied territory, and 2) once the first condition was met, the future was to be resolved through a plebiscite or a freedom, as promised by the Indian governor general and the prime minister. Accordingly, plebiscite has remained a recurring national symbol for the resistance narrative in Kashmir Valley. Since 1948, the resistance, whether mild, strong or violent, sporadic/ad hoc or organized, the slogan which reverberates in the Valley is: *Yeh Kashmir hamara hai iska faisla hum karaingay* (This is our Kashmir and we will decide its future).

Meanwhile, the Indian Constituent Assembly defined Jammu and Kashmir's political relationship with the Indian state in 1950. Due to the unique circumstances of the state's accession to India, a specific constitutional provision, Article 370, giving special and differential status in the Indian federation, was enshrined in the Indian Constitution. Significantly, this provision at that time was intended to be temporary. This provision restricts the Union's legislative powers to the areas of foreign affairs, defence and communication and allows the state to legislate on residuary powers, thus giving the state autonomy in all internal matters. The Indian Parliament needs the state government's concurrence for applying all other laws. Any constitutional amendment approved by the Parliament, applicable to all states, is not automatically applicable to the state of Jammu and Kashmir.

The Jammu and Kashmir Constituent Assembly (convened and popularly elected in 1951) approved the state's new constitution in November 1956 and was officially promulgated on January 26, 1957. One of its features included a provision with regard to the citizenship of the people of Kashmir and their classification into a special category of 'Permanent Residents'. While respecting Article 5 and its application of Indian citizenship to the people of the state and the criteria for citizenship as defined by the maharaja promulgations of 1927 and 1932, the Constituent Assembly made a single modification pertaining to the nomenclature. State-subjects were reclassified into a 'uniform class of Permanent Residents'. The permanent Residents are

> all those people who were born and residing in the territories of the state,
> when it was founded by the Maharaja Ghulab Singh in 1846, the people who

settled in the state later but before 1885, the people who settled in the state under special permission before 1911, and the people who took permanent residence in the state and acquired immovable property under the 'Ijazat Nama Rules' before May 1944.

(Teng et al., 1999, 210)

Article 370 and Section 35A have remained sacrosanct amongst the Kashmiri population and any attempt on the part of the Indian government to amend or abrogate it has in the past generated a huge political volatility in Kashmir Valley. On the other hand, the Hindu nationalist population, although a small minority in Jammu region – the support base of the RSS and the BJP – has made the special status as its rallying point. Since 1952, they have demanded Jammu and Kashmir's complete accession and integration with the Indian Union, thus making a demand for the abrogation of Article 370 and Section 35 A. For them, the Indian nation is one, its constitutional principles are applicable to all citizens and no exceptions can be made because of a distinct identity. Over the years, these integrative voices have become louder. The dynamics of the conflicting, but mutually reinforcing relationship between Jammu's integrationists and the Valley's nationalists (the latter constantly worrying about the distinct political identity of the state), explain to a large degree the tensions amongst its two regions. What has emerged during the last seven decades is the negative synergy of the symbiotic politics of the two regions: the more the Hindu population of Jammu raise the integrationist cry (with its slogan *Bharat Mata ki Jai* – Hail Mother India), the more defensive the Valley becomes in asserting its nationalism (*Hum kaya chahte* – *azadi, azadi* – what do we wish, freedom, freedom) which, in turn, further alienates the Jammu population. The multiple identity politics influences the direction of the politics of the state. Since the linguistic–cultural identities overlap with the regional identities, it becomes important to discuss the regional identities. Region forms not only an important marker of sociocultural identity but also becomes the basis of political specificities within the state.

The post-1947 politics of Jammu and Kashmir has followed different directions in its three regions. While the Kashmir region has been involved in the politics of contestation of the state's relationship with India, Jammu's politics has been scripted by the politics of regional deprivation and regional discrimination. Ladakh's dominant politics meanwhile has been characterized by the demand for Union Territory status. Without going into the details of each region's politics, the integrative politics, pursued after the arrest of the Kashmir nationalist leader Sheikh Abdullah in 1953 and the installation of centrally approved state governments, were to frame, on the one hand, the politics of secession and autonomy in the Valley, and on the one hand, the politics of removing all asymmetrical federal relationships of the state within the Indian Constitution was to dominate in its other two regions.

The years 1956 to 1976 witnessed the slow and steady erosion of the political distinctness, which Article 370 of the Indian Constitution had guaranteed to the state of Jammu and Kashmir. Article 370 has been amended several times, with the concurrence of the Jammu and Kashmir Legislature, to make most of the provisions of the Indian constitutional applicable to the state (Tremblay, 1996–7, 483–484). The more salient features of this integration (or abrogation/erosion of the initial intent of Article 370) include the application of various entries in the Union and the Concurrent Lists of the Indian Constitution, the application of Article 365 empowering the central government to impose the President's rule, the extension of Article 248, 249 and 250 giving the authority to the centre to legislate in matters of state jurisdiction, standardization of state designation for governor and chief minister (previously known as sadar-i-riyasat and premier). In 1967, the Jammu and Kashmir Representation of the Peoples Act was brought into conformity with the central law, enabling the Election Commission to appoint retired judges of the High Courts of other states as members of the Election Tribunal. It also authorized the Commission to intervene during the elections at the vote-counting stage in case of suspected irregularities. Similarly, the jurisdiction of the Supreme Court has been extended to the state in all aspects. Moreover, fundamental rights apply to the citizens of the state with one exception relating to the privileges of the permanent residents. However, the only exceptions (till the August 5 revocation decision) which remained intact were Kashmiri citizenship requirements and the property and employment privileges that lie in the 1927 and 1932 promulgation by Maharaja Hari Singh, known as the Permanent Resident requirements.

During this integrative period, the state was governed though a system of patronage politics delivered by a centrally approved government, which disallowed any dissenting political space to the ones who opposed the government. While the state was to remain relatively stable, the challenges to the government were to emerge at the margins of state politics. In the Valley, until 1989 when there emerged a full-fledged mass resistance accompanied by political insurgency, the demand fluctuated between *raishumari* (plebiscite) and autonomy. Meanwhile in the Jammu region, its demands took two shapes–integration vs devolution – the former (the Integrationists), with unmistakable Hindu communal overtones, raising the slogan of 'complete accession' and 'full integration within the Indian Union'; the latter (the Devolutionists), on the other hand, asking for the extension of the federal asymmetrical principle to the three distinct regions of the state. For the Devolutionists, the internal autonomy of the state of Jammu and Kashmir, granted to it constitutionally by India, ought to be accompanied by the internal autonomy of its three regions, Jammu, Kashmir and Ladakh. While they did not have much success in pursuing their agenda, the Integrationists have remained dissatisfied despite the extension of various integrative measures to the state. For them, Article 370 had continued to maintain very important exceptions. Consequently, an antagonistic symbiotic relationship between Jammu's Hindus and the Valley's Muslim population had become deeply embedded in the state politics, each reacting to the other. The more the Hindu population of Jammu raised the integrationist cry, the more defensive the Valley became in asserting its nationalism. By the end of the 1970s, the regional and religious cleavages had sharpened in the state, resulting in a strong religious–regional polarization.

After Jammu and Kashmir's accession to India, the first popular elections involving 75 seats for the state's Constituent Assembly were held in September 1951 (Tremblay, 1992, 164).[4] The Constituent Assembly was also to act as the legislative assembly for the state until the constitution was officially proclaimed in January 1957. For the legislative assembly, 87 seats are allocated as follows: Jammu 37, Kashmir 46 and Ladakh 4. There are six parliamentary constituencies – three in Kashmir (Srinagar, Baramullah and Anantnag), two in Jammu (Udhampur and Jammu), and one in Ladakh. A sharp religious–regional polarization of the Assembly seats was to become evident in the 1977 Assembly elections of the state. Up until 1972, Kashmir politics, particularly that of the Valley, was completely dominated by the National Conference party. In 1957, the National Conference (NC) won 66 out of 72 seats – all 40 in the Valley, 24 in Jammu and 2 in Ladakh. Again, it was the dominant party in 1962, winning 69 out of 75 seats, capturing 41 out of 43 in the Valley. In 1964, the NC leader Sadiq converted the ruling National Conference party into Indian National Congress party in order to 'join the mainstream of national political life' (Tremblay, 1995, 90). This newly merged party dominated the electoral scene in 1967 winning 61 seats, 33 out of 42 in the Valley. The year 1972 was a watershed in Kashmir politics. Jamait-i-Islami, which had been building a political space for itself through its social and religious functions carried out through its mosque network, contested its first election and won five seats in the Valley. This was the first time a clearly pro-Islamic, pro-Pakistan minority entered the political arena challenging the dominant secular ethos. In 1975, Sheikh Abdullah who reentered Kashmir politics as a result of the Kashmir Accord with Indira Gandhi revived the NC which was to remain the dominant party till the secessionist movement in 1989. In the Jammu region, the Bhartiya Jan Sangh (later the BJP) was the major spokesperson for the Hindu nationalists. Its success was to remain limited until the 2014 Lok Sabha elections. Indeed, while in the 1957 elections it had won five seats, in the subsequent three Assembly elections of 1962, 1967 and 1972 it barely managed to garner three seats.

The year 1988 would see an open challenge in Kashmir Valley to the Indian state. The immediate cause was the rigging of the 1987 Assembly elections, denying victory to all the dissenting candidates who had contested elections under a unified political group, the Muslim United Front. This was the catalyst for reactivating the until-then quiescent secessionist movement, leading to the transformation of Kashmiri demands from autonomy to *azadi*. Putting aside their differences, two prominent Valley-based groups – Hizbul-Mujahideen, espousing unification with Pakistan and the Jammu and Kashmir Liberation Front, demanding the unification of Pakistani- and Indian-administered Kashmir and their establishment into an independent state – came together (with Pakistan's help) to demand freedom for Kashmir. The year 1989 was to usher in a secessionist/nationalist movement in the Valley with mass public support, which, while experiencing its ups and downs, does not seem to have died down.

In 1996, after a seven-year president's rule in the state, an electoral process was initiated to reengage the Muslim population in the Kashmir region through a governance agenda. Since then, 11 sets of elections have been conducted – four Assembly elections and seven parliamentary elections. Despite the reactivation of the electoral process and the formation of popularly elected governments, demands for *azadi* have not waned. In 2002, the People's Democratic Party (PDP) and the Congress formed the government, rotating the post of chief minister, Mufti Sayeed until 2005, and Ghulam Nabi Azad until 2008 when the Amaranth Land row led to the resurgence of calls for *azadi* (Tremblay, 2009). In 2008, the NC, under Omar Abdullah, led the government, once again in coalition with the Congress party. The 2014 Assembly elections resulted in a clear split in the legislature between Hindu-majority Jammu and predominantly Muslim Kashmir, with the PDP winning 28 seats, almost all from the Kashmir Valley, and the BJP with 25 seats from the Jammu region; this necessitated the formation of a 'partnership government' in 2015, solely on pragmatic grounds, in order to deliver the governance agenda. The ideological differences between the two partners on several issues – significantly about the special status of the state and a dialogue with the separatists in the Valley – led to the collapse of the coalition government. In June 2018, the BJP pulled out of the PDP-led Mehbooba Mufti government of Jammu and Kashmir and yet again, president's rule was imposed on the state.

On and off, the Valley erupted; the 2008 Amaranth Land row, the 2010 youth protests, the February 2014 hanging of Afzal Guru, the prime accused in the attack on the Indian Parliament in 2001, and post-Burhan Wani (when in July 2016 Kashmir unrest became manifest in the Valley following the killing of a local youth) are all reminiscent of the events of the late 1980s that culminated in the Kashmir Valley's mass-supported opposition to India, the breakdown of the administrative framework and a reliance on the security forces to deal with the escalating ethno-nationalist upsurge. No popularly elected regional government has been able to convince the central government to revoke the Armed Forces Special Powers Act (AFSPA), which grants unbridled powers to Security Forces. The AFPSA Act remains a constant reminder to the people of the Valley that they are effectively under occupation. Under the Act, the Kashmir Valley was declared a 'Disturbed Area' in 1990.[5] Despite the insistence on the withdrawal of the AFSPA by both mainstream Valley-based political parties, the National Conference and the People's Democratic Party, security considerations, as vocally and vehemently articulated by the leadership of the Indian Army, have remained at the forefront of the central government's Kashmir policy.

The latest context of the continuing mass resistance and the demands for *azadi* are a consequence of the 2016 killing of Burhan Muzafar Wani, the 22-year-old homegrown commander of the Hizbul Mujahideen and two of his associates by the security forces (including the Jammu and Kashmir Police, Rashtriya Rifles and the CRPF), when the Valley was in the midst of Eid festivities; this incidence was to unleash a state of pandemonium. Burhan, who had emerged as one of the most recognizable faces of the militancy and who introduced the Valley to social media-driven militancy, was to instantaneously acquire the status of *shaheed* (martyr) along with Maqbool Butt and Afzal Guru (the former hanged on February 11 in 1984 and the latter on February 9, 2013) for openly challenging the dominant state power and keeping alive Kashmiri resistance against the Indian state. The public grieved for their local hero, which included 40 funeral prayers for Burhan's *janaza*. Both Guru's hanging and Wani's killing have given an impetus to local militancy, spurring angry young Kashmiris to join militant ranks. Groups such as Hizbul Mujahideen, Lashkar-e-Taiba and Jaish-e-Mohammad have been able to recruit more than 280 youths in three years, between 2015 and 2018.

The Valley has remained in the throes of a mass-supported protest politics since 1989 that has shown no signs of closure. In order to deal with this, on August 5, 2019 the government of Prime Minister Narendra Modi, with unexpected sud-denness, abolished the special constitutional status of the Muslim-majority state of Jammu and Kashmir and changed its regional status within the federation. The Indian Parliament passed two resolutions. The first revoked Article 370 and the sec-ond demoted the state by splitting it into two union territories: Jammu and Kashmir (with a legislature) and Ladakh (without a legislature). Anticipating a strong reac-tion from the Muslim-majority Kashmir Valley, more than 35,000 additional central forces personnel were deployed in the Valley. For the first time ever, the Amar-nath Yatra (pilgrimage) was cancelled. Hindu pilgrims, tourists and non-Kashmiri students of professional educational institutions were asked to return home. All educational institutions were closed and all major political leaders (including for-mer chief ministers Omar Abdullah and Mehbooba Mufti) were placed in custody or shifted to government jails. While there is jubilation in Hindu-majority Jammu and in Buddhist Ladakh, the Valley itself, remaining virtually under curfew and with no internet connectivity for more than five months, has been eerily silent. On August 8, Modi, in a speech to the nation, described the new era that has dawned. He said that with the abolition of special status, all citizens of India were now equal. He said that the citizens of Jammu and Kashmir could now see enhanced economic and social development, previously hampered by the state's special status. A new era, he said – a 'New India' – has been ushered in. What is yet to be seen are the impli-cations for the Indian nation and the character of its politics and society; and how (and whether) these actions of the Modi government might lead to ruptured, com-plicated trajectories of secularism, secularization and desecularization processes.

Notes

1 Wordsworth identifies five characteristics of foundational intersectionality: 1) 'Key social categories were defined and constituted through each other'; 2) 'Systems of domination are interlocking. Institutional histories interact'; 3) 'Subordination and privilege depend on more than one interlocking system of power'; 4) 'Political Experience and fate seen as intricately (structurally) linked'; 5) 'Hierarchies of privilege and subordination can exist across identity categories in same person/group.' See Wordsworth (2011, Table 1, p. 204).
2 Inasmuch as the now-iconic phrase 'wall of separation' is attributed to early nineteenth-century United States President Thomas Jefferson, an imagined, modern Western sev-erance between religion and politics does not necessarily make a suitable engraftment within all global settings.
3 This date is disputed, depending upon which narrative of accession one ascribes to.

4 In September 1951 a general election was held for 75 Constituent Assembly seats. Jammu's Hindu Nationalist party, the Praja Parishad (later to merge with Bhartiya Jan Sangh), which protested the limited integration of the state into the Indian union, boycotted the election. Consequently, all 75 seats were won without contest by the National Conference. For a detailed discussion, see Reeta Chowdhari Tremblay, 1992 'An Autonomous Jammu'.

5 The Act was imposed in 1990 in order, first, to respond to security threats arising as a result of the secessionist/nationalist activities and violence; second, to effectively deal with cross-border terrorism; and third, to assist with maintenance of law and order in the state in order to ensure adequate daily governance.

References

Asad, Talal. 1993. *Genealogies of Religion: Discipline and Reasons of Power in Christianity and Islam*. Baltimore and London: Johns Hopkins University Press.

Asad, Talal. 2003. *Formations of the Secular: Christianity, Islam, Modernity*. Stanford, CA: Stanford University Press.

Barr, Michael D. 2010. 'Religious Nationalism and Nation-building in Asia: An Introduction'. *Australian Journal of International Affairs*, Vol. 64, Issue 3, 255–261.

Bhatia, Mohita. 2014. 'Dalits in Jammu and Kashmir: Resistance and Collaboration in a Conflict Situation'. *Asian Survey*, Vol. 54, Issue 5 (September–October), 941–965.

Brubaker, Rogers. 2012. 'Religion and Nationalism: Four Approaches'. *Nations and Nationalism*, Vol. 18, Issue 1, 2–20.

Brubaker, Rogers. 2015. *Grounds for Difference*. Cambridge, MA: Harvard University Press.

Das Gupta, Jyoti Bhushan. 1968. *Jammu and Kashmir*. The Hague, Netherlands: Martinus Nijhoff.

Iqtidar, Humeira, and Sarkar, Tanika, editors. 2018. *Tolerance, Secularization and Democratic Politics in South Asia*. Cambridge: Cambridge University Press.

Rai, Mridu. 2004. *Hindu Rulers, Muslim Subjects: Islam, Rights, and the History of Kashmir*. Princeton: Princeton University Press.

Teng, Mohan Kishen, Bhat, Ram Kishen, and Kaul, Santosh. 1999. *Kashmir: Constitutional History and Documents*. Second edition. Jammu: Jay Kay Book House.

Tremblay, Reeta Chowdhari. 1992. 'Jammu: Autonomy Within an Autonomous Kashmir', in Raju G. C. Thomas (Ed). *Perspectives on Kashmir: The Roots of Conflict in South Asia*. Boulder, CO: Westview Press, pp. 153–167.

Tremblay, Reeta Chowdhari. 1995. 'Kashmir: The Valley's Political Dynamics'. *Contemporary South Asia*, Vol. 4, Issue 1, 79–102.

Tremblay, Reeta Chowdhari. 1996–97. 'Nation, Identity and the Intervening Role of the State: A Study of the Secessionist Movement in Kashmir'. *Pacific Affairs*, Vol. 69, Issue 4, 471–497.

Tremblay, Reeta Chowdhari. 2009. 'Kashmir's Secessionist Movement Resurfaces: Ethnic Identity, Community Competition, and the State'. *Asian Survey*, Vol. 49, Issue 6, 924–950.

Wordsworth, Nancy D. 2011. 'Intersectionality in California's Same-Sex marriage Battles: A Complex Proposition'. *Political Research Quarterly*, Vol. 64, Issue 1, 200–216.

Zutshi, Chitralekha. 2000. 'Religion, State, and Community: Contested Identities in the Kashmir Valley, c.1880–1920'. *South Asia: Journal of South Asian Studies*, Vol. 23, Issue 1, 109–128.

2

MOVING BEYOND SECULAR–RELIGIOUS BINARIES

A framework for understanding the interaction between religion and politics

Andrew M. Wender and Mohita Bhatia

The Kashmir conflict is intertwined simultaneously with competing nationalisms, religious and regional identities. Kashmiriyat – a regional identity (seemingly perceiving no contradiction in viewing the citizens of the Valley as being both Kashmiri and Muslim) – co-exists with Islamic and Hindu fundamentalisms, sometimes openly and at other times intersecting with political and regional nationalisms.[1] In order to make sense of the growth of ethnic nationalism and the assertion of religious fundamentalism in Kashmir, we must keep in mind Willfried Spohn's words: "the secularization process do not dissolve religion, but they develop in different patterns combining religious and secular components and proceed in oscillating movements of secularization and desecularization" (Spohn, 2003, 269).

In order to understand the unique pattern of the interaction between religion and politics in India and the state of Jammu and Kashmir, our objective in this chapter is to set up a theoretical framework for the complex discussion of constructed modern concepts of religion and politics/secularity which are strategically deployed as instruments of governing control. An important question to ask here is why we should discuss the scholarly discourse, global as well as South Asian, and what it has to do with the ongoing, protracted Kashmir conflict. We assert that academic discourse and debates frequently result in policy outcomes with serious, positive implications for social cohesion as well as the resolution of conflicts. But they can also have the opposite effect – exaggerating the socio-political cleavages in the society. The scholarly discourse, privileging particular ways of seeing and codifying certain practices, often gets translated into a political discourse with its potential impact on public policy.

This chapter begins with the central question – why talk about religion and politics and why now? We divide our discussion into two parts: the first portion highlights the broad contours of the global discussion about the intersection of religion and politics; the second portion points to the debates taking place in South

Asia, India in particular, regarding the secular domain and the processes of seculari-zation. In general, the global debate is a product of the European Enlightenment discourse which relegates religion to the realm of the private, whereas the South Asian discussion deals with a different context. Here the state-generated conceptu-alization of a secular state, different from the European version of secularism, finds a place for religion in its own unique version of secularism. The Indian Constitu-tion, adopted in 1950, scrupulously avoided the terms "secularism" and a "secular state". It was only in 1976, that the word secular was added to the constitution's preamble. Predating the Western debate on religion (especially Islam) and politics that intensified after the events of 9/11, the debates and discussions in India about secularism and its relationship to religion as a mode of organization and daily reli-gious practices as a mode of identification were to take place during the 1980s. They emerged with the rise of Khalistan, the Kashmir autonomy movements, the protection of personal laws for the Muslim community and the ensuing strength of Hindu fundamentalism in response to these demands. T. N. Madan notes that these debates took several different shapes.

> While some secularist intellectuals in the Nehruvian mold called for a reas-sertion of the principles of the Enlightenment (including scientific temper as well as the primacy of science and technology as instruments of social transformation), others boldly questioned these principles, drawing attention to the flawed character of "the modernity project" and advocating the revival of traditional cultures.
>
> *(Madan, 2003, 64)*

After reviewing both the global and the South Asian debates, this chapter points out, particularly in the South Asian context, that religion cannot be understood as a stand-alone analytical category but as one that is intertwined with other social cat-egories such as gender, ethnicity and class. In other words, a discussion of religion cannot be considered in isolation from its social context that presents how it is lived out in the daily lives of the people. The phenomenological realm of everyday reality underscores the fact that the fuzzy, diverse and overlapping socio-religious realities remain resilient to categorization and political homogenization.

The discourse about the Kashmir conflict fluctuates between these global and South Asian debates on secularism, thus making it imperative to underscore out the significance of this dual discussion. Kashmir's social fabric, interaction between Muslims and Pandits (Hindus) of Kashmir and political events leading to displace-ment of Kashmiri Pandits have often been analyzed from the lens of conventional Western secularism debate. Even terms like "Kashmiriyat" and its romanticized con-notations derive much from this canonical debate, that puts secularism on a higher pedestal, operating neatly, free from any local or regional conflicts. Newer studies of Kashmir (Mridu Rai, C. Zutshi) have departed from these generalized projections of Kashmiri secularism. Just like the contemporary Western debates on secularism that have problematized the neat religion–secular binary, some of the recent scholars on Kashmir have also challenged these compartmentalizations and harmonious conceptualization about the idea of Kashmiriyat. We take a step further, and in this chapter explore the Jammu and Kashmir discourse, in the context of the local South Asian dynamics. We delve into the scholarship which looks at the manifold, and look at the manifold social, religious, regional, caste, and political factors and their complex interactions to analyze the processes of secularization in Kashmir. We use the process of secularization to understand secularism not just as a state-driven process but as a more organic and multilayered process emerging from within the society.

This chapter concludes with the elephant in the room question – is Islam compatible with secularism – and our assertion, in response, that the discourse suggesting Islam's incompatibility with "secular" or "democratic" values must be refuted.

Why talk about religion and politics, and why now?

In the face of global and local realities that negate any strict boundaries between the "secular", "religious", and "political", many Western and non-Western debates on secularism have creatively re-envisaged the concept and highlighted its variegated meanings. Yet, these debates have sometimes been unable to locate secularism (and religion, by virtue of its characteristic exclusion from the conceptualization of secularism) in lived phenomenological realities. Our assertion is that the present enquiry is necessary because academic debates frequently have policy implications, and scholarly discourse often becomes strategically deployed by governing elites to control their diverse populations. The anthropologist Talal Asad, who has played a key role in revealing how conceptual constructions of religion and politics intersect with forces of power, recently explained:

> words like "modernity," "religion," "politics," "secularism" and their associated, shifting vocabularies are intertwined with modes of life. It is attention to the particular character of that intertwining, to what opponents claim or reject as the "proper" meaning of these terms (as their "essence") that should be our primary concern in trying to understand what people expect or demand from or dislike about "the secular" or "the religious" – and why they do so.
>
> *(Asad, 2018, 147–148)*

In short, there are everyday consequences to how the conceptualization of religion in relation to the political – and, with that, the secular realm to which politics is typically imagined as belonging – is undertaken and marshalled within the political arena.

Only a few decades ago, the academic study of interrelations between religion and politics might have been presumed obsolete, given the imagined, modern irrelevance of religion to politics. This presumption would have reflected then-dominant intellectual expectations that, under the supposed logic of historical progress, the forward march of secularization had relegated religion to the distant periphery of public life. As termed by Elizabeth Shakman Hurd, "the politics of secularism in international relations" captures International Relations practitioners' long-running bias against recognizing religion's global political import (Hurd, 2008). Such an outlook was implicated in various scenarios wherein analysts had presupposed that the maintenance of security "necessitated drawing a line between politics and religion" (Sheikh and Wæver, 2012, 275). However, the erroneousness of presupposing that such a line can be drawn is exemplified merely by a few of the United States' notorious Middle East policy debacles. Take, for instance, that country's failure to appreciate how a supposedly stable, pro-US monarchy in late 1970s Iran could be on the cusp of turning into a revolutionary theocracy, bitterly resentful of Western secularist impositions.[2] Or consider the US's ignorance of colonially exacerbated, intercommunal divides that might have foreseeably stood in the way of remolding post-Saddam Hussein Iraq into a Western-styled democracy (Hurd, 2008; Burleigh, 2018, 7–8).

In fact, in the perspective of numerous observers, religion is presently undergoing a global resurgence from its ostensible, secularizing decline. On the one hand, this resurgence is read as a broad socio-cultural and intellectual phenomenon, manifested in "rising levels of religious belief worldwide", and "the growing prominence of post-secular thinking in several disciplines" (Shortt, 2019, 25). Crucially, though, from the standpoint of scholarly as well as public engagement with politics, religion's putative reemergence is often seen as being typified by a worldwide proliferation of religious violence – with Islam regularly perceived and depicted as playing a singular role, above all in the form of militant Jihadism (Juergensmeyer, 2000; Toft et al., 2011).[3] The Cold War's close may have inspired premonitions of an end to history in which supposed, secular liberalism would stand peaceably triumphant; yet, today's world is said to witness an "age of anger" whose prevailing condition of "global civil war" often takes religious overtones (Fukuyama, 1989; Mishra, 2017, 35).[4] Some would now go so far as to construe the impossibility of "politics . . . divorcing itself from the sacred" (Nathans, 2017; Slezkine, 2017). Therefore, the worldwide relationship between politics and religion has transformed into the subject of robust scholarly debates.

Similar inter dynamics between religion and secularity need attention in the academic explorations of Kashmir's society and politics. Politics and religion in Kashmir are deeply intermeshed in intricate ways, and any debate on the Kashmir conflict would be inadequate if the interrelation between two is not apprehended. The timing now is particularly pertinent to talk about religion and politics, given the communal polarizations engendered by the present ruling party and the grave implications these national political scenarios have on Kashmir. The religion binaries between Hindus and non-Hindus (particularly Muslims) are being reinforced in both national and regional levels, making it imperative to analyze, contest and explain the complicated secularization processes in the Jammu and Kashmir society.

The global debate: religion and politics/secularity as artificially created modern concepts, strategically deployed as instruments of governing control

While perhaps preferable to an outmoded perception of thoroughgoing, global secularization, the notion of religion's having reappeared following a period of relative absence is far from unproblematic, even dangerously misleading (Gray, 2018, 5; Slezkine, 2017). Depicting religion as a formerly buried object that has somehow resurged from the historical past uncritically accepts the modern, Western construct rendering religion and politics (with politics supposedly belonging, by rights, to the secular realm) as an oppositional pair (Armstrong, 2015 [2014]; Cavanaugh, 2009; Fitzgerald, 2015). By presupposing either the fact of resurgent religion, or that resulting violence is attributable to Islam and further traditions, one remains ensnared in a false conceptual binary between religion and secularity that bears damaging policy implications. One representative implication would be feeding a post-9/11 appetite, stoked anew in the period since ISIS (Islamic State of Iraq and al-Sham) burst into the popular mind as unparalleled "monsters, savages, and killers", for battlefield-ready, terrorism research proving all too prone to "superficial" treatment of pertinent "religious dimension[s]" (Gerges, 2016, ix; Lewis, 2017, 2). Beyond holding forth the readily demonized specter of Islamic terrorism, the binary leads toward facile, dehumanizing, and politically counterproductive over-simplifications reducing religion to a unique cause of bloodshed. Fostered, thereby, are caricatures of one's political opponent, in a fashion playing into today's global ethos of endemic polarization. Given the intellectual and institutional forms of power accruing to the essentially contested concepts, religion, politics, and secularity, debates over the legitimacy of invoking them are no superfluous exercise in terminological pedantry.[5] Rather, it is crucial to reveal how these ideas have been strategically deployed as instruments of governing control.

The following overview of academic discourses surrounding religion and global politics underscores the extent to which the conceptual construction, and strategic deployment, of the categories religion, politics, and secularity bear implications for policymaking and civic life. The discussion is divided into four parts: a) the artificial bifurcation between religion, on the one hand, and secularity/politics on the other; b) the manner in which the modern, Western creation of a binary between religion and secularity/politics has given rise to implements of disciplinary power; c) secularism: a non-neutral idea with an uncertain future; and d) assessing the concept of religion within contemporary global politics – issues of violent conflict, identity, and the regulation of religious difference, especially the "politics of religious freedom" (Sullivan et al., 2015).

a) The artificial bifurcation between religion and secularity/politics

William Cavanaugh has coined "the myth of religious violence" to describe how the religion–secular binary was created in tandem with the modern state's self-representation as an authoritative guardian of worldly life, responsible for countering religion's violent propensities (Cavanaugh, 2009; Fitzgerald, 2015, 304). This act of creation occurred amidst the sixteenth- and seventeenth-century assemblage of European states, as a response to Catholic-Protestant "wars of religion" – wars that actually had a good deal more to do, Cavanaugh maintains, with such mundane interests as political strategizing and economic gain (Cavanaugh, 2009). Nonetheless, as the ostensibly secular state sought to carve out its own, self-legitimating monopoly over truth, power, and violence, it proved itself to be an author of quasi-religious orthodoxies (Asad, 2003, 21–66). The binary, "religious-secular" system of classification is therefore an illusory historical artefact of political dynamics (Casanova, 2012, 210).

The misleading mindset imagining that the modern world has become emptied of transcendence, and thereby "disenchanted", displays vast political ramifications.[6] In reaching back to Thomas Hobbes's 1651 maxim that the "great LEVIATHAN" is the "*Mortal God*", the German jurist Carl Schmitt called into question, shortly following World War I, the idea that the mundane realm is devoid of sacred power, particularly when it comes to the foundations of state sovereignty and governance (Hobbes, 1996 [1651], 114; Schmitt, 2005 [1922]). Thus arose Schmitt's formulation of political theology, holding that "[a]ll significant concepts of the modern theory of the state are secularized theological concepts, in which the political sovereign's sole authority to [decide] on the exception" serves to re-embody the power of a divine miracle worker (Schmitt, 2005 [1922], 36, 5). Coming in the wake of Schmitt, there have been arrayed inquires on how political theology, as well as often-apocalyptic political religions (e.g., the Nazism with which Schmitt was associated, and no less so Nazism's Bolshevik nemesis), appear within the contexts of modern state sovereignty and ideology (Voegelin, 2000). An upsurge in post-9/11 readings of Schmitt attests to his unfolding relevance for early twenty-first-century political dilemmas. One example is the implied, metaphysical absoluteness of sovereigns who accord to themselves perpetual emergency powers, allegedly justified by a ceaseless state of emergency and insecurity (Agamben, 2005; Kahn, 2011). Another manifestation is Islamic regimes' paradoxical attempts to claim transcendentally legitimated authority within a modern, Westphalian state that actually brooks no competitor to ultimate worldly power (Hallaq, 2013).[7] Thus, the underlying foundations and exceptional powers of modern political sovereignty reveal sacralized roots belying the religion–secular binary.

Moreover, the notion of a disenchanted world from which divine magic has receded occludes the presence of innumerable, alternative manifestations of sacredness (Weber, 1958 [1946]; Josephson-Storm, 2017). This point has important implications for revealing diverse ways of being religious within the setting of people's lived experiences. Such manifestations of sacredness might take inner-worldly, rather than primarily or even partially transcendent forms. These forms may integrate and alter pre-existing traditions, and frequently impart messianic promise to – in addition to sacralized politics – economics, sciences, arts, technology, and the worship of nature as well as of human societies and individuals themselves

(Voegelin, 2000; Josephson-Storm, 2017; Taylor, 2007; Gentile, 2006 [2001]; Noble, 1999). Moreover, because dominant notions of modern disenchantment postulate a world-historical account that was extrapolated primarily from European experiences, the bifurcation between religion and secularity/politics can be shown to lack its pretended, universal global validity. Within societies formerly colonized by the West (far from least, India), colonially engrafted paradigms of "secular disenchantment" have been resisted through myriad embodiments of "traditional religion . . . [that] seek transcendence" through everyday experiences like "art . . . music, and . . . festivals" (Kaviraj, 2016). Further countering Western dominance, China offers a complex illustration of state power that seemingly exemplifies a global, ideological turning away from transcendence, even as this officially communist state seeks to appropriate its population's diverse "spiritual revival" (Johnson, 2017, 397).

b) The religion–secular binary: an implement of disciplinary power

The artificial binary between religion and secularity/politics thus proves dubious, as it is unable to maintain its pretense to have progressed beyond, or at least strictly delimited, pervasive human quests for transcendence. Further interrogating the "religion" half of the binary illuminates how the categories, religion and secularity, have acted as implements of disciplinary power.

During the early 1960s, Wilfred Cantwell Smith advanced the landmark insight that invoking "the word and the concept 'religion'" is so fraught an exercise in objectification that the term "would be better dropped" (Smith, 1978 [1962], 19, 174). Accordingly, numerous scholars broadly concerned with religion have recently been deconstructing the conceptual raison d'être of their inquiries (Vries, 2008). Resulting analyses show how the ancient Latin term, *religio*, once filtered through unfolding doctrinal versions of Christian history, eventually metamorphosed into a circumscribed, "modern Western category of 'religion'" that was inapplicable across differing times, places and traditions (Casanova, 2012, 192–193; Nongbri, 2013). Thereby, a normative model of religion became predicated on post-Enlightenment constructs like "true *belief*" that could be interiorized within the individual, and separated from the supposed, superstitious ritualism of "primitive minds" (Asad, 2012, 40). Such a paradigm made possible nineteenth- and early twentieth-century Europeans' invention of a plurality of "world religions" like Buddhism and Islam (Masuzawa, 2005). These "religions" were then subject to being taxonomically ordered, and codified within the policies of colonial officials, helping to enable colonialists' conceptualizing and governing of non-Western Others (Chidester, 2014; Said, 1979 [1978]).

The genealogy underlying colonial conceptualizations of religion has made it possible for the religion–secular binary to be wielded as an implement of governmentalizing control (Asad, 1993).[8] The "historical category" of religion, once it sprang from Western origins to be made "universal", has been shaped in a way that enables governing authorities' forcible disciplining of behaviors deemed relevant

(Asad, 1993). Examples of such behaviors might be ritual practices of sacrifice presumed antithetical to rational, self-fulfillment-oriented liberalism; or, public speech that some find blasphemous, while others think it appropriately protected (Asad, 1993, 2009; Eagleton, 2018). The colonially imposed, disciplinary regulation of religion might have purported to travel in the name of enlightened reformism and the civilizing mission. However, deeply damaging worldwide effects have followed from such tactics as the carving of effectively antagonizing, administrative delineations among various religions, sects, and castes; and the radical reconfiguration of a vastly encompassing juridical tradition like *sharīʿa* to a narrowly tailored basis for addressing personal status matters like "family law" (Cook, 2014, 53–122; Makdisi, 2000; Weiss, 1998; Hallaq, 2010 [2009], 1–23; Asad, 2003, 205–256).

c) Secularism: a non-neutral idea with an uncertain future

As the other half of a binary construct wielding great disciplinary power, the idea of secularity carries orthodoxies of its own. Despite characteristic pretenses to the contrary, secularity does not denote a metaphysically neutral space where political life can play out in a rational, enlightened fashion, free from religious incursions that are blocked off by a watchful governing authority (Asad, 2003; Fitzgerald, 2015, 304). Given the porous, contested boundaries between religion and secularity/politics – if these boundaries can even be properly spoken of – it follows that "claims [religious, secular, or otherwise] about the Truth will have political consequences" (Laine, 2014, 233; Martin, 2014). What promises to remain, then, of the vigorously contested political doctrine that is secularism (Asad, 2003, 1)?

In its diverse formulations as an agent of state power, secularism typically claims to safeguard the sphere of worldly affairs, while holding the duty of neutrally arbitrating among competing truth claims. Yet, this claim is undergirded, paradoxically, by secularism's self-bestowed, ultimate truth-granting authority. The result has been endlessly variable sites of ongoing contestation, across the ideological spectrum of state-based politics. One broad realm of implications involves the historical legacies, and arguable continuance, of deaths perpetrated in the name of varying secularist ideologies like Bolshevism, fascism, Maoism, North Korean *Juche* (self-reliance), and crusading liberalism, including contemporary humanitarian interventions (Cavanaugh, 2009; Slezkine, 2017; Mishra, 2018). Within postcolonial settings, secularism's seizing of the doctrinal dominance that it denies to religion is illustrated by statist regimes whose modernization mantra has underwritten an absolutizing of state authority, over and against religious institutions. A still-reverberating case in point is authoritarian Egypt, following the short-circuited, post-2011 uprisings (Asad, 2015). Then, too, there is secularism's unmet promise to offer genuine emancipation in pursuit of a social principle like gender equality, an end goal that is arguably more undermined than advanced by the compulsory removal of "headscarves, veils . . . niqabs[,] and . . . burkinis", as well as by "sexual liberation" (Scott, 2018, 170). As the sociologist of religion Peter Berger asserted in 1999, to the extent that there remain people committed to the notion of secularity's offering an emancipatory antidote to religion, this commitment tends to be the restrictive province of a "globalized *elite*" "subculture composed of people with Western-type higher education" (Berger, 1999, 10).[9] It seems difficult to overstate the degree of Berger's prescience: consider current populist backlashes against the alleged fake news disseminated by secularist, globalizing elites who presume to substitute their purported, expert knowledge for the religiously infused, ethno-nationalist allegiances being voiced by "real people" and their chosen leaders, from the US to Russia, Turkey to India, Israel to Myanmar (Müller, 2016).

Much global debate surrounds the quandary of what might come "after secular law [and politics]" – with the attendant notion of a "post-secular" epoch hinging on the troubled premise that secularity can somehow be sealed off and overcome, in a sort of counter-modern triumphalism (Sullivan et al., 2011; Gorski et al., 2012; Warner et al., 2010). For one matter, the state-centric paradigm of political sovereignty underlying secularism is being fundamentally challenged (today's revanchist statists notwithstanding) by such transboundary forces as migration, capital flows, and rapid changes in communication. Accordingly, diverse forms of "transnational religion" hold the potential for helping to shape visions of society alternative to modern secularism (Rudolph and Piscatori, 1997). Secularism's uncertain future holds especial importance for postcolonial settings like India, where debate persists over whether it is an illegitimate, Western colonial implantation, or a civic model capable of renewal. In this latter vein, Rajeev Bhargava has raised the possibility of addressing "the crisis of secularism" by "rehabilitating" the idea (Bhargava, 2011). Bhargava proposes reimagining secularism within India, specifically, in a fashion that "see[s] . . . [no] necessary opposition between the secular and the religious"; but rather, "conceiv[es] a world inhabited by both religious and nonreligious people", while "minimiz[ing], if not altogether eliminat[ing]" forms of domination historically exercised by doctrinal communities against one another (Bhargava, 2011, 111). He goes so far as to invert the often-voiced notion that secularism is a Western colonial implantation, illegitimately forced into non-Western soil. Instead, Bhargava postulates, "[a] good, hard look at Indian secularism could also change the self-understanding of other Western secularisms", from the sometimes-draconian French *läicité*, to "a very individualist American liberal" variant (Bhargava, 2011, 110).

d) Assessing the concept of religion within contemporary global politics – violent conflict, identity, and the regulation of religious difference

Violent conflict

Amidst what some have regarded (however contestably) as a violence-scarred global religious resurgence, a burgeoning body of scholarship engages with outflows from "the enduring relationship of religion and violence" (Juergensmeyer et al., 2017 [2013]). An illuminating trend has been the application to historical and contemporary politics of insights from René Girard, whom a recent biography paints as "one of the few real thinkers we have had in our times" (Haven, 2018, 4). According to Girard, religion constitutes a fundamental human phenomenon that has developed in conjunction with violent social dynamics of sacrifice, victimization, and scapegoating (Girard, 1979 [1972], 1987 [1978]). Viewing humans as inherently mimicking (i.e., "mimetic") creatures who desire that which is possessed by their mirroring rival can shed light on the propulsive, resentment-fueled trajectories of violent conflict (Palaver and Schenk, 2018; Farneti, 2015; Antonello and Gifford, 2015; Mishra, 2017). Such trajectories play out across a diversity of present perils: from seemingly secular scenarios like contention over responsibility for addressing climate change, to ostensibly religious circumstances like Myanmar's ruling elites' cultivating the notion of a "Muslim 'Other'" whose presence within the country allegedly threatens the Buddhist majority's recent democratic political gains (Wade, 2017). As construed against this backdrop, secularism's colonially tainted tendency to repress, rather than acknowledge, the sacred significances of social dynamics has the effect of exacerbating, not ameliorating, resentment and violence (Mishra, 2017; Dupuy, 2013 [2008]).

Picking up on the scapegoating motif, Karen Armstrong seeks to counter the paradigmatic modern tendency that, by assigning religion unique causal blame for driving conflict, makes "a scapegoat of faith" (Armstrong, 2015 [2014], 3). Her position draws on Cavanaugh's assertion that "the myth of religious violence" emerges from the modern state's sought justification of its own supreme, worldly power. On Armstrong's interpretation, factors like historical struggles over resource allocation and geostrategic influence, modern nationalism, and reactions against Western colonial domination are in fact chief drivers of political violence; yet, these drivers are all too often cloaked in the sanctifying garb of religious symbolisms (Armstrong, 2015 [2014]). Notable work from among the vast literature on global jihadism – the ISIS embodiment and otherwise – often moves in an analogous spirit. Emphasized are the amalgamated historical conditions and political forces (e.g., postcolonial state tyranny, and destructive Western interventionism) that have helped give rise to jihadism's modernist framing and mobilization of Islamic discourses; this is as opposed to designating any essential Islam, per se, as a cause of violence (Hamid and McCants, 2017; Maher, 2016; McCants, 2015; Filiu, 2015).[10] In an interrelated vein, today's ominous public references to, and political opprobrium directed toward religious sectarianism as a supposed source of violence are critiqued by scholarship questioning whether postcolonial, intercommunal hostilities are actually the product of primordial hatreds. Underscored, instead, are rivalrous categories of identity, hardened through legacies of colonial divide-and-rule tactics (Hashemi and Postel, 2017; Makdisi, 2000).[11]

Identity

Categories of identity are greatly in flux, given present dynamics of globalization and transnationalism, and various reactions against these forces (e.g., recrudescent, exclusionary forms of nationalism and imperialism) (Bounds and Patterson, 2005). Moreover, the "post-Enlightenment assumption of human progress" has seen "the partial displacement of religion, as a basis for identity, by the nation state, class and ethnicity"; yet, this displacement is continually called into question by complex intersections among, and joint political mobilizations of these dimensions of identity (Benthall, 2019; Llobet, 2018). How, then, can scholars meet the politically freighted challenge of according full due to diverse, irreducible religious facets of identity? Ashutosh Varshney maintains that distinguishing religion from "ethnicity . . . attributes" like "common descent, language, history, culture, race. . . (or some combination of these)" is especially crucial "when ethnicity and religion clash (East and West Pakistan before 1971, Kashmiri Hindus and Muslims, Irish Protestants and Catholics, black and white American Christians)" (Varshney, 2009 [2007], 277). Then too, it is important to remember that one must distinguish between violence and conflict (Varshney, 2009 [2007], 278). Conflict enmeshing some aspects of contending identities is simply a fact of political life; as such, it may be that conflict is more usefully acknowledged in the pursuit of productive forms of civic engagement, than attempted to be quashed beneath enforced, illusory consensus (Mouffe, 2013). As categories of identity prove evermore destabilized, it is crucial to take each global scenario on its own terms, free from the superimposition of theoretical overgeneralizations (Bilgrami, 2014, 217–259).

Regulation of religious difference

States' recognition and regulation of differing religious communities present further, important policy ramifications for how religion is conceptualized (Mahmood, 2016). Critics of the "politics of religious freedom" point to how a historically Protestant, belief-based notion of religion delimits the modes of religious practice deemed worthy of the liberal state's emancipation and protection (Sullivan et al., 2015). Forms of religion falling outside those bounds of control are viewed by the modern state with disfavor, even repression. Under this line of critique, the belief-based ethic of religious freedom delivers not liberalism's promised safety and emancipatory rights, but rather, the sometimes hazardous status of being demarcated as a minority (Mahmood, 2016).[12]

Moreover, a belief-based, modernist idea of religion fails to acknowledge the welter of everyday, lived practices that find themselves presumptively relegated to a pre-modern past (Hurd, 2015; Orsi, 2012). The innumerable manifestations of "everyday religion" efflorescing beyond the modernist confines of state-sanctioned, doctrinaire belief emblematize the religious environments of today's world (Orsi, 2012, 150). On Robert Orsi's explanation, the variegated settings of day-to-day life show forth "how most of the world is religious today",

> from the alleys of Egypt to the new religions of African and Asian cities, to the shrine culture re-emerging across Southeast Asia; in the plethora of

religious improvisations in the United States; and in the resurgence of devotions to the saints across former Soviet space.

(Orsi, 2012, 150)

So, how might one conceptualize diverse, lived practices that do not lend themselves to tidy categorization as either religious or secular? As Cécile Laborde has recently argued, one approach might be to "disaggregate" religion into various "discrete features" that are also exhibited by "nonreligious conceptions" of "the good", such as "conscience, truth claims, culture, projects and preferences, modes of association, political ideology, community, ways of life" (Laborde, 2017, 240). By acknowledging a multiplicity of approaches to life and the sacred – without requiring their confinement to either side of the religion–secular divide – politics could be freed from the repressiveness that has accompanied this false binary.[13]

To gain insight into the complex and multiple ways of being religious and secular, without reifying the two distinct yet interrelated categories, we now move on to a summary of the South Asia debate on the interaction between religion, secularism, and politics. An analysis of the lived quotidian practices in South Asia enables de-fetishizing these categories. The chapter concludes by posing the burning question – is secularism compatible with Islam?

The South Asian context: secularism and religion

Although the postcolonial South Asian societies have added many new and competing dimensions to the meaning of secularism and its relationship to religion, this process has not been without contradictions or dilemmas. The South Asian debates have been, in particular, regarding the definition of secularism, what it means within the Indian context, and whether it is a useful concept in relation to the interlocking relationship between the religious and the secular, public realm. The colonial history, consequent fetishization of religious identities, and lately, the surfacing of religious and ethnic conflicts, have led scholars to rethink the process of secularization in South Asia. In India, particularly in the context of the political resurgence of the Hindu right, liberal academics such as Asghar Ali Engineer (1989) claimed that communalism has impaired secularism. Others, such as Madan (1998), Chatterjee (1994) and Nandy (1998), alleged that secularism – enforcing a decoupling of religion and politics – is a derivative discourse from the West, and is thus inapplicable to the Indian situation. Chatterjee argues that the secular vocabulary is inadequate to combat Hindu majoritarianism, and instead proposes "religious tolerance". He recommends incorporating a politics of representative democracy among religious groups, so that they generate internal reforms free from reformist interventions by the state and create conditions for mutual tolerance. Rajeev Bhargava (2011) negates the "inapplicability of secularism" thesis and states that the Indian version of secularism is not simply an "imitation", as it digresses significantly from the formulaic Western ideal. He moots the term "contextual secularism" to describe the Indian version, wherein the state adopts the stance of "principled distance". This implies that the state either intervene or refrain from interference, subject to which of the two positions is compatible with the values of religious liberty, freedom, and equality of citizenship. While acknowledging the limits of secularism, he argues that the best way forward is to rehabilitate it by thinking beyond the liberal framework.

Bilgrami (2012) also emphasizes the continued relevance of secularism, but suggests reimagining the concept. Criticizing Nandy for his simplistic anti-modernist stand and romanticism for past traditions, Bilgrami posits that the crisis of secularism is not because it was a modern imposition into an essentially traditionalist population, but rather because it was an imposition from the top that resisted negotiations between communities. He proposes secularization from below to facilitate dialogue between the state and various communities. Without dismissing the indispensability and empowering potential of universal categories such as secularism, modernity, public and private spheres, Chakrabarty (2000) acknowledges their inadequacies and exclusionary tendencies. He suggests renewing, questioning, and transforming these categories by and from the margins. Chakrabarty recognizes the inability of the scientific secular language to comprehend the religious world view and argues that "'disenchantment of the world' is not the only principle by which we world the earth. . . . The supernatural can inhabit the world . . . and not always as a problem" (1998, 27). Peter Van der Veer also affirms the continuities and links between the secular and the religious. He states that secular conceptions, although derived from the West, have been distinctively engaged by Indian political and cultural traditions.

Tejani (2008) also affirms that secularism is not simply a static idea borrowed from the West. She demonstrates that "rather than being distinct from community and caste, nationalism and communalism, liberalism and democracy, Indian secularism was a relational category that emerged at the nexus of all of these" (p. 15). Pandey (1999), without dispensing with the ideas of "modern" or "secular", situates secularism within the "totalizing" and "homogenizing" drive of the nation state. He maintains that the principle of secularism is integrated with the nationalist discourse that seeks to subsume diversities and differences within the dominant majoritarian culture. Pandey suggests unyoking the pair of "state" and "nation", so that the state does not represent the interests of the majoritarian community that presents itself as the "nation" (2007). Kumar (2008) argues that secularism has come to "connote an ideal of tolerance" and peaceful coexistence among various communities. However, the underlying essence of the notion of tolerance is not "so much to arrive at equality", but rather how to tolerate or put up with minorities or non-hegemonic groups. She suggests moving beyond the secular-liberal framework of tolerance or recognition of minorities to "more substantial questions about equality, democratic participation, and power sharing" (Kumar, 2008, 36). Prakash (2007), along with Gyanendra Pandey, also argues for moving away from the minority/majority discourse of Indian secularism toward a society of "multiple minorities", where there is no place for a permanent majority.

In the context of Sri Lanka, a similar critique of secular discourse as privileging the majoritarian religious community comes from David Scott (1999). Scott demonstrates how colonial modernity intervened to produce a "rational", "secular", and "codified" form of Buddhism, and crystallized the Sinhala-Buddhist identity. Sinhala-Buddhist nationalism not only challenged Christianity and colonial rule, but also proclaimed superiority over other socio-religious groups in post-colonial Sri Lanka. Instead of renewing the secular democratic apparatus, Scott calls for replacing it with a politics based on a recognition of communities and differences – a suggestion that is highly controversial as majoritarian and homogenizing tendencies may emerge within and between communities themselves.

Secularization debates concerning Pakistan have tended to focus on the Islamization process that is claimed to have deeply divided the country and superseded Jinnah's vision of a secular nation, exemplified in the work of Ian Talbot (2005). This view, however, has been challenged by many scholars who contend that it overlooks the nuances within Pakistan's society and politics, and simplistically equates Pakistan with "Fundamentalism" and "Islamism", thus proclaiming its utmost incompatibility with secularism. Humeira Iqtidar (2011) questions such readings that assume an inextricable connection between Pakistan, Islam, and fundamentalism. Not only does her work separate Islamists from other Muslim fundamentalists, but it also explores the complex relationship between Islamism, secularism, and secularization. Similarly, Magnus Marsden (2005) has brought to the fore the dialogic tradition present within Pakistan's society.

Moving beyond the theoretical frame: South Asia and lived religious practices[14]

Despite the divergent positions reflected in these debates, there is unanimity among scholars that the narrative of progressive rationalization needs to be shunned. Rather than the straightforward thesis of "decline of religion", a more complicated and entwined relationship is envisioned among religious, secular, public, and private spaces. A significant lacuna of the current debate is that scholars refashioning the secular/religion debate have remained largely in the theoretical realm, and have not located their conceptual propositions within the phenomenological realm of everyday reality. As a result, despite venturing beyond the conventional Western-liberal framework and challenging the absolute religious–secular divide, the current theories fail to capture the vivid, fluid, and multifunctional essence of religion as it is practiced in society.

Instead of overemphasizing the potency of dominant religious practices and their assimilating thrust, many scholars underscore the fuzzy, diverse, and overlapping socio-religious realities that remain resilient to categorization and political homogenization. Peter Gottschalk, in his study of a village in Bihar (2000), demonstrates how people in the village use past narratives and memories to exhibit multiple and shifting group identities that coexist with – and frequently cut across – religious and communal identity markers. Gottschalk refutes the idea of conceptualizing South Asia through the bifurcated lens of "Hindus" and "Muslims", and argues that it is difficult to define many religious and cultural practices as "Hindu" or

"Islamic" due to their internal perplexities, shifting dynamics, and shared nature. He alleges that not only do Western scholars, informed by the ideas of "secularism" and "rationality", simplistically label South Asian societies as essentially religious, but secular writers within South Asia also assume homogeneity and mutual exclusivity of religious categories, overlooking diversities, multiplicities, and interdependencies. Similarly, referring to regional cultural practices in the Sundarbans (a mangrove forest in the southern region of Bangladesh and West Bengal), Sufi a Uddin (2011) points to the female deity of forests, Bonbibi, who is believed to be the daughter of Ibrahim, a faqir (saint) from Mecca. Both Hindus and Muslims residing in close proximity to this forest and depending on it for their livelihoods worship Bonbibi, looking to her to protect them from tigers and other dangers. Uddin explains that typically, "at a Muslim shrine one would find a tomb of the saint where offerings are made. Here, instead, we have an image of a female holy personage that is by all appearances a Hindu goddess being venerated by both Muslims and Hindus" (ibid., 61). Although Hindus and Muslims venerate Bonbibi differently and accord divergent meanings to her, Bonbibi provides a common regional and cultural identity to them. The local practices, Uddin argues, are not merely "syncretic" or mutual borrowing. Syncretism, she holds, implies "improper mixing of two things of different origins". Rather, the local practices of people in the Sundarbans form a more complex and dynamic process that cannot be simply defined as either "Hindu" or "Islamic".

A similar argument is put forward by Dominique-Sila Khan (2004), who notes that the notion of "Hindus" and "Muslims" as two monoliths and binary opposites is misleading. It overlooks the socio-historical complexities of their evolution, as well as the convergence of their lived practices, cultures, and experiences. She further explains that convergence does not imply a linear relationship between two well-defined traditions, but is in fact the merger of a number of sectarian, ritual, and cultural practices that may ambivalently be defined as belonging to a broader spectrum of "Hindu" and "Muslim" modes of practices. Khan points out the limitations of the labels "syncretism" or "hybridization", which suggest a "temporary", "improper" or "exceptional" interaction between the religious communities. She instead introduces the term "threshold", or an open door or middle ground, where various traditions meet and intermix. Rather than a "temporary" space, it is a permanent opening for intermixing, where groups can retain their respective religious identities, or identities can blur without having to choose one side or another. The role of religion in public life as it facilitates not just competition but also dialogue, sharedness, and accommodation is illustrated in Anna Bigelow's (2010) work on three sacred spaces in the Punjab region. One of the sites, a "dargah" or tomb shrine of Haider Shaykh (a fifteenth-century Sufi saint), is in Malerkota region that has a largely Sikh and Hindu population and a minuscule number of Muslims. Two categories of ritual specialists take care of the shrine – "khalifas", the descendants of the saint, and "chelas", who are mainly Sikhs and Hindus and are said to be possessed by the saint's spirit. Bigelow argues that the fact that the saint is revered differently by "khalifas" and "chelas" – as well as by pilgrims of the different religions – could be a potential source of conflict. However, the very essence of the shrine, symbolized by "diversity of human kind and plurality of perspectives", wanes the possibilities of conflict, and in fact enables complex forms of convergences and sharedness. The other two sites described by Bigelow similarly point to a consensual process of shared-ness through a series of struggles and negotiations. As she explains, this did not "occur through an uncontested, spontaneous or unconscious acknowledgement of the site's identity. Rather this came about through dialogue and a series of compromises" (Bigelow, 2012, 39). Bigelow, Uddin, and Gottschalk point to the resilience of local religious and cultural practices that refuse to be assimilated into the hegemonic "Hindu" or "Muslim" political categories.

Is Islam compatible with secularism?

Nuancing the debate further, Roy (2007) addresses an oft-repeated question: Is Islam compatible with secularism? He points to the prejudiced understanding of Islam as a religion deeply immersed in a homogeneous traditional culture. Separat-ing religion and culture, Roy demonstrates that the rise of radical religious move-ments is rather a consequence of globalization that de-culturalizes individuals and enables them to articulate their views in transnational settings. According to Roy, Islamism also acts as an unintentional agent of secularization as it "individualizes and de-socializes religious practices" (2007, 76). Mahmood (2006, 344) states that the political project undertaken by the US to reform Islam reflects the normative force of secularism, which seeks to produce "a particular kind of religious subject who is compatible with the rationality . . . of liberal political rule". She advo-cates thinking outside the bounds of the prescribed secular-liberal imagery. In her study of Egyptian women's participation in the Islamic revivalist movement, she locates their agency in the willingness of women to inhabit religious norms and pious morality. These modes of flourishing are not captured in the restricted secular feminist discourses of individual autonomy and freedom. Joan Wallach Scott (2007) and Sherine Hafez (2011) have also contested the disciplinary vocabulary of secu-larization, which pronounces certain ways of being human as "progressive" while denouncing others. Rather than debating the intricacies that define the relationship between the "secular-liberal" and the "religious", Judith Butler (2011, 70) claimed that "depending on which religion we have in mind, the relation to the public will be different". Based on her study of the Israel–Palestine situation, she suggests a process of secularization based not on tolerance but cohabitation – the idea of plurality or polyvalence rooted in the diasporic traditions within Judaism – that enables a criticism of Israeli state violence coming from within the Jewish frame-works of social justice. Butler thus retrieves the potential of religion to invigorate political criticism.

Academic notions about Islam's incompatibility with "secular" or "democratic" values have been refuted by ethnographic works focusing on the secularization processes within various Muslim societies. Marsden's ethnographic study of the

Chitral area (2005) questions the assumption that Pakistani society has come under the conformist grip of a homogeneous, fanatic form of Islam. He alleges:

> it is often assumed that because Islam is a religion of submission . . . there is little place for the expression of individual creativity in the living of a Muslim life, and that morality in Muslim societies is a readymade and uncontested category simply deriving from a single set of scriptural codes.
>
> *(2005, 54)*

Contrary to this, he illustrates that despite pressure from various radical groups seeking to present a singular version of Islam, different groups among Muslims do not unthinkingly accept or reject any religious norm or political ideology. Chitral Muslims engage in critical and thoughtful debates about a number of issues, including music, poetry, dance, and a variety of ways to be good Muslims. Upholding a conversational tradition, these Muslims "do not think that it is only formally educated Islamic purists or 'modern' secular people who have the capacity to live rational, discerning, intellectually acute and morally sophisticated lives" (ibid., 10).

Facile notions about the relationship between Islam and secularization have also been contradicted by Iqtidar (2011). She not only points out fragmentations and heterogeneity within Islamist groupings, but also challenges the assumption of a sharp divide between "religious right" and "secular left". Through her ethnographic research focusing on Pakistan, she has problematized the taken-for-granted linear relationship between secularism and secularization. She proposes disentangling the two terms and exploring the nature of the relationship they share. Iqtidar demonstrates that secularization and secularism may at times move in very different directions. Certain state-initiated strategies of secularism may in fact stall the secularization process, "just as secularization may be supported by the very elements that oppose the ideology of secularism" (ibid., 35). Conducting an in-depth study of two Islamist parties in Pakistan–Jama'at-e-Islami and Jama'at-udda'wa – she illustrates that Islamists, though opposed to secularism, are in fact facilitating the secularization of society. By engaging in political competition with each other and claiming to offer a better model of piety, the Islamist groups are unintentionally bringing Islam into the forum of public and political debate. This increasing critical awareness about the various meanings of Islam is turning religion into a matter of objective, conscious choice of the individual, thus leading to secularization within Muslim societies.

This theoretical debate is essential to contextualize the processes of secularization in Jammu and Kashmir society, and the ways in which these processes influence the conflict discourse and vice-versa. It enables complicating the romanticized notion of Kashmiriyat and comprehending the tangled complex relationship between Kashmiri struggle for self-determination and religion without objectifying the connection between the two. Deconstructing the secularism debate and interrogating the notion of a linear, all-pervasive progression of secularism also enables understanding the prevalent contradictions and crisis within Indian secularism and its problematic relationship with the Kashmiri movement.

Notes

1 The term, fundamentalism, is regularly invoked to describe – and, problematically, some-times to impugn – adherents across a variety of worldviews whose distinctly modern modes of practice are characterized by traits like the literalist reading of scriptures (Arm-strong, 2009). Here, it is employed in the full awareness that scholars continually debate the legitimacy of extending the idea beyond its originating, early twentieth-century North American context: namely, where some Protestants reacted against the perceived excesses of modern secularity by advocating such "'fundamental' beliefs. . . [as] the iner-rancy of the Bible; [and] the direct creation of the world, and humanity, *ex nihilo* by God (in contrast to Darwinian evolution)" (Ruthven, 2005, 11).

2 "As one State Department official remarked in some exasperation after the revolution, 'Whoever took religion seriously?'" (Sick, 1985, 165).

3 The imagining of Muslims to be uniquely violent, as a premise underlying current expressions of "Political Islamophobia," actually extends back greater than a millennium to Western Christendom's representation of itself as the ostensible antidote to Muslim violence (Arjana, 2015).

4 This having been said, one might well regard secular liberalism as an ideology more fairly described, in actuality, as one "evangelical faith" among others – including, not least, liberalism's chief Cold War antagonist, Marxism (Gray, 2018, 5; Slezkine, 2017).

5 There would seem little doubt that religion, politics, and secularity are all essentially contested concepts, as in W. B. Gallie's classic sense that they "essentially involve endless disputes about their proper uses on the part of their users" (Connolly, 1993, 9–44; Gallie, 1955–56). The same might be said of the chronically demonized and politically appro-priated historical construct, terrorism (English, 2016; Hoffman, 2017, 1–44).

6 The archetypal understanding of a modern, secularized society is expressed in Max Weber's century-old dictum that "[t]he fate of our times is characterized by rationaliza-tion . . . and, above all, by the 'disenchantment of the world'", thereby draining "public life" of "the ultimate and most sublime values" (Weber, 1958 [1946], 155). As part of the intellectual genealogy comprising a purported, modern science of society, this claim had followed in the nineteenth- and early twentieth-century wake of August Comte's, Karl Marx's, and Émile Durkheim's asserting the socially constructed, fictitious char-acter of transcendent divinity (Aldridge, 2013). For that matter, one could probe to such late-medieval building blocks of modernity as "the [fourteenth-century] nominal-ist revolution" that, in ironically helping to reveal the actual inseparability of religion and secularity, imbued "theological origins" within the premise that the natural world's nameable phenomena are nondependent on transcendence (Gillespie, 2009 [2008]).

7 Beyond his 2013 argument asserting that a genuine Islamic state is, under modern conditions, impossible to achieve, Wael Hallaq has gone on to emphasize that the self-absolutizing modern state is merely one (albeit paradigmatic) organ of a colonizing, modernist worldview that seeks hegemonic domination over all worldly reality. Accord-ingly, any notion of secularity as distinct from religion belies modernity's utterly domi-neering metaphysical impulses (Hallaq, 2018).

8 Asad's signal contributions in this respect are consonant with those of the French phi-losopher Michel Foucault. Foucault sought to unearth the historical conditions of possi-bility amidst which power and knowledge converge in ideas that enable human subjects to be imagined, defined, and disciplinarily controlled (Foucault, 1972, 1994 [1966]). This dynamic is indicative of governmentality, meaning that subjects become ruled through the operation of "thinking involved in practices of government. . . [that is] embedded in language and other technical instruments but is also relatively taken for granted, i.e. it is not usually open to questioning by its practitioners" (Dean, 2010, 25). Given the ability of ideas to animate governmentalizing force, disciplinary control carries the mul-tiple connotations not only of disciplining a human subject, as in the sense of physically restraining a person with shackles, but also corralling a domain of knowledge (e.g., a target of study like religion) within the walls of an academic discipline.

9 Regarding itself as "the principal 'carrier' of progressive, Enlightened beliefs and values", this subculture manifests its high degree of influence in its "control [of] the institutions that provide the 'official' definitions of reality, notably the educational system, the media of mass communication and the higher reaches of the legal system" (Berger, 1999, 10). In posing these insights, Berger famously "recanted" his erstwhile, standard-bearing belief in the onward historical march of secularization (Aldridge, 2013, 66).

10 On the impossibility of subjecting Islam's "plenitude of meaning", as this meaning is variably made for "one-fifth of humanity", to an essential objectification, see Ahmed, 2016.

11 The question does arise as to whether sectarianism reflects a deep human propensity toward tension and contestation among worldviews. Some scholars suggest that such an impulse traces, in part, to fissures emerging as long ago as within the so-called great Axial Civilizations of the first millennium BCE (for instance, Zoroastrianism, the biblical prophetic tradition, Chinese thought, Greek philosophy, and Buddhism) (Eisenstadt, 1999; Taylor, 2011, 367–379). For that matter, Jan Assman has recently maintained that the Axial Age – while cautioning that this "global" historical demarcation is prone to being overstretched – saw the emergence, specifically with the Book of Exodus, of the revelatory outlook that would ultimately make possible "an idea of religion that has come to dominate much of the world", not least through political dimensions (Assman, 2018, 7, 338). Digging to still deeper strata of human history, sectarianism has also been attributed, alternatively, to a basic trait of tribalism (Fox, 2011).

12 The problematic limitations inhering in a belief-based right to religious freedom arguably point, further, to necessary critiques of human rights' presumed universality, and of hegemonic political projects justifying themselves in the name of "civilization" and "democratic values" (Nasir, 2016; Marshall, 2016). Although, not everyone concurs that the liberally conceived right to religious freedom is more worthy of being deconstructed than pursued. Some have assailed these so-called "new critics", together with their "guru" Asad, for their alleged, ivory-tower protected hostility to the urgent imperative for "religious freedom advocacy... [in a world where] human beings are killed, tortured, imprisoned, detained, robbed of their property, deprived of their houses of worship, and denied jobs, economic opportunities, and positions in public service on account of their religion" (Philpott and Shah, 2016, 389, 394–395).

13 As Hamid Dabashi asserts, while refuting any notion of Islam as the fixed, doctrinaire entity imagined by Western colonialists, and no less so by clerics acting in the service of a supposed Islamic Republic: "[i]n Iran, where I was born, Islam has always been integral to all phases of its unfolding cosmopolitan cultures, but never definitive of any one of them" (Dabashi, 2013, 153). On this basis, "Being a Muslim in the World" requires un-naming the religion and secularity that have become fetishized, commodified mirror images of one another. The space that "dis-invent[ing] religion and re-world[ing] the world" opens for "imagining the multiple universes, varied worlds, that [religion and all its ruses (from militant secularism to colonial modernity)] ... has historically denied, denigrated, and overcome" invites possible extension to the endlessly unnameable, lived experiences of many – Muslim or otherwise (Dabashi, 2013, 149).

14 Some of the discussion of this section has appeared in Bhatia Mohita, 'Secularism and Secularization: A Bibliographical Essay', *Economic and Political Weekly*, Vol. 48, No. 50, 2013, 103–110

References

Agamben, Giorgio. 2005. *State of Exception*, translated by Kevin Attell. Chicago and London: University of Chicago Press.

Ahmed, Shahab. 2016. *What Is Islam? The Importance of Being Islamic*. Princeton and Oxford: Princeton University Press.

Aldridge, Alan. 2013. *Religion in the Contemporary World: A Sociological Introduction*, Third Edition. Cambridge, UK and Malden, MA: Polity Press.

Antonello, Pierpaolo, and Paul Gifford, eds. 2015. *Can We Survive Our Origins? Readings in René Girard's Theory of Violence and the Sacred*. East Lansing, MI: Michigan State University Press.

Arjana, Sophia Rose. 2015. *Muslims in the Western Imagination*. Oxford and New York: Oxford University Press.

Armstrong, Karen. 2009. *The Case for God*. New York and Toronto: Alfred A. Knopf.

Armstrong, Karen. 2015 [2014]. *Fields of Blood: Religion and the History of Violence*. Toronto: Vintage Canada.

Asad, Talal. 1993. *Genealogies of Religion: Discipline and Reasons of Power in Christianity and Islam*. Baltimore and London: Johns Hopkins University Press.

Asad, Talal. 2003. *Formations of the Secular: Christianity, Islam, Modernity*. Stanford, CA: Stanford University Press.

Asad, Talal. 2009. 'Free Speech, Blasphemy, and Secular Criticism', in *Is Critique Secular? Blasphemy, Injury, and Free Speech*, edited by Talal Asad, Wendy Brown, Judith Butler, and Saba Mahmood. Berkeley: The Townsend Center for the Humanities, University of California.

Asad, Talal. 2012. 'Thinking About Religion, Belief, and Politics', in *The Cambridge Companion to Religious Studies*, edited by Robert A. Orsi, 36–57 Cambridge, UK and New York: Cambridge University Press.

Asad, Talal. 2015. 'Thinking About Tradition, Religion, and Politics in Egypt Today', *Critical Inquiry* 42: 166–214.

Asad, Talal. 2018. *Secular Translations: Nation-State, Modern Self, and Calculative Reason*. New York: Columbia University Press.

Assman, Jan. 2018. *The Invention of Religion: Faith and Covenant in the Book of Exodus*, translated by Robert Savage. Princeton and Oxford: Princeton University Press.

Benthall, Jonathan. 2019. 'In God's Name: Is Violence Built into the "DNA" of Sacred Texts?' *The Times Literary Supplement* 6058: 24–25.

Berger, Peter L. 1999. 'The Desecularization of the World: A Global Overview', in *The Desecularization of the World: Resurgent Religion and World Politics*, edited by Peter L. Berger, 1–18. Washington, DC and Grand Rapids, MI: Ethics and Public Policy Center and William B. Eerdmans Publishing Co. University Press.

Bhargava, Rajeev. 2011. 'Rehabilitating Secularism', in *Rethinking Secularism*, edited by Craig Calhoun, Mark Juergensmeyer, and Jonathan VanAntwerpen, 92–113. Oxford and New York: Oxford University Press.

Bhatia, Mohita. 2013. 'Secularism and Secularization: A Bibliographical Essay', *Economic and Political Weekly* 48 (50): 103–110.

Bigelow, Anna. 2010. *Sharing the Sacred: Practicing Pluralism in Muslim North India*. Oxford: Oxford University Press.

Bigelow, Anna. 2012. 'Everybody's Baba: Making Space for the Other', in *Sharing the Sacra: The Politics and Pragmatics of Intercommunal Economic & Political Weekly*, edited by G. Bowman, 39. Relations Around Holy Places. New York: Berghahn, December 14, 2013.

Bilgrami, Akeel. 2012. 'Secularism: Its Content and Context', *Economic & Political Weekly*, XLVII (4): 89–100.

Bilgrami, Akeel. 2014. *Secularism, Identity, and Enchantment*. Cambridge, MA and London: Harvard University Press.

Bounds, Elizabeth M., and Bobbi Patterson. 2005. 'Intercultural Understanding in a Community School', in *Religion in Global Civil Society*, edited by Mark Juergensmeyer, 171–188. Oxford and New York: Oxford University Press.

Burleigh, Michael. 2018. *The Best of Times, The Worst of Times: A History of Now*. London: Macmillan.

Butler, Judith. 2011. 'Is Judaism Zionism', in *The Power of Religion in the Public Sphere*, edited by E. Mendieta and J. VanAntwerpen. New York: Columbia University Press.

Casanova, José. 2012. 'Religion, the Axial Age, and Secular Modernity in Bellah's Theory of Religious Evolution', in *The Axial Age and Its Consequences*, edited by Robert N. Bellah and Hans Joas, 191–221. Cambridge, MA and London: The Belknap Press of Harvard University Press.

Cavanaugh, William T. 2009. *The Myth of Religious Violence: Secular Ideology and the Roots of Modern Conflict*. Oxford and New York: Oxford University Press.

Chakrabarty, D. 1998. 'Minority Histories, Subaltern Pasts', *Postcolonial Studies* 1 (1): 15–29.

Chakrabarty, D. 2000. *Provincializing Europe: Postcolonial Thought and Historical Difference*. Princeton: Princeton University Press.

Chatterjee, Partha. 1994. 'Secularism and Toleration', *Economic & Political Weekly* XXIX (28): 1768–1777.

Chidester, David. 2014. *Empire of Religion: Imperialism & Comparative Religion*. Chicago and London: University of Chicago Press.

Connolly, William E. 1993. *The Terms of Political Discourse*, Third Edition. Princeton: Princeton University Press.

Cook, Michael. 2014. *Ancient Religions, Modern Politics: The Islamic Case in Comparative Perspective*. Princeton and Oxford: Princeton University Press.

Dabashi, Hamid. 2013. *Being a Muslim in the World*. New York: Palgrave Macmillan.

Dean, Mitchell. 2010. *Governmentality: Power and Rule in Modern Society*, Second Edition. Los Angeles: Sage.

Dupuy, Jean-Pierre. 2013 [2008]. *The Mark of the Sacred*, translated by M. B. DeBevoise. Stanford, CA: Stanford University Press.

Eagleton, Terry. 2018. *Radical Sacrifice*. New Haven and London: Yale University Press

Eisenstadt, Shmuel. 1999. *Fundamentalism, Sectarianism, and Revolution: The Jacobin Dimension of Modernity*. Cambridge, UK: Cambridge University Press.

Engineer, Asghar. 1989. *Communalism and Communal Violence in India: An Analytical. Approach to Hindu-Muslim Conflict*. New Delhi: Ajanta Publications.

English, Richard. 2016. *Does Terrorism Work? A History*. Oxford: Oxford University Press.

Farneti, Roberto. 2015. *Mimetic Politics: Dyadic Patterns in Global Politics*. East Lansing, MI: Michigan State University Press.

Filiu, Jean-Pierre. 2015. *From Deep State to Islamic State: The Arab Counter-Revolution and Its Jihadi Legacy*. Oxford and New York: Oxford University Press.

Fitzgerald, Timothy. 2015. 'Critical Religion and Critical Research on Religion: Religion and Politics as Modern Fictions', *Critical Research on Religion* 3 (3): 303–319.

Foucault, Michel. 1972 [1969]. *The Archaeology of Knowledge & the Discourse on Language*, translated by A. M. Sheridan Smith. New York: Pantheon Books.

Foucault, Michel. 1994 [1966]. *The Order of Things: An Archaeology of the Human Sciences*. New York: Vintage Books.

Fox, Robin. 2011. *The Tribal Imagination: Civilization and the Savage Mind*. Cambridge, MA and London: Harvard University Press.

Fukuyama, Francis. 1989. 'The End of History?' *The National Interest* 16: 3–18.

Gallie, W. B. 1955–56. 'Essentially Contested Concepts', *Proceedings of the Aristotelian Society* 56: 167–198.

Gentile, Emilio. 2006 [2001]. *Politics as Religion*, translated by George Staunton. Princeton and Oxford: Princeton University Press.

Gerges, Fawaz A. 2016. *ISIS: A History*. Princeton and Oxford: Princeton University Press.

Gillespie, Michael Alan. 2009 [2008]. *The Theological Origins of Modernity*. Chicago and London: University of Chicago Press.

Girard, René. 1979 [1972]. *Violence and the Sacred*, translated by Patrick Gregory. Baltimore: Johns Hopkins University Press.

Girard, René. 1987 [1978]. *Things Hidden Since the Foundation of the World*, translated by Stephen Bann and Michael Metteer. Stanford, CA: Stanford University Press.

Gorski, Philip S., David Kyuman Kim, John Torpey, and Jonathan VanAntwerpen, eds. 2012. *The Post-Secular in Question: Religion in Contemporary Society*. New York and London: New York University Press.

Gottschalk, Peter. 2000. *Beyond Hindu and Muslim: Multiple Identity in Narratives from Village India*. New York: Oxford University Press.

Gray, John. 2018. 'Un-liberty–some Problems with the New Cult of Hyper-liberalism', *The Times Literary Supplement* 6000: 3–5.

Hafez, Sherine. 2011. *An Islam of Her Own: Reconsidering Religion and Secularism in Women's Islamic Movements*. New York: New York University Press.

Hallaq, Wael. 2010 [2009]. *Sharīʿa: Theory, Practice, Transformations*. Cambridge, UK and New York: Cambridge University Press.

Hallaq, Wael. 2013. *The Impossible State: Islam, Politics, and Modernity's Moral Predicament*. New York: Columbia University Press.

Hallaq, Wael. 2018. *Restating Orientalism: A Critique of Modern Knowledge*. New York: Columbia University Press.

Hamid, Shadi, and William McCants, eds. 2017. *Rethinking Political Islam*. New York: Oxford University Press.

Hashemi, Nader, and Danny Postel. 2017. *Sectarianization: Mapping the New Politics of the Middle East*. Oxford and New York: Oxford University Press.

Haven, Cynthia. 2018. *Evolution of Desire: A Life of René Girard*. East Lansing, MI: Michigan State University Press.

Hobbes, Thomas. 1996 [1651]. *Leviathan*, edited by J. C. A. Gaskin. Oxford and New York: Oxford University Press.

Hoffman, Bruce. 2017. *Inside Terrorism*, Third Edition. New York: Columbia University Press.

Hurd, Elizabeth Shakman. 2008. *The Politics of Secularism in International Relations*. Princeton and Oxford: Princeton University Press.

Hurd, Elizabeth Shakman. 2015. *Beyond Religious Freedom: The New Global Politics of Religion*. Princeton and Oxford: Princeton University Press.

Iqtidar, Humeira. 2011. *Secularizing Islamists? Jama'at-e- Islami and Jama'at-ud-Da'wa in Urban Pakistan*. Chicago: University of Chicago Press.

Johnson, Ian. 2017. *The Souls of China: The Return of Religion After Mao*. New York: Pantheon Books.

Josephson-Storm, Jason Ā. 2017. *The Myth of Disenchantment: Magic, Modernity, and the Birth of the Human Sciences*. Chicago and London: University of Chicago Press.

Juergensmeyer, Mark. 2000. *Terror in the Mind of God: The Global Rise of Religious Violence*. Berkeley and Los Angeles: University of California Press.

Juergensmeyer, Mark, Margo Kitts, and Michael Jerryson, eds. 2017 [2013]. *Violence and the World's Religions Traditions: An Introduction*. New York: Oxford University Press.

Kahn, Paul W. 2011. *Political Theology: Four New Chapters on the Concept of Sovereignty*. New York: Columbia University Press.

Kaviraj, Sudipta. 2016. 'Disenchantment Deferred', in *Beyond the Secular West*, edited by Akeel Bilgrami, 135–187. New York: Columbia University Press.

Khan, Dominique-Sila. 2004. *Crossing the Threshold: Understanding Religious Identities in South Asia*. London: I. B. Tauris.

Kumar, Priya. 2008. *Limiting Secularism: The Ethics of Coexistence in Indian Literature and Film*. Minneapolis: University of Minnesota Press.

Laborde, Cécile. 2017. *Liberalism's Religion*. Cambridge, MA and London: Harvard University Press.

Laine, James W. 2014. *Meta-Religion: Religion and Power in World History*. Oakland: University of California Press.

Lewis, James R. 2017. 'Introduction', in *The Cambridge Companion to Religion and Terrorism*, edited by James R. Lewis, 1–10. New York: Cambridge University Press.

Llobet, Anaïs. 2018. 'It's About Russia, Not God', translated by Charles Goulden, *Le Monde Diplomatique* 1804: 10–11.

Madan, T. N. 1998. 'Secularism in Its Place', in *Secularism and Its Critics*, edited by Rajeev Bhargava. New Delhi: Oxford University Press.

Madan, T. N. 2003. 'The Case of India', *Daedalus* 132 (3): 62–66.

Maher, Shiraz. 2016. *Salafi-Jihadism: The History of an Idea*. Oxford and New York: Oxford University Press.

Mahmood, Saba. 2006. 'Secularism, Hermeneutics, and Empire: The Politics of Islamic Reformation', *Public Culture* 18 (2): 323–347.

Mahmood, Saba. 2016. *Religious Difference in a Secular Age: A Minority Report*. Princeton and Oxford: Princeton University Press.

Makdisi, Ussama. 2000. *The Culture of Sectarianism: Community, History, and Violence in Nineteenth-Century Ottoman Lebanon*. Berkeley and Los Angeles: University of California Press.

Marsden, Magnus. 2005. *Living Islam: Muslim Religious Experience in Pakistan's North-West Frontier*. Cambridge: Cambridge University Press.

Marshall, Ruth. 2016. 'Beyond Religious Freedom: Re-thinking Religion in a Political Scientific Wilderness', *The Immanent Frame: Secularism, Religion, and the Public Sphere*. Available at: https://tif.ssrc.org/2016/07/22/rethinking-religion-in-a-political-scientific-wilderness/, accessed on June 15, 2019.

Martin, David. 2014. *Religion and Power: No Logos Without Mythos*. Farnham: Ashgate.

Masuzawa, Tomoko. 2005. *The Invention of World Religions: Or, How European Universalism Was Preserved in the Language of Pluralism*. Chicago and London: University of Chicago Press.

McCants, William. 2015. *The ISIS Apocalypse: The History, Strategy, and Doomsday Vision of the Islamic State*. New York: St. Martin's Press.

Mishra, Pankaj. 2017. *Age of Anger: A History of the Present*. New York: Farrar, Straus and Giroux.

Mishra, Pankaj. 2018. 'The Mask It Wears', *London Review of Books* 40 (12): 9–13.

Mouffe, Chantal. 2013. *Agonistics: Thinking the World Politically*. London and New York: Verso.

Müller, Jan-Werner. 2016. *What Is Populism?* Philadelphia: University of Pennsylvania Press.

Nandy, A. 1998. 'The Politics of Secularism and The Recovery of Religious Tolerance', in *Secularism and Its Critics*, edited by Rajeev Bhargava. New Delhi: Oxford University Press.

Nasir, Muhammad Ali. 2016. 'Governing (Through) Religion: Reflections on Religion as Governmentality', *Philosophy and Social Criticism* 42 (9): 873–896.

Nathans, Benjamin. 2017. 'Bolshevism's New Believers', *The New York Review of Books* 64 (18). Available at: www.nybooks.com/articles/2017/11/23/bolshevisms-new-believers/, accessed on June 15, 2019.

Noble, David F. 1999. *The Religion of Technology: The Divinity of Man and the Spirit of Invention*. New York: Penguin.

Nongbri, Brent. 2013. *Before Religion: A History of a Modern Concept*. New Haven and London: Yale University Press.

Orsi, Robert A. 2012. 'Afterword: Everyday Religion and the Contemporary World: The Un-Modern, or What Was Supposed to Have Disappeared But Did Not', in *Ordinary Lives and Grand Schemes: An Anthropology of Everyday Religion*, edited by Samuli Schielke and Liza Debevec, 146–161. New York and Oxford: Berghahn Books.

Palaver, Wolfgang, and Richard Schenk, eds. 2018. *Mimetic Theory and World Religions*. East Lansing, MI: Michigan State University Press.

Pandey, Gyanendra. 1999. 'Can a Muslim Be an Indian', *Comparative Studies in Society and History* 41 (4): 608–629.

Pandey, Gyanendra. 2007. 'The Secular State and the Limits of Dialogue', in *The Crisis of Secularism in India*, edited by A. D. Needham and R. S. Rajan. New Delhi: Permanent Black.

Philpott, Daniel, and Timothy Samuel Shah. 2016. 'State of the Field Essay: In Defense of Religious Freedom: New Critics of a Beleaguered Human Right', *Journal of Law and Religion* 31 (3): 380–395.

Prakash, Gyan. 2007. 'Secular Nationalism, Hindutva, and the Minority', in *The Crisis of Secularism in India*, edited by A. D. Needham and R. S. Rajan. New Delhi: Permanent Black.

Roy, Olivier. 2007. *Secularism Confronts Islam*. New York: Columbia University Press.

Rudolph, Susanne Hoeber, and James Piscatori, eds. 1997. *Transnational Religion and Fading States*. Boulder, CO: Westview Press.

Ruthven, Malise. 2005 [2004]. *Fundamentalism: The Search for Meaning*. Oxford: Oxford University Press.

Said, Edward. 1979 [1978]. *Orientalism*. New York: Vintage Books.

Schmitt, Carl. 2005 [1922]. *Political Theology: Four Chapters on the Concept of Sovereignty*, translated by George Schwab. Chicago and London: University of Chicago Press.

Scott, David. 1999. *Refashioning Futures: Criticism After Postcoloniality*. Princeton: Princeton University Press.

Scott, Joan Wallach. 2007. *The Politics of the Veil*. Princeton: Princeton University Press.

Scott, Joan Wallach. 2018. *Sex & Secularism*. Princeton and Oxford: Princeton University Press.

Sheikh, Mona Kanwal, and Ole Wæver. 2012. 'Western Secularisms: Variation in a Doctrine and Its Practice', in *Thinking International Relations Differently*, edited by Arlene B. Tickner and David L. Blaney, 275–298. New York: Routledge.

Shortt, Rupert. 2019. *Does Religion Do More Harm Than Good?* London: Society for Promoting Christian Knowledge.

Sick, Gary. 1985. *All Fall Down: America's Tragic Encounter With Iran*. New York: Random House.

Slezkine, Yuri. 2017. *The House of Government: A Saga of the Russian Revolution*. Princeton and Oxford: Princeton University Press.

Smith, Wilfred Cantwell. 1978 [1962]. *The Meaning and End of Religion*. San Francisco: Harper & Row.

Spohn, Willfried. 2003. 'Multiple Modernity, Nationalism and Religion: A Global Perspective', *Current Sociology* 51 (3–4): 269.

Sullivan, Winnifred Fallers, Elizabeth Shakman Hurd, Saba Mahmood, and Peter G. Danchin, eds. 2015. *Politics of Religious Freedom*. Chicago and London: University of Chicago Press.

Sullivan, Winnifred Fallers, Robert A. Yelle, and Mateo Taussig-Rubbo, eds. 2011. *After Secular Law*. Stanford, CA: Stanford University Press.

Talbot, Ian. 2005. *Pakistan: A New History*. Basingstoke: Palgrave Macmillan.

Taylor, Charles. 2007. *A Secular Age*. Cambridge, MA and London: The Belknap Press of Harvard University Press.

Taylor, Charles. 2011. *Dilemmas and Connections: Selected Essays*. Cambridge, MA and London: The Belknap Press of Harvard University Press.

Tejani, Shabnum. 2008. *Indian Secularism: A Social and Intellectual History*. Bloomington: Indiana University Press.

Toft, Monica Duffy, Daniel Philpott, and Timothy Samuel Shah. 2011. *God's Century: Resurgent Religion and Global Politics*. New York and London: W. W. Norton & Company.

Uddin, Sufia. 2011. 'Beyond National Borders and Religious Boundaries: Muslim and Hindu Veneration of Bonbibi', in *Engaging South Asian Religions: Boundaries, Appropriations, and Resistances*, edited by M. N. P. Schmalz and P. Gottschalk. New York: SUNY Press.

Varshney, Ashutosh. 2009 [2007]. 'Ethnicity and Ethnic Conflict', in *The Oxford Handbook of Comparative Politics*, edited by Carles Boix and Susan C. Stokes, 274–294. Oxford: Oxford University Press.

Voegelin, Eric. 2000. *The Collected Works of Eric Voegelin, Volume 5: Modernity Without Restraint: The Political Religions; The New Science of Politics; and Science, Politics, and Gnosticism*, edited by Manfred Henningsen. Columbia, MO and London: University of Missouri Press.

Vries, Hent de, ed. 2008. *Religion: Beyond a Concept*. New York: Fordham University Press.

Wade, Francis. 2017. *Myanmar's Enemy Within: Buddhist Violence and the Making of a Muslim 'Other'*. London: Zed Books.

Warner, Michael, Jonathan VanAntwerpen, and Craig Calhoun. 2010. 'Editors' Introduction', in *Varieties of Secularism in a Secular Age*, edited by Michael Warner, Jonathan VanAntwerpen, and Craig Calhoun, 1–31. Cambridge, MA and London: Harvard University Press.

Weber, Max. 1958 [1946]. 'Science as a Vocation', in *From Max Weber: Essays in Sociology*, translated and edited by H. H. Gerth and C. Wright Mills, 129–156. New York: Oxford University Press.

Weiss, Bernard G. 1998. *The Spirit of Islamic Law*. Athens, GA and London: University of Georgia Press.

3

SECULARIZATION, RELIGION AND IDENTITY

Resistance in Kashmir Valley

Reeta Chowdhari Tremblay and Shahnawaz Gull

There is a general perception that the Kashmiri Azadi movement in the Valley is increasingly being framed in terms of Islamic radicalism. The 'New Age Militancy' – indigenous tech-savvy, gun-carrying youth – has, in this view, shifted the resistance movement away from the secular (the traditional ethnic identity Kashmiriyat) towards a conservative-, religious- and patriarchally inspired praxis. But simply to term the present Kashmiri resistance as an Islamic radical movement, one dominated by armed and stone-pelting young men, is at once too simple and off the mark. Such a description takes away from the phenomenon's multidimensional and variegated character. Resistance, which is an oppositional practice to the relations of power and whose fundamental objective is to undermine a system of domination, comes in different types, modes and shapes. Resistance is "manifest individually or collectively, at the local level or at the level of the state, as a first response or a last resort" (Faulkner and MacDonald, 2016, 11). Different modalities of resistance accompany varying types of agency, ranging from compliant to open and confrontational. In particular, ever since the 1989 mass-supported political insurgency, it is evident that the Kashmiri 'Other' is vibrant with agency and has the will to resist.

Kashmir's secessionist/nationalist conflict, as Spencer asserts, is "both an 'old war' as well as a 'new war', and therefore needs to be evaluated with an approach reflecting the dynamics of ground realities" (Spencer, 2013, 77). The seeds of political contestation, i.e. the assertion of Islamic identity as a counter-identity to Hindu nationalism as well as dissatisfaction with the governance agenda were sown at the very moment the Indian army was air-dropped into the Valley in order to liberate Kashmir from the tribesmen in 1947. Since then, each period of Kashmir's political history would contribute to the collective memories and conscience of the population, shaping and reshaping the nature of resistance, both in the everyday life of Kashmiri Muslims and in an open collective assertion of nationalism against the Indian state.

The Kashmir Valley is a place where both past events and a collective memory, never quite effacing what came before, play significant roles. The Valley's public discourse has incrementally progressed: from the demand for *raishumari*, then for autonomy, and finally, for *azadi*.[1] However, azadi carries within it multiple meanings: raishumari itself (the right to self-determination, *haq e khud iradiyat*, as promised by Nehru, and then later confirmed by the UN Security Council resolution of 1948); the protection of Article 370 and Article 35A; the restoration of Kashmir as a nation and not as a *riyasat* (state within India); and the protection of the Kashmiri Muslim religious identity and the promise of a life of dignity, and the protection of human rights. These meanings are sometimes used singly and sometimes in combination by different actors and depending upon the specific context. Most significantly, the azadi/autonomy demands are framed in secular nationalist terms. Religiosity, of course, plays a prominent role (and that role has increased with the ongoing secessionist/nationalist struggle and with the demographic homogenization of the Valley resulting from the minority Hindu exodus in 1990) but it is both conflated with and subservient to the political/nationalist demands.

In this chapter we make three major points. First, we argue that Kashmir Valley's secular nationalism intersects in a dynamic, complex manner with the fluid and multidimensional processes of secularization and resistance. The 'shared public understanding of the nation' in the Valley continues to be filtered through the lense of secular politics; indeed, the word 'political' has become synonymous with 'secular'. It is the operative phrase to describe the 'legitimate' resistance of the Kashmiri Muslim population to the Indian state as well as the seeking of a solution to the Kashmir conflict. We maintain that in the Kashmir Valley, the secular political project is built in the wake of secularization and that the protracted on-going secessionist/nationalist movement in the Valley against the Indian state has maintained a continuity of the idiom 'secular nationalism' with the 1940s' Kashmiri nationalist movement against the Hindu Dogra rule. This particular version of secular nationalism, first witnessed in the Valley's resistance to the Hindu ruler, and now to the Indian state has, on the one hand, been consciously separated from religious nationalism, and, on the other hand, has been built upon the inherited and the ongoing dynamic and complex processes of secularization.[2] Secularization, however, adjusts to qualitative shifts over a period of time in 'how religious thought and practice are imagined within society'. It involves, as Mohita Bhatia states, "diverse sociocultural and religious sanctions and religious interactions, conflicts, dialogue and compromises with variable outcomes that take place within the realm of everyday life" (2013, 106). Religiosity has been consistently framed and vocalized by the Kashmiri Muslim population as tolerance – the continuing reaffirmation of a tolerant Kashmiriyat ethnic identity (entailing the peaceful coexistence of all religious communities). In other words, secularization is the basis upon which resistance has been and continues to be framed: in terms of a secular/political movement, whether the demands be for increased autonomy within the Indian state or for outright azadi. In this framing, religiosity (or the Islamic identity) is not being denied but is managed through secular nationalism and secularization. It is through the medium of the present and the past processes of secularization that religion and nationalism are intertwined. Although religious imagery takes different shapes, depending upon the context, the time and the actors, the imagining of the future state project (whether an independent 'state' or a distinct part of the Indian federal state with internal autonomy) has been consistently articulated as secular (read 'political') in the Valley – inclusive of all communities and three distinct regions of the state.

Second, we suggest that the processes of secularization are not without contradictions. We explain these contradictions through our discussion of the 2016 post-Burhan Wani developments in the Valley (the so-called New Age Militancy), often associated with the rise of Islamic nationalism. Religiosity is no longer hidden. Political activism is conflated with Islamic resistance. Masculinity and virility in the protection of mothers and daughters are being played out in the political confrontation between the 'colonized' (the Kashmir Muslims) and the 'colonizer' (India). Yet, the Valley's distinct processes of secularization are often repeated while adhering to the political project of azadi, acknowledging the religious heterogeneity of the society. The small minority of Islamists, like Zakir Musa, who oppose secularism and have supported the Islamic State have inadvertently facilitated secularization. The organized separatists, under the umbrella group of Hurriyat, have openly opposed Musa's platform. The Burhani group, as well, quickly ousted him from the leadership position for suggesting that the Kashmir fight is to establish Sharia. There is a clear recognition that the global Islamic nationalism of Musa and a few others undermines the azadi movement, alienating the progressive elements in India and in the international community.

Third, we point out that as opposed to the young militants like Wani and others, for the common citizenry, particularly the middle class, the secularization processes entail negotiation and dialogue in shifting the boundaries between religion, culture, politics and community. The middle class resist through compliance. They participate in competitive professional educational and administrative programmes and challenge the state from within. In their quotidian resistance where accommodation and resistance operate simultaneously, we see secular nationalism interacting with class and ethnicity to generate diverse trajectories of secularization – a far more complex and dynamic secularization process than is generally recognized.

Secularization, resistance and the secular nationalism project

Joya Chatterjee in her essay, 'Secularization and Partition Emergencies', suggests that the violent partition of the Indian subcontinent along religious lines in 1947, resulting in displacement of the population and disorder for the two new nation-states, "generated tendencies towards secularization in both India and Pakistan". She goes on to point out that "the process of secularization occurred while communal attitudes were pervasive, sometimes despite, and sometimes because of, extreme violence" (2013, 42). However, in the case of the state of Jammu and Kashmir, we suggest that secular nationalism is built upon underlying processes of secularization with which the contemporary resistance/azadi/protest politics maintain an uninterrupted continuity. It is founded upon the fourteenth-century historical symbol of *Kashmiriyat* – an ethnic and cultural identity where the "traditions followed by Kashmiri Muslims, the indigenous method of practicing their faith, and following customs, sometimes to the extent of modifying the rules of Islamic jurisprudence makes them distinct from their co-religionists" (Punjabi, 1992, 136).

However, the secularization processes are not without contradictions. First, on the one hand, the concept of Kashmiriyat is invoked by Kashmiri Muslims to point to the indigenous philosophies, traditions, practices of Islam (Sufism) and Hinduism (Shaivism) in the Valley, differentiating both religious communities from their counterparts elsewhere, generating tolerance at the societal level. Cherar-e-Sharif, the Sufi shrine (known as the Nanda Shrine to Hindus and Shiekh Nur-ud-in Shrine to Muslims), is regularly visited by both Hindus and Muslims. This and various other traditions point to the convergence of the two communities' lived practices, culture and experiences. Underlying this convergence is a plurality of perspectives, a consensual process of shared-ness through dialogue, negotiations and compromises. Following Dominiqiue-Sila Khan, it would be appropriate to point out that this process of secularization presents a middle ground where the two traditions meet and intermix (2004). It is a permanent opening for intermixing where each community maintains and seeks to protect its particular religious identity. Kashmiriyat, for the Valley's Muslims, points to the resilience of the lived culture and practices of tolerance. However, this middle ground is also based on an explicit understanding between the two communities that their religious and ritual differences are to be negotiated but to be neither refined nor erased. If this process of negotiation, termed as the practices of proximity by Dipesh Chakrabarty (2002, 148), is not followed, the product could be communal chaos, thus harmful to the political cause of asserting Kashmir's distinct identity. One such example of communal chaos was the 1967 episode when a young Kashmiri Pandit (Brahmin) girl, Parameshwari, married a Muslim boy. The Kashmiri Hindu minority, which has carefully guarded its religious identity by maintaining social exclusivity and no inter-religious marriages, were outraged. The Valley became the scene of strong protests and demonstrations in which the Muslims were accused of forcibly converting and kidnapping the Hindu girl. The Muslims counter protested protecting their daughter-in-law who was renamed as Parveen Akhtar (when she converted during her marriage). Communal passions had already been let loose.

Second, and on the other hand, the indispensability of the historical tradition or the myth of Kashmiriyat for serving the objectives of nationalism leads to the erasure of conflicts and struggles from memory. In other words, the socio-historical complexities tend to be overlooked. The Valley's demographically insignificant Hindu minority, who have traditionally occupied elite positions, have run the risk of being absorbed into a Muslim state of Kashmir. Every time there has been an exodus of this community, they have blamed Muslim oppression. It is asserted that during Sultan Sikander's rule (1398–1413), all Hindus except 11 families fled the Valley because of the Sultan's order forbidding Hindus to wear their religious mark on their foreheads and his melting down of all golden and silver Hindu idols, converting these into money. Similarly, the Hindus point out that the violence against the community at the start of the 1989 political insurgency accompanying the secessionist movement led to their exodus from the Valley in 1990. The Valley's Muslims see it differently. A large majority suggests that historically the Kashmir Pandits have left the Valley for brighter economic prospects or green pastures and the present migration of the minority community follows a similar path.

Third, Kashmiri Muslims have always remained anxious of losing their religious identity and thus have been vocal in expressing their fears. In June 1931, Kashmiri Muslims were outraged by the reports that the Dogra government had prevented the Muslims from offering their prayers in a mosque in Jammu and that some pages of the Holy Koran had been found in a public latrine. Kashmiri Muslim processions in the Valley were met with police fire which killed 22 people, an event since commemorated as Martyr's Day and celebrated annually in the Valley. This existential anxiety was evident in 1947 when the first Sikh regiment landed at the Srinagar airport to get rid of tribal invaders in the Valley. The regiment raised their religious slogan, *Jo Bole So Nihal, Sat Sri Akal* (a Sikh slogan literally shout of victory, triumph or exultation); Srinagar's Muslims were upset. Sheikh Abdullah had to calm them down explaining the religious ritual and its significance for creating unity amongst the Sikh soldiers. Similarly, the December 27, 1963 disappearance of the holy relic from the Hazratbal shrine and the consequent daily demonstrations was another significant episode in Kashmiri history when Muslims expressed anger at the regional government for not protecting their religious identity. These fears and anxieties have often led to the counterpoising of the Kashmiri Muslim identity with the secular Kashmiri identity – Kashmiriyat.

Nevertheless, Kashmiriyat appears to have worked well for both Hindu and Muslim communities in their struggle against the Dogra rule. Secular nationalism, as conceived in the 1940s by Kashmiri Muslim elites (in collaboration with the progressive Hindu community) against the Dogra rule, was to be built upon the so-called already existing processes of secularization, unique to the Kashmiri nation. In the late nineteenth and early twentieth centuries, the princely state of Jammu and Kashmir was incrementally integrated into British India. Through the administrative offices of the British resident in Kashmir, administrative and political reforms were introduced which included a Council of Ministers, a partly elected and partly appointed legislative assembly, the Praja Sahib, and an administrative review of land settlement. The latter resulted in the introduction of partial land tenure reforms and land revenue assessment policies. The missionaries introduced English education to the Valley and medical missionaries helped to bring Western medicine and established hospitals. Meanwhile, the Hindu ruler, Maharaja Hari Singh, responding to protests from Jammu's Hindus and the Kashmiri Pandits (the Valley's Hindu minority) against the predominant presence of British citizens in the state's administrative structure, introduced 'state-subject laws', restricting government employment and ownership of property exclusively to the citizens of the state. However, the middle-class Muslims of the Valley were to fare poorly under this new governance structure. In 1931 the Muslim Conference led by Sheikh Abdullah launched a protest. The Sheikh was quick to realize that a full-fledged nationalist movement against the Dogra rule could only be successful if it were framed as secular (to recruit the influential minority Hindu community in the Valley) and socialist (to make poverty in the Valley an issue in order to gain the Congress party's support in India). In 1939, Abdullah was to transform the Muslim Conference into a mass-based secular, socialist nationalist movement under a new organization, the National Conference. While continuing to mobilize the Kashmiri Muslim population through the religious venue of the Hazratbal shrine, Islam was to remain prominent. Its secular-progressive discourse was (and continues to remain) mediated by the use of religious idioms and symbols. It, nevertheless, allowed the emerging Kashmiri Muslim elite to secularize its approach, first, in order to broaden the legitimacy of their nationalist movement against the hundred-year-old Hindu rule, and, second, to forge its constitutional alliance with the Indian state so that it would continue to keep intact its geographical political identity, a product of British colonialism. To the prominent slogan to unite the Muslim community, *Nara-e-Takbir* (God is great), was added the call for unity of Hindus and Muslims − *Sher-I-Kashmir ka kya irshad − Hindu-Muslim-Sikh etihad* (what is the message of the lion of Kashmir − Sheikh Abdullah − Hindu-Muslim-Sikh unity). After Kashmir state's liberation from Hindu Dogra rule, the processes of secularization would therefore serve two purposes: define the state's distinctness within India and maintain the unity of its three religiously/linguistically differentiated regions. Thus began the dialogic and interactive relationship between secularization and secular nationalism, which not only became the foundational legal/constitutional framework of Jammu and Kashmir's distinct status within India, but has also to this day both structured and organized everyday Kashmiri Muslim resistance to the Indian state.

Resistance and the institutional design

Over the years, the Kashmir Valley has been a witness to multiple strands of contestation: cultural, religious, class and political. However, it is the initial design of political institutions between 1947 and 1952, in naming a secular Kashmiri political identity by simultaneously recognizing differences and similarities (Kashmir's own distinct secularization processes embedded in its Kashmiriyat identity and India's secularism), which has generated a framework within which resistance has been and is being played out. Kashmiri resistance is both a product of and a response to this institutional framework.

Resistance is deeply contingent upon institutional forms and their evolution over a period of time. Institutional configurations are central in determining how and when politics becomes nationalist, the nature of resistance to the dominant political power − whether it is organized or muted, structured or unstructured as in everyday resistance − and in determining how the processes of secularism and secularization interact. In other words, political institutions and their initial design emerge as central and crucial forces in creating a political context shaping agency and identity landscapes (religion's complex and contingent intertwining with other elements of ethnic and/or civil identity and secular politics). Whether in naming, amending or reformulating identity, institutions generate the foundational narrative not only with regard to the processes of identity construction, transformation and mobilization, but also in the establishment of mechanisms of inclusion and exclusion and group differentiation. As Lecours points out, "political institutions contribute, independently of agency, in the creation, crystallization, and politicization of territorial identities through the boundaries they set in the subjective and political universe of citizens" (2005, 184). Consequently, the agency of the resister is greatly conditioned by the institutional context. In short, "agency does not occur in an institutional vacuum" (Lecours, 2005, 185). The legal, institutional space for ethnic and political identity, once it has been constructed by the state, has far reaching consequences for the future actions and choices of both the state itself and the various fragments of the civil society. Resisters in their oppositional activity to the dominant political power operate within the legal and institutional framework.

Between 1947 and 1952, the Indian state, through its legal and constitutional apparatus and by virtue of an elite alliance (between Sheikh Abdullah and the Nehru government) based on ideological grounds (secularization and secular nationalism and the exigencies of political power), had a significant input in constructing and shaping Kashmiri ethnic as well as political identity. Within the context of the October 1947 Treaty of Accession (whereby the Hindu ruler of the princely state joined the newly formed Indian state after the tribal invasion supported by Pakistan) promising the people of Kashmir the right of self-determination, the Indian state created two constitutional/legal provisions, first in 1950, Article 370 in the Indian Constitution recognizing a special status for the State of Jammu and Kashmir, and later on through a 1954 Presidential Order, the incorporation of Article 35 A.

For its part, the Indian state through these legal categories, simultaneously embraced its similarity and difference with the state, particularly its Muslim population. It recognized the cultural and political identity of the Kashmiri population (the Valley's fourteenth-century ethnic identity 'Kashmiriyat' of syncretism and tolerance by the Muslim Sufi community of other religions and traditions), thereby privileging the Valley and its traditions over the other regions' (Jammu and Ladakh) practices and history. Thus, in forging a new identity for the Kashmiris, the Indian state was to appropriate a particular history and cultural identity at the cost of denying the actual or perceived experiences of both the Hindu and Buddhist communities. Yet, it asserted that the similarities between Kashmir and the Indian state were based on the socialist, democratic and secularist agenda of Sheikh Abdullah's government (secularist in view of India's assertion in the new Indian Constitution of its own secularism and of the post-princely Dogra-ruled Kashmir's secularism based on its inherited processes of secularization).

The Kashmir conflict, most significantly, the resistance in Kashmir to the Indian state, cannot be understood independently of these early legal and political structures. Through the naming of a political and ethnic identity, these institutions have moulded the subjective and political universe of the citizens of all three distinct regions of the state. The state has come to be known for its societal commitment to the Valley's unique civilizational experience, the religiously tolerant Kashmiriyat identity, but which neither Jammu's Hindus nor Ladakh's Buddhists were party to. However, the structures of the early Jammu and Kashmir, especially the federal asymmetric provisions of the Indian Constitution and the prescribed follow-up to the Treaty of Accession by the implementation of the promise of 'plebiscite' failed to accomplish what they had been designed to do. Plebiscite was not to take place due to the enduring India-Pakistan conflict. Most significantly, a slow and steady integration of the state began to take place after 1953, both undoing the initial bargain of treating Jammu and Kashmir as distinct as well as bringing about institutional change which would become instrumental in ushering in a complex nationalist politics. And this brought about multilayered and changing patterns of resistance at different critical junctures in the Kashmir Valley (which has recently also given a substantial boost to identity-based politics and a process of de-secularization, as shown by Mohita Bhatia in the next chapter of this volume).

Article 370, a constitutional provision giving Jammu and Kashmir a special and differential status in the Indian federation, was included in the Indian Constitution in 1950 but was intended to be temporary. Its inclusion was due to the unique circumstances surrounding the accession of the state to India and not because of any 'distinct identity' of the state's population. Article 370, however, did establish a specific political identity for the state, different from other regional governments in India: under its provisions, Jammu and Kashmir was granted much more internal autonomy than any other state in the Indian federation. Part XXI of the Constitution of India, which deals with 'Temporary, Transitional and Special provisions', restricts the Union's legislative powers to the areas of foreign affairs, defence and communication and allows the state to legislate on residuary powers, effectively granting the state autonomy in all internal matters. The Indian Parliament needs the state government's concurrence for applying all other laws. Any constitutional amendment approved by the Parliament, applicable to all states, is not automatically applicable to the state of Jammu and Kashmir. The President issues an order proposing the parliamentary approved changes which must then be approved by the state government and its legislative assembly in order to take effect; it is only in this way that any amended provision can be applied to the state. The Delhi Agreement of July 1952 between the Indian Prime Minister Nehru and the Kashmir leader Sheikh Abdullah (who was then heading the National Conference government in the state) echoed the provisions of Article 370 in determining the centre–state relations.

Article 370, reiterated in the Delhi Agreement, defines the political identity of Jammu and Kashmir and its citizens. In addition, two instruments give affirmation to a distinct, state-determined, set of citizenship requirements – who is included and who is excluded in the membership to the Jammu and Kashmir community, namely the 1954 Presidential Order The Constitution (Application to Jammu and

Kashmir) Order, 1954 and the exceptionality, Article 35A – Permanent Resident Requirements (which received its concurrence by the Jammu and Kashmir Constituent Assembly and its enshrinement as Section 6 of the state's constitution). Through the permanent resident requirements and several other legislative acts, the Jammu and Kashmir state has chosen unambiguously to protect its citizens from others settling in the state and prevent any settlers to lay claim on the acquisition of immovable property and public employment. Section 95 of the J&K Cooperative Societies Act, 1960, Section 17 of the J&K Agrarian Reforms Act, 1976, Section 4 of the J&K Land Alienation Act, 1995, Section 4 of the Land Grants Act, 1996, Section 20-A of the Big Landed Estates Abolition Act, 2007 – all these impose a complete ban on the acquisition of immovable property by non-permanent residents of the state. Similarly, certain political rights are also denied to non-permanent residents. Section 12 (b) of the Jammu and Kashmir Representation of People Act disqualifies a non-permanent resident of the state from participating in any election in the state. A non-permanent resident cannot occupy the office of chief minister or become a minister. He or she cannot be a member of the legislature in the state. Section 8 (a) of the Village Panchayat Act also disqualifies any non-permanent resident from being elected or appointed as a member of a panchayat. Similarly, Rule 17 (a) of the Jammu and Kashmir Civil Services (Classification, control and Appeal) Rules, 1956 prohibits any person from appointment to any service by direct recruitment unless he or she is a permanent resident of the state.

These legal provisions have become symbolically and emotionally inter-twined with the special status and distinct identity of the state and inform the major narrative of resistance. Despite the fact that Article 370 has been eroded substantially and does not exist in its original form,[3] it evokes strong reactions both within and outside the state and among the state's different regions. In Kashmir itself there are two divergent opinions, all strongly held, yet all subscribing to the dominant secularization framework of the overarching 'Kashmiriyat' identity. On the one hand, within the Valley, the leadership of the mainstream Kashmir-based political parties (the National Conference and the PDP) views Article 370 as the only link or bridge between the state and India. They see this constitutional provision as providing and assuring a distinct status to the state on the basis of its history, culture and its own specific identity. Moreover, Article 370 is not seen as a temporary measure but a clear articulation of the special status of the state within Indian federation. Thus, all autonomy demands (reverting to the 1953 status as defined by the Delhi Agreement) emanate from this particular context. On the other hand, at the other extreme stand the secessionist groups of the Valley who consider Article 370 as conditional and provisional. For them, this provision was included in the Indian Constitution due to the conditional acceptance of the state's accession to India; the accession is not final and Kashmiris' wishes regarding their political association must be ascertained through a plebiscite, a promise made by the Indian leadership and confirmed by the United Nations. What is common in these competing nationalism narratives is their insistence that that their resistance is fundamentally based on the principles of secular nationalism (the Kashmir conflict is political) and they remain committed to the societal entente of the inherited, historically negotiated secularization.

Conceptualizing and mapping the terrain of resistance

Contrary to the claims that the roots of Kashmiri alienation can be traced to the 1953 arrest of Sheikh Abdullah and that the militancy began after the rigging of the 1987 state legislative assembly elections, we suggest that the roots of the Kashmiri resistance can be found as early as 1947–1948. Resistance, an oppositional act carried out in relation to power, represents agency in various forms "nationalist as well as resistant, hegemonic as well as subaltern, and every day as well as orchestrated" (Klein, 2001, 92). The seeds of political contestation, the assertion of Islamic identity as a counter to Hindu nationalism, and dissatisfaction with the governance agenda were sown, indeed, at the very moment the army parachuted into the Valley to liberate Kashmir from the tribesmen in 1947.[4] Since then, each period of Kashmir's political history was to contribute to the collective memories and conscience of the population, shaping and reshaping the nature of resistance, both in the everyday life of the Kashmiri Muslims and in open collective assertion against the Indian state. And the 'practice of remembering' emerges as one of the essential ingredients for creating 'counter-history' and 'counter-memory' (Vinthagen and Johansson, 2013, 130)

The essence of Kashmiri Muslims' discontent can be broadly captured under three headings: first, a perceived threat to their agency over the control of their territory (thus the demand for self determination is at the core of resistances, questioning the state's accession to India); second, fear and anxiety of losing their religious identity (which translates into worries about the changing composition of Kashmir's demography and the erosion of Kashmir's Islamic identity); and third, the Kashmir Valley's disappointment with the governance agenda. Some of the easily visible actors of resistance can be identified as: the mainstream regional political parties – often labelled as soft nationalist (pro-Indian state with the demands for continuing recognition of the distinctness of the state, e.g. the National Conference, the PDP); the organized anti-state groups, both local as well as Pakistan-sponsored militant groups (including the young new age militants); and the subaltern Kashmiris who carry out acts through their everyday politically intended resistance which fluctuates between conscious, semi-conscious and habitual activities. The latter also include those who challenge the state domination through both cultural and ideational resistance. Increasingly poets, artists, photographers, writers and journalists have joined the ranks of the discontented public by an open protest through their art. To these actors/agents of resistance, we would like to add another, though less visible, category, to use Gyan Pandey's term 'the better-positioned members' or the middle-class members of the Kashmiri community. With the modernization of the state of Jammu and Kashmir, the growing middle class have been major beneficiaries of the state's economic development (higher education, professional jobs – engineers, doctors, government employees). These 'middle class subalterns', with their relative affluence in the society, are in a "perpetual tightrope walk between rejecting and embracing the status quo as one of the beneficiaries" of the state's development agenda (Pandey, 2010, 4). These are the 'straddlers' with their feet 'in both the dominant and subordinate communities'. As Klein points out, "agency at this level can have multiple objectives and effects (e.g., opposing one center of authority but supporting putting another in place), engender a variety of trans-formative tactics, and can be both oppositional and hegemonizing" (p. 90). This ambivalence or the paradoxical nature of resistance has been evident for more than six decades in the Valley. Kashmiri Muslim masses have at times resisted the state power and embraced the goals of the secessionist/nationalist groups, while at other times, they have reversed their allegiance and sided with governmental institu-tions promising material benefits and personal security, modulating their political responses to the elected government of Jammu and Kashmir between the poles of accommodation and resistance.

In short, the protracted seven-decade old Kashmir conflict is complex and multi-dimensional. Resistance is neither monolithic nor solely directed from above by the separatist groups, such as the Hurriyat or its new incarnation, the Joint Resistance Movement. To the contrary, there are different modalities of resisting Kashmiri Muslim agency. Some resist and openly challenge the political power where others act out their agency through compliance rather than resist-ance, and some others adopt the approach of 'constructive resistance' *a la* the regional mainstream Valley's political parties' version (Sorensen, no date).[5] And still others practice resistance in their daily lives but waffle between compliance and resistance and choose time and space for their engagement with "different types of actors, techniques, and discourses" (Vinthagen and Johansson, 2014, 111). This explains why, despite the fact that there are sometimes short and sometime long periods of normalcy the resistance movement continues. It explains the ambigu-ous and even paradoxical choices that the Kashmiri Muslims make. It helps us to understand, for example, why Kashmiri Muslims participate in elections while still challenging the state; why the young compete for the limited number of seats in the professional colleges (medical, engineering); or why they compete for admission to the prestigious, highly competitive Indian Administrative Services (IAS) and yet challenge the Indian state and support Kashmiri dignity and the freedom cause.

Modalities and repertories of resistance: increasing usage of religious symbols within the secularization framework

As suggested earlier, resistance is a variegated practice, comes in various forms and need not follow a simple single matrix. Resistance can range from a direct, open, violent challenge (armed resistance, stone pelting, etc.) to cultural and ideational resistance (music, photography, street art, poetry) to quotidian practices (everyday resistance). The nature and content of the resistance narrative has continued to shift with critical junctures in the state's seven-decade old history, the last one after the

2016 killing of Burhan Wani, the local home-grown youth leader, which has acted to accelerated the pace and intensity of nationalist and resistance politics.

Since 1948, the resistance discourse has incrementally progressed from the demand first for *raishumari* (self-determination), then for autonomy (restoring the pre-1953 distinct, federal asymmetric status of the state within Indian federation), then in 1989 for azadi (the demand for freedom from the Indian state) to the recent narrative of combined objectives: azadi, a life of dignity with the protection of human rights, and the pursuance/protection of religious identity. Commonly known as New Age Militancy and popularized by Burhan Wani (a former teenage stone pelter in 2010 who emerged as the leader of the Hizbul in 2103), this most potent vocal contemporary discourse accompanied by violent militancy has the recovery of Kashmir's land from India ('the occupier') as its central narrative of resistance. Its adherents, working through social media, describe one of the goals of their resistance as the protection of Kashmiri Muslim women. In this narrative, a 'public masculine identity' (Gutman, 1993) is interwoven with the development of nationalism and resistance. The Kashmiri Islamic nation is constructed in a specific gendered way, both symbolically and physically. Its liberation becomes one of the foundational pieces of this patriarchal nationalism legitimizing violence against the Indian state as well as anyone else supporting the 'enemy'. They describe themselves as carrying on a *jido-jehad* (a struggle) against the Kashmiri enemies. In this *tahreek* (movement), they see themselves as soldiers/warriors.

The New Age Militancy has broadened and shifted the discourse in terms of land and Islam but it remains dominated by a relatively small number of indigenous young men (local boys). They are very aware that they operate in an interacting, mutually constitutive relationship with other acts of resistance. Despite their open and vocal religiosity, they reference a Kashmiri society where all religious communities are welcome and they would like to see the return of the 'Kashmir Pandits' to the Valley. Carefully avoiding the narrative of religious nationalism, they support the protection of Article 370 and Article 35 A. A very small minority under the leadership of Zakir Musa, who has spoken in favour of the establishment of 'Caliphate', have been either sidelined by other New Age Militants or taken to task by the organized separatist groups like the Hurriyat. By reaffirming that the Kashmir issue is political and that it needs to be resolved through a three-party dialogue (India, Pakistan and Kashmir), Hurriyat and other resisters continue to support secular nationalism and inadvertently its foundational basis – the historical processes of secularization.

Burhan Wani and the re-emergence of the secessionist movement

The July 8, 2016 killing of Burhan Muzafar Wani, the 22-year-old home-grown commander of the Hizbul Mujahideen and two of his associates by the security forces (including the Jammu and Kashmir Police, Rashtriya Rifles and the CRPF), when the Valley was in the midst of Eid festivities, was to unleash a state of pandemonium in the Kashmir Valley. Burhan, who had joined the Hizbul after the 2010 unrest (when 112 young men were killed) was to emerge as one of the most recognizable young local faces of the militancy. In 2015, in an open challenge to the Indian security forces, he released through the social media the now famous photograph of Burhan surrounded by 11 other armed men, all holding AK47s with a clear message to the security forces to come and kill them and that they were not afraid. There was no need to hide their faces, unlike their predecessors who were almost always masked. Upon his death, Wani acquired the status of *shaheed* (martyr) along with Maqbool Butt and Afzal Guru (the former had been hanged on February 11 in 1984 and the latter on February 9, 2013).

Since July 8, 2016, following the public grieving for their local hero (which included 40 funeral prayers for Burhan's *janaza*), Kashmir Valley has remained engulfed in continuing violence. Stone pelting crowds (including women and children) have been responded to harshly by the security forces' zero tolerance policy. The Modi government's two-pronged strategy (first with its alliance partner the PDP and now under president's rule) of providing development assistance while simultaneously using force against the militants through special projects like Operation All-Out ('neutralizing' the home-grown militant and 'eliminating' Pakistan-sponsored militants) has not gone unanswered. Indeed, local mass resistance (protests, demonstrations, shut-downs and funeral processions as well home-grown local and Pakistan-sponsored militancy have increased manifold in the last three years.

Under the security-driven state policy following Burhan Wani's death there has been an increase in momentum of the home-grown youth militancy. According to one recent estimate (June 2018), the number of these indigenous militants is approximately 280. While the number of militants killed has increased successively every year from 110 in 2014 to 218 in 2017, and during the last three years, 10 of the armed men in Wani's photograph have been killed by the security forces while one voluntarily left the group,[6] the Hizbul Muhjahideen have been successful in recruiting local youth in increasing numbers. Through its recruitment drive in social media (for example, '*Burhan Bharti* –- Burhan Recruitment), the year 2017 saw 126 local youth joining the Hizbul, the highest number since 2010 (this number varies in different reports of the Indian army and the Jammu and Kashmir State Assembly). One often hears stories of young men joining groups such as the Hizbul or the foreign-based group Lashker-e-Taiba after the killing of their neighbours or friends or bystander civilians after security–militant–civilian encounters. Some of these have included professional young men, such as the 21-year-old Zakir Rashid Bhat, a Chandigarh-based civil engineering student joining Wani in 2015 or the 32-year-old Mohmmad Rafi Bhat, a sociology lecturer at the University of Kashmir who left his academic job and joined the militant group in May 2018 and was subsequently killed in an encounter with the security forces, or the 26-year-old Junaid Ashraf Sehrai, 26, an MBA degree holder from Kashmir University, and son of Mohammed Ashraf Sehrai (who took over as chairman of Tehrek-e-Hurriyat from Syed Ali Shah Geelani). Sehrai's recruitment was important because it was the first time that the son of a senior separatist leader of the stature of Sehrai had joined the militancy in Kashmir. All new recruits are given a new name. Junaid Ashraf Khan in an undated image, circulated on WhatsApp, was shown in army fatigues, carrying an AK47 gun, with his birth name, his new name (Aamar Bhai), his father's name and father's affiliation with the Hurriyat, his locality and his educational qualifications and the date of his entering active duty with the Hizbul Mujahideen – March 24, 2016. The aim is clear: openly challenge the dominant state power and keep alive Kashmiri resistance against the Indian state.

The funerals, a pan-Kashmir phenomenon, have taken on a new meaning – to pay tribute to all 'martyred mujahideens' and to affirm that the responsibility for the loss of these valued human lives lies with India. The quotidian practice of burial of the dead, now taking the form of a solemn funeral procession generates the "collective production of novel political and cultural identities" (Escobar, 1992, 396–397). In public bereavement on city streets, the showing of grief is to "make the disappeared visible and perhaps reclaim the dead" (Ipsita Chakravarty, 2016). Each funeral witnesses a huge coming together of men and women from neighbouring towns and villages. In earlier protests the crowds were comprised mostly of men but recently women have begun to attend. The funerals have also become an unprecedented expression of anger against state violence. The mass grieving also gives rise to stone pelting by the young targeting both the security forces and the police who respond through their fire power, killing civilians. Violence is very much on the rise and the killings by the security forces produce, in response, mass protests, violent encounters with the army and the police, shut-downs of towns through curfews and the suspension of internet and train services. The general population defies curfews, attends the funeral processions of the killed militants shouting anti-India slogans and provides shelter to the local young jihadis. With few exceptions, parents refuse to ask their militant children who left to join the militant movement to return home. One mother remarked to an army man who had come to persuade the parents to ask their son to surrender, "I want him to martyr himself for the cause. If he comes home, I will kill him myself." The doctor brother of Zakir Musa (who replaced Burhan Wani after his death as the Hizbul Commander) expressed the opinion, like many others on the streets, that the young men, from whom stone pelting as a weapon of resistance was taken way, had no choice but to resort to guns in challenging the Indian state. In a video interview with journalist Burkha Dutt, he states: "There is no shame in picking up the gun when you have taken away their right to protest with stone pelting."

State actions to control the mass protest through the use of force, denial of public space for protest, severe restrictions on the physical and virtual mobility of the Valley's already angry and grieving population have also been accompanied by a hysterical, often provocative, response in certain sectors of India's media, resulting in further alienation and resistance in the Valley. The day Burhan was killed, the Indian news channels, some with great bravado, talked in detail about the army operation to capture Burhan and his two colleagues and dead militants' faces were shown repeatedly on television – apparently without realizing the consequences of such coverage. For the Kashmiri masses, while most of them abhor violence, did admire the courage and commitment of these local young men to openly challenge the Indian state. What Burhan's father, Muzaffar Wani, a government school principal, had to say about his son's death, "It gives a satisfaction that he has achieved martyrdom", no doubt echoes what the ordinary Kashmir Muslim feels and thinks. It is clear that the dominant narratives such as 'a terrorist is a terrorist', 'jihadi militant and religious radicalization', 'Pakistan intervention in India's internal affairs', 'Kashmir a law and order problem' fail to grasp the Kashmiri reality, Kashmiri Muslims' grievances, their ongoing resistance against the Indian state and their demands for azadi.

The New Age Militancy is dominated by technology-savvy young men, potent, armed and more deeply committed to the cause than the generation in the 1990s (who had crossed over the border to seek military training and weapons and who had either been killed by the armed forces or a rival militant group or quit fighting after witnessing the armed struggle fall apart). No apologies are made for invoking Islam within which the cause of azadi is framed, unlike the 1990s' Islamic based groups such as the Harkat-ul Ansar, or Hizbul Mujhaddin or the Lashkar-e-Taiba who clearly were pro-Pakistani or the secular Jammu and Kashmir Liberation Front which maintained that the Kashmir nationalist movement was exclusively political rather than based on any religious demands. For the new generation, Kashmir jihad is both the protection of Islamic identity and freedom from the Indian 'occupation'. For the first time in a decade or so, the ratio between indigenous and foreign militants has changed in favour of the former. Most significantly, the local population actively supports these young militants whether by providing them shelter, hiding them from the security forces or marching in huge funeral processions. But the 'New Age' militants are also aware that the general citizenry of the Valley are not necessarily committed to waging a religious jihad. Thus, they adhere to the common narrative – the Kashmir conflict is political and their demands do not envision setting up an Islamic state.

The New Age Militancy: Islam, gendered nationalism and Kashmiri jido-jehad[7]

As one senior Intelligence officer points out,

> Burhan Wani's killing changed the discourse in Kashmir. Kashmiri youth started vociferously taking to 'jihad'. They started joining camps that would train them in one week and send them for operations against security forces, where they would obviously get killed. These home-grown militants are also responsible for the increased cases of weapon snatching in the Valley.
>
> *(Das, 2018)*

The new militants display their guns and present themselves in social media as warriors in army fatigues. While the weapon of choice happens to be AK47,

Sameer Tiger, one of the 2010 stone pelters-turned militants and one of the 11 comrades of Burhan Wani, appeared in a social media picture with an American M4 carbine, leading to much speculation in the media as to how he might have acquired the gun.

For this small organized, armed militant group the jihad is against the Indian oppression (*zulm*) within the context of Islam and the Quran. For them, political activism is conflated with Islamic resistance. Without any doubt, the Kashmiri Muslims have always been protective of their religious identity, but it has taken on a different tone and different emphasis in the Burhani and post-Burhani Hizbul discourse. After the 1990 exodus of virtually the whole minority Hindu population from the Valley, the post-1989 insurgency generations have grown up in an exclusively single-religion environment, losing the hitherto dialogic daily experience of negotiating differing religious identities with their Hindu neighbours. They have grown up surrounded by perpetual violence, of both the state and non-state variety along with school and market shut-downs, curfews, and restrictions on their mobility (both physical and virtual). Moreover, they have grown up with the increasing influence of Hindu fundamentalism, both in India and in the Hindu-dominated region of Jammu. Within this framework, 'what constitutes Kashmiri identity' is being defined in uncritically accepted mutually exclusive polarities. This narrative of dualities represents regional (distinct Kashmir) and religious (Kashmiri Muslims, non-secular) identities in opposition to an inclusive national identity (India, Hindu India/secular India) and it clearly tends towards a resolution in favour of the Hindu. For them, under this religious/secularity polarity, a Kashmir Muslim identity cannot be counterpoised with the secular and Indian identity. Moreover, for Hindu nationalists of all stripes, the demand for recognition of the state's distinctness, based on both religious and political identity, is seen as incompatible with the requirements of the Indian nation. Religion, in this new context, has taken on a very different emphasis for the New Age Militancy.

A characteristic example of the pre-New Age Militancy discourse of religiosity is the December 27, 1963 disappearance/theft of Moi-e-Muqqadas, a sacred beard hair of the Prophet Mohammad. The protests and demonstrations against this occurrence (discovered during the Friday *deedar* [showing] at the Hazratbal Shrine) was a memorable event in terms of conflating the demands for *raishumari*, good governance and the protection of Kashmiri Muslim identity. Kashmiri protests at that time were largely confined to the framework of the secular praxis of the ethnic Kashmiri identity, Kashmiriyat. Hindus joined Muslims in the protests demanding a quick recovery of the sacred relic. The New Age Militancy's resistance to the Indian state, on the other hand, is both religious and political with a strong reinforcement of patriarchal values. But they are quick to emphasize that their 'new war' is fundamentally a continuation of the 'old war'.

Burhan Wani, in two videos released a few days before he was killed, explains in Urdu that, first of all, he and his comrades are carrying on the resistance movement which was begun by the previous generations. In other words, their struggle/resistance against the Indian tyranny/oppression (zulm) is not new but a continuation of their fathers' and forefathers' struggle for azadi for Kashmir. Second, the struggle aims to get back their land and free it from the occupier. Third, the goal is to "establish Khilafat in Kashmir. Not only in Kashmir but we will establish Khilafat in whole world." This third goal gets abandoned quickly in the face of vocal opposition from the Hurriyat leadership. The struggle is deemed unique to Kashmir. Consequently, a small minority under the leadership of Zakir Musa quit the Hiz-bul group in pursuance of global jihadism, remaining a fringe movement.

Similarly, Riayz Naikoo (one of Burhan Wani's original 11 who took over the leadership of the Hizbul in May 2017) in his video message (made in response to the army's efforts to ask the family members, particularly the mothers of the militants, to surrender in exchange for amnesty and a promise of employment) invokes the concepts of nation and religion as the justification for resorting to an armed militancy. "We picked up the gun not on anybody's direction nor will we leave on anybody direction. We won't betray Nation. India can't bend us. We will fight till India exits."

All video messages are in Urdu, begin with Islamic verses, and the Quran is invoked throughout. Burhan in his video messages points out that the young left home, took up guns not to only to get their land back and fight oppression but also to protect their mothers and daughters. The Kashmiri nationalist, Islamic discourse is about protecting women's dignity and their purity.

The video messages are used similarly to recruit other young people but also to warn those who are India supporters and those who bring harm to the militants and to their cause. To the youth, Naikoo's message was to seek their help in carrying on jido jehad (struggle/resistance) against India (*Bharat*).

"We want to send a message to the whole valley, especially we want to give message to youths that you come and join us, support us. . . . If you cannot join us, you can still help us in many other possible ways, so that we defeat BATIL (falsehood). . . . So that you get success here and hereafter." After a lengthy quote from the Quran, he points out its significance. "Believe in Allah and his prophet after that do Jihad with your wealth and life. It is good if you possess knowledge. Leave your family, your friends, your mother, and your sisters . . . and after leaving everything, leaving worldly happiness and your comfort, sacrificing you future, then stay focused in your cause so that the dignity of mothers and sisters of our nation can be protected."

In this jido jehad, he issues a warning against all those who do not fall in line with the cause: 'those boys and girls who are working as informers for the army'; the police 'who picked up guns against us and they are supporting India and harming our families'; the media; and even the Moulvis (the Kashmiri Ulemma). The latter should, during the Friday prayer meetings, inform the general population of the ongoing Kashmiri situation, making them aware of their responsibilities. Although he proposes a collective forgiveness to those 'who have derailed'. Especially those boys and girls "who are working as informers of army we warn them to restrain or be ready to embrace death".

Confident in their ability to inflict physical harm to the police and their families, army informants and other 'so-called' supporters of India, he nevertheless pointedly invokes the Quran, points to Islam and its injunction that Islam does not permit them to harm the families of these 'derailed' individuals. Oneness of the nation, one God is equated with the responsibility of all to protect the 'mothers and daughters' of the nation.

> As far as police is concerned they picked up guns against us and they are supporting India. They have been always causing harm to our families. If we wish we could also make their families unsafe. However this nation is one, Quran is one and God is one. Moreover Islam also do not permit us to harm their families. We treat their families the same as we would ours. Their mothers and sisters are our mothers and sisters. We left our homes to protect all mothers and sisters.

Naikoo concludes his video by saying,

> At the end I want to tell you all that the sun of Haq (truth) has dawned and sun of BATIL (falsehood) has set. And thank God Kashmiri youth is ready to die for the supremacy of Islam and this struggle will continue till death. Our blood will lead to Islamic supremacy.

In another video, he warns that police would be attacked if they do not stop harassing the youth. He asks the youth to act as informants for the militants. He provides advice to them on how to deal with the police and the army if they enter their homes or their neighbourhoods. "This land belongs to us."

> I appeal to those youth who want to join us to collect complete details of cops of their respective areas; of their role towards militancy and handover the details to us. We will also recruit them at the right opportunity.
>
> If you (police) care about your lives, remain inside your police stations, don't put barricades on roads and stop harassing youth. Those who will do this will be responsible for their life. . . . I want to tell police that you are our brothers and our real enemy is India but you fail to understand that India makes us fight among ourselves. Train your guns on the Indian Army and help in our freedom movement. It doesn't make any difference to India whether a militant or a cop dies. They are pitting us against each other.
>
> If any policeman, army or anybody supporting the Indian cause tries to enter any home at any place in any corner of Kashmir, kick them out. Every Kashmiri has our support, Inshallah. And pelt stones to quell the army when they come to your areas because this land belongs to us.

In an audio message, similarly, Naikoo also urges young men to post their experiences on social media if army "pushes them" to provide information about militants. He advises the youth to share with village elders and on the social media their experiences of the army "detaining them from the streets, calling them to camps and torturing them mentally and physically to become army informers".

He interweaves a public masculine identity with Kashmiri nationalism.

> We have got information that army and policemen are developing relationships with women particularly school girls to prompt them to provide information about militants. Army men are developing contacts with these girls to get them do wrong things.[8]

He cautions parents and teachers against sending their wards to army-sponsored educational tours (the army's re-education programmes to socialize the young away from militancy):

> I am at a loss to understand how parents allow their daughters to go on tours with army officers like Major Gogoi. . . . Army and education are two separate departments and they are not connected to each other even remotely. Army tours are a conspiracy so that they can reach our sisters. Then they lure them to do wrong things and then blackmail them to work as informers for army.

Then he threatens them:

> We will not spare those parents and teachers who allow their children to go on tours which are directly or indirectly connected to army.

In another episode, reacting both to state police chief S. P. Vaid's appeal to mothers to ask their militant sons to abandon arms and return home and to football-player-turned-militant Majid Khan's surrender in November 2017, Naikoo once again urges the youth to make use of the social media to counteract the Indian narrative of success. In his message to subvert the state-led directive, his masculinist narrative of the nation challenges the Indian gendered approach (for Naikoo Kashmiri mothers are being used by India to subdue the armed struggle of the youth) and to ensure that another '*konan poshpura*',[9] would never take place. The aggressive Kashmiri male warrior will continue the jido jehad to protect the dignity of the women of Kashmir. As Gutmann suggests, the "question of virility and definitions of manliness' are being played out in both the cultural and political confrontations between the colonized (the Kashmir Muslims) and the colonizer (India)" (Matthew Guttmann, 1997, 389).

> You people know, that from the day Majid Khan, the football player from Pahalgam, returned home from militancy on the emotional advice of his mother, the Indian army has been approaching the houses of our militants and forcing mothers to issue emotional videos so that their sons return home.

Yes, in certain cases the army has been successful in compelling the militant's family to send videos messages to their sons asking them to abandon militancy and come home. Actually, India wants to show the world that young men are joining the militancy by force. *Moreover, it tells our mothers that India loves them as well as their sons. And if the mothers succeed in bringing them back, India will liberate them from militancy and provide them with employment. But I want to tell my people categorically that India loves neither our mothers nor our young people. If India had loved our mothers and sisters, then there would have been no Kunan Poshpora. If India had loved our youth, then they would not have killed thousands of youth in Kashmir. They would have not blinded them.* Actually India wants us to abandon our freedom struggle. . . . It wants us to drown our struggle but the sun of freedom will rise again. . . . When we picked up the gun, it was not at anyone's direction and when we put it down, it will also not be at anyone's direction. We won't betray our Nation. India cannot bend us. We will fight until India exits. (italics ours)

Naikoo quickly conflates the masculine project with religious nationalism. He maintains that Majid Khan was released not because his mother appealed but because he wanted to return home ("we do not force anyone to join us . . . the recruits must possess wisdom and join voluntarily"); and that the Kashmiri struggle is a religious one, therefore making it obligatory for the leadership to follow Islamic direction (*deen*) and not the direction of the parents.

We do not have recruitment problem. A huge number of boys want to join but we want to activate only a few in the field. We respect emotions, love and pain of mother. We know how much a mother loves her son, but our *Deen* teaches us that we should love Allah and prophet more than our parents. If not us, who will fight for us? If we want freedom, blood must be shed. . . . Freedom demands blood. My dear mother, we released Majid Khan not on his Mother's appeal but because he himself wanted to return. In Kashmir, it is our religious obligation to join this war. We don't need permission from parents.

Yet, this religious obligation is typically framed as an indigenous movement which neither subscribes to global jihadism nor shares its goals with either al-Queda or ISIS. Zakir Musa, who was appointed commander of Hizbul Mujahideen following the death of Burhan Wani in 2016, was quickly ousted from the leadership position when he declared that the Kashmir fight is "only and only to establish Sharia and an Islamic state"; and "whenever we are fighting with gun or throwing rocks, this should not be for nationalism but for Islam". He threatened the separatist leaders of Kashmir (the Hurriyat) to behead them at the Lal Chowk of Srinagar for calling the Kashmir issue political. For him, this was an 'interference in the Islamic struggle' in Kashmir. For him, the resistance had to be about establishing a Caliphate in the Valley. Not only was he to receive outright condemnation from the Hurriyat leaders but the Hizbul Mujahideen chief, Syed Salahuddin, similarly issued a statement distancing his organization from Zakir Musa's threat, terming it condemnable. The Hurriyat leaders, Syed Ali Shah Geelani, Mirwaiz Umar Farooq and Yasin Malik made speeches pointing out that that the Kashmiri movement is local in nature and indigenous in character and that there was no role for international terror outfits like ISIS and al-Qaeda within the movement. In 2017, Musa formally separated himself from the Hizbul organization and created an Al-Qaeda cell in Jammu and Kashmir called Ansar Ghazwat-ul-Hind. Although there are only a negligible number who support Musa's hard-core Islamic agenda, still, in Kashmiri everyday resistance, anyone who takes on the Indian state immediately receives the status of a hero, irrespective of the group they belong to. This was evident during the funeral in March 2018 of Eisa Fazili, who had left his engineering studies the year before (he had been studying outside the Valley) in order to join the Tehreek-ul-Mujahideen, a relatively small Islamist group. It is believed that he was one of three militants to start the Kashmir branch of ISIS–ISJK, the Islamic State Jammu and Kashmir. With his body draped in the ISIS black flag, during his funeral, rival resistance narratives were being played through slogans: "We want freedom. . . . This nation is ours, we will decide its face"; "Kashmir will become Pakistan"; "Musa, Musa, Zakir Musa". And later, in May 2019, Musa's death at the hands of the security forces evoked similar responses. In Noorpora village, Musa's home town in south Kashmir's Pulwama district, thousands assembled to participate in his funeral procession. People offered multiple rounds of prayers after the police handed over Musa's body to his family early in the morning. Even the Hurriyat Conference chairman Syed Ali Shah Geelani called for a shut-down of all businesses to protest his killing.

What is striking is that the New Militancy has maintained its politically confrontational but religiously tolerant view of the Hindu–Muslim relationship in the Valley, in complete continuity with Kashmiri secularization. Both Burhan Wani and Naikoo seemed in no way to reject the sharing of Kashmir land with the small Kashmiri Hindu community. Indeed, before taking on the leadership, Naikoo invited the Kashmiri Hindu minority to return home. "We will welcome those (Kashmiri Pandits) warmly and there is always place for them in our hearts. They are part of our nation. We are their protectors and not their enemies" (Pandit, 2017). However, there is a clear objection to the plan of the BJP government to create a separate township for them – a policy rejected by Kashmiri Muslims of all stripes. Moreover, Burhan and Naikoo, in their respective messages, reinforced their assurances that the annual religious pilgrimage of the Hindus to the Amarnath cave would not be compromised. In one of his videos, Burhan is categorical: "We aren't planning to carry out any attacks on Amarnath pilgrims who will be here to perform their religious rites." Similarly, Naikoo in 2018, in an audio clip released on social media, stated in categorical terms, "Amarnath Yatra is not our target. They come here to perform their religious rituals. They (yatris) are our guests. . . . We have never attacked the Amarnath yatra. We are not at war with the yatris. . . . We are at war with those who forced us to pick up gun. We are fighting for our rights and our freedom" (see you tube, www.youtube.com/watch?v=-gBxmHfXmTs, accessed February 5, 2020).

This indirect reaffirmation of secularization is largely a response to the quotidian practices which give strength to the organized militancy. Kashmiri Muslims, whether they act in their oppositional politics through the articulation of a collective subaltern Kashmiri consciousness or in mobilized response to the urgings of the secessionist/nationalist groups, are the main force in determining the dynamic nature of engagement with different types of actors, techniques and competing discourses. The leadership of the New Age Militancy are conscious: a) that the consensus regarding resistance against India is fundamentally about protecting a distinct Kashmir identity (both religious and political – Articles 370 and 35 A); b) that Kashmiri Muslims' self-representation (whether it bears any relationship to the ground realities or not) effectively subscribes to a public discourse that they are religious (confident about their Islamic identity) while at the same time remaining committed to the 'secular' Kashmiri identity – Kashmiriyat; c) that an ideology of Islamic fundamentalism, were it to prevail, would clearly be to the detriment to the Kashmiri's political demands; d) that, most significantly, the aspiring middle classes occupy a crucial space and complicated position in Kashmiri society which impacts how resistance gets payed out.

The subaltern middle-class resistance, nationalism and secularization

The middle classes are an essential constituent component of the everyday resistance. Their agency modulates between, on the one hand, demands for increased improved material security, and on the other hand, maintenance of Kashmir's distinct identity and resistance to the violation of Kashmiri human rights and the autocratic state control over civil society. That middle classes move between strategic compliance and resistance is neither unnatural nor contradictory but is contingent upon changing contexts and situations. Thus, as is the case with the new youth militancy leadership, a polymorphous agenda operates in both the organized and the everyday resistance of the middle classes – the rationale, however, is different for these two sets of agents.

The everyday resistance of the middle class has a complex, at times ambiguous relationship with organized resistance as well as with the political power which they seek to resist. This explains why the acts of resistance include accommodation and "ambiguity of political activity" (Sherry Ortner, 1995, 175). As Jean-Klein states, "agency at this level can have multiple objectives and effects (e.g., opposing one center of authority but supporting putting another in place), engender a variety of transformative tactics, and be both oppositional and hegemonizing" (Jean-Klein, 2001, 90). Jean-Klein uses the term 'duplexity' to describe the lack of consistency in different agents' resistance practices. She points out that "subalternness is a relational and situational positioning" (Jean-Klein, 2001, 91). In these practices, resistance may not necessarily be consistent and may contain contradictory simultaneous practices of compliance/accommodation (to the directives of the dominant power/s) and resistance. For example, the Kashmiri population in their resistance, while protecting their religious and political identity vis-à-vis the Indian state's harsh integrative and assimilative security practices, also do not want to find themselves in the chaotic ungoverned spaces which sometimes result from the oppositional activities of the secessionist/nationalist groups. Similarly, Vinthagen and Johansson suggest that "accommodation is not necessarily the opposite of resistance" and that the usage of contradictory practices or "utilizing creative and complex combinations" amounts, in practice, to resistance acts on the parts of common citizenry (Vinthagen and Johansson, 2013, 26). Jean-Klein takes this point further and describes the dynamics of these ambiguous practices of everyday resistance: "activists have no need to deny or hide the double-edgedness of their activities – to be duplicitous – because they do not view them as invalidating one another. Finally, as regards the question of consistency of impetus, energy, and belief, duplexity of process (and of morality) does not rule out intermittency, doubt, or pauses" (Jean-Klein, 2001, 92).

The middle classes in Kashmir Valley have been the beneficiaries of land reforms (initiated by Sheikh Abdullah in 1948), Western education (the seeds of which were sown by the missionaries in the late nineteenth century), the establishment of state public education institutions including professional medical and engineering colleges by the Dogra rulers and the post-1947 Kashmir government, the developed network of a public health care system (again initiated by the medical missionaries in mid to the late nineteenth century but with rapid development in the post-accession Kashmir government), and the growth of public sector employment.[10] As compared to the pre-1947 scenario when only a miniscule minority could take advantage of education, there has been a huge growth in the school- and college-going population. Both primary and higher education are free in the state. Rather and Thanikodi point out in their study on peace and the development of education in Kashmir that "during the decade 2001–2011, literacy rate increased from 55.50% to 68.74%" (2016, 10). Of 364 colleges, 123 are government colleges, 241 private colleges. There are eight universities in the state: two central, two state and four state-supported universities; Rather and Thanikodi note that these have an (annual) intake capacity of 11,400 students and "15 offsite campuses of Universities of Kashmir & Jammu have been approved, out of which 9 campuses have been established, mostly in far -flung areas" (2016, 13).[11] However the state has lagged behind the rest of India in annual economic growth and per capita income growth. In order to enhance its legitimacy, the state government has relied on providing public employment incurring a significant drain on its revenue but developing a strong patron–client relationship with its citizens. The *Indian Express* noted during the 2016 budget season that the government's expenditure on salaries and pension was approximately half of its total expenditure:

> according to data from the J&K budget in 2015–16, the government's total expenditure was Rs 51,670 crore, out of which capital expenditure stood at Rs 14,473 crore, while spending on pensions and salaries was a massive Rs

20,770 crore. Out of total revenue receipts of Rs 51,460 crore in 2016–17, total Central grants – including plan and non-plan grants – were estimated at Rs 27,721 crore. In the previous financial year, total Central grants were at Rs 21,373 crore out of the total revenue receipts of Rs 40,904 crore, while in 2014–15, Central grants stood at Rs 16,149 crore out of total revenue receipts of Rs 28,938 crore.

(Sasi, 2016)

The growing middle class in the Kashmir Valley, however, remain tied to the political and cultural marginality of Kashmir. As Pandey notes in his excellent edited volume on *Subaltern Citizens and Their Histories*, "middle class . . . has always been defined by a series of exclusions: in other words, by what it is not. Central among these, although not always fully recognized, have been exclusions based on ideas of race, gender and religion" (2010, 16–17). The growing saffronization of India, particularly since the 2014 elections and the formation of the Modi BJP national government, means that the Kashmiri Muslim is increasingly seen as the enemy of the Indian 'Hindu' nation and that the demand for a distinct Kashmir and azadi is perceived as anti-patriotic. This is evident in the open public hostility against Kashmiri students which has surfaced on Indian campuses. For example, in 2016, a Kashmiri student was expelled from Aligarh Muslim University (AMU) for posting 'objectionable' comments on Facebook over the Pakistani-sponsored terror attack on the army base in Uri. In another incident, a group of 8 to 10 unidentified men assaulted a Kashmiri scholar at Barkatullah University in Bhopal, Madhya Pradesh. In February 2018, two students of the Central University of Haryana (CUH), Aftab Ahmed, 23, and Amjad Ali, 22, both pursuing MScs, were thrashed by a group when they were returning to the campus after offering Friday prayers at a nearby mosque. Another four Kashmiri students were beaten up in a College campus in Punjab for allegedly cooking beef. After the February 14, 2019 militant attack in Pulwama (South Kashmir) on an army convoy, killing 30 Indian soldiers, many Kashmiri students faced threats and harassment across many major cities in India.

At home in the Valley, through public art (graffiti), poetry, photography, music and films, the young educated middle class youth is expressing its anger over violations of human rights in Kashmir resulting from the repressive actions of the security forces; increased securitization of the state; and the loss of personal dignity. Graffiti has now emerged as an important artistic form of resistance. In 2016, a group of Kashmir university students transformed a fallen Chinar tree into a 50-ft long piece of art with a "collection of images depicting Kashmir's culture and the suffering of its people – of barbed wire, tortured souls, shattered houses, women smoking hookah and bidi" (Qazi, 2016). This was captured in the 2017 documentary "In the Shades of Fallen Chinar" made by Fazil NC and Shawn Sebastian from Kerala. Many young documentary and photo journalists are recording the daily life, resistance and the ongoing conflict in the Valley; quite often the images are posted on Facebook, Instagram and circulated through other social media. To cite a few examples: in 2017, Yawar Nazir Kabli (one of the most notable photo journalists in the Valley) posted a poignant photograph of a boy smiling boy covering the bullet hole which pierced through the glass of a shop during a shootout between Indian government forces and Kashmiri rebels in Srinagar; Kamran Yousf, who works for the Kashmir English daily *Greater Kashmir*, often posts photographs of ordinary people, young militants challenging the state security system and their funerals. In an online posting in 2017, Rouf Sadiq Tantry described the works of nine emerging photojournalists, educated young professionals, but victims of police harassment and brutality. In another venture, in 2009, artists and performers in the Valley created a platform called, 'Kashmir Art Quest', a tranquil resistance project to reinvigorate their identities as Kashmiris that they asserted to have been compromised since 1947. Cartoonist Mir Suhail's work went viral on social media in 2016 when he digitally manipulated a poster of the hit 1964 Bollywood film *Kashmir Ki Kali* which showed actress Sharmila Tagore with a bandaged eye and her face pockmarked with pellets. The cartoon did its job – bringing wide attention to the post-Burhan Wani killing and blinding of the civilian population. These are all instances of a youth resistance movement, parallel to but outside the frame of the New Age Militancy, driven by young people who are both products of growing middle-class privileges as well as victims of the prevailing institutionalized violence in Kashmir.

We close with a recent and potentially significant example of educated middle-class resistance. Shah Faesal, who had topped the Indian Administrative Services (IAS) competitive exam in 2010, resigned from the service in January 2019, in protest

> against the unabated killings in Kashmir, and lack of any sincere reach-out from the Union government; the marginalization and invisibilization of around 200 million Indian Muslims at the hands of Hindutva forces reducing them to second-class citizens; insidious attacks on the special identity of the J&K state and growing culture of intolerance and hate in the mainland India in the name of hyper nationalism.
>
> *(Nazir Massodi, NDTV, January 9, 2019)*

Shah has launched a new political party, the Jammu and Kashmir People's Movement (JKPM), with a secular, socialist agenda with the objective of "giving justice to the people of all the regions without any consideration for the region, colour, creed and caste". The processes of secularization are well and alive in his message about the resolution of the Kashmir issue, "we have to understand the people, talk to them and work to bridge the gap and maintain unity as we all are brothers" (NDTV, April 1, 2019). Interestingly, the Muslim aspect of the party's identity was acknowledged during its launching ceremony of the party, its name posted in the colour green and its new slogan '*Hawa badlegi*' (the wind will change) written in Urdu.

The aspiring Kashmiri middle class occupies a crucial space and complicated position in Kashmiri society which impacts how resistance gets played out. In their subaltern resistance lies the continuation of the dynamic and complex relationship between the processes of secularization and secular nationalism, encompassing simultaneously the demands for human rights, inclusive development, internal autonomy and finally azadi.

Notes

1 A very small section of the new militancy groups are pleading for Caliphate.
2 Martin Sökefeld in his essay, 'Secularism and the Kashmir Dispute', correctly points out that the case of Kashmir is "inscribed in a complex, multiple and at times contradictory entanglement of religion and politics and cannot be sorted out in a simple opposition of the secular versus the religious. Both categories do not have a fixed and transparent meaning" (p. 102) in Bubandt and van Beek (2011).
3 All successful integrative measures, leading to the erosion of this constitutional provision, were a result of three interconnected factors: a) the incarceration in 1953 of Sheikh Abdullah (who had begun to entertain the question of an 'independent' Kashmir) and the centrally approved regional governments of Bakshi Ghulam Mohammed and G.M. Sadiq (the latter was boldly to convert the ruling National Conference party into the Indian National Conference with the intent to join the mainstream national political life); b) the virtual absence of political opposition in the Valley accompanied by a large-scale patronage system; and c) a sustained inter-regional harmony despite Jammu's grievances of discrimination by the Valley-dominated politics.
4 When the first Sikh regiment landed at the Srinagar airport to deal with the tribal invasion in 1947, their slogan 'Jo Bole So Nihal, Sat Sri Akal' caused anxiety amongst Srinagar's Muslim population. Sheikh Abdullah had to explain in a public meeting that that particular slogan was 'a war of cry for the Sikh regiment' whose sole purpose in Srinagar was to protect them. In another incident, seven people (some belonging to the National Conference militia), all Muslims except one, were inadvertently killed by soldiers unable to differentiate between the Kashmiri Muslim population and the tribesmen. The local population was outraged and carried the dead bodies in procession through the main roads of the city. For details see Tremblay (2017).
5 Sorenson describes constructive resistance as one "which covers initiatives in which people start to build the society they desire independently of the dominant structures already in place. This is initiatives which not only criticise, protest, object, and undermine what is considered undesirable and wrong, but simultaneously acquire, create, built, cultivate and experiment with what people need in the present moment, or what they would like to see replacing dominant structures or power relations." Majken Jul Sørensen, 'Constructive Resistance–Conceptualising and Mapping the Terrain', JRS, no date, http://resistance-journal.org/2017/08/constructive-resistance-conceptualising-and-mapping-the-terrain/. Last accessed March 18, 2020.
6 According to one report, with the launch of Operation All-Out, there was a relocation of an additional 2,000 army troops in south Kashmir – the hotbed of militancy and a source of major local recruitment of the young into Hizbul. Riyaz Wani, in his insightful piece in *The Diplomat* on May 31, 2018, 'Kashmir: Killing Militants Won't Kill Militancy', reported that "In 2017, 119 local youth were recruited, despite the ambitious Operation All-Out (OAO) launched by the security forces in January that year. OAO began with the relocation of 2,000 more army troops to South Kashmir. Six new army camps were set up and 1990s-style Cordon and Search Operations (CASO) revived. J&K Police were issued new fighting gear and equipment, including armored vehicles and bulletproof vests (which even the Indian Army has been struggling to get as standard equipment for nine years now). The year ended with 218 militants killed, the highest since 2011. But, despite OAO's sweeping mobilization, 45 local youth took up arms in January-April 2018." See Riyaz Wani, 'Kashmir: Killing Militants Won't Kill Militancy',

The Diplomat, 31 May 2018. https://thediplomat.com/2018/05/kashmir-killing-mili tants-wont-kill-militancy/. Last accessed March 18, 2020.
7 Ethnographic research for this section (speeches and statements of the New Age Mili-
   tants) was compiled by Shahnawaz Gull through Facebook pages, blogs, video recording
   of speeches (YouTubes) circulated by Burhan Wani, Riyaz Naikoo and Zakir Musa.
8 Major Gogoi (perhaps the most detested man in the Valley and the most celebrated in
   Indian patriotic circles) who made headlines in 2017 after he tied a Kashmiri civilian to
   the front of his vehicle and claimed that he did so to prevent stone-pelters from targeting
   his convoy, was caught with a Kashmiri girl in a hotel room.
9 The Kunan Poshpora incident occurred on February 23, 1991, when a unit of the Indian
   army launched a search and interrogation operation in the twin villages of Kunan and
   Poshpora, located in Kashmir's remote Kupwara District. It is reported that at least 100
   women were gang raped by soldiers that night. However, human rights organizations
   including Human Rights Watch have said that the number of raped women could be as
   high as 150.
10 See for details on the growth of the education and health sector, Mufti (2013).
11 Also see Mohd Ummer Jan Padder and P. Shanmugam, 'A Study on Growth of Higher
   Education in Jammu and Kashmir', *European Academic Research*, Vol. III, No. 4, July 2015.
   http://euacademic.org/UploadArticle/1841.pdf. Last accessed March 18, 2020.

References

Bhatia, Mohita. 2013. "Secularism and Secularization: A Bibliographical Essay". *Economic and Political Weekly*, Vol. 48, Issue 50, 103–110.

Bubandt, Nils, and van Beek, Martijn, eds. 2011. *Varieties of Secularism in Asia: Anthropological Explorations of Religion, Politics and the Spiritual*. London: Routledge.

Chakrabarty, Dipesh. 2002. *Habitations of Modernity: Essays in the Wake of Subaltern Studies*. Chicago: University of Chicago Press.

Chakravarty, Ipsita. 2016. 'Funeral Processions for Militants in Kashmir Have a Troubling Message for Government'. *Scroll.In*. http://scroll.in/article/805088/in-pictures-funeral-processions-for-militants-in-kashmir-have-a-troubling-message-for-government, last accessed on May 21, 2019.

Das, Shaswati. 2018. "Rise of Home-grown Militants in J&K Sets Alarm Bells Ringing". *Live Mint*, June 27. www.livemint.com/Politics/DH74I7rZ31AkPTuUzK8FoK/Rise-of-homegrown-militants-in-JK-sets-alarm-bells-ringing.html, last accessed on May 21, 2019.

Escobar, Arturo. 1992. "Culture, Practice and Politics: Anthropology and the Study of Social Movements". *Critique of Anthropology*, Vol. 12, Issue 4, 395–432.

Faulkner, Ellen, and MacDonald, Gayle. Summer 2016. "Introduction: Agency and Resistance: Debates in Feminist Theory and Praxis", in Elizabeth Comack, Gillian Balfour, Ellen Faulkner, Gayle MacDonald, A. J. Withers, Kiran Mirchandani, and Wendy Chan (Eds). *Gender, Law and Justice*. Nova Scotia: Fernwood Publishing: Black Point.

Gutman, Matthew C. 1993. "Rituals of Resistance: A Critique of the Theory of Everyday Forms of Resistance". *Latin American Perspectives*, Vol. 20, Issue 77, 74–92.

Gutman, Matthew C. 1997: "Trafficking in Men: The Anthropology of Masculinity". *Annual Review of Anthropology*, Vol. 26, 385–340.

Jean-Klein, Iris, 2001. "Nationalism and Resistance: The Two Faces of Everyday Activism in Palestine During the Intifada". *Cultural Anthropology*, Vol. 16, Issue 1, 83–126.

Lecours, André Lecours. 2005. *New Institutionalism: Theory and Analysis*. Toronto: University of Toronto Press.

Mufti, Guljar. 2013. *Kashmir in Sickness and in Health*, Kindle Edition. New Delhi: Partridge India, Penguin Books India Pvt. Ltd.

Nazir, Masoodi. 2019. "IAS Topper Shah Faesal Resigns, Says 'Kashmiri Lives Matter', in Tweet" NDTV. January 9. https://www.ndtv.com/india-news/ias-topper-shah-faesal-resigns-says-kashmiri-lives-matter-in-tweet-1975171, last accessed on March 19, 2020.

NDTV. 2019. "Shah Faesal Says His Party Is Open to Politicians with Unblemished Record". April 1. www.ndtv.com/india-news/shah-faesal-says-jkpm-jammu-and-kashmir-peoples-movement-is-open-to-politicians-with-unblemished-rec-2015663, last accessed on June 20, 2019.

Ortner, Sherry. 1995. "Resistance and the Problem of Ethnographic Refusal". *Comparative Studies in Society and History*, Vol. 37, 173–193.

Padder, Mohd Ummer Jan, and Shanmugam, P. 2015. "A Study on Growth of Higher Education in Jammu and Kashmir". *European Academic Research*, Vol. III, Issue 4 (July). http://euacademic.org/UploadArticle/1841.pdf.

Pandey, Gyanendra Pandey, editor. 2010. *Subaltern Citizens and Their Histories: Investigations from India and the USA*. London: Routledge.

Pandit, M. Saleem. 2017. "Tech-savvy Militant Is New Hizbul Commander in Kashmir". *The Economic Times*, May 29. https://economictimes.indiatimes.com/news/politics-and-nation/tech-savvy-militant-is-new-hizbul-commander-in-kashmir/articleshow/58887786.cms, last accessed on May 21, 2019.

Punjabi, Riyaz. 1992. "Kashmir: The Bruised Identity", in Raju G. C. Thomas (Ed). *Perspectives on Kashmir: The Roots of Conflict in South Asia*. Boulder, CO: Westview Press, pp. 131–152.

Qazi, Sehar. 2016. "Kashmir: Bringing Alive a Dead Chinar with Resistance Art". *Catch News*, May 21. www.catchnews.com/culture-news/kashmir-bringing-alive-a-dead-chinar-with-resistance-art-1463813922.html.

Rather, Mudasir Ahmad, and Thanikodi, A. 2016. "Peace and Development of Education in Jammu and Kashmir". *Asia Pacific Journal of Research*, Vol. 2, Issue XXXV II (March 10–19). http://apjor.com/downloads/2403201618.pdf, last accessed on March 19, 2020.

Sasi, Anil. 2016. "Jammu & Kashmir: An Economy in Turmoil". *The Indian Express*, September 13. https://indianexpress.com/article/business/business-others/jammu-kashmir-an-economy-in-turmoil-tourism-jobs-unrest-economic-growth-3028034/.

Sökefeld, Martin. 2012. "Secularism and the Kashmir Dispute", in Nils Bubandt and Martijn van Beek (Eds). *Varieties of Secularism in Asia: Anthropological Explorations of Religion, Politics and the Spiritual*. London: Routledge, pp. 101–120.

Sørensen, Majken Jul. 2017. "Constructive Resistance–Conceptualising and Mapping the Terrain". *JRS*, no date. http://resistance-journal.org/2017/08/constructive-resistance-conceptualising-and-mapping-the-terrain.

Spencer, Dustie. 2013. "The Subaltern Kashmir: Exploring Alternative Approaches in the Analysis of Secession". *Hydra: Interdisciplinary Journal of Social Sciences*, Vol. 1, Issue 1, 77–84.

Tantry, Rouf Sadiq. 2017. "Online Posting". http://withkashmir.org/2017/08/19/9-emerging-photographers-from-kashmir/, last accessed on May 21, 2019.

Tremblay, Reeta Chowdhari. 2017. "Contested Governance, Competing Nationalisms, and Disenchanted Publics: Kashmir beyond Intractability?" in Chitralekhas Zutshi (Ed). *Kashmir: History, Politics, and Representation*. Cambridge: Cambridge University Press.

Ummer, Mohmd, Jan Padder, and Shanmugam, P. 2015. "A Study on Growth of Higher Education in Jammu and Kashmir". *European Academic Research*, Vol. III, Issue 4 (July). http://euacademic.org/UploadArticle/1841.pdf, last accessed on March 18, 2020.

Vinthagen, Stellan, and Johansson, Anna. 2013. "Everyday Resistance: Exploration of a Concept and Its Theories". *Resistance Studies Magazine*, Issue 12, 1–46.

Vinthagen, Stellan, and Johansson, Anna. 2014. "Dimensions of Everyday Resistance: An Analytical Framework". *Critical Sociology*, Vol. 42, Issue 3, last accessed on March 18, 2020.

Wani, Riyaz. 2018. "Kashmir: Killing Militants Won't Kill Militancy". *The Diplomat*, May 31. https://thediplomat.com/2018/05/kashmir-killing-militants-wont-kill-militancy/ last accessed on May 21, 2019.

You tube, "Youth Being Forced to Spy upon Militants, Riyaz Naikoo Releases Fresh Audio" *https://www.youtube.com/watch?v=r7fs8YtFnV4* " Last accessed April 14, 2020.

4

SECULARIZATION AND DESECULARIZATION IN JAMMU

Interrogating the canonical approaches

Mohita Bhatia

This chapter examines the secularization and desecularization processes in the Jammu region. Of the three major regions of the ex-Indian-administered state of Jammu and Kashmir – Jammu, Kashmir and Ladakh – Jammu was a major part of the state that had significant stakes in the politics of conflict and any dialogue aiming toward its resolution. Presently part of the Union territory (UT) of Jammu and Kashmir, it still has a crucial position in the conflict politics. The various ways in which religion and nationalism operate in this region impact the socio-political sensitivities of the entire UT. This chapter will analyze the state-oriented politics based on religion or nationalism as well as the ways in which these realities are variously performed in society. It is in the context of social and cultural performances of religion that I use the term secularization. As this book illustrates, the state enforced 'secularism' is different from the society-oriented processes of secularization; albeit both may entangle or influence one another at various moments. Here, I engage in exploring the possible political spaces of secularism and its engagement (or disengagement) with the everyday secularization processes in the Jammu region.

This chapter, while illustrating these complex trajectories, makes three important points. First, secularization[1] and desecularization[2] are not completely antithetical processes; they often form a part of the non-linear dialogic processes involved in socio-cultural and religious interactions, conflicts, as well as political struggles. Secularization and desecularization may be intertwined, simultaneous or discrete realities contingent on specific temporal, political or spatial contexts. Second, as against the inherently coherent secularism thesis, this chapter takes its cue from Chatterji's observations on secularism to point at the ruptured, complicated trajectories of secularism, secularization and desecularization processes.[3] Third, it argues that state-oriented discourses of secularism may or may not influence the societal performances and practices of secularization and vice-versa. The latter may, at times, function independently or even depart from the state's version of secularism.

An analysis of Jammu's changing socio-cultural and religious trajectory points to this complex, dialectical and multi-directional understanding of the secularism and secularization processes.

Changing facets of secularization in Jammu's society

Departing from the unilinear and straightforward conceptualization of secularism and secularization, this chapter brings out their different facets in Jammu since historical times. It briefly looks at monarchial rule, post-accession period and moves on to more contemporary times to reflect on these facets. Yet, it maintains that at no particular time did secularism/secularization surface as a coherent or all-pervasive reality. Religion itself has remained a fluid, differentiated category and has interacted with other social senses of belongings, politics and nationalism in diverse ways.

The princely state of Jammu and Kashmir was established in 1846. Gulab Singh, the Hindu Dogra Rajput ruler of Jammu, joined hands with the British in defeating the Sikh kingdom. In return for his services, the British ceded the Muslim majority Kashmir to him in lieu of Rupees 75 lakhs (105,000 USD) under the treaty of Amritsar.[4] The Kashmir Valley was added to Gulab Singh's territorial possessions of Jammu and Ladakh, thus also accomplishing Britain's quest for a centralized state of Jammu and Kashmir (Rai, 2018). Scholars have maintained that previous overlapping sovereignties involving multiple religious and political influences were nullified to form a centralized 'Hindu' state (Rai, 2018; Marsden, 2011). It distinctly oppressed and discriminated against its Muslim subjects (Rai, 2004; Behera, 2000). Kashmiri Muslims were particularly treated unfavorably and callously by the Dogra monarchs, since Kashmir was considered a 'conquered' territory.[5]

While concurring to the argument of waning multiple sovereignties and increasing political awareness of religious identities, it is crucial to point out some of the fallacies and over-generalizations inherent in the narrative that suggests the 'Hindu' identity of the state. More than the 'Hindu' identity, it was the martial Rajput caste identity that defined the Jammu-based Dogra rulers and their political performances vis-à-vis their 'subjects' to a large extent. Rajputs belonging to Jammu were the most benefitted community even at the cost of other upper-caste Hindus including the Brahmins (Bhatia, 2014). Despite their somewhat pro-Hindu stance, these rulers did not unambiguously uphold their 'Hindu' identity. A more complex interplay of caste–class nexus characterized their rule, whereby the Dogra rulers allied with the elite Muslims and Hindus of Kashmir and Jammu regions and offered many privileges to these classes. Within Kashmir, not just Hindu Pandits but also the small influential class of Muslim Pirs and Sayyids were co-opted by the Dogra rulers, and were exempted from various oppressive taxes as well as the system of forced labor known as *begar* (Zutshi, 2004, 62). Chitralekha Zutshi notes that apart from the sizable Hindu landed elites, peasantry also faced exploitation from these Muslim elites of Kashmir who took advantage of their religious authority to extract food grains from them.

These entangled structures of hierarchy clearly point to the incomplete, partial and ambiguous 'Hinduization' of the princely state of Jammu and Kashmir. The rulers came to symbolize a 'Hindu' regime even though they were mainly prejudiced in favor of their own clan, employing mostly Rajputs in the state services and army. Entrenched Hindus belonging to other castes were also placed in an advantageous position (Bazaz, 1987, 94–108). However, as Prem Nath Bazaz notes, the Rajputs among these Hindus were the most privileged and satisfied class under the Dogra regime.[6] The Brahmins resented the elevated position of Rajputs, although a few educated and upper-class Brahmins aligned with the royalty and were co-opted by the rulers. Traders and 'shahukars' or moneylenders (mainly belonging to the Mahajan caste) also benefitted from the exploitative feudal practices (Bazaz, 1987, 303).

Reference to the oppressive character of the feudal Dogra regime is generally made with respect to the peasantry, artisans and the working classes of Kashmir. Not much attention is paid to the equally exploitative relationship of Dogra ruling classes with the Dogra peasantry, lower castes and working classes in Jammu. The condition of a vast majority of Hindus and Muslims was as miserable as that of the large number of Kashmiris. One of the Dogra poets said, 'People say this is Dogra rule, but what Dogra rule is this where Dogras don't get even saag (spinach).' Being feudal in character, the contradictions of the Dogra regime were defined more by its class character rather than by its regional or religious character. Various entrenched Hindu and Muslim communities allied for political and economic interests and repressed the lower classes. The most oppressed and pauperized sections in Jammu were the peasantry and artisan classes, as well as other landless sections; comprising both Hindus and Muslims. Among Hindus, Dalits or ex-untouchables and Other Backward Classes were at the receiving end of monarchial subjugation. Dalit impoverishment was a consequence of not just the most draconian of taxation systems but also the deep structural prejudices against this community that caused their social denigration and everyday humiliation. Languishing in abject poverty, Dalits were also the target of the *begar* system. While a vast majority of Muslims in Jammu suffered economic distress, there were a few landed Muslim elites who enjoyed the patronage of the Dogra royalty. Besides, Muslims of Jammu also served in the Dogra administration as well as the army. They comprised a substantial proportion of the J&K army.[7] Muslims from Jammu were also part of the Dogra police and constable services. As compared to Kashmiri Muslims, Muslims of Jammu were economically better placed and employed in government services (Chowdhary, 2015).

These intricate levels of hierarchies, competing patronages and alliances characterized the Dogra rule in Jammu. Caste and class collaborations often subsumed religious interests of both the Hindu and Muslim privileged sections; allowing some space for secular politics on the top. These alliances often neutralized the religious stance of the Dogra rulers. Religious differentiations further enabled rupturing of any cohesive 'Hindu' or 'Muslim' identity. Zutshi, for instance, points to the power struggles within Muslim elites such as Hamadanis (pro-shrine) and Mirwaizs (wahabi followers) in Kashmir. Similarly, the influential class of Kashmiri Pandits blamed the Dogra rulers for unfair treatment in favor of Rajput Hindus of Jammu as well as the Punjabi Hindus (Zutshi, 2004).[8] These contestations and associations engendered a secular political outlook that suited the interests of the entrenched classes, and co-existed with the religious concerns of these groups. The politics of the elite did not directly result in secularization or desecularization of Jammu's society; yet it reflected on the caste-based divisions of the 'Hindus'. 'Hindus' comprised of many caste or class-based groups, scattered spatially and did not represent any cohesive community. A few lower castes were not even considered 'Hindus', and existed as discrete caste/clan/class-based communities. Ties and conflicts were more prevalent between peasantry than between 'Hindus' and 'Muslims'. These ill-defined religious boundaries started to become sharper by the early nineteenth century with the advent of the nationalist movement.

Nationalism, political awareness and religious identities in Jammu

Political consciousness in both the Kashmir and Jammu regions began to sharpen in the early twentieth century, albeit differently. Politicization in Kashmir started as educated youth raised awareness regarding the oppression of Muslims by the 'Hindu Dogra' rulers.[9] Giving voice to the subjugated Muslim peasantry, the Kashmiri political consciousness also sharpened 'Kashmiri Muslim' versus 'Hindu Dogra' identities. Even as the politics in Kashmir gradually took on a relatively progressive outlook and allied with the 'secular' Congress-led nationalist movement, it always fluctuated between using religious or 'Islamic' idioms and articulating secular politics (Zutshi, 2004).

Politics in Jammu acquired a different shape as unlike Kashmir it was bereft of any organized progressive leadership. Although the peasantry of Jammu were extremely impoverished and suppressed, no intellectual or organic leadership could emerge to mobilize the lower classes (Bhatia, 2014). A few like-minded Jammu-based individuals, leaders and groups that supported the cause of the peasantry and lower classes of the region did not secure the support of any organized national or regional leadership to enable them to consolidate and further their agenda. While the organized leadership of Kashmir, under the banner of the National Conference, failed to move beyond Kashmir and engage meaningfully with these Jammu leaders, the latter also did not get any support from the National Congress party that took an exclusive interest in Kashmir's politics. Dispersed and isolated, these intellectuals and groups remained as lone voices and could not be the face of Jammu's politics.

Despite the lack of any organized political coalescence, Jammu was influenced by a variety of nationalist and religious ideas, mainly coming from the bordering state of Punjab. Religious movements co-existed with nationalist politics, often sharpening the religious consciousness of Hindus, Muslims and Sikhs as well as appealing for a secular political space. Many religious organizations stood for consolidating religious identities and yet urged for a united national struggle against the colonial regime. The swadeshi movement[10] and Mahatma Gandhi's ideas also triggered a widespread response among the people of Jammu, especially students in school and colleges (Kaur, 1996, 82–83). Nevertheless, a heightened political consciousness, through an amalgam of religious–nationalist–secular ideas, changed the social character of Jammu, as elsewhere in India. The previously blurred sense of belongings among people were transformed into specific social, political, and even religious categories. Jammu's peasantry, lower classes and castes were now assigned religious and regional identities.

During this period, the work of Arya Samaj among Hindus is particularly noteworthy. Well grounded in Punjab, this revivalist Hindu organization had also gained prominence among Hindus of Jammu including the lower castes, through its *shuddhi* movement – reconversion of non-Hindus and bringing them back into the 'Hindu' fold. Arya Samaj's critique of other religions and its reconversion drive also led Muslims to form religious groups on the lines of the Samaj (Kaur, 1996, 54–59). Communal fault lines began to appear with the communal and nationalist politics of Punjab influencing and luring the peasantry of Jammu. In this context, Rekha Chowdhary explains that 'Despite the fact that there were similar economic reasons for discontent among masses in Jammu region as in Kashmir region, politics did not acquire mass base here' (Chowdhary, 2015, 176). She notes that in many parts of Jammu such as Mirpur, Kotli or Rajouri, where peasantry were mainly Muslims, the influence of the religion-based politics of Punjab was significant. 'The Punjab based All India Kashmir Conference and the Majlis-e-Ahrar succeeded in turning the discontent [of the peasantry] into a communal direction.' Many incidents of violence targeting the Hindu Dogra landlords were reported in these areas of Jammu.

Many Muslims of Jammu had joined hands with the Kashmiri leader, Sheikh Abdullah, in the formation of the Muslim Conference in 1932 and raising awareness about repression of Muslims at the hands of 'Dogra Hindus'. When Sheikh Abdullah and a few other Kashmiri leaders decided to expand their political base beyond religious lines and convert the Muslim Conference into the National Conference in 1939, many Muslims leaders of Jammu parted ways with Abdullah. They went on to emphasize the religious identity politics and revived the old Muslim Conference in Jammu (Chaudhary, 2015). The Muslim Conference, affiliated itself with the All-India Muslim League, a nationalist party that stood for politically safeguarding Muslim interests of the Indian subcontinent. Unlike the National Conference or the Congress, the Muslim Conference, as well as the Muslim League, endorsed the feudal status quo and rallied in favor of the Dogra maharaja (Chaudhary, 2015).

Akin to conservative Muslim politics, in the early twentieth century Hindus of Jammu were also inclined toward the Hindu-oriented organizations such as the RSS and the Hindu Mahasabha that were supporting the Dogra ruler's idea of independent Jammu and Kashmir in the early twentieth century. In fact, the passivity of the All India Congress leadership in mobilizing the people of Jammu on a mass-scale enabled the Hindu-based groups to capture the socio-political space in Jammu. Steadily, religion-based politics started gaining ground in Jammu, outweighing any moderate political influences. Both the RSS and the Hindu Mahasabha had established themselves in various parts of Jammu and led the process of communal mobilization in Jammu. Initially, these groups represented the interests of the feudal upper classes and firmly opposed the National Conference's political struggle to abolish monarchy and its proposal to introduce land reforms in the state. Gradually, these organizations also claimed to speak for the marginal Hindu classes. The discontent of the latter was channelized in 'religious' and 'regional' terms. These Hindu-based groups, in the absence of any other potent political force, became the predominant political voice of Jammu, representing the 'Hindus' of the region and their grievances (Bhatia, 2014).

Despite these status-quo-ist and religion-based predominant political influences, Jammu also had political space for a few progressive and revolutionary voices. Ved Bhasin and Balraj Puri, along with many other young and educated activists formed the Jammu Students Federation. They described it as a 'secular' student group that represented the diverse religious communities of the state.[11] The Federation, having a progressive political outlook, participated in anti-colonial and anti-monarchial struggles and also endorsed the radical land reforms that were implemented in the post-accession period in the state. Dogra Sadar Sabha was another organization formed in Jammu in 1904. It emphasized the word 'secularism' in its agenda and comprised Dogri and Pahadi speaking residents of Jammu. As the organization grew, it began to engage with the politics of the state. As its members, many progressive-minded activists, poets, writers and theatre artists have been writing on various aspects of Jammu, including the repressive regime of Dogra rulers. Ram Nath Shastri, and Dinoo Bhai Pant, revolutionary Dogri writers, were among the founding members of this organization. They have penned down what may be called a 'people's history' of Jammu, describing the gendered, class and caste dimensions of Jammu's history and society, and provoking reactionary responses from the conservative and upper-caste sections of Jammu.

These discrete voices and groups could not turn into a robust mobilizing force, and remained at best the critical and intellectual segments of Jammu's society. Consequently, more organized organizations – the RSS, the Hindu Mahasabha and the Muslim Conference – were successful in disseminating their ideas among the masses and to an extent desecularizing Jammu's society. The context of partition of the subcontinent and the violence associated with it also influenced the political psyche of people in Jammu, as elsewhere in India. The many riots and killings of minority groups – both Hindus and Muslims – in different parts of Jammu were reported before and during the partition of the state of Jammu and Kashmir in 1948. Many Muslims were brutally massacred in the Hindu majority Jammu city, while many Hindus were killed in Muslim-dominated regions such as Muzaffarabad, Mirpur and Rajouri (Mehta, 2005; Bose, 2003; Chattha, 2016; Khan, 2007). Violence had an amplified effect in Jammu due to the bi-fold processes of the partition – of the Indian subcontinent in 1947 as well as of the state, mainly the Jammu belt, in 1948.

Communal violence notwithstanding, desecularization processes that accompanied the nationalist politics were neither linear nor absolute. During the turbulent times of partition violence and displacement, people of Jammu region manifested a mix of emotions, often contradictory and fractured. Many student activists, community leaders and even common people shielded the members of the other communities from communal violence. Communal outrage by some people was simultaneously responded to by acts of humanity and generosity by many other members of the society. Acts of secularization and desecularization went together, and often manifested many contradictions and ruptures. In my interview with an elderly, former journalist of Jammu who had witnessed partition turbulence and displacement, he commented:

> Not every secular person avoided violence. Some men, no matter of what political ideology, used violence as an opportunity to assert their masculinity over women; some men found the turbulent situation as an opportunity to loot and make some money. Similarly, not all religious-minded men and women indulged in communal violence. Many of them compromised their own safety to protect people of other religions.

Many such contradictions were explained by my respondents during my fieldwork on issues of partition and borders (conducted between 2013 and 2015). While explaining them is beyond the scope of this chapter, it is worthwhile to mention here the insecurities that led some individuals to act in certain ways during the times of partition. I was told that rumors and actual incidents of violence had prompted people in certain areas to arm themselves. Their insecurities in that situation, rather than just a 'communal' psyche impelled them to be prepared for violence. An old woman, who was displaced from Kotli (now in Pakistan administered Jammu and Kashmir) to the Indian administered part of Jammu, told me: 'Who knew who was who in those times? Good people turned bad. People we thought were bad helped us. No one could be trusted in those times. Nobody.' 'One of our Muslim friends in the other village who was known to help everyone . . . Hindus, Sikhs, Muslims. . . . We were shocked to know that he had weapons. He killed women of his family. He killed many Hindus,' she narrated. These societal contradictions explain the fragmented and incomplete nature of the secularization/desularization processes, not just in chaotic times like partition but also in normal situations of everyday life. The next sections lay out such normal, not so chaotic phases and the intricate socio-political life of Jammu in the post-accession and more contemporary times.

Post-accession to contemporary everyday life

In the post-accession phase, it took some time for people of Jammu to rebuild their lives and recuperate from the shock of violence. Nevertheless, this period offered peace a chance and over the years people again started building relationships of trust with other religions, communities and classes. Due to partition, post-accession Jammu lost its earlier Muslim majority character and was now a Hindu majority region. However, many regions of Jammu such as the border belt of Poonch-Rajouri (that adjoin the Pakistan administered Jammu regions), or the Doda-Kishtawar areas (that adjoin Indian administered Kashmir) were the Muslim majority parts of Jammu. Also, among Hindus of Jammu, a bulk comprised the Dalits who despite the land reforms were still at the margins of society. A small percentage of Jammu's population also comprised Sikhs and Christians. It would be spurious to comprehend Jammu's demography in simply religious terms; Jammu's vast diversity is defined through its various sub-regions (Jammu city and vicinity; hilly belts of Rajouri-Poonch; Doda-Kishtawar-Bhadarwah belt that adjoin Kashmir), languages (Dogri, Punjabi, Pahari, Gojri, Sarazi, Kishtawari, Bhaderwahi, Pogli), cultures, communities (Gujjars, Bakerwals, Paharis, Dogras, Punjabis, Kashmiris). Religious communities of Jammu are widely spread throughout various sub-regions and divided into these varied cultural and linguistic categories. This amalgam of communities and cultures also prevented any cohesiveness on religious lines and facilitated a process of constructive socio-cultural interchange.

At the level of Jammu's political discourse, however, a different narrative was constructed. During this post-accession period, the predominant political discourse of Jammu continued to articulate an anti-Kashmiri politics. Dominated by Hindu Dogra elite and mobilized by the right-wing parties mentioned earlier, it constructed a 'Jammu versus Kashmir' rhetoric and assumed a chauvinist, ultra-nationalist outlook (Bhatia, 2014). In line with the national politics, it questioned Kashmir's loyalty toward India and demanded complete integration of the state with the Indian Union.[12]

It was in this context that the 'liberals' and 'seculars' labeled the politics of Kashmir as 'secular', while the political discourse of Jammu was categorized as 'communal'. The 'communal' content of the right-wing brand of politics cannot be dismissed. Yet, it may be argued that the potential of this politics to penetrate was not just due to its 'religious' content. The fact that the 'secular' politics of Kashmir could not come out of its 'Kashmir' and 'Kashmiri Muslim' locus standi and reach out to other parts of the state, also reinforced and led to the popularity of chauvinist Jammu politics. Not just Jammu's political rhetoric but Kashmiri politics had also become quite exclusive and parochial (Bhatia, 2014). While Jammu's politics has been explicitly 'communal' on certain occasions, Kashmiri political narratives have also often used religious symbols and vocabulary in many subtle ways. Both versions of the dominant politics sustained one another. Another related factor here was the preeminence of the authoritative 'secular' Kashmiri politics in the state of Jammu and Kashmir and its reluctance to accommodate and address the aspirations of people of Jammu. The dominant Kashmiri politics created a 'marginalization' of Jammu psyche. The regional grievances of the people of Jammu were quite successfully manipulated and incorporated into the political agenda by the Hindu-oriented parties. These arguments are not intended to simply accuse the Kashmiri discourse for parochializing Jammu's politics, but rather to point out the over-simplified 'secular' versus 'communal' label. Not only is the 'religious' component a part and parcel of both Kashmir and Jammu's politics, though in different ways; even the most blatantly parochial politics of Jammu incorporated an intricate mix of elements, not just religion. Further, it is crucial to point out the limits of Hindu-oriented discourse. Few sections of Jammu's Hindus endorsed this political rhetoric, yet this process of political mobilization was never complete till quite recently. Till the rise of BJP's Modi in national politics in 2014, the Hindu nationalist BJP had to face serious electoral competition from other relatively moderate parties such as the Congress, National Conference and other regional parties in many constituencies having a substantial Hindu population (Chowdhary, 2015).

In the post-accession period, the simultaneity of the rise of conservative politics and the secularization of society is noteworthy. While the politics of Jammu was assuming a parochial and at times communal shape, the society was witnessing a process of secularization and building trust among various communities. The socio-cultural everyday secular performances thrived despite political conservatism. In many areas, people lived in mixed communities, visited religious and social ceremonies in their neighbourhood, articulated a common sub-regional and cultural identity and even a shared political subculture. For instance, in the hilly, border belt of Poonch-Rajouri, there has been a strong assertion of 'Pahari' identity and politics. This politics has been demanding cultural recognition and economic development of these areas. In these contexts, religious affiliations have coincided with the other social and political identities. This is not to narrate a story of perfect communal harmony. In fact, conflicts based on religion, caste, class or other social factors have co-existed with secular performances. Further, 'secularization' here does not exclude religion in any way. In fact, religion—culture have amalgamated in interesting ways to facilitate secularization of Jammu's society, for instance in 'sufi' places of worship and sacred spaces of local village deities.

Secularization sans secular politics

Jammu's case points to a process of secularization of society that can take place without secular politics in place. There were many factors that enabled this process. One, as mentioned earlier, the demography and diversity of Jammu with multiple cultures, sub-regions and ethnicities inhibited construction of any large-scale homogeneous religious enclaves. It, thus, provided a social space for blooming of multiple and differentiated senses of self and cultural belongings, with religion being one of the significant identity markers. For instance, people residing close to the Line of Control borders would form a strong border identity, having a distinct culture and political sense of self.[13] Similarly, those living in the more developed Jammu district[14] and its vicinity are mainly Dogras or Punjabis and would identify themselves with a different set of socio-political issues. Furthermore, the displaced communities from Kashmir and remote parts of the state, settling in the Jammu district – due to heightened militancy in the 1990s – also add to the cultural and political diversity of the region. These complex interactions, competitions and mutual ties have led to opening up of the socio-political space in Jammu. Nevertheless, at the level of political rhetoric, Hindu-based politics would often unite many sections of Hindus, across sub-regions and cultures, especially in politically sensitive situations such as in the insurgency period, Amarnath agitation[15] or more recently the rise of the BJP in the national political space. These contradictions have often marked Jammu's social and political persona.

Second, the structural anatomy of Jammu and the associated cultural practices also suggest co-existence and acceptance of different religions and cultures. In most parts of Jammu, whether the foothills or hilly regions, it is quite typical to have sufi shrines built adjacent to temples; or mosques, temples, shrines and gurdwaras constructed next to one another. For instance, 'Gumat', a prominent area in the old Jammu city, is known by its two religious structures standing opposite to each other. A very famous Dargah (shrine) of Pir Roshan Ali Shah complements the Hanuman temple. The narrow and congested street of the Gumat market caters to low- and middle-income groups who come to shop as well as pay respects to the dargah or/ and the temple. While Jammu is popularly known as the city of temples, there are numerous mosques and shrines interspersed throughout the districts of Jammu. A Sufi cultural orientation is what allows these mixed community spaces to exist and even connect side-to-side. The Sufi shrines offer an interface between different castes, communities and religions. In fact, many of these Sufi shrines are managed and taken care of by the Hindu families. The identity of the *peer* (Sufi saint) of a few such shrines is ambiguous, while in other cases the *peer* is viewed and worshipped by all communities as a 'Muslim *peer*'. One of the shrines that is located in a village close to Jammu city and run by a Hindu family has a very interesting and unconventional decor. When I visited this shrine in 2010, I noticed that like many other shrines, this one is also adorned with a sparkly green cloth from the outside; however, the inside of the shrine carries both Hindu and Muslim religious symbols. Pictures of 'Macca' co-exist with photos of the Hindu Gods Rama and Krishna.

Another example is of a shrine, locally known as Pir Badesar, very close to the Line of Control (LOC) area. Although a militarily heavily guarded area, both Hindus and Muslims visit this place after taking formal permission from the local administration. In local parlance, the term 'Pir Badesar' refers to the grave of the Muslim peer. Yet, there is another Hindu narrative that marks this place. There is an old Shiva temple, known as Veer Badreshawar, standing next to the grave. According to the Hindu narrative it was constructed by King Kanishka in 142 AD. Additionally, a newer Shiva temple has been constructed close to the old one by the army. The new temple, managed by the Indian army, is beautifully adorned with thousands of bells of various shapes and sizes. It is this temple that occupies the central space; while the *aasthan* (place) of the *peer* is located a little down below. Is this area visited or worshipped as a shrine of a Muslim 'peer' or as a temple or both? What is the original name of this place – pir badesar or Veer Badreshawar? Local residents have no definite answers to these questions. People across religious boundaries go to visit this place, appreciating the temple adorned with bells as well as venerating the Muslim *peer*. Pir Badesar, thus, perfectly signifies the layered, multivocal, one might even say polyphonic, cultural spaces that do not require a definite closure. Pervasiveness of shrines, *ziyarats* (holy graves) and worship places of local deities define Jammu's cultural milieu. An illustration of a sufi cultural orientation of

Jammu is not intended to romanticize inter-communal relations. Rather, it suggests a simultaneity of everyday secular performances alongside the social conflicts and a 'communal' political discourse. At times these inter-mixed religious realms such as the *ziyarats* enable neutralizing or even transcending the effects of polarized socio-political narratives.

The third factor that facilitated the secularization of Jammu's society is its caste structure. Broadly, Rajputs, Brahmins and Baniyas (traditionally traders) comprise the economically, socially and politically influential castes in this region. Various Other Backward Castes (OBCs) and Scheduled Castes have a subordinate status within the 'Hindu' community; despite the educational and economic progress that these castes have made since the post-accession period. Purposely overlooking these social fissures, Jammu's upper-caste-based politics has often projected Hindus as a cohesive group. While this politics has been partially successful in connecting Jammu Hindus of various castes, classes and cultures at the ideological level, their claims lie flat when it comes to everyday social life. Due to an absence of any vocal or organized Dalit or subordinate politics, the lower castes have not been able to contest the dominant politics of Jammu; in fact, on many occasions they have endorsed the nationalist, pro-Jammu and Hindu-based elements of this politics. Nevertheless, at the social level, there is an ongoing contention of the upper- and middle-caste cultural and religious practices. Though covert and often indirect in nature, these everyday struggles create possibilities for cultural critique, dissidence and at times dialogue in Jammu's society (Bhatia, 2014). Thus, even when backing the vocal Jammu politics, the lower castes constantly engage in contestation of the upper-caste values and practices; thus aiding in secularization of the social realm. The ruptures within 'Hindus' at the cultural level have prevented formation of a cohesive religious community even when such a cohesiveness is at times achieved at the political level.

These secularization processes in Jammu's society have never been linear or unambiguous. Rather, there have been occasions of communal discord and distrust. Reasons for the polarization of society have ranged from trivial ones like an India–Pakistan cricket match, to more sensitive reasons such as insurgency. A simple event such as a cricket match has often become a point of tension in the otherwise peaceful Danidhar village of the Muslim-majority border district of Rajouri. During my doctoral fieldwork in 2010–2011, elder residents of Danidhar expressed concern regarding the skirmishes during India–Pakistan cricket matches. I was informed that 'Hindu' and 'Muslim' youth often engage in heated arguments and clashes. 'When India is winning, the Hindu boys would tease Muslims. They would allege that Muslims are never happy when India is winning and would provoke a fight. When Pakistan is winning, and if any of the Muslim boys cheer, there would be a communal clash. Muslims are assertive in our region, so they also reply back,' an elderly Muslim narrated. I was also told that in such circumstances, even close friendships between Hindu and Muslim friends are jeopardized. 'In our village, Dalits have close relationships with Muslims. But in one instance of serious clash between Hindus and Muslims during the cricket match series between India and

Pakistan, even these relations became tense . . . but not for a long time. These tensions are short-term and get resolved very soon,' a Dalit youth informed me.

Many trivial incidents may produce communal tensions but these rifts are generally short-lived, not widespread and limited to certain areas of Jammu. However, insurgency was one such episode that impacted almost the entire districts of Doda, Kishtwar and Bhaderwah and left lasting impressions of conflict and violence. These districts are closer to Kashmir and have a large Muslim population. Despite having their own specific culture and politics, Muslims of these areas were influenced by Kashmiri separatist politics. That being so, when Kashmir-based insurgency spread to parts of Jammu in the late 1990s and early 2000, many Muslim youth of these districts joined insurgency alongside Kashmiris and many extremist Pakistan-backed groups. Insurgency, thus, took a brutal shape when it hit these regions and many communal killings have been recorded during those periods. Hindus were targeted and killed in a few villages, during marriage ceremonies and while travelling in buses (Swami, 1998, Puri, 2008). In these districts, the responses of the Hindu communities was also extreme, as many vehemently endorsed the right-wing politics. The rift between the 'Hindus' and 'Muslims' was clearly felt in those times, and an overwhelming Dalit–upper caste political unity was achieved. Although the tension between the two communities did resolve over time, in certain areas a sense of distrust and cynicism still prevails. Nevertheless, it is important to note that during the period of insurgency, other parts of Jammu were also affected. Yet, it did not alter the inter-community dynamics to any great extent. Muslims, in other parts of Jammu, were as affected as other communities by the militant violence; and this brought all the communities together in sharing their fears and losses. It is interesting to note that while the militancy period led to the desecularization of Doda, Kishtwar and Bhaderwah regions of Jammu, it opened up channels for trust and mutual dependence among various groups in other parts of Jammu; thus enabling a process of secularization.

National rise of BJP and modified Jammu – a move toward desecularization

Since the 2014 elections, India has witnessed the rise of the Hindu nationalist BJP. What is peculiar about the post-2014 era is the presidential nature of the BJP's campaign that relies entirely on the growing popularity of the BJP leader and current prime minister, Narendra Modi. Both 2014 and 2019 parliamentary elections were successfully won by the BJP, projecting Modi as a larger-than-life figure. The digital, technological and social media machinery of the BJP has done an excellent job of building a grand persona of Modi as the most decisive national leader and the most audacious proponent of 'Hindu' majoritarian rights. Modi's campaign team has also cashed in on issues of national security, India–Pakistan antagonism and anti-terrorism to construct and strengthen the pan-Indian narrative of ultra-nationalism. Simultaneously, any viable opposition, specifically the Congress, has been electorally wiped out, leaving no space for political dissent. The triumphant 'Modi wave', in these years, has not waned despite some flawed economic policies of the BJP. The Hindu majoritarian politics of hate has affected the social fabric of the nation, deeply polarizing the communities. At the level of social discourse, a 'Hindu–Muslim' antagonistic narrative is being produced, subsuming various cultural, caste, class and regional diversities. Modi's politics has been legitimized at the political and social domains, as articulated by Pralay Kanungo (Kanungo, 2019):

> What made matters even more difficult for the opposition is that the 2019 election was not only substantially presidential, but also significantly cultic. The Modi cult overshadowed every other political leader and political party, from his own to the opposition. It has also dominated every constitutional and democratic institution due to his sheer political weight. And now with resounding popular approval, this cult has been legitimized as all powerful.

Jammu has not been aloof from the rising Modi-cult effect. The vocal politics of the BJP had not translated into any huge electoral successes all these years.[16] But in sync with the growing adoration of Modi, the BJP registered a historic grand victory in the 2014 assembly elections and formed a government in the then state of Jammu and Kashmir for the first time. The BJP has strengthened its position among large sections of Hindus since its coming to power for the second time at the national level in 2019. It has taken some unexpectedly sensational political steps such as de-operationalizing Article 370 of the Indian Constitution that offered a special status to the state of Jammu and Kashmir. It also divided the state of Jammu and Kashmir into two Union territories (UTs) – UT of Jammu and Kashmir and UT of Ladakh. It is debatable whether the people of Jammu will gain from these changes, especially the de-operationalizing of the special status. In fact, on the economic front, Jammu may stand to lose on some fronts – some of its jobs and land that were exclusively reserved for the people of the Jammu and Kashmir may now be open to the people from outside the state. Yet, these changes imply an emotional victory for those sections of Jammu that viewed Article 370 as a hinderance to the integration of the state with the Indian Union. The demand for abrogation of Article 370 was part of the chauvinistic nationalist discourse that wanted to rid Kashmir of its unique status. This anti-Kashmiri politics has been very much part of Jammu's political vocabulary. In some ways, to the residents of Jammu Article 370 implied Kashmir's political dominance as Kashmiri leadership used it to deny resident status to many groups such as West Pakistan Hindu refugees or Punjabi Dalits who had settled in Jammu back in 1950s. Turning the political rhetoric of the 'abolition' of Article 370 into a reality offers an emotional victory for the people of Jammu, mainly Hindus.

These drastic and draconian political changes, overlooking the wishes of Kashmiri Muslims, have not just further severed connections between Kashmir and Jammu regions but also divided the 'Hindus' and 'Muslims' of the Jammu region. The ties between the communities that had survived various provocations including insurgency may come under political strain this time. What would these drastic national and political changes, that are majoritarian in character, entail for the people

of Jammu? Will these processes of desecularization erode the secularized public performances? Will they obstruct discourses of social interface? What will be the impact
of desecularization that denies any particular religion an absolute authority on anonymous cultural/religious realms? These questions need to be explored in the coming
times. Nevertheless, it may be affirmed that secularization or desecularization may
not be viewed as an inherent essence of any society, including Jammu.[17] The case of
Jammu suggests that these processes are often inter-linked, non-linear and fractured,
one more hegemonic than the other in a particular political and social context.

Notes

1 For an elaborate reading on 'secularization' in the South Asian context, see Humeira
   Iqtidar (2011) and Mohita Bhatia (2013).
2 The term desecularization is used aptly by Sadia Saeed in context of the shifts in the
   political landscape of Pakistan. She argues that 'In deploying the term "desecularization,"
   I do not mean to suggest that secularization processes are reversible in the sense of restoring a bygone enchanted world. Nor is my suggestion that the two are empirically discrete processes representing distinct historical phases. . . . Desecularization is an instituted
   process, typically centred around the state, and entails specific actors, interests, practices
   and discourses through which the political importance of religion is reflected, reformed
   and transformed over time' (Saeed, 2016, 22). In this chapter I have used the term loosely
   to imply assertion of religious identities, whether by the state or at the social level.
3 See Chatterji (2013).
4 The Treaty of Amritsar was signed between Raja Gulab Singh and the British on
   March 16, 1846. The British, having conquered the Sikh kingdom, gave away the Kashmir Valley and all regions of the Sikh empire east of the river Indus and west of river
   Ravi to Gulab Singh in lieu of Rs 75 lakhs. For details, see http://jklaw.nic.in/treaty_of_
   amritsar, accessed August 30, 2019.
5 It is implied that 'Hindu-Muslim' religious identities were drawn with Dogra rulers
   privileging Hindus; albeit with the overt or covert backing of the British. For instance,
   Mridu Rai points out that the Department of Archeology created in 1904 was used by
   the Dogra rulers to protect Hindu monuments and temples while responding indiffer-
   ently to the Muslim archeological structures (Rai, 2018)
6 Prem Nath Bazaz remarked that the 'large part of the state Army is their monopoly. . . .
   Civil services are, of course, open to them too' (p. 298). Further he states that 'Jagirs have
   been granted to the Rajputs out of all proportion to their number' (pp. 299–300).
7 Choudhary notes that along with Hindu Rajputs, among Muslims the Rajputs, Suddans,
   Jats and Gujjars of Jammu province were prominently employed in the British India
   forces. He states that 'the Muslims also made a significant percentage of the J&K State
   Army and possibly they were all from Jammu province' (Choudhary, 2015, 24).
8 Dogra rulers preferred Punjabi Hindus over the Pandits for higher administrative positions as the former were considered more educated and efficient.
9 In the 1930s, a few educated and left-leaning young Kashmiri intellectuals formed a
   Reading Room group to discuss literary as well as political issues. This group then
   started participating in the politics that opposed Dogra oppression; thus bringing about
   political consciousness among the people of the Valley.
10 The Swadeshi movement was part of the Indian anti-colonial struggle that emphasized the use of Indian-manufactured goods and boycott of British-made products. The
   Swadeshi movement was brilliantly pioneered by Mahatma Gandhi.
11 Interview of Ved Bhasin in Kashmir Lit, www.kashmirlit.org/riots-changed-jk-politics/,
   accessed August 15, 2019.

12 Through Article 370 of the Indian Constitution, the state of Jammu and Kashmir enjoyed special status and is exempted from the Indian Constitution; except Article 1 and Article 370. Article 370 has been de-operationalized recently, in 2019, by the BJP government against the wishes of the Kashmiri population.
13 Within this border belt, a further differentiation is manifested by Paharis and Gujjars – the two competing communities. While Gujjars are a traditionally nomadic community of Muslims that speak Gojri, the Pahari-speaking, settled and relatively more economically developed Paharis comprise both Hindus and Muslims in that sub-region. Both these communities of the border belt have been competing for economic and political resources, contesting each other's claims.
14 The Jammu administrative unit comprises of 10 districts – Jammu, Kathua, Udhampur, Samba, Reasi, Ramban, Doda, Kishtwar, Rajouri, Poonch.
15 For a detailed reading on the Amarnath agitation, see Bhatia (2009) and Tremblay (2009).
16 It is interesting to note that prior to 2014, despite the electoral competition that the right-wing politics had to face vis-a-vis other political parties like the Congress, National Conference and other regional parties, its ultra-nationalist narrative remains the common sense discourse in Jammu region. It is mainly because the other parties have not made any serious effort to aggressively challenge or create an alternative discourse. For more details, see Bhatia (2014).
17 See Ravinder Kaur's article on secularism (Kaur, 2019) for an insightful reasoning on the impermanence of these ideas.

References

Bazaz, Prem Nath. 1987. *Inside Kashmir*. Mirpur: Verinag.

Behera, Navnita. 2000. *State, Identity and Violence: Jammu, Kashmir and Ladakh*. New Delhi: Manohar.

Bhatia, Mohita. 2009. "Women's Mobilisation in the Jammu Agitation: Religion, Caste, Community, and Gender". *Economic and Political Weekly*, Vol. 44, Issue (26–27): 447–453.

Bhatia, Mohita. 2013. "Secularism and Secularization: A Bibliographical Essay". *Economic and Political Weekly*, Vol. 48, Issue 50.

Bhatia, Mohita. 2014. "Dalits in Jammu and Kashmir: Resistance and Collaboration in a Conflict Situation". *Asian Survey*, Vol. 54, Issue 5.

Bose, Sumantra. 2003. *Kashmir: Roots of Conflict, Paths to Peace*. Cambridge: Harvard University Press.

Chatterji, Joya. 2013. "Secularization and Partition Emergencies. Deep Diplomacy in South Asia". *Economic and Political Weekly*, Vol. 48, Issue 50.

Chattha, Ilyas. 2016. "The Long Shadow of 1947: Partition, Violence and Displacement in Jammu & Kashmir", in Amritjit Singh, Nalini Iyer, and Rahul K. Gairola (Eds). *Revisiting India's Partition: New Essays on Memory, Culture, and Politics*. Lenha, MD: Lexington Books, pp. 143–156.

Chaudhary, Zafar. 2015. *Kashmir Conflict and Muslims of Jammu*. Srinagar: Gulshan.

Chowdhary, Rekha. 2015. *Jammu and Kashmir: Politics of Identity and Separatism*. New Delhi: Routledge.

Iqtidar, Humeira. 2011. *Secularizing Islamists? Jama'at-e-Islami and Jama'at-ud-Da'wa in Urban Pakistan*. Chicago: University of Chicago Press.

Kanungo, Parlay. 2019. "The Rise of the Namo Cult". https://thewire.in/politics/narendra-modi-cult-bjp-election-victory, last accessed on August 21, 2019.

Kaur, Ravinder. 2019. "Lessons from the Verdict". *The Indian Express*, September 14.

Kaur, Ravinderjit. 1996. *Political Awakening in Kashmir*. New Delhi: APH Publications.

Khan, Yasmin. 2007. *The Great Partition: The Making of India and Pakistan*. New Haven: Yale University Press.

Marsden, Magnus. 2011. *Fragments of the Afghan Frontier*. London: Hurst and Co.

Mehta, Krishna. 2005. *Kashmir 1947: A Survivor's Story*. London: Penguin Books.

Puri, Luv. 2008. *Militancy in Jammu and Kashmir: The Uncovered Face*. New Delhi: Promilla & Co., Publishers in Association with Bibliophile South Asia.

Rai, Mridu. 2004. *Hindu Rules, Muslim Subjects: Islam Rights and History of Kashmir*. New Delhi. Permanent Black.

Rai, Mridu. 2018. "Kashmir: From Princely State to Insurgency". https://oxfordre.com/asia nhistory/abstract/10.1093/acrefore/9780190277727.001.0001/acrefore-9780190 277727-e-184?rskey=KrHlM0&result=6, last accessed on August 12, 2019.

Saeed, Sadia. 2016. *Politics of Desecularization: Law and the Minority Question in Pakistan*. Cambridge: Cambridge University Press.

Swami, Praveen, 1998. "A Summer of Massacres". *Frontline*, Vol. 15, Issue 17.

Tremblay, Reeta Chowdhari. 2009. "Kashmir's Secessionist Movement Resurfaces: Ethnic Identity, Community Competition, and the State". *Asian Survey*, Vol. 49, Issue 6.

Zutshi, Chitralekha. 2004. *Languages of Belonging: Islam, Regional Identity and the Making of Kashmir*. Oxford: Oxford University Press.

5

THE DYNAMICS OF KASHMIR IDENTITY AND ITS CONTEMPORARY CHALLENGES

Noor Ahmad Baba

An identity that defines the characteristic features of a people is reflected in their culture in terms of their value-orientation, social attitudes, folklore, literature, art and architecture. It is a dynamic, constantly evolving process involving factors that can be internal to a place or emerge out of a confluence with the surrounding socio-culture communities. In this context the Kashmir identity and its cultural personality are outcomes of the evolution of a community with thousands of years of history.[1] Kashmir has been unique in a number of respects. Globally, very few ethno-regional and cultural communities exhibit such a directly marked, manifest and discernable relationship between people and their place of habitation with a defined geography as in Kashmir.[2] This underscores the need for any discussion on the identity of people in Kashmir to be contextualized in their evolution in history, in their interface with the place they live in and also in relation to its surroundings. As an ethno-cultural community, it is clearly defined by its continuity within the Valley of Kashmir surrounded as it is by high mountains and inhabited by people with strong identity markers in terms of a common language, values, culture and its symbols and manifestations in dress, architecture, literature, folklore, rituals, etc. Marc Aurel Stein (1862–1943), in his translation of *Rajtarangni*, notes that "We find here (Kashmir) a fertile plain embedded among high mountain ranges, a valley large enough to form a Kingdom for itself and capable of supporting a highly developed civilization" (Stein, 1900, 388). The mountainous surroundings of Kashmir have helped it to shape itself differently from its neighboring areas. It is not only Kashmir's borders but also the nature of its topography and profuse endowment with natural assets that have helped to reinforce and strengthen the uniqueness of its culture – a culture reflected in the day-to-day idiom of ordinary men and women, folklore evolved through centuries of living together in interface with serene natural surroundings, language and literature.

It has all been influenced by the "capitulating beauty of its meadows, mighty mountains, forests, water bodies and the general ambience of variety in changing seasons" (Lawrence, 1967, 12–28).

For many observers, Kashmir has everything that can stimulate creative genius, compelling passion and ever refining and innovative art. According to a nineteenth-century geologist and ethnographer, Frederick Drew, who had stayed in the Valley for a decade-long service, "the Kashmiri people are doubtless physically the finest of all the races that inhabit the territories we are dealing with and I have no much hesitation in saying that in size and in features they are the finest on the whole continent of India. Their physique, their character and their language are so marked as to produce a nationality different from all around as distinct from their neighbors as their country is geographically separated" (Drew, 2008, 124). Kashmir has remained the home of knowledge, learning and debating ideas since ancient times (Bazaz, 2003, 22–33). It has contributed to the growth of philosophy, science, language, literature and discourses in religion. Within the whole of the Indian subcontinent Kashmir is the only region that can claim the distinction of possessing an uninterrupted series of written records of history (Stein, as quoted in Lawrence, 1967, n. 4, 179). *Rajtarangni* is based on the works of historians who were living much before Kalhana Pandit undertook to compiling/writing this work in 1148 AD.

The Kashmir identity has evolved not only in relation to its own internal dynamics but also in relation to its uniquely rich and composite surroundings. It needs to be noted that Kashmir for the past five thousand years of its history has remained at the crossroads of civilizational interface as a meeting point of Chinese, Central Asian, Indian and Persian civilizations, cultures and economies (Puri, 2009). All these important civilizational traditions have had an enriching impact on Kashmir (Banday, 2009). Along with this economic and cultural interface, Kashmir also has been at the crossroads of transition of many important spiritual and religious traditions like Hinduism, Buddhism and Islam, and has also been impacted by other religious traditions that evolved in its proximity like that of Zoroastrianism in Iran and the Confucian tradition in China. Kashmir even now continues to be a meeting point of four great religious traditions (Baba, 2016, 4–11).

It seems evident as well that Kashmiri society must have constantly been fertilized by its interface with its surrounding peoples through social, cultural and economic interaction (Baba, 2016, 4–11). Having surroundings is not unique to Kashmir. All socio-cultural communities live and interact with their neighborhood. But what has been unique about Kashmir is the variety and the richness of these surrounding traditions and the fact that in spite of being surrounded by a number of such great civilizations, it retained the uniqueness of its cultural personality as manifested in the language, dress, food habits, social moorings, etc. of its people. It did change with and in relation to changing times, challenges and incoming influences from its surroundings, but it absorbed these changes in a manner that did not fragment its social fabric and did not create significant cleavages that could have distorted the unique collective personality with which it is still identified. It has been a strongly consensual society that has changed without uprooting itself from its inherited socio-cultural possessions and legacy. Kashmir has truly been a melting pot that has absorbed various influences from within and from its surroundings without being undermined or overtaken by any one of these dominant civilizations and that has instead formed its own uniqueness. With all these influences coming from left and right, north and south, near and far, it has retained its personality as a distinct cultural community about which its people remained strongly conscious and possessive (Baba, 2016, 4–11). In the words of Balraj Puri in the Kashmir Valley, "Kashmir identity has been the most persistent and dominating urge of people" (Puri, 2009).

The by-and-large peaceful and gradual transition of faiths without violent disruptions and enriching interface with many great civilizational traditions has given Kashmir's people a culture of inclusivity, a cosmopolitan outlook and creative ingenuity that are reflected in their approach to arts and crafts, literature and in their approach to politics even in very trying situations. One of the important features of this uniqueness has been the remarkable degree of civility and a composite cultural outlook that became a defining feature of Kashmir's social living and identity and which has promoted an intercommunity living with common cultural references. And this composite living and social inclusivity endured even after Islam emerged as the dominant religion of its people and became a very important component of its identity. Indeed, Kashmir continued to be defined by the culture of interfaith peace and understanding in which its own unique *Rishi* mystic tradition has played a very important role. Two iconic individuals who successfully embodied and symbolized Kashmir's identity with all the richness of its cultural genius and spiritual ethos were, Lala Eshware/Laleshware (Hindu) better known as Lal Ded (Mother Lala) and Shaikh-ul-Alam Shaikh Nuruddin Wali (Nund Rishi, Muslim), the most revered saint of Kashmir representing a composite legacy (Zutshi, 2003, 18–19). Historically speaking both have occupied the cultural and literary imagination of people in Kashmir across religious lines. Both have been hugely influential in shaping the socio-psychological consciousness and identity of Kashmiri society and in symbolizing intercommunity harmony and the tolerant character of its society. The duo "became synonymous with Kashmiri identity" and its syncretistic culture (Accardi, 2018, 247–264). But it may well have been Shaikh Nuruddin who came closest to and best symbolized the Kashmiri identity with all its cultural genius and richness of spiritual personality as he laid the foundation of the *Reshi* mystic tradition with its syncretic attributes and thereby came to be recognized as the national saint of Kashmir (Baba, 2009, 51–58). Historically, Kashmir's "Patron Saint", exercised a deep and pervasive influence in shaping the socio-psychological character of Kashmiri society and in promoting its intercommunity harmony and tolerant character (Puri, 2009). Not surprisingly, he became the epitome of Kashmir's cultural and spiritual personality (Puri, 2009). And, both as a person and as an institution, came to personify Kashmir's national personality as well. He and his legacy continued to inspire the people of Kashmir for peace, reconciliation and harmony. Through all these influences Kashmiri society, in spite of the various challenging situations with which it was faced, by and large remained pacifist and nonviolent.

Kashmir was able to retain this uniqueness in spite of its changing political fortunes. This has been the case when its political authority extended beyond its natural borders and even when it lost its political independence as a kingdom in 1586 with its annexation by Emperor Akbar who brought it under the jurisdiction of the Mughal Empire. During the Mughal rule Kashmir retained its status as a politico-administrative provincial unit. It is no exaggeration to say that the Mughal empire, because of its enlightenment, prosperity, civilizational grandeur, syncretic policies and rulers' fascination for the place, contributed to the economic wellbeing, administrative reforms, architectural and landscape refinement, as well as to the enrichment of art, culture, literary and intellectual life of the place that have left permanent and positive marks on its identity. With the weakening of the empire the Valley came under Afghan rule from 1756 which, in the words of Lawrence, meant passing "to a time of brutal tyranny, unrelieved by good works, chivalry, and honour" (Lawrence, 1967, 197). It remained under the Afghans till it was captured by Maharaja Ranjit Singh and annexed to the Sikh Kingdom of Punjab in 1819 and remained so till 1846. Sikh rule was no better. It was crudely discriminative, oppressive and extortionist in its approach to people and the place (Bazaz, 2003, 113–117; Schofield, 1997, 33–38). Both Afghans and Sikhs were political novices, culturally coarse, bereft of any refinement and notably insensitive to human suffering. Due to the oppressive, partisan, and fleecing character of the Sikh regime, Kashmiris had to undergo a very trying situation in their battle for survival. However, in response to the extremely repressive nature of these regimes the people developed tactics of adaptability for survival that prompted them to be tactful and shrewd (Bazaz, 2003; Schofield, 1997).

During the first Anglo-Sikh war (1846), the British East India Company defeated the Sikh state with clandestine support from Gulab Singh, then the Raja of Jammu and the functioning prime minister of the Sikh state. After defeating the Sikhs, the British contrived to constrain the Sikh state to cede the control of Kashmir Valley over to Gulab Singh through the treaty of Amritsar, mainly as a reward for the help that he had rendered them to defeat Sikh state (Singh, 1988, 105–122). The acquisition of the Kashmir Valley by Gulab Singh in 1846, under the British colonial design, and its incorporation into his Dogra Kingdom marked a major boost to his political fortunes. Kashmir, it should be pointed out, represented a long political and civilizational history, a gifted people, a stable economy, and recognition as a center of learning with which no other unit of his kingdom could hope to compete. The acquisition of Kashmir transformed Raja Gulab Singh of Jammu into the maharaja of a new construct, called the Jammu and Kashmir state, with multiple layers of ethno-regional plurality within which the valley of Kashmir alone was a homogeneous region, representing predominantly a single geo-ethnic and cultural unit (Singh, 1988, 105–122). But, for Kashmir, it marked political and economic marginalization and the beginning of a new and, from the point of view of the present study, crucial phase in its checkered contemporary history. Many of its present-day problems can be traced to these conditions. In this process, Kashmir's former position of centrality in relation to its surroundings was lost to a new political equation under which Jammu (a hilly, as opposed to mountainous terrain without much of significant political history) emerged as a center of power and a parallel capital to Srinagar in Kashmir. It happened so because of the ruling dynasty's ethnic, religious and political roots in the region. As compared to Kashmir, Jammu considerably benefitted within the new equation. From being a *rajwada* (principality) confined to Jammu's central hills, its provincial status saw itself expanded to include a large number of newly conquered regions and territories that historically had each enjoyed their own ethno-cultural identity and politico-economic significance regardless of what might become of Jammu.

Under the new dispensation, which was to last for more than a century, the Dogra dynasty, on account of the very nature of state formation and also because of the character of its politics, became partisan of the Dogra community in particular (which constituted less than 15 percent of the state's population but to which it ethnically belonged) and in general to Hindus (Snedden, 2013, 10). Dogra rulers designated the princely state as Hindu, giving it a partisan communal character in spite of the fact that Muslims overall constituted almost 80 percent of its population and more than 95 percent of the population in the Kashmir province of the state (Rai, 2004, 7, 80). Under this partisan arrangement, Muslims in general and Kashmiri Muslims in particular suffered a number of disadvantages resulting in their alienation, deprivation and suffering. They suffered these disadvantages on account of discrimination in services, heavy taxation on handicraft, forced labor, etc. (Khan, 1988, 11–31). The regime projected Kashmir as a purchased territory which therefore deserved no empathy and consideration. During the Dogra rule, the people of the state suffered a lot because of the institution of the jagirdari system which the rulers installed and operated (Khan, 1988, 11–17). The privileged class of mainly Hindus (Dogra Rajputs, Kashmiri Pandits and Punjabi Hindus) received the maximum benefits and were bestowed jagirs by the regime for their service to the Dogra rulers. In fact, the majority of the higher posts were held by Dogra Rajputs themselves. The Kashmiri Pandit community filled the rank and file of the state services (Verma, 1994, 12). As a result, the condition of the common masses, comprised mainly of Muslims, was pathetic on almost all indicators. In the Kashmir region, Muslims remained bereft of any position of privilege or power compared to the tiny compatriot minority of Kashmiri Hindus, the Pandits (mainly constituted of Brahmins). Because of their presence in all sectors of administration, Kashmiri Pandits came to represent, in the eyes of the common Kashmir Muslim, the state and its oppressive manifestation. This situation, therefore, structurally created conditions for the growth of polarizing communal consciousness, sowing the seeds of political mobilization and identification on communal lines for communities with divergent interest and loyalties. Such policies had serious implications in the light of the increasingly emancipative and anti-colonial atmosphere developing in and around the state and at the larger level of the colonized world (Baba, 2007; Verma, 1994, 11). However, the situation of communal polarization did not impact the social relationship between Kashmiri Hindu and Muslim communities, in part because of Kashmir's ethos, in part because of the Pandit community's dependence on Muslims at all levels of the day-to-day chores of their social existence and for various household and other services. Their belonging, by and large, to one privileged social caste (Brahmin) has been inherently antithetical for their identification as a class with the masses and to developing empathy with their sufferings. Therefore, what followed in 1931 was the assertion of Kashmiri Muslim identity in response to the discriminative and oppressive policies against the Muslims of the state in general and in the Kashmir Valley in particular.

The 1931 uprising was preceded by many important developments, which suggests that emancipative forces were already at work in Kashmir. The symptoms of these forces included: the *Shawl-baf* agitation in 1865, the establishment of the first Muslim school in 1889 and the subsequent transformation of the initiative into a movement in the form of *Anjumani Nusrat-ul-Islam* (1905) with a reformist agenda and as a means of providing Kashmiri Muslims leadership on a number of issues and problems concerning the community, the Silk factory workers agitation (1924), etc. These developments became reflective of the growing awakening and agitation of Kashmiri Muslim masses against the policies of personalized, oppressive and discriminative feudal order. One of the important developments of the time included the submission of a memorandum to the Viceroy of India in 1924 by some concerned and prominent Kashmiris highlighting the problems and disadvantages suffered by Kashmiri Muslims and soliciting their redressal. The focus of the memorandum was on extension of rights on land for peasants, greater representation for Muslims in the state services and steps to be taken for improving their educational status. All this was indicative of the growing awareness and assertion of their rights by the Muslims who, in spite of constituting an overwhelming majority of the state's population, found themselves marginalized in almost all walks of life (Baba, 2007). It also demonstrated their growing willingness to stand up and strive for what they perceived as their rightful place. One important factor that we need to take note of in the context of Kashmir is the role played by Kashmiri (mainly Muslim) diaspora settled across northern India in general and the Punjab in particular, that included some eminent members like Allama Mohammad Iqbal, Sonaullah Amratseri, Mohammad din Fauq, Saifuddin Kichloo. This diaspora did its utmost to help alleviate the plight of what it called the Kashmiri nation. A number of periodicals/papers were published from Lahore solely devoted to the awakening of the Kashmiri Muslims by invoking their consciousness as a community that suffered deprivation, and focusing on their plight (Baba, 2007). This was a natural response to the avowedly Hindu regime that was discriminating against Muslims.

In spite of the invocation of Muslim consciousness, the freedom movement that emerged in the state remained non-violent and committed to secular demands for education, employment, representation in the governance process and government services, taxation reforms, land rights for peasants, etc. The agitation was also joined by the Muslims of Jammu. However, in the context of the time and in response to the nature of the regime the political movement that was formed to pursue the grievances or demands of people was named the Muslim Conference (MC). The MC was intended to work toward the empowerment of Muslims who had remained marginalized within the state. But just within less than a decade of its formation, reflecting Kashmir's inclusive and composite ethos, the organization was renamed as the National Conference (NC), with a vocal commitment to the secular values of national emancipation, democracy, inclusiveness and progressive empowerment of all sections of society, irrespective of caste, creed and sex. In Kashmir, the experiment had at best only partial success as only a small number of non-Muslims (Pandits) joined the organization and became active members since an overwhelming majority of them were intrinsically privileged as a social caste/class and had developed a vested interest in the state and its partisan character (Bazaz, 2003, 157–160). However, in 1939, soon after this change, the Jammu chapter of the organization resurrected the Muslim Conference to suit the relatively more polarized political orientation of the Jammu region. This new division was subsequently to have a far-reaching impact on the politics of the state and that of subcontinent as a whole. In 1944 the National Conference adopted what is called a *Naya Kashmir* Agenda as a manifesto for shaping Kashmir as a progressive, egalitarian, and a welfare-oriented independent state (Whitehead, 2018, 70–88).

The difference in the anti-colonial orientation between the Muslim League (ML) and Indian National Congress (INC) in British India had a serious bearing on the politics of the state with far reaching implications. Gradually, the two branches of the freedom movement in the state, the Muslim Conference and the National Conference developed a political proximity with rival political forces in the Indian mainland depending on their politico-ideological orientations. That meant that the National Conference developed a closer proximity with the Indian National Congress and its leadership, particularly with Jawaharlal Nehru and Mahatma Gandhi.

The most important thing to note here is that during the time of the British withdrawal and the partition of India in 1947 into India and Pakistan, Kashmir remained peaceful even when all border regions were rife with violence and bloodshed. Even within the state, Jammu region saw violence and large-scale intercommunity killings while the Muslim majority Kashmir remained calm and peaceful. So much so that at that time of communal frenzy and darkness Gandhi saw a ray of light in Kashmir and its conduct.[3] Subsequently at the crucial juncture of the challenging situation that emerged in Kashmir, the National Conference leadership endorsed Maharaja Hari Singh's belated accession with India on October 27, 1947. There is some evidence to suggest that at that time the National Conference would have preferred a secular, democratic and independent Kashmir in line with the Naya Kashmir Manifesto of 1944 (Whitehead, 2018, 70–88). However, given its limited options, Sheikh Abdullah and the NC leadership supported accession to India in the hope of securing a meaningful autonomous status for the state, which he thought to be necessary for translating the NC's vision of Naya Kashmir into actual practice.[4] The leadership probably thought that it would not be able to secure such a position within Pakistan. Part of the reason for this was that during the crucial years preceding 1947, Sheikh's relations with the Muslim League leadership were considerably strained and that he had gained greater proximity to the ideology and the leadership of the Indian National Congress. So, at this crucial juncture, the

NC supported accession with India on the assumption of the validity of its democratic and secular credentials. It supported the reservation of substantial powers to the state as per the terms of the accession deed signed by Maharaja Hari Singh. The maharaja, through the instrument of accession, had surrendered his jurisdiction to the dominion government only on defense, foreign affairs and communication.

Of the three regions – Jammu, Kashmir and Ladakh – Kashmir alone stood by and large intact and undivided at the end of India–Pakistan active confrontation and war in November 1949.[5] That also meant that the NC leadership, rooted in Kashmir, stood there to provide the only viable leadership to the state during that crucial phase. Naturally their political thinking reflected their own vision of state building and state formation. Consequently, when the question of defining the state's relationship under the constitution arose (which was being worked out within the Constituent Assembly of India) it was the interim government of the state (that had been formed under the leadership of Sheikh Abdullah) which determined the center–state relationship (India and the state of Jammu and Kashmir) exactly in line with the terms of the instrument of accession.[6] The new Kashmiri leadership, while supporting the accession to India, strongly wanted Kashmir's special identity to be preserved and safeguarded. This urge was mainly rooted in their identity consciousness as Kashmiris. They were also aware of the need to retain the Muslim character of the state which if divided could be more vulnerable.[7] It also wanted to secure enough powers to implement the emancipative agenda for social engineering that it had adopted in 1944 as an instrument of social change in Kashmir (Whitehead, 2018, 70–88).

There were several rounds of discussions and a number of drafts exchanged between the state representatives and the Government of India before the two parties came to agree on what became Article 370 of the Indian constitution (adopted in November 1949).[8] The agreed draft was prepared by Shree Gopalaswami Ayyangar, who had taken over as Minister of Kashmir Affairs in India, in consultation with Kashmiri NC leader Mirza Afzal Beg and other National Conference members nominated for the constituent assembly of India (Baba, 2012a, 191–208). Therefore, on the promulgation of the constitution on January 26, 1950, it became clear that only two of its Articles, viz. Article I, declaring India as the union of states, and Article 370, which defined the relationship of the state with the Indian union, became applicable to the state directly and completely. Under Article 370, Jammu and Kashmir was made an exception to the application of Article 238, which regulated relations between Group 'B' of the Indian states and the Union government.[9] It explained that the power of Parliament to make laws for the said state shall be limited to the subjects mentioned in the instrument of accession, that is, defence, foreign affairs and communication. The president of India had to identify matters in the central and the concurrent list "in consultation with the government of the state" which correspond to those specified in the instrument of accession (Sathe, 1992, 14). In essence, therefore, the state obtained a special position within the Constitution of India in tune with its leadership's distinctive aspirations.

So far so good, but Kashmir's assertion of a progressive, secular and inclusive identity that seemed to be going well came to face serious external and internal challenges. Pakistan had assumed that, as per the partition framework, Kashmir would accede to it because of its Muslim character and due to its greater geographical proximity with it. Consequently, the tribal invasion supported by Pakistan's regular army along with the conflict that had begun in Jammu with the revolt of Muslims in its Poonch district, culminated in the effective division of the state between what became the Indian and Pakistani controlled parts of Jammu and Kashmir.[10] In addition, the Pakistani contestation of the maharaja's accession, the Indian commitment to referring the issue of final dispensation of the state to its people, the internationalization of the issue and the UN endorsement of the right to self-determination of the people – all these factors combined together were subsequently to make Kashmir the object of multiple pulls and pressures that would continue to strain its identity (Gupta, 1966, 110–139). The result was a serious challenge to Kashmir's political identity and major predicaments for the leadership and its vision for the state's future development. After having lost the option for an independent state, envisioned in its Naya Kashmir (New Kashmir) Manifesto, in the complex context of politics created by the division of the subcontinent on religious lines, the national movement rooted in Kashmir Valley, which had demonstrated preference in favor of what it assumed to be a secular democratic India (Whitehead, 2018), had been able to secure a special status within the Indian Constitution which allowed the security of the Muslim majority character of the state and which gave it sufficient powers for implementing the progressive vision it had for the state.

In the changed context, the progressive and emancipative outlook of the secular democratic leadership of National Conference had a very long-term impact on the Kashmir society. One instance was the land reforms that were initiated in 1950 whereby landless peasants gained land ownership. It contributed to the long-term empowering of most of the so-far dispossessed peasantry who at that time in the Kashmir Valley were mostly Muslims. Other measures that further reinforced this emancipative trend included free universal education and health care. These measures with the passage of time produced a new generation of educated Muslim youth with a claim for government services which till then had been almost the sole prerogative of the minuscule Kashmiri Pandit (Hindu) community. This process of equalizing was resented by the Pandits who had traditionally enjoyed a sort of monopoly of government jobs partly because of the low education levels among Muslims (who otherwise constituted more than 95 percent of the population in the valley) and partly because of the discriminative policies of the princely state. But in spite of this emerging competitiveness between Pandits and Muslims in the valley, the social relations between the communities continued to be cordial and harmonious. However, there was a greater challenge to community relationships and to the regional equation. It was due to the following three reasons:

1   As stated earlier, within the political construct of multi-ethno-regional Jammu and Kashmir, Kashmir had lost its geo-political eminence and autonomy as a result of Gulab Singh's taking over its possession in 1846 when the British facilitated its transfer to him as part of their own colonial political project.

After 1947, because of the effective division of the state, the regional polarization on the Indian side was further reinforced because of the changed demographic situation of the three regions – Jammu, Kashmir and Ladakh – creating
a distinct majority religious character in each region.[11] In this situation, the
progressive nationalist vision of the NC leadership (that was mainly rooted in
the Valley) came to be resented by the dominant elites in Jammu and Ladakh.
These created internal fissures within the state facilitating external intervention and subsequently undermining the whole autonomy project.

2   The NC leadership in its visualization had seen India through the prism of
Nehru and Gandhi and their secular and pluralist plan for the country. However, soon after the accession of the state to India and after the drafting of the
Indian Constitution, alternative non-secular forces began to assert an assimilationist agenda for the country and to lobby for undoing Kashmir's autonomy.
These forces even supported/promoted communal polarization within the
state. That brought on greater strains in the relationship between the governments in Kashmir and of the Indian union, a product of which was the
dismissal of Sheik Abdullah's government and his imprisonment on August 9,
1953. This further complicated Kashmir politics by undermining people's trust
in secular democratic credentials of the Indian state. After having dismissed the
most popular leader, whose endorsement of accession had been considered
essential by the Indian leadership in 1947, the Government of India had to
depend on unpopular leadership to run the state that required elections to
be manipulated. It was the outcome of the assimilationist mindset that got
activated on the issue in which the RSS and its leaders like Shama Prashad
Mukherjee, the founder of the Jana Sangh, took the lead.[12]

3   The Indian leadership publicly went back on its promise of the right to self-
determination to the people of Kashmir around the middle of the 1950s on
the pretext that Pakistan had entered into an alliance with the United States.
To the ordinary Kashmiri, this was an absurd explanation. They were being
deprived of their right because of the actions of a third party and for none of
their own fault. To say the least, in the words of Jayaprakash Narayan, it had
no moral basis. According to him "it is forgotten that the offer or the pledge
had been given but to the people of Kashmir. There could be no justification
for punishing the latter (Kashmiris) for the actions of the former (Pakistan)"
(Narayan, 1964). The Government of India never considered the people of
Kashmir and did not view them as a serious stakeholder in the problem.[13] The
result was that the Indian leadership lost its moral case vis-à-vis the people of
Kashmir.

The combination of these factors continued to complicate Kashmir politics and
considerably strained its inclusive and syncretic character. This undermined the
faith that the secular democratic leadership had placed in India's secularist and
pluralist vision and weakened their influence. In a way it vindicated the protago-
nists of the two-nation theory in the state. This strengthened the Pakistani case and

its ideological underpinnings for the two-nation theory: by implication it meant that the Muslim identity of Kashmir could not be secured within what it said was primarily a "Hindu" India with a secular facade. In this context, within the state and within the valley dormant supporters of the two-nation theory gained a new lease of life. The contention of secular Muslim leadership had been considerably weakened.

However, the movement for self-determination that was launched in 1955 under the leadership of Sheikh Abdullah continued to be committed to secular, pluralistic and nonviolent values and methodology.[14] But it began to be undermined because of a number of factors. The Sheikh's political compromise with Indira Gandhi in the 1975 accord resulted in his regaining power by abandoning his plebiscite claim and without undoing the erosion to the state's autonomy which had been carried out in the more than two decades between his dismissal in 1953 and his return to power in 1975. It undermined him and his brand of secular politics and eventually the Islamist forces, committed to self-determination for the state with accession to Pakistan as a preference, began to assert themselves as soon as the towering personage of Sheikh Abdullah got removed from the scene with his death in 1982. Then Mrs. Gandhi's personalized government at the center pushed for undemocratically engineering the dismissal of Farooq Abdullah's popularly elected government (Nehru, 1997, 601–641). This further weakened the people's faith in the democratic credentials of the Indian state in relation to Jammu and Kashmir. More importantly, it encouraged the traditional leadership, inclined toward a more Islamist agenda, to get activated and become assertive within a globally facilitating context. It began with a number of developments within the Muslim world that saw the assertion of political Islam particularly in and after the 1970s with impact on South Asia. It happened along with technological changes that brought in television to the global stage as an effective tool of transmission of news, ideas and influences across countries and regions. This facilitated an effective news interface between the Muslim lands and Kashmir. Three major developments that created a facilitating context for the emergence of political Islam can be identified:

1   After the 1967 Arab defeat vis-à-vis Israel, the secular forces within the Arab world led by President Nasser of Egypt declined considerably and the conservative Gulf regimes led by Saudi Arabia gained ascendancy within the Arab–Muslim world. In the 1970s some new developments in the vicinity of South West Asia began to have a very profound impact all across the Muslim South West Asian region. It began with conservative monarchies in the Gulf led by Saudi Arabia which, with the world's largest discovered oil reserves, gained enormous financial clout as a result of soaring oil prices (as, given the rapidly increasing global demand for oil, the Organization of Petroleum Exporting Countries [OPEC] was able to push for increasing oil prices) (Baba, 1992, 3–22).

2   The Iranian revolution of 1978–1979 generated revolutionary appeal across the Muslim world. Its revolutionary rhetoric and message for a revolutionary

Islam, democracy and republicanism had a destabilizing impact on the conservative and hereditary regimes in the Gulf region. It prompted these conservative regimes with their growing financial clout to counter Iran by invoking Sunni consciousness among the Muslims. This began to polarize Muslim societies, including in South Asia, on sectarian lines. It particularly had an impact on a vulnerable Pakistani society that began to get polarized under these external stimuli with a facilitating regime under Zia-ul-Haq (1978–1988) who had his own project of Islamization. The polarization along Shia–Sunni sectarian lines was further reinforced after the Iran–Iraq war that began in September 1980 and lasted for almost a decade as both antagonists in the war began to invoke support within their own side of the sectarian fault lines. In this situation, Saudi Arabia with its growing resources began to push for and promote a more literal and hardline interpretation of its own Wahhabi brand of Islam. Not only were Muslim societies divided on Shia–Sunni lines but they also witnessed the Sunni fragmentation on various *maslaki* (sub-sectarian) lines. The worst case of this extreme multi-level fragmentation of Muslim society occurred in Pakistan where violent attacks led to mass killings in mosques and other shrines of various historically revered saints. Such sectarian sentiment did impact Kashmir to the extent that a host of new mosques started coming up with sectarian identification, most prominently Salafi mosques reflecting Saudi influence and funding.[15] But probably because of the character of Kashmiri society all this did not lead to the significant levels of social fragmentation and violence on sectarian lines of the kind witnessed elsewhere in some Muslim societies.

3   A third development that had a very serious impact on the region was the Soviet invasion of Afghanistan in 1979 that continued for more than a decade and plunged Afghanistan into an unending turmoil. It brought in a number of politically motivated powers led by the United States of America together to prop up a new crop of conservative and radical *jihadists* in defense of "Muslim Afghanistan" in an active resistance to the "atheistic communist" power, the Soviet Union. This development further impacted Pakistan which was used as a frontline state by the United States against the Soviet occupation. It radicalized sections within its society, granted legitimacy to non-state violence and facilitated the flow of weapons. It was to undermine both the Pakistani state and the liberal sections within its society. In spite of various efforts, the Pakistani state has not been able to overcome this problem completely so far. It impacted the Kashmir situation all the more severely because of the existence of the on-going political problem of Kashmiri resentment caused by its non-resolution and the growing alienation of its society during the 1980s, particularly after the emergence of militancy.

Because of these influences combined with the growing communalization of Indian politics, the idiom of politics in Kashmir began to draw increasingly from the Islamism that was gaining ground in Pakistan. Such trends gained strength with the weakening of secular, democratic and nationalist elements in Kashmir politics.

The major turning point in this connection can, to a great extent, be traced back to the unjustified and even "unconstitutional" dismissal of Farooq Abdullah's government in July 1984 and the installation of a regime which, for its survival, had to impose a curfew for about 70 days of its initial 90 days' existence to preempt any protest demonstrations in the valley (Nehru, 1997, 609–641; Abdullah, 1985). This exposed the hollowness of the Indira–Abdullah Accord that had brought the National Conference back to power with the promise of restoring the autonomous position to the state that had been lost since 1953 (Baba, 2012b, 111–112). It was during the subsequent governor's/president's rule in 1986–1987 that signs of communal polarization in Kashmir politics started emerging and gaining strength. Parties with proved secular, nationalist credentials like the National Conference, that for a long time had remained synonymous with Kashmiri identity, started losing ground and new forces with a more radical non-secular Islamist tinge began to flourish in the Valley. This situation became one of the factors prompting Farooq Abdullah to enter into an alliance with his erstwhile foe, the Congress party that was then in power in Delhi. It meant compromising on the NC's historical assertion of the political identity of Kashmir.

This alliance totally undermined Farooq and his capacity to represent the distinctive Kashmiri aspirations, and to respond to the identity demands of the people. In other words, it blocked the normal and moderate channels of expression of Kashmiri sentiments, thereby paving the way for Islamist forces to replace them as vanguards of the people and promote their own interests in the state. These forces grouped together under the name of the Muslim United Front (MUF) and became a major force in Kashmir politics. So much so, that NC–Congress alliance felt obliged to resort to the large-scale rigging of elections in order to secure a clear majority in the State Assembly and prevent the MUF from winning a respectable number of seats. This exposed the NC–Congress alliance further and undermined its democratic credentials. The people effectively lost faith in democracy and the younger elements felt that in order to obtain justice the only alternative left to them was to resort to armed violence. More significantly it marked the resurgence of a separatist movement in the Valley with a vigor never witnessed earlier.[16] It was in this context that the emergence of militancy in Kashmir took place. The first group of young men to take to violence consisted mostly of those who had actually worked on the side of the Muslim United Front (MUF) during the 1987 elections. They were subjected to severe torture for their association with the opposition alliance. It is clear that the objective situation provided a good opportunity for Pakistan to get involved in Kashmir as never before. Because of the regional and international atmosphere, the militancy began to draw from the Islamist idiom growing globally and locally due to factors indicated earlier. Thus, it was this squeezing of the political and democratic space which pushed the increasingly frustrated youth in Kashmir to initiate a violent uprising in the late 1980s. The experts have almost unanimously held the view that one of the most important factors contributing to the post-1989 turmoil in Kashmir has been the total lack of credibility of its electoral practice.[17]

A number of factors created a context of hope for the success of the movement. These significantly included the Soviet withdrawal from Afghanistan (1989) which had a symbolic significance. A small country defeating a superpower became a big inspiration. This also meant that the Pakistan security establishment that had gained expertise and experience in Afghanistan would have the confidence to focus on Jammu and Kashmir. Finally, the breakdown of the Soviet Union (1991) that followed the Soviet withdrawal from Afghanistan resulted in the independence of six Muslim states in Central Asia and Caucasus which became a big inspiration for the people in Kashmir.

So the context was quite encouraging and gave hope to the militants, their supporters in Pakistan and the general masses in Kashmir. It needs to be noted that militancy in the early 1990s as it emerged was mainly symbolic and nominal. It was the whole-hearted massive support from general masses all across the Valley that made the movement a major challenge for the Indian state to deal with. Massive public demonstrations with over a million people's participation became a regular feature in the valley in 1990.[18] The all-out mobilization of the repressive machinery by the Indian state gave rise to the issue of human rights violations. So much so that it is generally admitted that Kashmir began to earn the dubious distinction of having the heaviest military presence within a civilian area in the world.[19] This was also the time when Hindutva forces began to gain greater ground within mainland India. The increasing mobilization of these forces culminated in the demolition of the Babri Masjid in Ayodhya by Hindu mobs in 1992 (Pasha, 1994). This not only led to communal polarization within India but it also had a bearing on the balance of forces in Kashmir. It was within this overall atmosphere of the communal polarization that the Islamist and pro-Pakistan Hizbul Mujahidin began to gain ascendancy over the otherwise secular nationalist JKLF that had initiated the armed resistance in Kashmir. Thus, while Islamism was increasingly to become the idiom of politics, it by and large continued to espouse political objectives like *azadi* (freedom)/ accession with Pakistan without any significant admixture of pan-Islamic aspirations and other extremist objectives.

However, Islamic slogans combined with demand for *azadi* and an overall atmosphere of insecurity as a result of the violent discourse was a factor in frightening large sections of pro-India Kashmiri Pandits and even many Muslims. Their migration from the Valley in large numbers has been a major setback to Kashmir's syncretic and pluralist identity with far-reaching implications (Bose, 2005, 71–80). And greater harm to the cause of the inter-communal relationship was also done because the BJP and the RSS began to play their own polarizing politics on the issue (Bose, 2005, 75).

By the mid-1990s, the state and its coercive agencies along with what came to be known as pro-government/renegade militants (*Ikhwan*) seemed to be succeeding against what till then had been a predominantly local militancy. But that proved temporary as militancy re-emerged with greater vengeance and sophistication. During the latter part of the 1990s, one saw militancy being confined to people with a high degree of motivation, dedication and skill drawn both from within and without. In the process, militancy also gained a greater degree of cross-border Islamic dimension and non-local groups like *Lashkari Toiba* and *Harkatul Ansar* gained ascendancy over local groups like *Hizb-ul-Mujahiddin*. However, the militants continued to find local recruits in addition to the contingents of support that they were drawing from outside.

That the state authority in Kashmir largely depended on coercive and repressive agencies became a reflection of its weakness rather than its strength. It was in this context that the then army chief, S. Padmanabhan, and the then defense minister of India, George Fernandes, echoed the considered view that Kashmir is fundamentally a political problem and requires a political settlement. This was the view that was also shared by then prime minister of India Shree Atal Bihari Vajpayee. As well, the people in Kashmir who have been historically used to living a peaceful life within the comfort of serene surroundings could not sustain violence for long. They have always responded positively to the call for peace in a situation of hope. Moreover, it was the changing international situation in the context of the 9/11 attacks that became the basis for an initiative for dialogue.

Kashmir began to change for the better on account of the following two factors: first, the de-legitimization of non-state violence as a means of realizing political objectives with even Pakistan finding it more difficult to support the cross-border militancy; and second, the strengthening of a positive political environment and a strong political will to work toward a peace process that began to consolidate particularly after 2003–2004. In the context of an evolving peace process some significant initiatives were taken like Cross-LoC (Line of Control) Bus service and the opening of trade points across the LoC in Jammu and Kashmir (Baba, 2005). These were in addition to the 2003 Indo-Pak agreement on cease-fire across the LoC. These steps were viewed positively by both Kashmiris and non-Kashmiris. It was in this situation of overall hope that a significant effort was made to resolve the Kashmir issue on a permanent basis through a very creative approach. Musharraf's four-point proposal (2006) to resolve the Kashmir issue was generally seen as a realistic option to resolve the issue on permanent basis. In this situation militancy got considerably weakened across Kashmir. In the words of a well-grounded Kashmiri journalist "Kashmir is the first conflict-ridden Muslim region in the world where people have consciously made a transition from violence to non-violence, and this includes the staunch Islamists too" (Jaleel, 2008).

However, the hope for peace proved to be short-lived. A series of developments and a combination of factors aggravated the situation, beginning with the collapse of the peace process. By 2007, Musharraf, as a result of lawyers' agitation against him, began to lose his grip on power. After the 26/11 (2008) Mumbai attack, India suspended all peace talks with Pakistan. The ceasefire agreement that was reached in 2003 began to be breached thereafter. The internal situation in Kashmir began to worsen as a result of changed policies. Then a series of summer unrests occurred in Kashmir beginning in 2008 and continuing in 2009. It was the prolonged public protests and a chain of *hartals* (shut-downs), combined with stone pelting, which came to define a new mode of agitation. The major setback came in June 2010 with news of a fake encounter killing of three Kashmiri youths by the army at Macchil (a village in Kupwara district in Kashmir), that the military initially had claimed were "Pakistani infiltrators". This paved the way for a prolonged agitation that saw more than 100 youths being killed during the public demonstrations that continued for a number of months. It was followed by the execution of M. Afzal Guru in February 2013, who had been accused of attacking the Parliament. The general impression in Kashmir was that he did not get a fair trial.[20] The secretive manner in which he was executed, not allowing his family to meet him, and not handing over his dead body to his family for proper burial added to the mass anger (Rising Kashmir, 2018).

The non-empathetic and non-responsive nature of the Indian state and its purely coercive handling of the situation angered the Kashmiri youth. This marked the emergence of a new phase of militancy that was rooted locally, drawing mainly from the educated young, that used the new media to connect to the people in general and to the youth in particular. The typical representative of this phase of militancy was Burhan Wani from South Kashmir. He became popular through his proficient use of social media which allowed a greater interface with the masses. He began appealing to the Kashmiri youth to join militancy. Burhan quickly rose to become the commander of the Kashmiri militant group *Hizbul Mujahideen*. Rather than being seen as someone involved in violent actions, he came to be viewed a symbol of political defiance in the state.[21]

But, instead of redressing the situation through creative responses, the state continued with its repressive policy of using disproportional coercion even against the peaceful and stone pelting protests which had begun to gain an increasing currency with the growing alienation of the population. The new militancy continued to be rooted locally mostly as part of the Hizbul Mujahiddin that kept a conscious distance from the emerging radical Islamist trends that had begun to emerge and operate in Muslim West Asia. However, the situation began to worsen after the Hindu Nationalist Party, the BJP, wedded to a more muscular and assimilationist policy in relation to Kashmir, took over power in Delhi during 2014. The situation took a turn to the worse in 2015 after the BJP became a coalition partner of the People's Democratic Party (PDP) in forming the state government. The PDP aligned with the BJP in spite of the fact that the latter had been completely rejected by voters within the valley. The BJP's ascendancy increasingly began to create apprehensions about the undermining of the Kashmiri political identity and autonomy that was incorporated within the Indian Constitution, carefully designed to safeguard the special character of the state. The situation deteriorated further in 2016 when Burhan Wani, who had by then gained considerable popularity as a symbol of resistance, was killed along with several of his colleagues in a security trap on July 8 that year. This led to massive protests, particularly in South Kashmir.

The state handling of these protests resulted in a heavy loss of life and produced public protests/agitation that broke all records of the past in terms of its longevity, the expanse of areas affected and the number of civilian causalities. There were protests all across Kashmir, even extending to Muslim districts within Jammu and

Ladakh. The state as usual used coercion in dealing with the protests that resulted in prolonged shut-downs, hundred plus causalities, thousands injured and maimed that included the blinding (full and partial) of several hundred children/youth (including girls) across Kashmir. As a result of all this, public anger has continued. Public protests and stone pelting encounters with the security forces have become a regular feature more particularly in South Kashmir that had hitherto remained relatively peaceful even during the hey days of militancy.[22] The pronounced use of this muscular policy in dealing with Kashmir, bereft of any initiative for meaningful dialogue and peace, has resulted in the further alienation of the Kashmiri youth, enabling their recruitment into local militant groups, educated young men in particular.

It is worth noting that the Kashmir militancy had remained by and large immune to ultra-radical ideologies with pan-Islamist agendas even when there was a dramatic rise of groups like ISIS/Daesh destabilizing large parts of the Arab–Muslim region and sending alarm bells across the globe. Kashmir, in spite of the abnormal politics, violence, repression and vulnerability, has not seen serious inroads of radical religious extremism because of its particular ethos. That is why groups like ISIS have not found much appeal among the angry youth (Meraj, 2018). It is because the social evolution of people in Kashmir has been different from places like Afghanistan which fortunately makes it difficult to sustain violence beyond the point where it becomes a mass phenomenon, indiscriminatory and intensely destructive. However, if immediate remedial measures are not taken Kashmir's vulnerability to such phenomena is likely to grow because of the following factors (Bhushan, 2018):

1   Kashmir is a predominantly Muslim society that is undergoing a raging conflict as a result of which its youth are caught in a situation of suffocation and hopelessness, and could therefore be vulnerable to various undesirable influences.
2   The use of a hard-line muscular approach to the situation in Kashmir and the absence of hope for dialogue and peace has increased the vulnerability to such influences as we have witnessed during the past year or two. And within India, a growing religious intolerance and obscurantist forces have been gaining traction, further adding to such vulnerabilities.
3   Because of recent technological advances there has been social erosion in Kashmir as elsewhere in the world. The process of socialization of younger generations in accordance with the age-old traditions and ethos through intensely living and experiencing together has been undermined by exposure to new social media. In the changing atmosphere, the new generations, instead of witnessing social cohesion, live in the virtual world devoid of the real world society. Therefore instead of being socialized into a syncretic social setting they are prone to get exposed to all kinds of influences (Bhushan, 2018). With this, their vulnerability to extraneous and mostly undesirable influences is growing.
4   The new generations remain connected mainly with technological devices, experiencing the outer world through them and frequently getting into

gaming and its fictional, artificial characters and through these into a heartless competition in the virtual world where pain and suffering, life and death lose the psychological value of requiring empathy and compassion. Life and death come to be seen merely as winning and losing and not as pain and suffering. Such an upbringing is likely to dehumanize human conduct vis-à-vis others.

This is so at a time when extremist radical ideologies globally, mainly through social media, are impacting upon the impressionable minds within Muslim societies. So, as mentioned earlier, vulnerabilities are growing and some youth in Kashmir, even if their number remains small, have been attracted to groups like ISIS. It seems clear that the best way of meeting the challenge is to address the situation of conflict through a peaceful dialogue that generates a process of reconciliation and a situation of hope. Kashmiri society has already lost some of its inherited virtues. Its experience of and its experiments with composite living have considerably been compromised after the large-scale Pandit migration from the valley. A whole new generation has grown that has no experience in multi-faith composite living. Within the discourse of violence and protests, there is a situation of hopelessness and growing economic desperation. The almost daily and rampant scenes of death and destruction have created large-scale psychological traumas. And, not surprisingly, this situation has promoted drug addiction among the youth. All this has undermined many of the traditional attributes that once defined the identity of Kashmir – the syncretic living, the social cohesion and the cosmopolitan outlook of the society. The Muslim/religious identity in Kashmir has become somewhat more pronounced. Kashmir's naturally gifted assets that have defined Kashmir identity over time are rendered vulnerable. But still there are many who have reason to believe that Kashmiri society in its internal functioning and in relation to people visiting Kashmir from outside are exhibiting civility of conduct, humanity and generosity in trying situations and a general dislike for violence, showing empathy and hospitability toward one and all.[23] Even while living in a situation of distress, its youth are showing great promise through their achievements in their careers and ingenious contributions to art, literature, sports, and knowledge and the creative areas of life. The challenge for all concerned within and outside Kashmir is to build on the positives by creating and sustaining a situation of hope, dignity, reconciliation and peace.

Postscript

On August 5, 2019, the ruling BJP abrogated Art. 370 of the Indian constitution (along with Art. 35 A) which, despite its considerable erosion over the years, had symbolically reflected and secured Jammu and Kashmir's special identity and its nationalist aspirations. This action of the central government was done unilaterally and the government was able to seek parliamentary approval on the strength of its overwhelming majority status. It also divided the state into two union territories, thereby undermining its political positioning as a state within the Indian Union and bringing it under the direct control of the central government. All this was done against the norms of democracy and federalism, without taking the state and its people into confidence and incarcerating the entire spectrum of Kashmir's political leadership. The Valley was also put under a long spell of crippling restrictions. It was and continues to remain cutoff from the world by restricting the internet connectivity for an indefinite period. This disempowering act is probably the greatest challenge to Kashmir's identity in recent history, the consequences of which are unpredictable and long term.

Notes

1 For a view of the Kashmir evolution in relation to the forces and the factors, see Balraj Puri (2009).
2 Ibn Khaldun (1332–1406) has been an important propounder of this view. He stresses on the impact of environment on social organization and economic process that define value, prosperity and culture. See Muhsin Mahdi (1964).
3 As is well known, the partition resulted in the mass killings and collapse of the political process. See Sisir Gupta (1966, 13–14). For mass killings of Muslims in Jammu with the connivance of state administration see Snedden (2013, 54–55).
4 For a discussion on the Kashmir special status see Ram Hari (1983, 58–59). For further details see M. K. Teng and Santosh Kaul (1975).
5 After the 1963 Chinese aggression the former princely state of Jammu and Kashmir was divided into three parts under the control of three different sovereign states. Out of the total area of 222,236 sq. kms. of what constituted Jammu and Kashmir till 1947, 35.15% i.e. 78,114 sq. kms., is presently under the control of Pakistan, 2.29% i.e. 5180 sq.kms., has been ceded by Pakistan to China, 16.92% (3755 sq. kms) has been occupied by China from India during the 1963 aggression and 45.64% (1,01387 sq. kms.) remain with India. "Some Facts and Figures About Jammu and Kashmir", Manthan, New Delhi, October 1991.
6 In October 1947 as Emergency Administrator, Changed into Prime Minister in March 1948. A S. Anand (1994, 117–118).
7 The Muslim proportion of the population of the state as it existed before its partition was about 79% of its total population. After its effective division between the Indian and Pakistani parts the proportion of Muslims on the Indian side of the state come down to about 68% as per the 1961 census.
8 For a detailed account of the process through which Article 370 evolved and divergent perceptions on the issue, see Teng and Kaul (1975, 34–49).
9 This Group (B) of states consisted of former princely states that included Jammu and Kashmir. Even though a princely state, it was to be governed differently from the rest under Article 370.
10 As a result of the Karachi agreement of 1949 that created a ceasefire between India and Pakistan under the supervision of the United Nations Commission for India and Pakistan (UNCIP), the former princely state of Jammu and Kashmir got divided in de facto terms into what is known as Indian- and Pakistani-controlled Kashmir.
11 In the united Jammu and Kashmir till 1947 all the three regions had a Muslim majority. But with the division Jammu and Ladakh on the Indian side became Muslim minority regions. Jammu became a Hindu majority region and Ladakh was identified as Buddhist.
12 This rethinking on the Article 370 had agitated Sheikh Abdullah and he had questioned as to why Dr. S. P. Mukherjee did not "think of these matters at the time when he was one of the members of Government of India at the time of framing the constitution". See A. G. Noorani (2011, 189).

13 The argument looked more strange because India itself in the initial years had sought similar proximity with the US for the sake of securing its support on its position on Kashmir, see Noorani (2011).
14 The movement for self-determination was launched in 1955 under the banner of Plebiscite Front by Mirza Afzal Beg under the patronage of Sheikh Abdullah.
15 According to one estimate, during the reign of King Fahd (1982 to 2005), over $75 billion was spent in efforts to spread Wahhabi Islam. The money was used to establish 200 Islamic colleges, 210 Islamic centers, 1,500 mosques, and 2,000 schools for Muslim children in Muslim and non-Muslim majority countries.
16 In the words of Sumantra Bose, "I stress that the roots of the crisis that erupted in 1989–90 lie in a post-1947 history of denial of democratic rights and institutions to the people of J&K, particularly those of IJK". (2005, 7).
17 For a more detailed account of the democratic deficit in the state, see Sumantra Bose (1997, 23–54) and Widmalm (1997).
18 Over a million people's participation became a regular feature in the valley in 1990 in Kashmir.
19 As per Shubh Mathur, according to conservative estimates there are about 500,000 military/paramilitary personnel present in the state. See Shubh Mathur (2012, 42).
20 Even many others in India and across the globe shared this view. See Arundhati Roy (2018).
21 There was no significant evidence of Wani participating in any encounter with security agencies.
22 "Hundreds of our bright children have lost their eyesight shattering their dreams in life. Thousands are maimed and grievously injured. Many of our civil and political leaders and youth are being detained under various repressive laws." Noor Ahmad Baba (2016).
23 The author has received testimony from some of the senior members of the security agencies confirming this claim.

References

Abdullah, Farooq. 1985. *My Dismissal*. New Delhi, Vikas.
Accardi, Dean. 2018. "Embedded Mystics: Writing Lal Ded and Nund Rishi into the Kashmir Landscape" in Chitralekha Zutshi, ed. *Kashmir: History, Politics Representation*. New Delhi, Cambridge University Press: 247–264.
Anand, A. S. 1994. *The Constitution of Jammu and Kashmir*. New Delhi, Universal.
Baba, Noor Ahmad. 1992. "Nasser's Pan-Arab Radicalism and the Saudi Drive for Islamic Solidarity: A Response for Security" *India Quarterly, New Delhi, Indian Council of World Affairs*, January–June, Vol. XLVIII, Nos. 1–2: 3–22.
Baba, Noor Ahmad. 2005. "Kashmir Bus: Small but a Step in the Right Direction" in *Peace & Conflict*. New Delhi, Institute of Peace and Conflict Studies, April.
Baba, Noor Ahmad. 2007. "Contextualizing 1931 Uprising in Kashmir" *Greater Kashmir*, 13 July.
Baba, Noor Ahmad. 2009. "From Conflict to Reconciliation: The Relevance of Shaikh-ul Alam" *Alamdar: A Journal of Kashmir Society & Culture*, Shaikh-ul Alam Chair, University of Kashmir, Vol. III, No. 3: 51–58.
Baba, Noor Ahmad. 2012a. "Democracy & Governance in Kashmir" in Nyla Ali Khan, ed. *The Parchment of Kashmir, History, Society and Politic*. New York, Palgrave Macmillan.
Baba, Noor Ahmad. 2012b. "Kashmir Special Status: Myth and Reality" in V. R. Raghavan, ed. *Conflict in Jammu and Kashmir*. New Delhi, Vij Books.

Baba, Noor Ahmad. 2016. "Kashmir Protests: Case for a Critical Reflection" *Greater Kashmir*, October 25.

Banday, Ajaz A. 2009. "A Recent Discovery of Hellenistic Image of Gaja-Lakshmi from Kashmir: Style and Development" *The Journal of Central Asian Studies*, Vol. XVIII, No. 1: 75–86.

Bazaz, Prem Nath. 2003. *History of Struggle for Freedom in Kashmir*. Srinagar, Gulshan Publishers.

Bhushan, Bharat. 2018. "Waiting for Moderators: Kashmiri Youth Are No Longer Amenable to Sagacious Advice" *Outlook*, 16, April.

Bose, Sumantra. 1997. *The Challenge in Kashmir: Democracy, Self-Determination and a Just Peace*. New Delhi, Sage.

Bose, Sumantra. 2005. *Kashmir: Roots of Conflict, Pathways to Peace*. New Delhi, Vistaar Publications.

Drew, Frederick. 2008 (originally published in 1875). *The Northern Barriers of India and Jammu and Kashmir Territories, Reprinted*. Srinagar, City Book Centre.

Gupta, Sisir. 1966. *Kashmir: A Study in India-Pakistan Relations*. Bombay, Asia Publishing.

Hari, Ram. 1983. *Special Status in Indian Federalism: Jammu and Kashmir*. New Delhi, Seema Publications.

Jaleel, Muzamil. 2008. "Kashmir's Unarmed Freedom Fighters" *The Guardian*, August 31.

Khan, G. H. 1988. *Freedom Movement in Kashmir: 1931–1940*. New Delhi, Light & Life Publishers.

Lawrence, Walter R. 1967. *The Valley of Kashmir*. Srinagar, Kesar Publishers.

Mathur, Shubh. 2012. "Life and Death in the Borderlands: Indian Sovereignty and Military Impunity" *Race and Class*, Vol. 54, No. 1.

Meraj, Zafar. 2018. "Groups Like ISIS Have Got No Public Support in Kashmir" *Multimedia*, July 15.

Muhsin, Mahdi. 1964. *Ibn Khaldun's Philosophy of History: A Study of the Philosophical Foundation of the Science of Culture*. Chicago, University of Chicago Press.

Narayan, Jayaprakash. 1964. "The Need to Re-Think" *Hindustan Times*, New Delhi, May 15.

Nehru, B. K. 1997. *Nice Guys Finish Second: Memoirs*. New Delhi, Viking India.

Noorani, A. G. 2011. *Article 370: A Constitutional History of Jammu & Kashmir*. New Delhi, Oxford University Press.

Pasha, A. K. 1994. "Communal Revivalism in India: Its Impact on Ties with West Asia and North Africa" in Muchkund Dubey, ed. *Communal Revivalism in India: A Study of External Implications*. New Delhi, Har Anand.

Puri, Balraj Puri. 2009. "5000 Years of Kashmir" *Early Times*, Jammu, May 13.

Rai, Mirdu. 2004. "Hindu Rulers" in *Muslim Subjects*. New Jersey, Princeton University Press.

Roy, Arundhati. 2013. "The Hanging of Afzal" *The Guardian*, Guru is a stain on India's democracy. www.theguardian.com/commentisfree/2013/feb/10/hanging-afzal-guru-india-democracy (accessed 5/2/2020).

Sathe, S. P. 1992. "Art 370 and Jammu and Kashmir: For a Future Federalisation of Polity" *Mainstream*, July 25.

Schofield, Victoria. 1997. *Kashmir in the Crossfir*. New Delhi, Viva books.

Singh, Bawa Satinder. 1988. *The Jammu Fox: A Biography of Maharaja Gulab Singh of Kashmir, 1792–1857*. New Delhi, Heritage Publishers.

Snedden, Christopher. 2013. *Kashmir: The Unwritten History*. Noida, Harper Collins.

Stein, M. A. 1900. (Notes on Translation.) *Kalhana's Rajtarangni: A Chronicle of Kings of Kashmir*. Westminster, Archibald C. and Co.

Teng, M. K. and Kaul, Santosh. 1975. *Kashmir Special Status*. New Delhi, Oriental Publications.

Verma, P. S. 1994. *Jammu & Kashmir at Political Crossroads*. New Delhi, Vikas Publications.

Whitehead, Andrew. 2018. "The Rise & Fall of New Kashmir" in Chitralekha Zutshi, ed. *Kashmir: History, Politics Representation*. New Delhi, Cambridge University Press: 70–88.

Widmalm, Sten. 1997. *Democracy and Violent Separatism in India: Kashmir in a Comparative Perspective*. Uppsala, Uppsala University.

Zutshi, Chitralekha. 2003. *Language of Belonging: Islam, Regional Identity and Making of Kashmir*. New Delhi, Permanent Black.

6

THE SACRED AND THE SECULAR

Religion and politics in Jammu and Kashmir

Nyla Khan

I start from the premise that the syncretic ethos of Kashmir has been violated by the outburst of religious nationalism, secular nationalism, and ethno-nationalism that have facilitated political and social structural violence. The well-crafted theoretical fiction of a syncretic culture by the advocates of a Kashmiri polity empowered them in a circumscribed fashion to choose an idiom within which they could arbitrarily remove the distinction between religion and politics. Religious and political rhetoric remains simply rhetorical without a stable and representative government.

Using self-reflexive and historicized forms, drawing on my heritage and kinship in Kashmir, I explore the construction and employment of the Kashmiri political and cultural landscape, and gender, in secular nationalist, religious nationalist, and ethno-nationalist discourses in Jammu and Kashmir(J&K). I question the exclusivity of cultural nationalism, the erosion of cultural syncretism, the ever-increasing dominance of religious fundamentalism, the irrational resistance to cultural and linguistic differences. I also question the victimization and subjugation of women selectively enshrined in the prevalent regressive social discourse and the uncritically rendered folklore of traditional Kashmiri Islamic and Hindu cultures. In the years prior to 1938, under the rallying banner and political ideology of the Muslim Conference (MC) in Jammu and Kashmir, Sheikh Abdullah mobilized a collective sense of pride in regional Kashmiri identity. He had the political will and astuteness to create an efficiently organized network of young people who were committed to the party's ideology. His initial emphasis on a shared Muslim identity, which promised social and political enfranchisement, was a light at the end of the tunnel for an abject and politically disenfranchised people.

The formation of secular local political organizations that espoused a nationalist and socialist ideology in the twentieth century in the erstwhile princely state, such as the Kashmiri Youth League (post-1947), Peasants Association (1946), Students Federation (1934), Silk Labour Union (1924), Telegraph Employees Union, and so on, enabled popular political leaders to shift their focus on to the structural ineq-uities legitimized by the state rather than on just religious and sectarian conflict. Although the MC won 14 out of 21 seats allotted to Muslim voters in the State Assembly,[1] the assembly had only consultative powers. Two years later, however, fresh elections were held, because the elected members of the legislature fiercely protested their restricted powers. The Sheikh's disillusionment with the superses-sion of nationalist aspirations by sectarian ones inspired him to forge a secular movement in the state. In order to disseminate his progressive ideas, the Sheikh and a Kashmiri Pandit secularist, Prem Nath Bazaz, founded an Urdu weekly, *Hamdard*, in 1935. Consequently, the MC was replaced by the secular All Jammu and Kashmir National Congress (NC), presided over by the Sheikh, in June 1938.

In order to align itself with the purportedly secular and nationalist Indian National Congress, the younger generation of MC leaders strove to transform a religiously oriented political movement into a secular movement for political, eco-nomic, and social reforms. The nature of this transformation was articulated by the Sheikh in his address to the MC's annual session in March 1938:

> We desire that we should be free to set our house in order and no foreign or internal autocratic power should interfere in our national and human birthrights. This very demand is known as Responsible Government. . . . The first condition to achieve Responsible Government is the participation of all those people . . . they are not the Muslims alone nor the Hindus and the Sikhs alone, nor the untouchables or Buddhists alone, but all those who live in this state. . . . We do not demand Responsible Government for 80 lakh Muslims but all the 100% state subjects. . . . Secondly, we must build a com-mon national front by universal suffrage on the basis of joint electorate.
>
> *(Quoted in Hassnain, 1988, 88)*

In 1944, the NC sought reconstitution of the political, economic and social systems of J&K, and it came to be identified with socially leftist republicanism and the personality of the Sheikh (Bose, 2003, 21). Its particular context of an indigenous political movement against the Dogra House helped the evolution of a distinct entity, which was Kashmiri nationalism.

This won the approbation and full-fledged support of emancipated Hindus and Muslims. The aim was to forge connections between the group's agenda for socio-economic transformations with the agenda of other groups impacted by autocracy, feudalism, and communalism. As the NC made its support of secular principles and its affiliation with the All India National Congress more forceful, the gulf between the upholders of secularism and the guardians of an essential Muslim identity became wider. The Muslim Conference (MC) characterized itself as representing the Muslim segment of society attempting to undermine the political dominance of the Dogra maharaja and create a state in which primacy would be given to Islamic laws and scriptures. In that environment, the NC found itself gasping for breath in the quagmire created by the maharaja's duplicitous policies. For example, the maharaja's government had passed a special ordinance introducing two scripts, Devanagari and Persian, in Kashmir's government schools, signaling the metaphoric dislocation of Kashmiri culture. Language was seen in relation to an array of matters: political, power, ethnicity, and cultural and psychological denigration. Also, the Jammu and Kashmir Arms Act of 1940 had prohibited all communities except Dogra Rajputs from owning arms and ammunition. Such communally oriented policies created a rift between the Muslim leadership of the NC and their Hindu colleagues.

The rift within the organization was further widened by Mohammad Ali Jinnah's insistence that the Sheikh extend his support to the Muslim League and thereby effectively disavow every principle he had fought for. His refusal to do so sharpened the awareness of the Muslim League that, without his support, it would be unable to consolidate its political position. Initially, the Congress supported the Quit Kashmir movement and later reinforced the Sheikh's position on plebiscite. The Congress advised the maharaja, right up to 1947, to gauge the public mood and accordingly accede to either India or Pakistan. Nehru's argument that Kashmir was required to validate the secular credentials of India was a later development. Jinnah refuted the notion that Pakistan required Kashmir to vindicate its theocratic status and did not make an argument for the inclusion of Kashmir in the new dominion of Pakistan right up to the eve of partition. As Navnita Chandha Behera (2006, 24) writes, "If Kashmir was integral to the very idea of Pakistan, it is difficult to see why the Muslim League and the Muslim Conference did not ask the Maharaja to accede to Pakistan until as late as 25 July 1947." By then politics in Kashmir had acquired a purposive nature. This new politics was devoid of the narrow limitations of religion, and it enabled the creation of a political collectivity. I posit that the Sheikh perceived the evolution of Kashmiri nationalism in world-historical terms, as opposed to a domestic issue. He did not subscribe to the notion that a powerful global ideology like pan-Islamism, or communism, or fascism would effectuate a universal liberation. He advocated the creation of a political structure in which a popular politics of mass mobilization would be integrated with institutional politics of governance.

Complexity of the historical and political context of Kashmir

In order to further contextualize my perception of religion and politics in Kashmir, I examine the historical and political roots of the Kashmir conflict. The nation-states of India and Pakistan have employed aggressive strategies in the former princely state of Jammu and Kashmir and overtly imperialist methods since the inception of independence in 1947. The partition of India legitimized the forces of masculinist nationalism and enabled virile hatred for the "other" to irreparably mutilate a shared anti-colonial legacy and cultural heritage so systematically that the wounds inflicted by the partition are yet to heal. The geographical borders, political animosities, and religious hatreds dividing the two sides were not orchestrated just by British imperial cartographers but were ignited by nationalists of the Indian National Congress and the Muslim League as well. As historian Uma Kaura (1977) keenly observes, the partition of India was orchestrated not just by the machinations and quiet diplomacy of the British viceroy, but by the egregious mistakes made by the leadership of the Indian National Congress as well as by the acrimony and belligerence of the Muslim League (p. 170). Ever since the inception, in 1885, of pro-independence political activity in pre-partition India, the Muslim leadership insisted on the necessity for a distinct Muslim identity (Kaura, 1977, 164). Kaura also underlines the inability of the nationalist leadership to accommodate Muslim aspirations because its primary concern was to ingratiate itself with the militant Hindu faction, which would have created ruptures within the Congress. The creation of India and Pakistan were pyrrhic victories for their denizens because the political, socioeconomic, psychological, and cultural havoc wreaked by that momentous event is reflected in those pogroms, ethnic cleansing, proliferation of nuclear weapons, poverty, and riots that continue to cause seismic tremors in the Indian subcontinent. "The fundamental character of this relationship [between India and Pakistan] has been one of *strategic hostility*, unchanged and essentially unquestioned since the birth of the two as independent countries" (Chenoy and Vanaik, 2001, 125).

For India, Kashmir lends credibility to its secular nationalist image. For Pakistan, Kashmir represents the infeasibility of secular nationalism and validates the rationale of the partition, which occurred along religious lines. Once the Kashmir issue took an ideological turn, Mahatma Gandhi remarked, "Muslims all over the world are watching the experiment in Kashmir. . . . Kashmir is the real test of secularism in India." (Details of the accession of the princely state of J&K to India are amply covered in other chapters in this volume.)

The strategic location of Indian-administered J&K underscores its importance for both India and Pakistan. The state of J&K borders on China and Afghanistan. Although Pakistan distinctly expresses its recognition of the status of J&K as disputed territory, it avoids doing so in areas of the state under Pakistani control: advocating self-determination for the entire former princely state of J&K would severely damage Pakistan's political and military interests. The governments of India and Pakistan have been pursuing autocratic policies vis-à-vis Kashmir and have been accelerating the political, economic, and social impairment of the state. The unwillingness and inability of the two governments to enable the emergence of Kashmir as a bastion of democracy, secularism, and development speaks volumes about the disfigurement of the public diplomacy of the two nation-states. Josef Korbel (2002, 304) wrote with foresight that "whatever the future may have in store, the free world shares with India and Pakistan common responsibility for the fate of democracy and it awaits with trepidation the solution of the Kashmir problem. Its own security may depend on such a settlement."

Ethnic, religious, and religious divisions in Indian-administered Jammu and Kashmir

Clearly, any unitary discourse that claims to encompass the reality of Kashmir would inevitably be lop-sided and suspect. Democracy promises curative treatment as opposed to mere palliative treatment, and citizens of Jammu and Kashmir continue to hope for the restoration of self-determination, rule of law, a solution-oriented revival of internal political dialogue, negotiations, and, in the opening decades of the twenty-first century, many additionally seek accommodation of diverse ideological and political leanings of identities within a secularist framework, creating new openings for people, including the young, to discuss public issues and become active participants. The aims of that process should be to repair the frayed ethnic fabric in all parts of the state but the various ethnic, linguistic, and religious groups in Indian-administered Jammu and Kashmir, Kashmiri Muslims, Kashmiri Pundits, Dogra Hindus, and Ladakhi Buddhists and Shi'ite Muslims, have been unable to construct a shared cultural and historical legacy that would enable them to fashion a cultural alterity to that of the Indian nationalist one. Due to the regional sentiments that are becoming increasingly religionized, the ideology and rhetoric of a shared cultural and historical past have been unable to garner public support and mobilization for reconstruction and nation-building. The signifiers of nationhood in Jammu and Kashmir – flag, anthem, and constitution – have thus far not been able to move beyond a nebulous nationalist self-imagining. Regional political forces have effectively sabotaged attempts made to construct a unitary identity. The political acts of demanding the right of self-determination and autonomy for J&K have not been able to nurture a unity amongst all socioeconomic classes, but, on the contrary, are threatening to create unbridgeable gulfs (Rahman, 1996, 148–149; Ganguly, 1997, 78–79). Now more than ever, the three regions of the state of J&K are at daggers drawn about the future political configuration of the state. This doleful truth was forcefully brought home to me at the conference organized by the Government of India selected Interlocutors for Jammu and Kashmir on "Pluralism and Diversity in Jammu and Kashmir", held in Jammu, Jammu and Kashmir, July 11, 2011.[2]

The province of Jammu, in which Jammu city is predominantly Hindu, sees its unbreachable assimilation into the Indian Union as the only way to safeguard its future. However, of the original six districts of Jammu, the three predominantly Muslim ones, Poonch, Rajouri, and Doda, would undoubtedly align themselves with the predominantly Muslim Kashmir Valley. In the Ladakh region of the state, predominantly Buddhist Leh, which has always been critical of the perceived discrimination against it, has zealously been demanding its political severance from the rest of the state and pushing its demand for Union Territory status within the Indian Union, whereas the predominantly Shi'ite Kargil district in the Ladakh region does not perceive a jeopardized cultural and linguistic identity and advocates retention of its political alignment with the rest of the state. The resounding slogan of self-determination resonates loudest in the Kashmir Valley. Among the Dogra

Hindu populace of Jammu and the Buddhist populace of Ladakh, this slogan is perceived as exclusionary and insensitive to the diversities and divergences in the state. The political instability that has ensued in the wake of the rekindling of this slogan in 1989 is perceived as detrimental to the germination and evolvement of developmental projects, institutionalization of political processes that would enable the devolution of powers to the grassroots cadres by the aforementioned populaces of Jammu and Ladakh. That perception, however, is not shared by the Muslims of the Kashmir Valley, who live in the toxicity of a trust deficit between the state and the Government of India.

The confluence of religious nationalism, secular nationalism, and ethnic nationalism creates the complexity of the Kashmir issue. The political asphyxiation of a viable trajectory for Kashmir has further vitiated the political space of Kashmir, both mainstream and separatist. There is a plethora of opinions about the political, cultural, religious, and social complexity of Kashmir. Indian- and Pakistani-administered Jammu and Kashmir is a space in which conflicting discourses have been written and read. For more than 60 years the Kashmir conflict has remained like a long pending case in a court of law between the two nuclear giants in the Indian subcontinent, India and Pakistan: "Kashmir has been an enduring and intractable problem. For decades the greatest barrier to eliminating nuclear tension in South Asia was India's unwillingness to give up its nuclear option because of its more ambitious self-perceptions. . . . A new dimension – the possibility of a nuclear outbreak between the two countries – has been added to an already conflict-filled situation" (Chenoy and Vanaik, 2001, 127). The Kashmir imbroglio has worsened partly because of disillusionment with the perceived hollowness of Indian secularism, partly out of the ignominy that Kashmiris felt in being tied to a government and a polity that is getting increasingly religionized:

> The self-perceptions that have led to India taking up the nuclear option have everything to do with the rising popularity of a belligerent and aggressive form of nationalism among a frustrated and increasingly insecure elite. This is embodied in the rise of Hindu communalism and of the various cultural and political forces associated with it.
>
> *(ibid., 127)*

Sheikh Mohammad Abdullah's disillusionment with Indian democracy and his dismal reassessment of India's proclamation of republicanism, secularism, and democracy have proven uncannily prophetic. After Abdullah's death on September 8, 1982, the National Conference (NC) was led by his oldest son, Farooq Abdullah, until 2002, when he chose to step down as president of the party. Since then, however, the NC nominated Farooq Abdullah as its chief ministerial candidate for the 2008 Assembly elections, and he is currently the president of the political organization. Subsequent to Sheikh Mohammad Abdullah's death, Farooq Abdullah took over as head of government and led the NC to a resounding victory in the Assembly elections in 1983. At that time, Indira Gandhi was making overt and covert appeals to Hindu majoritarianism against grossly exaggerated secessionist threats from Muslim and Sikh minorities (for a thorough discussion of Hindu majoritarianism, see Bose, 2003). Indira Gandhi's mobilization of Hindu fanaticism worked wonders for the Congress in the Jammu region, where it won 22 out of 32 Assembly seats. But the performance of the Congress in the Muslim-dominated Kashmir Valley was dismal, where it won just three seats, and one in Ladakh. The NC had another landslide victory in the Valley, winning 35 out of 41 Assembly seats. The NC also won seven seats in the Jammu region and one in Ladakh, enabling it to form the state government with the Congress as a large opposition. But Indira Gandhi was not to accept the verdict of the people of Kashmir in a democratic fashion. She found particularly unacceptable the alliance that the NC had formed with other Indian parties in an attempt to unify anti-Congress forces as preparation for the parliamentary elections in late 1984. Indeed, by forging such a relationship with the opposition parties, Farooq was subverting a tacit clause in the 1975 Delhi agreement that had enabled Sheikh Mohammad Abdullah's release, whereby the NC would make no attempt to undermine Congress rule at the centre in exchange for the Congress government's non-interference in the political supremacy of the NC in J&K. In order to quell Farooq's declaration of autonomy, Indira Gandhi resorted to undemocratic and unconstitutional means as his government approached the end of its first year in 1984. The Congress government in New Delhi orchestrated the formation of a new political party, comprising 12 NC legislators who unconstitutionally quit their party, and formed a new government with the support of the Congress legislators in the J&K Assembly. The leader of this breakaway faction was Sheikh Mohammad Abdullah's older son-in-law, Ghulam Mohammad, who had cast his lot with Abdullah in the heyday of the Plebiscite Front (PF).

Dismissal of the Farooq government and installation of the Shah government

The purportedly autonomous status of J&K in the early 1950s provoked the ire of ultra-right-wing nationalist parties, which sought the unequivocal integration of the state into the Indian union, a unitary concept of nationalism that challenged the basic principle that the nation was founded on: democracy. In this nationalist project, one of the forms that the nullification of past and present histories takes is the subjection of religious minorities to a centralized and authoritarian state, thereby expunging the political autonomy endowed on the state by India's constitutional provisions. Deploying the rhetoric of soft Hindutva and grossly exaggerating threats of Muslim secessionism in Kashmir, Prime Minister Indira Gandhi dismissed a manifestly democratically elected government and instead provided support to an unpopular regime.

Ghulam Mohammad Shah, politically more experienced than Farooq, aimed to become Abdullah's successor. Ministerships were bestowed on the 12 NC defectors in the new government. Farooq Abdullah wrote as follows about this plot hatched by the Congress prime minister of India, Indira Gandhi:

> the Congress high command decided to work for my downfall through dis-gruntled elements in my party [National Conference] who were already in league with Mrs G.M. Shah [Farooq's older sister]. The plan to overthrow my government was given final shape on 23 June 1984. . . . The conspiracy had been hatched and the blueprint drawn up in 1 Safdarjang Road, New Delhi [Prime Minister Indira Gandhi's official residence]. The cast which performed as directed was presided over by Mrs Gandhi, who was the direc-tor and producer.
>
> *(Farooq Abdullah, 1985, 8)*

If those who forget history are condemned to repeat it, Farooq had to pay a heavy price for having forgotten New Delhi's treatment of his father. The 1984 *coup de grâce* was reminiscent of the 1953 *coup d'état*. Farooq's appeal for fresh elections was denied by J&K's New Delhi-appointed governor, Jagmohan. The dismissal of the Farooq government was perceived as a blow to the morale of the Kashmir people who had placed him on the political pedestal previously occupied by his father. I recall that divisive period as being a particularly difficult one for my maternal grandmother, Begum Akbar Jehan, and also for my mother, Suraiya Ali Matto. The protests that ensued in the Valley were brutally repressed by detachments of the Central Reserve Police Force (CRPF) and Indian paramilitary forces which were flown surreptitiously from Delhi to Srinagar the night before the coup (conversa-tions with the family in Kashmir, 2007). Salman Rushdie (1991, 43), in a display of political acumen, observed:

> The growth of Hindu fanaticism, as evidenced by the increasing strength of the RSS, the organization which was behind the assassination of Mahatma Gandhi, has been very worrying; and it has had its parallel . . . in the increased support for the Muslim extremist Jamaat Party in Kashmir – the support being, itself, the result of the toppling of Farooq Abdullah by the Centre, which seemed to legitimize the Jamaat's view that Muslims have no place in present-day India.

The beginning of representative government in J&K (in 1977) was summarily destroyed in 1984 in an act of callous disregard for the wishes and aspirations of the Kashmiri people which brought political apathy in its wake. Later that year, India's parliamentary elections were held. Indira Gandhi's Congress, led by her older son Rajiv Gandhi, availed itself of the sympathy wave created in the wake of Indira's assassination on October 31, 1984, and won by an overwhelming majority. But all three parliamentary constituencies in the Kashmir Valley, Srinagar, Baramulla and Anantnag, elected NC representatives with enormous majorities. The Congress won the two parliamentary seats from the Jammu region and one from Ladakh, but overall the NC made a wonderful recovery and a palpable dent in New Delhi's nefarious designs.

In 1986, the Congress government at the centre dismissed the G.M. Shah government and Governor Jagmohan took over as the representative of the central government and effective ruler of J&K. The rationale given by New Delhi to replace Shah with Jagmohan was the breakdown of the law and order machinery. This political move, in which Kashmiri politicians were shunted around like pawns, destroyed political autonomy and created institutional paralysis. During this election, the Farooq-led NC was ferociously opposed by Indira Gandhi's Congress. Quite a few writers on Kashmir have summarized the destructive effect of the policies deployed by New Delhi and India's political and military interference in the state during that fateful decade of the 1980s.

Ramifications of the despotic gubernatorial politics

In this section, I underline the repercussions of India's anti-democratic strategies in the state which instigated oppositional and dissident responses. I delineate the fundamental structural inequities in the J&K polity, exacerbated by political and military intrusions of the Pakistani administration and the engendering of political resistance. Despite the belligerence of gubernatorial policies, and the tenacious control of fundamentalist forces animated by a misplaced religious fervor stoked by a besmirched leadership, the leadership in India and Pakistan were unable to douse the conflagration that threatened to annihilate the entire region.

Jagmohan was adept at carrying out the oppressive policies of his patrons. He was responsible for the attempted extirpation of the secular Jammu and Kashmir Liberation Front (JKLF), which adhered to the ideology of an independent Kashmir. The incarceration and torture of its leader, Maqbool Bhat, occurred during Jagmohan's reign. Physical brutality began to be unapologetically employed as a tool for psychological degradation. Young Kashmiri men were arrested on suspicion, and tortured and killed by Indian soldiers. Kashmiri women, irrespective of age, were defiled and humiliated. This state-sponsored brutality boomeranged with young men subscribing to a form of militant nationalism and willy-nilly taking up arms to fight the Indian state (Ali, 2003, 246). Then, in late 1986, Farooq Abdullah forged an alliance with the Congress party at the centre. The creation of this alliance was a death-knell for regional political aspirations and cultural pride. Farooq's attempt to establish harmonious relationships with the Congress regime at the centre was met with contempt and derision by NC's popular base, but enabled his installation as head of government pending fresh Assembly elections in March 1987 (Akhtar, 2000, 12). His negotiations and purported compromise with New Delhi created a deep rift between the NC and its mass following. Elections were held in J&K in 1987 in order to constitute a Legislative Assembly and a state government. By then the NC had managed to alienate its popular base and represented only the interests of a powerful political elite.

During the 1987 elections, the NC was opposed by an unwieldy coalition of non-mainstream, anti-establishment groups, calling itself the Muslim United Front

(MUF). It was a conglomerate that lacked structure and a unifying political ideology. However, as the newsmagazine *India Today* (March 31, 1987, 26) observed during the campaign, the emergence of the MUF indicated that "the Valley is sharply divided between the party machine that brings out the traditional vote for the NC, and hundreds of thousands who have entered politics as participants for the first time under the umbrella provided by the MUF". Among the MUF's several component political organizations, the most important was the Jamaat-i-Islami, chaired by Syed Ali Shah Geelani. Despite having participated in the 1972, 1977, and 1983 elections, and as part of the MUF conglomerate in the 1987 elections, the Jamaat had been unable to make a mark on the political matrix of J&K. It had, however, succeeded in making an impact in religious institutions where young boys were indoctrinated by mullahs and which Sheikh Mohammad Abdullah had attempted to quell by closing down places of religious education (Verma, 1994, 74). In addition, Abdul Ghani Lone's People's Conference, G.M. Shah's breakaway NC faction, the Awami National Conference, and Maulvi Farooq's Awami Action Committee expressed unity of opinion, purpose or interest with the MUF. The ideological or experiential solidarity among a large number of opposition parties presented a formidable front. In the 1987 elections, the people of Kashmir unanimously expressed their wish to elect a party that would redress their grievances and nurture their aspirations (interview by the author with political activists of the National Conference and independent candidates, Kashmir, 2007). The emphasis laid by the MUF on Kashmiri nationalism and cultural pride enabled them to woo a large number of Kashmiri youths. The MUF underlined its ultimate objective of working towards Islamic unity and disallowing political interference from the Indian government in New Delhi (Verma, 1994, 159). But New Delhi was not willing to let anti-establishment organizations rule in a state in which it could exercise power only through proxy. As reported in *India Today* (April 15, 1987), the 1987 elections were characterized by rigging and booth-capturing. The predictable outcome was the landslide victory of the NC–Congress alliance, which won 63 seats and formed the state government without a hindrance. This instance of the erosion of democratic processes and institutions worked to the advantage of the Congress party which had been unable to form a mass base in Kashmir and had traditionally been perceived as the arch opponent of Kashmiri nationalism and cultural pride. There was an exponential rise of fundamentalist forces in the Kashmir Valley during this period (Balraj Puri, quoted in Verma, 1994, 141). However, while the resurgence of religious fanaticism may have provided the disgruntled youth of J&K with an ideological bastion, Islamist organizations in the Valley were unable to convince Shah's Awami National Conference and Lone's People's Party of the viability of forming a theocratic state.

Faulty electoral processes

Some of the current problems in J&K can be traced to the surging saffron wave in India. From the 1970s onwards, the effective generation in the Kashmir Valley came to be the new educated middle class which was witness to not only the tremendous work of their predecessors towards communal amity traceable to hundreds of years of collective zeitgeist, but found themselves victims of unemployment and a decrepit infrastructure. They were witnesses to the rising saffron wave in India. The Kashmir imbroglio has worsened partly out of disillusionment that was generated by the perceived hollowness of Indian secularism, partly out of the ignominy that Kashmiris felt in being tied to an increasingly religionized government and polity.

Subsequently, armed struggle gained impetus in the Kashmir Valley once the populace was disabused of the notions of regional integrity and autonomy it had once held. The subversive acts engineered by the JKLF in 1988 prognosticated political wreckage of extraordinary proportions. The disenchantment caused by diktats issued by the Indian government spawned resistance factions in various parts of J&K. "The JKLF, however, was singled out by the Indian authorities as being mainly responsible for the upsurge in internal disorder" (Schofield, 2002, 140).

In the late 1980s, anti-India sentiments in the Kashmir Valley engendered uncritical support for Pakistan. While 41 years of independence were being fervently celebrated in the rest of India on August 15, the Valley resonated with sounds of lamentation about its fate: "Whereas in 1947 the Pakistanis were deemed the invaders whilst the Indians were greeted as the liberators, by 1988 in the minds of the militants the roles had been psychologically reversed" (ibid.). On April 11, 1988 several people were killed in an ammunition dump in Ojhri in Pakistan, which had been used as a depot for arms intended for Afghan rebels. In order to express their solidarity with Pakistan, zealous pro-Pakistanis in the Valley coerced shopkeepers to keep their shops shut for a day as a symbolic gesture of sympathy for those killed. This day of mourning was marked by instances of clashes with the police, vandalism, arson, and brandishing of pro-Pakistan feelings. In the wake of these events, Indian nationalist parties critical of the politics of the Farooq-led government demanded his resignation (ibid.). Thus, as the decade of the 1990s dawned, the Kashmir Valley became a playground for Indian military and paramilitary forces, as well as for innumerable resistance factions that toed different ideological lines. The hitherto placid Valley began to shake with a rumbling energy that would prod the complacency of the governments of India and Pakistan and expose their complicity in the neglect of the peoples of the state of J&K.

Beginning of armed insurgency

The armed insurgency was driven by nationalistic and religious fervour: a movement in which religion and politics became conflated with a resulting lack of clarity preventing its integration with any resuscitation of progressive politics.

A large number of young men from various parts of the Kashmir Valley crossed the Line of Control (LOC) in search of ammunition and combat-training. Sumantra Bose (2003) eloquently outlines the gist of the contemporary problem in Kashmir: a conflict driven by nationalistic and religious fervour, with each side pointing to the violence and injustice of the other, and each side pointing to its own suffering and sorrow. The distrust, paranoia, and neurosis permeating the relationship between a large number of people of J&K and the Indian Union had intensified the conflict. Kashmir, which to most outsiders was a becalming tourist haven, had been engulfed by the conflagration of armed insurgency. "The armed insurgency which gathered momentum after the 1987 election caught the rest of the world unawares" (Schofield, 2002, 138).

The guerrilla war in the state has gone through a series of phases since 1990, but repressive military and political force remains the brutal reality, which cannot be superseded by seemingly abstract democratic aspirations (see Bose, 2003). For instance, on October 1, 1990, Indian paramilitary forces razed to the ground the bazaar of Handwara, a town located in the northwestern part of the Valley. This action, taken after a guerrilla attack, resulted in the indiscriminate killing of a large number of civilians. Ever since, the town has been garrisoned by Indian military and paramilitary troops. The landscape has been tarnished by shanty-like bunkers with firing positions adorned with Indian flags and nationalist slogans, underlining the brutal repression of regionalist and anti-establishment aspirations. Despite the conspicuous presence of Indian police and military forces, however, the dense forests of Handwara have provided a safe haven for the guerrilla fighters and have enabled them to wage a constant subversive war against the Indian army, which was heavily deployed in that area (ibid., 138).

While the popularity of the NC was steadily diminishing, a new phenomenon was emerging in J&K in 1988. A large number of young men had gone across the LOC in order to acquire arms and combat training to fight for the cause of Kashmiri independence. On July 31, 1988, bomb explosions occurred outside Srinagar's central telegraph office and at the Srinagar Club, an establishment for the political and business elite of the state. Although the attacks were launched by young Kashmiri men trained across the LOC, they had been planned by Mohammad Rauf Kashmiri, a Pakistani member of the JKLF, an organization committed to regaining the independent status of J&K (conversation with political activists of the National Conference and the Congress, Kashmir Valley, 2007). Again, events that were celebrated in the rest of India were overtly mourned in Kashmir: August 15 (Independence Day) and January 26 (India's Republic Day) were occasions that evoked a resentful and pain-filled response in the Valley.

Unfortunately, the state government's response entailed belligerent tactics, invoking the political and economic support of New Delhi and antagonizing the Kashmiri people who did not see a ray of hope in New Delhi (see Puri, 1995). As the insurgency began to spread, the authority of the state government began experiencing a progressive political decline. Farooq Abdullah's approach during this term was described as "a virtual abdication of power" (*India Today*, November 15, 1986: 43 and April 30, 1990, 10). Veteran journalist and author of *Sheikh Mohammad Abdullah: Tragic Hero of Kashmir*, Ajit Bhattacharjea, has critically analyzed Farooq's political prowess: "The last symbol of secular Kashmiriyat remained a lightweight given to helicopter sorties over the stricken Valley, to elitist projects to attract tourists, while basic facilities were ignored" (Bhattacharjea, 1994, 257).

In November 1989, another Indian parliamentary election was held in J&K, which the JKLF and other pro-independence groups asked the populace to boycott. The electorate responded by abstaining, resulting in an overwhelming victory for the NC. The NC won unopposed in Srinagar, and in Baramulla and Anantnag, the other two parliamentary constituencies in the Valley, it won enormous victories. But a large proportion of the state's population was not just alienated but palpably antagonistic towards New Delhi. Although there have been representative governments in J&K installed through democratic processes, notably in 1947–1953 and 1977–1984, the territory has otherwise been benighted by misgovernance and trammeled by a militarized culture.

By the late 1990s the purportedly secular policies of the Congress had been replaced by the Hindu nationalist politics of the Bharatiya Janata Party (BJP). In the Kashmir Valley, Islamist groups mushroomed as Afghan mercenaries came across the border to perpetuate the reign of terror. The main rival organizations during that period were the homegrown Hizbul Mujahideenand (HM), the Pakistani-sponsored and abetted Lashkar-i-Toiba and Harkatul Mujahidin (interview with political activists of the National Conference and independent candidates, Kashmir, 2007). These groups frequently assassinated each other's militants – HM and JKLF were belligerently opposed to each other, kidnapped Western tourists in order to extort money or for political mileage, harassed Kashmiri Pandits who had been an inextricable part of the region for centuries, took punitive action against Kashmiri Muslims who remained fiercely secular, and organized subversive action against Indian forces and officials. The factionalism in these groups disallowed them from joining hands in order to defeat the designs of the Indian administration and forces. Some of the Islamist groups in this region are the creation of Pakistani military intelligence (Ali, 2003, 251). Governor Jagmohan employed ruthless measures to neutralize whatever support they had managed to garner: night-long house-to-house raids became the order of the day. Indian soldiers kidnapped young men at gun point only to torture and kill them in custody (ibid., 247). Jagmohan's autocratic rule and the tyranny of the Afghan mercenaries resulted in the militarization of Kashmiri culture and the torture of hapless Kashmiri civilians. The sense of disenfranchisement in Kashmir was aggravated by New Delhi's rule, which lasted until 1996 when a civilian government came back to power. But the NC's coalition with the Hindu fundamentalist BJP further eroded the mass base of the organization.

J&K is an example of a neocolonial territory manipulated by New Delhi in collusion with comprador governments unrepresentative of the populace, and reliant on the political and military prowess of their patrons. This policy appears to have been formulated to circumscribe anti-India and pro-Pakistan allegiances. This strategy, however, has had the adverse effect of stunting the development of democratic and civic structures conducive to suffrage and participatory procedures. The conscious policy of the Indian state to erode autonomy, populist measures and democratic institutions in J&K has further alienated the people of the state from the "demonic" Indian Union (Bose, 2003, 97–98). The erosion of political opposition in J&K has delegitimized the voice of dissent and radicalized antagonism towards state-sponsored institutions and organizations. The exposure of Indian democracy as a brutal façade has instigated disgruntlement and antipathy towards Indian democratic procedures and institutions in the state. The cause of the independence and/or autonomy of J&K has been thwarted by both India and Pakistan. Beijing is also worried about the ramifications that Kashmiri independence would have in Tibet. In India, the BJP has been deviously planning the balkanization of J&K along religio-ethnic lines, first propounded in 1950 by Sir Owen Dixon, the United Nations representative for India and Pakistan.

Militant resistance to the Indian administration

This section delineates the fundamental structural inequities in the J&K polity, exacerbated by political and military intrusions of the Pakistani administration and the engendering of political resistance. I remain of the firm belief that the onus lies on those who claim to lead the political movement for autonomy and self-determination in Kashmir to separate religion and politics and to present this movement in a more ecumenical form.

The rebellion which had been simmering for over a year erupted into a conflagration in 1990, in brutal resistance to Indian occupation in the Kashmir Valley. Assassinations of individuals suspected of being Indian spies occurred in large numbers towards the end of 1989, atrophied the government machinery and rendered its intelligence apparatus dysfunctional. Contrary to general belief, some three-fourths of the victims (political or social bigwigs accused of collaborating with Indian forces, alleged spies, and local politicians who had either tacitly or overtly supported J&K's accession to India) were Muslims, the rest were Kashmiri Pandits. The parliamentary elections that were held in J&K in late November 1989 were boycotted by a large section of the population, rendering the process a sham.

In December 1989, Rubaiya, the daughter of Mufti Mohammad Sayeed, the Kashmiri Muslim Interior Affairs Minister in India's federal cabinet and chief minister of J&K from 2002 until 2005, was kidnapped by militants of the JKLF. This incident, evidence of a growing malignancy in a culture that had prided itself on shielding its women from political and religious turbulence, caused fear among young women all over the Valley. I recall the tangible tension and loaded silence in the examination hall at the Government College for Women where I was taking my British Literature examination the day after Rubaiya was kidnapped. Her captors demanded the release of six high profile JKLF activists then in incarceration. Rubaiya Sayeed was kept in captivity until the Government of India succumbed to the demands of her captors. The six JKLF activists who were released were welcomed by numerous Srinagar residents with happiness and triumph, undeterred by the Indian troops. The Government of India's choice to tread the path of least resistance bolstered the courage of organizations that deployed kidnappings, extortions, killings, and other violent methods as their modus operandi. In January 1990, Farooq Abdullah's defanged government resigned, citing a breakdown of civil order as the rationale.

Subsequently, J&K was brought under the direct rule of New Delhi. Jagmohan, who had played a treacherous role in J&K between 1984 and 1986, was sent back to Srinagar to govern with reinforced high-handedness and unaccountability (conversations with political activists and other civilians in Kashmir Valley, 2007). Huge demonstrations in support of independence surfaced in every part of the Valley. It was as if the unspoken urge for self-rule, lost among the debris of dismantled insurrectionist resolves, had begun to collect and cohere to form the certainty of this political demand. People from all walks of life marched with abandon along the uneven streets of various parts of the Valley. In a gesture of defiance, adolescent boys and girls pelted stones at the well-equipped Indian military and paramilitary forces. The response of the Indian administration was the implementation of blood-curdling repressive measures. The state-sponsored violence in the Valley escalated between July and September 1990 after the Indian government legislated an Armed Forces Special Powers Act and a Disturbed Areas Act that reinforced the powers of Indian military and paramilitary troops, and legitimized the barbarism, violence, and reprisal unleashed by them. Bose and his co-authors note:

> From our investigations . . . we found that the paramilitary forces and the Army jawans [soldiers] had no excuse of self-defence [sic] [as normally given when dealing with riotous mobs] when they fired indiscriminately upon what were crowds of unarmed demonstrators. A savage thirst for blood seemed to have gripped the CRPF, as evident from the calculated manner in which they went about pumping bullets into bodies of injured people in the Gow Kadal [Srinagar] area on 21 January 1990. The brutalities perpetrated by the Army jawans on 1 March 1990, call for serious disciplinary action against them. Attempts by the army authorities to justify their killing of bus passengers at Tengpora [Kashmir] on that day by inventing a false story, are a further blot on the country's defense forces who are required to be highly disciplined cadre dedicated to the task of protecting our people.
>
> *(Bose et al., 1991, 233)*

The attempt of the Indian administration to represent the Kashmiri as a fanatical terrorist is indicative of political and military discourses of exclusion that rely on tightly drawn boundaries to maintain the "authenticity", or purity, of their respective discourse. The Kashmiri, by his or her status as a secessionist traitor, served to reaffirm draconian authority that required opposition in order to assert itself.

Initially, the insurgent demand for autonomy resonated just through the Kashmir Valley, reminiscent of the 1930s and 1940s when the Valley had been festooned with the pennants of the PF and the NC, streaking the sky with the colour of liberation. The political rebellion of these two organizations was forcefully reiterated by the JKLF in the early 1990s in the Valley. The JKLF's unwavering commitment to the discourse of an independent state antagonized the Pakistani military's Inter-Services Intelligence (ISI), which abruptly withdrew its economic and political support to the organization (for the secular formation of the separatist group JKLF, see Khan, 1970).

As a retaliatory measure, the ISI patronized and facilitated the establishment of two pro-Pakistan organizations, Al-Umar Mujahideen and Ikhwan-ul-Muslimeen, which deployed guerrilla tactics to perpetrate a reign of assassinations and unbridled terror. The ISI also enabled the entrenchment of bigoted Islamic groups such as Harkat-ul-Ansar and Hizb-ul-Mujahideen (HM) in the Valley (interview with political activists of the National Conference and People's Democratic Party, Srinagar, 2007). The strategies employed by these organizations and their pro-Pakistan leaning created a generation of trigger-happy youth, engendering a malignant gun culture in the Valley. The fanaticism of the HM led to an upsurge of violence in the Valley. The rising strength of pro-Pakistani guerrilla outfits resulted in the marginalization of the JKLF. Sporadic disagreements leading to violent clashes between the JKLF and the HM occurred in 1991 and 1992 in various parts of the Valley. The HM had an uncontested dominance over the Islamist and pro-Pakistan outfits in the Kashmir Valley. In the early part of the insurgency, the HM claimed that its employment of guerrilla strategies would render J&K impregnable for the Indian military and paramilitary forces, intern the Indian forces in their restrictive camps and make them vulnerable. This spurious claim impaired the credibility of the HM, particularly after the increasing factionalism within the organization (ibid.). In the early part of 1992, the JKLF made an assiduous attempt to regain lost ground by organizing a march to the LOC to underscore the unity between Indian-administered Jammu and Kashmir and Pakistani-administered Jammu and Kashmir. The march was dispersed by Pakistani border troops who, firing indiscriminately, killed 21 marchers. This incident created a wave of sympathy for the JKLF, and 60,000 people convened at the Hazratbal shrine to express condemnation of the unwarranted show of strength by Pakistani forces, marking an overwhelming political victory for the JKLF (*India Today*, March 31, 1993, 27).

In 1993, over 30 political organizations joined hands to form a coalition group known as the All Parties Hurriyat Conference (APHC). The conglomerate comprised Syed Ali Shah Geelani of the Jamaat-e-Islami, Abdul Ghani Lone of the People's Conference, Maulvi Abbas Ansari of the Liberation Council, and Professor Abdul Ghani Bhat of the Muslim Conference (MC), and was headed by the then teenaged religious leader of the Awami Action Committee, Maulvi Omar Farooq. What bound these politicians and religious leaders of disparate ideologies was the goal of obtaining the right of self-determination for the people of J&K. the right of self-determination. But there was no agreement about whether independence was the most desirable solution for the troubled state, or whether unification with Pakistan was the better alternative. The APHC has since been joined by the leader of a breakaway faction of the JKLF, Yasin Malik. While most of the other components of the conglomerate lean towards unification with Pakistan, Malik tenaciously adheres to JKLF's ideology of independence for the former princely state. A leader of one of the core groups of the APHC, Abdul Ghani Lone, was assassinated in 2002 by the Lashkar-e-Toiba. Another unyielding Islamist member of the organization, Syed Ali Shah Geelani, severed ties with the APHC after Maulvi Omar Farooq seemed to do a volte face by beseeching the militant factions to adopt a more reconciliatory approach. It should be pointed out that Geelani was a member of the Jammu and Kashmir Legislative Assembly from 1972 to 1977, 1977 to 1982 and 1987 to 1990, and that during none of these tenures was he as vociferous about the illegitimacy of the accession of J&K to the Indian Union, nor did he publicly prioritize the autonomy of the state. The Omar Farooq-led APHC has been vacillating about its political stance vis-à-vis the status of the state, equivocating between reversion to the pre-1953 autonomous status of J&K within the Constitution of India and the unacceptability of any such solution. Despite the participation of its leadership in various international forums, the seemingly bona fide intentions of the organization have come under severe scrutiny, and political analysts as well as laypeople have leveled allegations of corruption and complicity with the law-enforcing agencies of both India and Pakistan.

Pakistan's attempt to chart the course of the insurrection created paranoia in the Valley and was resented by JKLF supporters. By the mid-1990s, the HM had become notorious for targeting not just JKLF's pro-independence supporters, but also members of nondescript militant groups. Many ex-militants, renegades or *baaghee*, and their families sought security – physical, financial, and otherwise – through collaboration with Indian counter-insurgency forces. The emergence of such collaborators, who were incorporated into the Special Task Force (STF) – a militia group comprising renegades – bolstered India's military and political campaign against Kashmiri insurgents and Pakistani infiltrators. Although the Government of Pakistan did not explicitly avow the legitimacy of insurgency in J&K in terms of acknowledging its financial and military support in the armed conflict, the perception in India was that Pakistan supported the insurgency through its formidable intelligence agency, the ISI. This common perception was created by the recognition of the centrality of the Kashmir issue to the theocratic and nationalistic identity of Pakistan (Desmond, 1995, 15).

Communal turn of the insurgency

The insurgency in Kashmir grew into a low intensity warfare made lethal by the firepower of two nation-states. This disastrous backdrop has remained the same for the past 30 years and has led to greater religious divides. In September 1989, a Kashmiri Pandit, Tikka Lal Taploo, an advocate of the High Court and a leader of the Hindu nationalist BJP was brutally killed. Soon after this incident, another Kashmiri Pandit, Neel Ganth Ganju, was remorselessly killed. Ganju was a retired sessions judge who had passed the death sentence on the iconicized founder of the JKLF, Maqbool Bhat (Schofield, 2002, 144). Reports of the desecration of women by militants did much to besmirch their image. In 1990, a Kashmiri Pandit nurse at the Sher-i-Kashmir Institute of Medical Sciences, Srinagar, Sarla Bhat, was reportedly raped and killed by JKLF militants for having informed the police/state authorities about injured militants at the medical institute. Asia Watch reported that while it was unclear that militant leaders willfully permitted such abuses, there was little indication that they had taken substantive action to prevent such gruesome incidents. Some of the victims and their families were accused of being police informers, and the brutal humiliation of these women was a tool wielded to wreak revenge and silence the detractors of militant organizations (Asia Watch, 1993, 98). The communal turn taken by the insurgency in the state was exacerbated with the grisly murder of 16 Hindu men who were taken off a bus on their way to Jammu and killed at pointblank range in August 1993. In 1995, a group of Western tourists was kidnapped by an obscure militant outfit, Al-Farhan. One of the tourists, a Norwegian, was decapitated; one of the Americans in the group surreptitiously escaped and the whereabouts of the other three are unknown to this date. Pro-independence and pro-autonomy organizations in the Valley are of the opinion that this gruesome incident, like the mass exodus of Kashmiri Pandits, was actually orchestrated by the Indian government to discredit insurrection in J&K, as zealot and talibanized. By 1996–1997, the coercive tactics employed by Indian counter-insurgency forces had successfully emasculated most of the guerrilla outfits and rendered the JKLF a moribund organization.

In 2000 the HM restored its damaged organizational ethos by engineering and executing a series of attacks reminiscent of the guerrilla tactics they had used in the 1990s, but with greater violence. These attacks were clearly designed to instigate communal dissension in J&K and to maintain the tenuousness of the India–Pakistan rapprochement. The horrifying phenomenon of suicide bombing surfaced in the state in 1999 and mounted in hostility in the early 2000s. The first suicide attack occurred in August 1999 when militants of the Lashkar-e-Toiba, a group purportedly consisting of ultra-orthodox Muslims from Pakistan but believed by many Kashmiri locals to be working in collusion with Indian paramilitary forces, stormed a Border Security Force (BSF) post in Kupwara district. The official estimate is that since then 50 suicide attacks have occurred in the Kashmir Valley, of which 29 took place in 2001. While most of the attacks have occurred in the Valley, the suicide bombers have made their mark in the Jammu region and in New Delhi as well. A suicide squad of the Lashkar-e-Toiba launched a bloody attack on an army garrison positioned inside the Red Fort in Delhi on December 22, 2001 (Ramachandran, 2002). The demand for autonomy made a foray into the Jammu region in the 1990s. In August 2002, an army colonel supervising counter-insurgency operations was killed in a mine blast in Doda district in Jammu. This attack was attributed to HM operatives in the area (*Kashmir Times*, August 20, 2002).

Towards the end of 2002 the Indian government, tarnished by the widespread and condemnable allegations of human rights abuses by its military and paramilitary forces, organized Assembly elections in the state in order to form a new state government. I was in the Kashmir Valley a couple of months before that election, in which the NC suffered a humiliating defeat. The first phase of the elections covered constituencies in Baramullah and Kupwara in the Kashmir Valley, Rajouri and Poonch in Jammu, and Leh and Kargil in Ladakh; the second phase covered constituencies in Srinagar and Badgam in Kashmir Valley and Jammu; the third phase covered constituencies in Pulwama and Anantnag in the Kashmir Valley, and Udumpur and Kathua in Jammu; and the fourth phase of the elections covered constituencies in Doda in Jammu division. The voter turnout in most constituencies was dismal, and demonstrations in favor of autonomy and against integration into the Indian Union were held at several places. The NC performed poorly, winning nine out of 37 Assembly seats in Jammu, 18 out of 46 seats in the Kashmir Valley and one out of four seats in Ladakh. The Congress secured 15 seats in Jammu and five in the Valley. In a curious turn of events, the Hindu nationalist Bharatiya Janata Party (BJP) was able to secure just one seat in the predominantly Hindu Jammu province. National and local newspapers reported attempts at intimidation and coercion by the Indian paramilitary troops. According to a rather dubious claim by Indian authorities, the voter turnout was 42.97 per cent in Baramullah district, 54.57 per cent in Kupwara district, 35.57 per cent in Poonch, 44.94 per cent in Rajouri, 76.89 per cent in Kargil, 43.82 per cent in Badgam, 12.83 per cent in Srinagar, 60.19 per cent in Jammu, 29.45 per cent in Pulwama, 24.43 per cent in Anantnag, 59.82 per cent in Udumpur, 62.35 per cent in Kathua and 53.24 per cent in Doda. These figures, however, included voters who were coerced to exercise their franchise. Interestingly, almost a million and a half citizens entitled to vote were just not registered and were therefore not included when estimating these figures. Apparently women did not participate either in large numbers or enthusiastically (interview with Observers of the Electoral Process in Kashmir, 2007). There were districts, however, in which the voting was impartially carried out. The politicization that was palpable in Kashmiri-speaking areas had not occurred in the predominantly Gujjar or Ladakhi constituencies, which did not harbor the antipathy towards the Indian state and its institutions that a large section of the Kashmiri Muslim population did.

Terrors of counter-insurgency

The muted voices of marginalized laypeople, particularly women, have not been raised loud enough against the atrocities to which they are subjected by Indian paramilitary forces, Pakistan-sponsored insurgents, counter-insurgency forces, and religious fundamentalists. As the decade of the 1990s dawned, the political, cultural, and socioeconomic fabric of Kashmir was severely impaired by the free rein given to Indian military and paramilitary forces to quell dissidence, and also by Pakistan-trained militants who, in a no holds barred conflict, inflicted atrocities on their co-religionists as well. New Delhi hadn't succeeded in consolidating democratic institutions in the state, which could have enabled effective participation. More than a decade later, in 2008, the Valley remained the hub of counterinsurgent activity. In March 2008, for example, Farooq Ahmad Sheikh, resident of Sopur, Kashmir, was coercively detained by a cohort of policemen in civilian clothes. His family, after frenetic inquiries were callously informed that he had drowned – his wife had been mercilessly widowed and his young son was now a waif ("Family Seeks Whereabouts of Youth", *Greater Kashmir*, March 25, 2008). In another incident in Sopur, Kashmir, students of the Sopur Degree College protested against the killing of a fellow student, Mohammad Ramzan Shah, by soldiers of the Indian army in an allegedly fake encounter. The police deployed unwarranted force to quell the protests and in the resulting violence, 30 people were injured ("Five Lecturers among 30 Injured: Protests Continue in Sopur", *Greater Kashmir*, September 15, 2007). In September 2007, 25 people were brutally beaten up by Indian soldiers when they voiced their resentment against the reign of terror unleashed by Indian military and paramilitary forces in Graw Gund Kulpora, Pulwama, in south Kashmir. Residents of that area lamented the inhumane treatment meted out to them by the police and military personnel ("Soldiers Go Berserk in Pulwana", *Greater Kashmir*, September 13, 2007).

Despite the sectarian and ethnic violence in J&K, the cultural syncretism of the state has managed to garner the strength of conviction to survive. In 2002, a large number of Kashmiri Pandits participated in a festival held at a Hindu shrine, Khir Bhawani, in a village close to Srinagar, where they enjoyed the hospitality and protection of the Muslims in the area. This occasion marked the return of many migrant Pandits to the Kashmir Valley. This celebration was held after a pain-filled hiatus of 18 years, and was conducted in a convivial atmosphere ("Sentimental Return for Pandits", *Tribune News Service*, 2000). The representative organization of dislocated Kashmiri Pandits, Panun Kashmir Movement, which is riven by factionalism as well, now acknowledges that the exodus of their community in 1990 was orchestrated by the Government of India ("GOI Responsible for Exodus of Kashmiri Pandits", *Greater Kashmir*, March 31, 2008).

Kashmiri women's vigilante groups: forms of subjectivity that reinforce essentialist and dichotomous state-nationalist subjects

What have been the effects of nationalist, militant, and religious discourses and praxes on a gender-based hierarchy? Sheikh Abdullah's strategic campaign to free J&K from the systemic violence perpetrated by the Dogra monarchy, which was launched in the early 1930s, had won strong support from the Kashmiri people, including the women. As the Kashmiri historian Mohammad Ishaq Khan (1978, 192) is quick to point out, "13 July 1931 was a historic day in the annals of Srinagar. The 'dumb-driven cattle' raised the standard of revolt. . . . Even the women joined the struggle and to them belongs the honor of facing cavalry charges in Srinagar's Maisuma bazaar." That political awareness manifested itself again in 1989–1990 when masses of women bolstered the JKLF's campaign to free J&K from Indian rule in the labyrinthine lanes of Srinagar city. In the 1970s and the 1980s, Indira Gandhi's Congress regime characterized every demand for local empowerment as potentially insurgent, and discouraged the growth of a progressive generation of Kashmiris (Ganguly, 1997, 84–85; Kohli, 1997, 341–342). Entrenched gender inequities are intensified in situations of armed conflict, in which the agency assumed by women in the public sphere is given legitimacy by male authoritative figures and is subsumed within masculinist discourse.

There are other instances of women's mobilization, which some Kashmir analysts might see as agential but, which I would argue, attempt to validate the "isolationist admiration" of Kashmir. For instance, the *Dukhtaran-e-Milat* (DM), instead of pressing for women's political empowerment sanctifies the reductive portrayal of a Muslim woman as a veiled sociocultural icon who is mobilized more for who she is than for what she believes in, ignoring the diverse interpretations and the rich heterogeneity of cultural traditions and the paradoxes within them. This assertion of the salience and meaning of the identity of a "Kashmiri Muslim Woman" takes the form of trying to legitimize sociocultural practices like veiling, polygamy, punitive action against behaviour deemed "un-Islamic," such as the mixing of sexes in public places, in an attempt to define the "proper" place of women. The regressive discourse propounded by this organization creates a determinate concept of Islam. In other words, it does not allow negotiation between different value systems, exacerbating the cognitive dissonance in the minds of these women. The DM comprises educated as well as uneducated women of the lower middle class. Its influence is restricted to the summer capital of Jammu and Kashmir, Srinagar city. The ideology and politics of this vigilante group have not seeped into grassroots cadres in rural areas.

On the other end of the spectrum is the Daughters of the Vitasta, a Kashmiri Hindu women's organization, which seeks the resolution of the Kashmir conflict in the creation of a separate homeland for internally dislocated Kashmiri Hindus within the Valley. The Daughters of the Vitasta is an exclusionary Kashmiri Hindu women's organization, comprising middle-class and professional women. Lower-middle-class Kashmiri Hindu women are not part of the upper crust of this organization.

These organizations are glaring illustrations of those insurgent manifestations of the armed rebellion and counterinsurgency in Kashmir that are striving for exclusionary and patriarchal nationalisms. My contention is that fundamentalist ideologies of organizations like the DM and the Daughters of the Vitasta have grown in spaces created by structural inequities, repression, and a sense of injustice by the Government of India. Although the Daughters of the Vitasta would align itself with an ultra-Indian-nationalist ideology, its growth is the blowback of the dislocation and displacement of the Kashmiri Hindu community subsequent to the inception of armed insurgency in 1989, and the inability of the Government of India to take substantive measures towards facilitating its return and rehabilitation in the Kashmir Valley. The Daughters of the Vitasta gives an essentialist Hindu identity a privileged place in political discourse, unambiguously defining that identity and projecting it in order to solicit support. Such political assumptions and claims are "a negation of the role of values, understanding and intellect" (Smith, 2001, 43). It is no surprise that, given the gender, ethnicity, and class status of the members of the DM and the Daughters of the Vitasta, they experience and recover from the effects of violence, displacement, and disenfranchisement differently. Also, both organizations espouse an identity politics that "appeals to that part of individual identity that is shared in a collective identity". But, "the question to ask about this kind of politics is, 'Which collective identity?' It is a question that is never asked in the process of political mobilization on the basis of identity; indeed, the question is often actively suppressed, sometimes violently" (Smith, 2001, 36). Given the essentialist politics of these two organizations, they feed on each other.

The oppositional positioning of such organizations, I argue, does not enable the forging of new paths "in this combat locked within action and reaction" (Grewal, 1997, 249). These organizations do not have clear nation-building programmes, which would involve reviving civil society, resuscitating the shattered economy, providing sources of income, and building social and political structures. How will these organizations pave the way for sustainable peace, human rights, and security which would diminish the potency of militarized peacekeeping, following closely on the heels of militarized interventions? It wouldn't be presumptuous to assume that members of the *Dukhatan-e-Milat* and Daughters of the Vitasta embrace intransigent and monolithic versions of Islam and Hinduism, respectively, as a viable way to find meaning in their origins, and also, perhaps, a rationale for their lack of access to the global market. This analysis of the politics of these two vigilante groups brings to mind Dan Smith's pertinent point about conservative gender politics: "people who make essentialist generalizations about women's roles are usually unable not just to explain but even to acknowledge the diversity of women's experiences and abilities" (p. 38).

Conclusion

We require constructive critiques of the inability of the religio-political organizations to practice politics of accommodation and negotiation. It is important for such organizations, including the Bharatiya Janata Party and the Jammat-e-Islami to pave the way for clear nation-building programmes, which would involve reviving civil society, resuscitating the shattered economy, providing sources of income, and building social and political structures. Political institutions cannot be subordinated to precepts and criteria determined by the clerical elite of any religion/faith whether these belong to temples, churches, synagogues, and mosques. Only administrators and politicians belong in political institutions, not clerics, yogis, priests, rabbis, and mullahs.

The political and social upheaval that followed upon the creation of India and Pakistan in 1947 has left legacies that continue to haunt the two countries. The partition enabled the thunderous forces of violence and displacement to tear the preexisting cultural and social fabric so systematically that the process of repair hasn't even begun. The borders that were brutally carved at the time of the partition of India have led to further brutality in the form of riots, pogroms, and organized historical distortions and cultural depletions with which the histories of independent India and Pakistan are replete. Mob lynchings, allegations of blasphemy, *ghar wapsi*, mass religious conversions in Uttar Pradesh are manifestations of the forces of yore that continue to eat away at the sociocultural fabric in both countries. The moulding of collective subjectivities by the evocation of pan-national religious affinities, particularly these days, results in the stifling of minority voices that express divergent cultural and social opinions

The partition is a vivid manifestation of the claim that postcolonial nations are founded in a bloody severance of the umbilical cord, one that fortifies borders between nation-states with irrational and remorseless violence.

In order to assert itself a nation-state needs to draw clearly etched borders, so it can define itself in opposition to other nations. But ultra-right-wing nationalisms in both India and Pakistan erase a shared past. Bloody manoeuvres to destabilize the British Raj were employed by the Muslims as well as Hindus of colonial India in a joint effort to oust the oppressor. The composite culture constructed by the two communities was an inherent part of pre-colonial India as well, but is expunged by ultra-right-wing nationalists in their attempt to disseminate the unitary discourse of nationalism. Militant nationalism must evolve into critical nationalism, which is an awareness that unless national consciousness transforms into social consciousness, so-called "liberation" would merely be a continuation of imperialism. Relentless violence and bloodshed cannot validate the "reality" of borders.

The Kashmiri struggle – for identity and autonomy for some, self-determination for others – has, historically, been a political one. Contrary to what some separatist organizations believe, Kashmiri culture is not homogeneous and nor is Kashmiri identity exclusively Muslim. Equally deserving of criticism are not only reactionary organizations but also current regional and national administrations for their insensitivity to the diverse interpretations of religious laws and to the heterogeneity of cultural traditions. Any attempt to homogenize Kashmiri society or the politico-cultural discourse on Kashmir would be a dangerously flawed exercise.

Finally, it is historically true that cultural, societal, and market constraints have denied women access to information about the outside world. But the sort of advocacy concretized by the intra-Kashmir women's conference could overturn the historical seclusion of women and provide them with routes to make forays into mainstream cultural and socioeconomic institutions. Perhaps the mobilization of women at the collective level would enable a metamorphosis, fostering the skills and ability of women to make informed decisions about issues in the non-domestic sphere.

Notes

1 The first legislative assembly of the princely state of J&K was established in 1934 by the then monarch Hari Singh.
2 At this intraregional conference, I was a member of the Kashmir delegation and I presented a paper on the restoration and revitalization of the autonomous status of J&K.

References

Abdullah, Farooq. *My Dismissal*, New Delhi:Vikas, 1985.
Akhtar, Shaheen. "Elections in Indian-held Kashmir, 1951–1999." *Regional Studies*, 18: 3, 2000: 12–29.
Ali, Tariq. "The Story of Kashmir." In *The Clash of Fundamentalisms: Crusades, Jihads and Modernity*, London:Verso, 2003: 217–252. Asia Watch, Reports, June 1993.

Behera, Navnita Chadha. *Demystifying Kashmir*, Washington, DC: Brookings Institution Press, 2006.

Bhattacharjea, Ajit. *Kashmir: The Wounded Valley*, New Delhi: UBS Publishers, 1994.

Bose, Sumantra. *Kashmir: Roots of Conflict, Paths to Peace*, Cambridge: Harvard University Press, 2003.

Bose, Tapan et al. "India's Kashmir War." In *Secular Crown on Fire: The Kashmir Problem*, edited by Ashghar Ali Engineer, New Delhi: Ajanta, 1991: 224–253.

Chenoy, Anuradha Mitra, and Achin Vanaik. "Promoting Peace, Security and Conflict Resolution: Gender Balance in Decision Making." In *Gender, Peace and Conflict*, edited by Inger Skjelsbæk and Dan Smith, London: Sage Publications, 2001: 122–138.

Desmond, Edward W. "The Insurgency in Kashmir 1989–1991." *Contemporary South Asia*, 4: 1, 1995: 5–16.

"Family Seeks Whereabouts of Youth." *Greater Kashmir*, 25 March 2008; www.greaterkashmir. com/full_story.asp?Date=26_3_2008&ItemID=54&cat=14 (accessed 20 March 2008).

"Five Lecturers Among 30 Injured: Protests Continue in Sopur." *Greater Kashmir*, 13 September 2007; www.greaterkashmir.com/full_story.asp?Date=14_9_2007&ItemID=52& cat=1 (accessed December 2007).

Ganguly, Sumit. *The Crisis in Kashmir: Portents of War, Hopes of Peace*, New York: Woodrow Wilson Center Press, 1997.

"GOI Responsible for Exodus of Kashmiri Pandits." *Greater Kashmir*, 12 November 2007; www.greaterkashmir.com/full_story.asp?Date=13_11_2007&ItemID=23&cat=1 (accessed 12 November 2007).

Grewal, Inderpal. "Autobiographic Subjects and Diasporic Locations: *Meatless Days* and *Borderlands*." In *Scattered Hegemonies: Postmodernity and Transnational Feminist Practices*, edited by Inderpal Grewal and Caren Kaplan, Minneapolis: University of Minnesota Press, 1997: 231–254.

Hassnain, F.M. *Freedom Struggle in Kashmir*, New Delhi: Rima Publishing House, 1988.

India Today. 31 March 1987: 26; 15 April 1987: 40–43; 15 November 1983: 43; 30 April 1990: 10; 31 March 1993: 27.

The Kashmir Times (Jammu), 20 August 2002.

Khan, Amanullah. *Free Kashmir*, Karachi: Central Printing Press, 1970.

Khan, Ishaq. *History of Srinagar, 1846–1947: A Study in Socio-Cultural Change*, Ann Arbor, MI: University of Michigan Press, 1978.

Kohli, Atul. "Can Democracies Accommodate Ethnic Nationalism? Rise and Decline of Self-Determination Movements in India." *Journal of Asian Studies*, 56, 1997: 325–344.

Korbel, Josef. *Danger in Kashmir*, Princeton: Princeton University Press, 1954; reprint, New York: Oxford University Press, 2002.

Kaura, Uma. *Muslims and Indian Nationalism: The Emergence of the Demand for India's Partition 1928–40*, Columbia: South Asia Books, 1977.

Political Activists of the National Conference and the People's Democratic Party (PDP), Srinagar, July 2006, 2007.

Puri, Balraj. *Kashmir: Towards Insurgency*, New Delhi: Orient Longman, 1995.

Rahman, Mushtaqur. *Divided Kashmir: Old Problems, New Opportunities for India, Pakistan, and the Kashmiri People*, Boulder: Lynne Rienner, 1996.

Ramachandran, Sudha. "Suicide, Just Another Way to Fight in Kashmir." *Asia Times Online*, 24 July 2002; www.atimes.com/atimes/South_Asia/DG24Df02.html (accessed March 2008).

Rushdie, Salman. "The Assassination of Indira Gandhi." In *Imaginary Homelands: Essays and Criticism 1981–91*, London: Granta Books, 1991: 41–46.

Shah, G.M., former Chief Minister of Jammu and Kashmir, and President of the Awami National Conference, April 2008.

Schofield, Victoria. *Kashmir in Conflict: India, Pakistan and the Unending War*, second revised edition, London: I.B. Tauris, 2002.

"Sentimental Return for Pandits." *Tribune News Service*, 2000; www.tribuneindia. com/2000/20000610/j&k.htm#3 (accessed January 2008).

Smith, Dan. "The Problem of Essentialism." In *Gender, Peace, and Conflict*, edited by Inger Skjelsbæk and Dan Smith, London: Sage Publications, 2001: 32–46.

"Soldiers Go Berserk in Pulwama." *Greater Kashmir*, 13 September 2007; www.greaterkash mir.com/NewsItem.asp?Date=14_9_2007 &Show=1 (accessed January 2008).

Verma, P.S. *Jammu and Kashmir at the Crossroads*, New Delhi: Viking, 1994.

7

RELIGION MATTERS

Religion and politics in Kashmir

Aijaz Ashraf Wani and Tabzeer Yaseen

In the Western discourse on modernity, the disengagement of the secular from the religious is its dominant feature. In the historical transformation of traditional societies into modern, secular and rational industrial nations, religion is supposed to decline and to occupy a space in the private realm. History has, however, disproved the overconfidence of Enlightenment scholars in the growing power of reason. Religion/ethnicity/caste/language and other identity markers continue to play a dominant role in the politics and the everyday life of the people (Phukon, 2002). This irrelevance of the secular–religious binary is aptly captured by Peter Berger.

> The world today, with some exceptions . . . is as furiously religious as it ever was, and in some places more so than ever. This means that a whole body of literature by historians and social scientists loosely labeled "secularization theory" is essentially mistaken.
>
> *(Berger, 1996–97, 4)*

In this chapter, we suggest that the relationship between state and religion has various dimensions. We delineate the role of religion in shaping the politics of the deeply plural state of Jammu and Kashmir (J&K) ever since it was formed in 1846. Drawing from various sources, we maintain, first, that the Dogra state (1846–1947) treated state and religion as complementary and thus, privileged the religion and religious community of the ruler, generating resistance among the majority community. The terms which the Muslim majority community used to describe the Dogra rule were *shakhsi raj* (personal rule of the maharaja), *dharam ka raj* (Hindu state) and *jagirdarana* and *chakdarana nizam* (feudal state) (Rai, 2004; Saraf, 2005; Hussain, 1931; Thorp, 1870). Second, we assert that Kashmir's nationalist movement against the Hindu ruler, though secular and progressive in orientation, had strong religious undercurrents. Religion and religious symbols were frequently used to mobilize the Muslim community. The Hindus, barring a few, on the other hand, opposed this movement both for maintaining their elite position as well as for defending the 'Hindu rulers' against the 'Muslim onslaught'. Thus "while the process of politicization of the community of Muslims of Kashmir was a result of the consciousness of their situation of deprivation and utter powerlessness, the politicization of the community of Hindus was a step towards maintenance of their position of dominance. That explains why the political movement that took shape in Kashmir in the decade of thirties had not much enthusiastic participation of Kashmiri Hindus" (Chowdhary, 1998, 7). Third, we speak to the regional divide on religious lines in the post-1947 politics of the state. After the demise of Dogra rule and the transfer of power to the new government led by Sheikh Abdullah (the Kashmiri Muslim who spearheaded the freedom movement), a new struggle was launched in J&K. It was led by the Hindu right-wing party, Praja Parishad, with the mass support of Hindu Dogras of Jammu in particular, and the non-Muslim communities of the state (particularly the Buddhists of Ladakh) in general. Pitted against the Abdullah government, the Praja Parishad agitation specially targeted the land reforms which had benefited largely the Muslim masses and lower-caste Hindus at the cost of the Hindu Dogras and Kashmiri Pandit landlords. Dubbing the new *sarkar* as the government of Kashmiri Muslims, the Hindu Dogras launched a virulent agitation against the special status of the state, for which they got the full support of Hindu nationalists from some parts of India as well. Creating a vicious circle, the agitation led to the dismissal and imprisonment of Sheikh Abdullah, who, in turn, sponsored the launching of the Plebiscite Movement, which, receiving mass Kashmiri Muslim support, divided the state into two opposite political camps – Jammu's Hindus demanding Kashmir's merger with the Indian Union, and the Kashmiri Muslims asking for a referendum to be held for the final solution of the Kashmir problem.

Although Sheikh Abdullah compromised on his long-standing position in 1975, the deeply embedded plebiscite sentiment re-surfaced violently in the late 1980s and received mass Muslim support. With the heating up of the demand for *raishumari* (plebiscite), the right-wing parties of Jammu and the Buddhists of Ladakh renewed with more force their long held demand of either the tripartite division of the state, or the merger of Jammu with the Indian Union and declaring Ladakh as a Union Territory. Significantly, however, Muslims of both Jammu and Ladakh distanced themselves from the politics of the Jammu Hindus and Ladakhi Buddhists. In recent times this was on wide display during the Valley's 2008, 2010 and 2016 agitations. This regional divide on religious lines was also patently visible during the 2014 and the 2019 parliamentary as well as 2014 state assembly elections. Thus, though Kashmir is often quoted to have defied the ideology of the two-nation theory, post-1947 J&K presents a stark example of Hindu/Buddhist vs Muslim politics – Hindus and Buddhists arraying on one side of the divide, and Kashmiri Muslims on the other side of it making it clear that religion continues to be an important category by which social consent is created. This is not to deny that there are individuals/scholars belonging to all religious communities who stand apart from the collective community discourse. Further, it is important to underline that the politics of the state (the nature of the state, centres of power, government policies and political contestations) has played a significant role in bringing religion into play.

State and religious demography

Jammu and Kashmir state is a colonial construct, bringing together three regions, each with a distinct history, culture, geography and ethnicity. The cultural plurality of the state crisscrosses the geographical and cultural landscape of Kashmir creating "multiple and layered identities" (Chowdhary, 2010, 1–22). The three main administrative entities within the princely state included the province of Jammu, with the Siwaliks and Outer Hills, which has been the heartland of Dogra control in the Punjab; the province of Kashmir, a structural basin that lies between the Pir Panjal and the Himadri, sold to the Dogra ruler by the British in 1846; and the provinces of Ladakh and Baltistan, regions of the greater Himalayas, the former conquered by the Dogras in 1834 and the latter in 1840. In addition, the Gilgit Agency, which the British attached to the princely state for political convince in 1889, was leased back to them in 1935. Similarly, Poonch was brought under the formal control of the state in 1936.

Jammu and Kashmir is not only a conglomerate of three distinct regions—Jammu, Kashmir and Ladakh – but there are regions within regions marked off from each other by their geography, culture and history. Religious heterogeneity has been the feature of the state and continues to be so. Though these regions were integrated into one single political entity in 1846, the politics of regionalism and sub-regionalism continue to be stubbornly informed by their respective histories and cultures, resulting in the politics of regional and sub-regional assertions, the politics of demands and counter-demands, movements and counter-movements, ideologies and counter-ideologies. Often these are shaped on religious lines, though an economic and political sense of deprivation (real or perceived) does play its part.

The princely state and religion

The formation of the state of Jammu and Kashmir in 1846 under the aegis of British paramountcy was not simply an act of stitching together different geo-cultural terrains into a single political entity, externally determined by the British and internally under the control of the maharaja; but it led to the transfer of the sovereignty of J&K into the personhood of the maharaja. The very nature of the Dogra state made the boundaries between religion and state politics blurred. Since the Dogra state, right from its inception, manifested its Hindu character, it led to the mix of religion with politics and governance of the state. The mixing of religion, state, region, class and defining state subjects fundamentally by their religious identity created its own perils. As Rai argues, the Hinduness of the state that was reflected in the patterns of its legitimacy "allowed the Hindus of Kashmir to exclude Muslims in the context for the symbolic, political and economic resources of the state" (Rai, 2004, 6). Since a vast majority of the subjects were denied economic, political and other rights fundamentally due to the religious character of the state; religion became a basis for producing a counter-narrative to the state. Therefore, as Rai argues, religious discourse became inseparable from the discourse of rights in Kashmir (Rai, 2004, 274).

A raja-centred and religion-centred polity was not an innovation. It was a continuity of the ancient and medieval times which the Dogra rajas carried forward faithfully even though the counter-wave of separating religion from politics was insisted upon by the colonial state. Thus as Rai states

> the legitimacy of Dogra sovereigns placed over the valley was sought from the arenas that had little relevance for the vast majority of the people their rule encompassed . . . these sources of legitimacy emphatically made no reference to and had no resonance among Kashmiri Muslims.
>
> *(Rai, 2004, 293)*

Prem Nath Bazaz similarly asserted, "Speaking generally and from the bourgeois point of view, the Dogra rule has been a Hindu Raj. Muslims have not been treated fairly, by which I mean as fairly as the Hindus" (Bazaz, 2002, 250).

Immediately after assuming power, Gulab Singh, the founder-ruler of the Dogra state, made it known that he would not allow the *Mohammandans* (Muslims) to practice all their religious rituals. He announced that as a Hindu, "he would have to give priority to the religion of Hindus" (Rai, 2004, 93). The rule of his successor, Ranbir Singh (1857–1885) saw a full-fledged Hinduization of the state. The British traveller, Colonel Torrens, who visited Kashmir during the rule of Ranbir Singh, observed that the Dogra Rule was the 'Hindu Rule' which was run by 'Hindu *faqueers*' dedicated to building temples and attacking Muslim places (Torrens, 1862, 300). Prior to Gulab Singh's rule, Persian had been the official language but Maharaja Ranbir Singh gave official patronage to Dogri, Sanskrit and Hindi. This was followed by a revival of Sanskrit schools (*pathshalas*) and making Hindi under the Devangari script one of the official languages of the state (Sufi, 1996, 790). However, with the subsequent involvement of the British government in the affairs of the state, Urdu was accorded the official status of state language. Although Pratap Singh (1848–1925) had declared in 1885 that he would treat all his subjects 'without any distinction of race or rank, creed or colour', the association of the state with the religion of the ruler continued to remain the dominant feature of the polity. This was evident from the emblematic representation of the state, public celebration of festivals patronized by the Hindu ruling house, closing down of all business in the state in deference to the performance of last rites of Maharaja Ranbir Singh as required by the Hindu tradition (disallowing the sacrificial rite of *Id-i-qurban* which coincided with the period of mourning), and coming down harder on Muslims on the issue of cows. Interestingly the demand of the Shia community that the cinemas be shut during the period of Muharram, the period of their mourning, was met with a rebuff by the maharaja, "the whole community could not be asked to observe mourning for the sake of Shias" (J&K Archives, 1922, 719). In another instance of selective polarization of the Pandit and Muslim community of the Valley, the maharaja came up with the Sri Pratap Jammu and Kashmir Laws Act of Samvat 1977 (AD 1920). This law set aside the age-old tradition of deciding property issues on the basis of customs common to both Pandits and Muslims and replaced it with the personal laws of the respective communities. Pratap Singh would never bear the sight of a Muslim in the morning (Khayal, 1997, 26–27), and had banned the burial of Muslims in a graveyard located at Sonawar (locality in Srinagar) as he did not want any Muslim funeral to pass his way (Bashir, 2017, 85).

In complete disregard for the religious sentiments of the Muslims, a large number of Muslim mosques and shrines were confiscated by the rulers and declared state property. For example, Khanqah-i-Sokhta, Idgah, Khanqah-i-Dara-Shikoh, Khanqah-i-Bulbulshah, Pather Masjid and many other important religious places in Srinagar and Bahu Mosque and Khanqah Sufi Shah in Jammu were confiscated and used as storehouses for grains and arms as well as stables (Glancy Commission Report, 1932, 3). Ranbir Singh even closed the Friday market in historic Jamia Masjid. Instead he opened a new one under the name of Maharaja Gunj (Saraf, 2005, 303). While Hindus had full freedom to preach and propagate their religion and popularize the *shudi* movement, Muslims were not allowed to preach Islam (Saraf, 2005, 303; Bashir, 2017, 85). On the issue of conversion, if a Hindu converted to Islam, he was to be deprived of his right to inheritance, whereas it was not the case the other way round (Hassnain, 1988, 30; Bashir, 2017, 85). Muslims were also forced to pay taxes like *ashgal*, to be used for the maintenance of Hindu priests and temples (Bates, 1873, 102; Lawrence, 1895, 416). The killing of a cow, ox or buffalo, commonly known as *hathai* (derived from the Saniskrit word *hathya*, murder), was declared a punishable crime. During the initial phase of the Dogra regime the punishment for such killings was the death sentence, which was subsequently reduced to life imprisonment (Knight, 1905, 115; Thorp, 1870, 51).

Immediately after assuming the title of maharaja of Jammu and Kashmir, Gulab Singh (r. 1846–1857) vested in himself the proprietary rights (*huquq-i-malikana*) of the entire Kashmir Valley, depriving the peasantry (overwhelmingly Muslims) of their proprietary rights. The government also revoked the *jagirs* and *inam* grants of the Muslims and transferred these to their co-religionists. Quoting from his personal notebook, Ellison Bates writes that Dr. Elmslie (a medical missionary who stayed in Valley between 1865 and 1872) noted that out of a total of 45 *jagirs* in the Kashmir Valley, only five were given to Muslims (Sunnis two, and Shias three) and the rest were given to Hindus (Bates, 1873, 30). This process of transferring land grants/assignments from the Muslim to the non-Muslim community was one of the consistent policies of the Dogra rule till its end. In 1947, the number of *jagirdars*, *chakdars*, and *mukarares* was 396, 9,000 and 2,347 respectively. And except for a thin slice, all these 'land lords' belonged to either the Rajput Dogra community or the

Kashmiri Pandits. This is the reason land reform was opposed by these groups and became one of the main reasons for their consistent opposition to Sheikh Abdullah, leading to his dismissal in 1953 (Wani, 2019a).

The administration was overwhelmingly dominated by the Kashmiri Pandits despite the fact that Muslims formed a majority of the total population of the State (95 per cent in Kashmir Valley). The revenue department from *patwari* (who keeps records regarding the ownership of land) to *naib-tehsildar* (assistant to an Indian district revenue officer), to *wazir-i-wazarat* (administrative head) was completely in the grip of the Pandits (Lawrence, 1895, 400–401). It is therefore no wonder that the Kashmiri Pandits took pride in identifying themselves with the government and the ruling class.

The very nature and the policies of the state resulted in discrimination against the largest segment of the society on the basis of their religious identity. The enmeshing of religion with the state politics resulted in privileging the Hindu community over the Muslim majority community in economic, political and administrative matters. This religious orientation of the state was clearly visible in its policies which decisively favoured Hindus. Therefore, the initial discourse of the Kashmiri political leadership was fundamentally in response to discrimination and the denial of their rights but mediated by religion.

Muslim resistance

In the last decade of the twentieth century, there was a general awakening among the Kashmiri Muslims with respect to their rights. Having suffered discrimination for decades together, they started showing signs of assertion. Although the first expression of Kashmiris' sense of assertiveness emerged in the form of asserting their religious rights, the religious manifestation of their response needs to be understood within the context of the socio-political-economic nature of the state. As Bazaz argues, though the emerging educated Muslim youth of Kashmir articulated their political demands speaking as Muslims, they were however, asserting their class rights (Bazaz, 1954, 165). This growing awareness among the Muslims of the Kashmir Valley was epitomized in the July 13, 1931 incident. The uprising of 1931 besides being a Muslim response was also a "manifestation of the dee- rooted discontent of the Muslim masses vis-a-vis the policies of Dogra rule" (Chowdhary, 2016, 9). However, the July 13, 1931 incident created a deep wedge among the two main communities of Kashmir. To quote Bazaz:

> In the killing of 21 persons by the police on 13 July, 1931, almost all the officials being Hindus and the Maharaja a Hindu and the 21 persons killed all Muslims, the public opinion among the Muslims had by the time crystallized on the point that the government and the Hindu community was inseparable and that one stood for the other.
>
> *(Bazaz, 2002, 130)*

The sense of being discriminated against by the Hindu Dogra state on religious lines ultimately fructified into the establishment of a Muslim political party – the All Jammu and Kashmir Muslim Conference (MC) – in 1932. It needs to be mentioned that though seemingly a communal organization (by virtue of its nomenclature), the demands of MC were quite secular and progressive in nature as is evident by the presidential addresses and its charter of demands. The organization was not against the Hindu rule per se or the maharaja in person but against the discriminatory policies of the state.

The basic reason for the denominational naming of the organization was the relentless position taken by the Kashmiri Pandit leadership on the recommendations emanating from the Glancy Commission (appointed after the massacre of July 13, 1931 to look into the demands of Muslims). In fact, they had disapproved the appointment of the Commission and had given a call to boycott it. Only one member of the community, namely, Prem Nath Bazaz, an intellectual par excellence, refused to buckle before the community pressure and stayed on as a member of the Commission. Immediately after the recommendations of the Commission became known, the Kashmiri Pandit leadership started an agitation known as the 'Roti Agitation', rejecting all those recommendations which were aimed at ameliorating the condition of the Muslim masses (Saraf, 2005, 442–445: Abdullah, 2013, 130–131). The Hindu press in Punjab provided the agitation unreserved support. The Kashmir movement was dubbed as a pan-Islamic movement by the non-Muslims in British India. The Muslim press played the same role for their co-religionists in Kashmir.

The Muslim leadership, on the other hand, did give a rallying cry – 'Islam in Danger' – to mobilize the people during and after the 1931 uprising (Hassnain, 1988, 96). During a public meeting convened by the Youngmen's Muslim Association on June 21, 1931 at the *Khanqah-i-Moulla*, Mirwaiz Moulvi Yosuf Shah declared that they must all join in the name of Islam in the struggle for various rights of the Muslims. All leaders took an oath in the name of the Holy Book that they would remain faithful to the cause of Islam (Bazaz, 1988, 42). However, to argue that it was a holy war would be a wrong conclusion. As Ian Copland argues,

> it would appear that religion was an essential factor in the process of mobilization, providing an avenue for organization and propaganda and a sense of communality among the Muslims which transcended the formidable barriers of class, education and region. But the root cause of the revolt was socio-economic-a determination on the part of the Muslims to win for themselves a prominent position in Kashmiri society.
>
> *(Copland, 1981, 257)*

In 1939, the Muslim Conference was converted into the National Conference to facilitate the process of making the freedom struggle a joint platform of all communities. Even after this bold decision taken by the Muslim leadership, only a few non-Muslims joined the organization; and they too parted ways subsequently. There were always differences between Sheikh Abdullah and the Hindu leaders of the National Conference. The secular-progressive discourse of the mass-based political party, the National Conference, was mediated by the use of religious idioms and symbols of the Muslims (Wani, 2007, 244–269). Religion was used as a political expedient to serve the basic agenda of winning the masses to a secular-progressive ideology. In fact, religion had played an important role in the rise of Sheikh Abdullah as a mass leader of Kashmiri Muslims. The use of religion and religious symbols was the most important mobilization technique for both the Muslim Conference and the National Conference, just as Hindus or Kashmiri Pandits used these for resisting any change in the status quo.

The Hindu members seriously objected to the raising of slogans like *Nara-i-Takbir* (God is Great) and reciting of Quran during the NC rallies and sessions on the plea that it went against the secular character of the National Conference (Abdullah, 2013, 179). However, Abdullah was a pragmatic politician. He firmly believed that no leader could muster "the courage to ask them to abandon their religion; and if he does so, then the masses will withdraw their support from the leader". He stressed that the "idiom of a slogan or speech was determined by the mental calibre of the audience and their culture and the idiom they were accustomed to" (Abdullah, 2013, 179). He believed that as religion played an important role in the lives of the people, there is no objection in using it in politics for just ends. He even referred to the Indian National Congress, which had adopted *Vande Mataram* as its national song, which, though it contained some parts inimical to Muslim sentiments, received support from the Muslims (ibid., 179). He further argued that the slogan '*Long Live Bharat Mata*' is often shouted at Congress meetings. Turning Bharat into a goddess, the slogan invoked the image of idol-worshiping which is completely against the religious beliefs of Muslims, although Muslims never objected to it (ibid.). But Abdullah was protective of his religious identity and it was the confrontational attitude of the Hindu community that was to push him to state that he was "Muslim first and a Muslim last" (Nehru Papers 102/2). From time to time, Hindu leaders who had joined the NC reacted strongly against the celebration of *Eid-e-Milad* in 1940 and the celebration of events like Martyrs Day on July 13 arguing that Abdullah was trying to soothe the religious sentiments of the Muslims.

To sum up, the partisan rule of the Dogras converted Kashmir from a plural society underpinned by amity and inter-dependence into a hotbed of hostilities between the communities, with enduring consequences. The majority of non-Muslims, who were the beneficiaries of the Dogra Hindu state, played "the historic role of anti-revolution to a finish" (Bazaz, 2002, 291). From now onwards both the communities were withdrawn into their own religious boundaries (Rai, 2004, 258) for political mobilization. This was further fuelled when the new government headed by Sheikh Abdullah reversed the sectarian and feudal policies of the Dogra maharajas, making the state a space perpetually torn by internal strife and divergent and mutually opposite positions on issues of crucial significance.

The conflict over Kashmir and the internal contestation of the nature of relations between the Union and the state, the shift of power from Jammu to the Valley and subsequent political developments creating a sense of discrimination and neglect among some regions and communities resulted in a contestation between and among regions that was largely shaped on religious lines.

Religion and politics after 1947

The division of the Indian subcontinent on the basis of religious demography and the lack of coherence between regions and communities led to a Kashmir dispute with external and internal dimensions. The external dimension involves India, Pakistan and the UN. The internal context of the dispute involves contending positions on the Kashmir issue and the divergent politics on its internal power structure and position of the state. The contesting positions within J&K oscillate between two extremes – demand for independence (*azadi*) and plebiscite to complete accession with India, mediated by a demand for autonomy. Although the contestation is fundamentally political in nature, given the nature of the regional divide the fault lines are largely shaped on religious lines.

While the Muslims in general demand the holding of a Plebiscite as per the accession agreement, a faction among them, represented by mainstream political parties especially National Conference and Peoples Democratic Party (PDP), demand the restoration of the autonomous position of the state. On the other hand the Buddhists of Ladakh and a significant majority of Jammu Hindus, have been demanding either trifurcation of the state or merger with India. There is also a potential voice urging for regional autonomy (Puri, 1999, 2008, 8–11). In order to mobilize people around these demands, the political elite of the state more often than not put "more emphasis on ethno-religious considerations than on culture, region or economic factors" (Verma, 1987, 562). Religious affiliations also play an important role in mobilizing the minority Muslims from Jammu to identify themselves with the Valley Muslims as well as for the minority Hindus from Kashmir to identify themselves with Hindus (ibid., 562.). These issues have created a permanent deficit of peace in the state; have strained relations between the centre and its local supporting structures, on the one hand, and religion-based intra-state tensions, on the other, with a cascading inimical impact on communal harmony, peace and development.

While Abdullah negated the religion-based two-nation theory by supporting J&K's accession to India, the deep-seated divide ceased to go away and kept resurfacing in one form or the other on almost all important issues concerning the state. Immediately after assuming power, as soon as the Abdullah government began implementing the *Naya Kashmir* Manifesto, there was a chain reaction from a section of Dogra Hindus. They launched an agitation seeking the abolition of the special position of J&K and demanded the complete merger of the state with India. Also the nature of the state and government created by Sheikh Abdullah which resembled a "one-party state, one organization (NC), one leader (Sheikh Abdullah) and one program (Naya Kashmir), was seen within Jammu and Ladakh as Kashmiri rule" (Behera, 2007, 109). All the subsequent moves by the Abdullah government were seen as favouring Kashmiri Muslims in "political, economic and administrative matters leaving Jammu and Ladakh feeling neglected and marginalized" (ibid.). Balraj Puri notes that "there were certain psychological factors that created anxiety in Jammu about the shift of power from its base in Jammu to that of Kashmir. Such anxiety was enhanced due to the advantages that Kashmir had in the post-accession period: 'its numerical superiority, internal homogeneity, established leadership and international importance'. As it acquired dominant position within the state, it generated resentment in other regions" (Puri, 1983, 188–189). The ideological differences on political issues along with a sense of neglect and discrimination fuelled the regional discontent in Jammu and Ladakh especially among Hindus and Buddhists. In order to mobilize the masses for political ends, religion can be seen used extensively by all parties post-1947.

Between 1949 and 1953, Praja Parishad launched three aggressive agitations demanding the abolition of Article 370, the complete merger of J&K with India or, at least, the merger of Jammu and Ladakh with the Indian Union. It sought the support of Hindu communal organizations, namely Bharatiya Jan Sangh, the Hindu Mahasabah, the Ram Rajya Parishad and the Punjab Arya Samaj. As a result of its intensive mobilization, emotionally surcharged slogans like: *ek desh mai do vidhan do nishan do pradhan, nahi chalanga nahi chalanga* (there cannot be two constitutions, two flags and two premiers in one state) or the cry for *ek vidhan, ek nishan, ek pradhan* (one constitution, one flag, one premier) reverberated Jammu. Rejecting the 1952 Nehru–Abdullah agreement, the Praja Parishad leadership proclaimed that "Our way is not with Kashmir. The Sheikh is not acceptable to us. We cannot tolerate Jammu and Ladakh going to the winds" (Puri, 1966, 93). Though this movement was basically a politico-economic movement engineered by the beneficiaries of sectarian and feudal princely order who had lost their privileged position after the transfer of power to the NC (Brecher, 1953, 166; Behera, 2007, 111), it however succeeded in giving it a communal colour. Although the Praja Parishad agitation petered out after the removal of Sheikh Abdullah, the discourse it generated was to have an enduring impact on Jammu politics.

Stunned by the open support of communal organizations of India and even some members of the Indian National Congress for the agitation launched by the Praja Parishad, Abdullah expressed his deep hurt by delivering fiery speeches questioning Kashmir's accession to India (see, Bazaz, 2009, 489; Puri, 1981, 99–100; Korbel, 1954, 235; Butt, 1981, 52; Mullik, 1971, 35). The events unfolding the agitation had an immediate and long-term impact. The agitation led to the polarization, communalization and subsequent regionalism in Jammu (Tremblay, 2009, 930). Moreover, it triggered an ideological shift in Abdullah's decision to demand independence of the state (the NC adopted a resolution in 1953 to that effect).

These events ultimately led to the dismissal of the Sheikh government in 1953 leading to a public uprising against the centre and subsequent state governments. Although the uprising was suppressed, the National Conference leaders channeled the popular unrest by launching the Plebiscite Front in 1955. The Plebiscite Front continued a sustained movement for two decades, demanding that the state's political future be decided through a plebiscite. The popular slogans that reverberated in every hamlet and *mohalla* of Kashmir were: *mahaz raishumari foran karau* (hold a plebiscite immediately), *jis Kashmir ko khun se sencha, woo Kashmir hamara hai* (Kashmir which we nourished by our blood, that is our Kashmir*), ye muluk hamara hai, iska faisla hum karangay* (this is our country, we will decided its political future). It was during these two decades that Kashmiri Muslim society was effectively mobilized around the Kashmir question culminating in a deep-seated separatist sentiment. Meanwhile the centre hollowed out the autonomous position of the state with the active cooperation of the cliental regional governments (see Noorani, 2011, 2013; Bose, 2003, 44–101).

No doubt Sheikh Abdullah reached a compromise with New Delhi in 1975, disbanded the Plebiscite Movement, revived the National Conference and followed the politics of governance; but the political mentality, which was created among the Muslims of the state through a sustained movement for 22 long years, refused to change. It first expressed itself in the formation of the Muslim United Front (MUF) in 1986 and the mass support it gained against the hegemonic power of the NC and ultimately the armed struggle in 1989–1990. Similarly, the demand made by Jammu Hindu Dogras and Ladakhi Buddhists was largely fulfilled by the central government, by hollowing out Article 370 with the active support of the installed governments in Kashmir. However, the Hindu nationalist forces of Jammu continued their agitational politics against the regional imbalances and Article 370. The struggle against 'Kashmiri domination' received momentum after the outbreak of militancy in the Valley. Since militancy received the mass support of Muslims in Kashmir, it was seen as an attempt to transform J&K into an Islamic state. This generated tremendous opposition among the Hindu community across the region. It was institutionalized in the formation of the Jammu Mokti Morcha (JMM), the Jammu Autonomy Forum (JAF) and the Jammu State Morcha (JSM). The JMM and its new incarnation JSM (formed in association with the RSS) demanded tripartite division of the state, which was also supported by the BJP state unit (see Om, 1996a; Tremblay, 1992, 153–167). The JAF, on the other hand, sought a federal constitution for the state. The Hindu nationalist forces of Jammu no doubt failed to garner much support in spite of representing the 'Jammu cause'. They could not win the support of Jammu Muslims who no doubt had grievances against the valley-based power centre but "were not in favour of the communal agenda either" (Behera, 2007, 111).

In Ladakh (its two regions are Leh and Kargil – the former predominantly Buddhist and the latter overwhelmingly Muslim), like the other two regions of the state, the mobilization, especially of Buddhists, for political demands involved the use of religion. The initial mobilization of the Buddhists was supported by Kashmir-based neo-Buddhist Kashmiri Pandits, who formed the Kashmir Raj Bodhi Maha Sabha (KRBMS) in 1932. On the authority of Ladakh's foremost religious leader, Shushok Stagtsang Rapa of Hemis Monastery, the KRBMS submitted a memorandum to the Glancy Commission (Kaul et al., 2004, 277–286). Interestingly, the memorandum did not touch the economic and infrastructural backwardness of the region and the plight of Ladakhi masses owing to the oppressive policy of the state and the Lamas; it only focused on educational development and the eradication of social evils (ibid.). The first local Buddhist organisation, the Ladakh Buddhist Education Society (LBES), was formed in 1933; and this too was formed at the instance and active involvement of the Arya Samaji writer-activist, Rahula Sankrtyayana who spoke to "the dangers of growing number of Muslims and the low birth rate among Buddhists due to monasticism and Polyandry" (Beek, 2004, 200). The LBES was replaced by the Young Men's Buddhist Association (YMBA), "which again had strong involvement of Kashmir Pandits, at least in the years until independence" (ibid., 201). Both the YMBA and the KRBMS continued raising the issue of Muslim progeny outnumbering the Buddhists in the region. "From the start, then," says Beek, "modern Ladakhi Buddhist activism was strongly informed by outsiders and their understanding of the Indian political system, as well as what they thought was good for Ladakhi Buddhists" (ibid.).

The identity politics of Ladakhi Buddhists was further nourished by the partition of India, the accession dispute, the Praja Parishad agitation in Jammu and the discriminatory attitude of the state government. The demand for autonomy was justified by "emphasizing the region's geographical, cultural and socio-economic uniqueness and later during 1989 this argument was reinforced by the use of the communal representation of Ladakh as Buddhist" (Beek, 1998, 36). Ladakhi leadership tried to make it clear that the agitation was aimed against the state of J&K and not the Union (ibid.). A memorandum submitted by Kalan Tsewang Rigzin, president of the Ladakh Buddhist Association (LBA), as the YMBA had renamed itself, in July 1949, to Prime Minister Nehru, asserted Ladakh's right to self-determination and the need for its secession from J&K state. It was argued that Ladakh was 'a separate nation' by all the tests – race, language and culture – determining a nationality. It pleaded for direct central rule over Ladakh, or its amalgamation with Hindu-majority parts of Jammu to form a separate province (Behera, 2000, 311–314). Although the most prominent Buddhist leader of the time, Kaushak Bakula, the head Lama of Siptuk monastery, was a member of the National Conference, he joined other forces in demanding the merger of Ladakh with the Indian Union in case Kashmir opted to stay autonomous. In 1952, Bakula sought federal status for Ladakh. And in the same year he delivered a fiery speech during the discussion of the budget session in the State Assembly accusing the government of neglecting Ladakh and threatened the government openly with the impending revolt. Despite the state having taken some steps like the creation of a special office for Ladakh affairs and the reservation of some ministerial berths for Ladakhis at the state, the complaint of discrimination and slow development continued, leading to the increasing demand for secession or greater autonomy for the region. As argued by Beek, three central themes emerge from the Ladkahi representations/agitations

Ladakh is a poor and backward region. . . . Kashmir's government has neglected Ladakh and has failed to develop the region; Ladakh's population are true patriots and dedicated to the nation. The same themes are found also in the more communal representations, where Ladakhiness is reduced to Buddhism; the Kashmir government is driven by communal motivations; and the secessionists in the Valley cannot be trusted precisely because they are Muslims, while as Ladkahis, Buddhists are naturally part of India.

(Beek, 1998, 36)

While the sentiment of discrimination is shared by most sections of the Ladakhi society, however, the use of religion for political ends has created cleavages on religious lines within the Ladakhi society. In the late 1960s the demand for the introduction of central administration along the lines of the system applied to the North-East Frontier Agency (NEFA) was consistently made (Beek, 2004, 202). And in the 1969 agitation, the leadership played the communal card that eroded the possibilities of a united Ladakhi movement (ibid., 203). In August 1989 the LBA launched a violent agitation for a Union Territory and mobilized the Buddhists on the basis of the Hindu–Muslim divide. The Buddhist agitators called for a boycott of the Muslims and called on the local population to 'free Ladakh from Kashmir'. The social boycott of the Muslims continued for the next three years (Behera, 2007, 115–116).

In their bid to win support at the national level and bring pressure to bear upon the central government, the LBA sought support from groups outside Ladkah. A national convention on Ladakh was organized in March 1990. The LBA delegation participated in the BJP convention in Jammu, during which Kashmiri Pandits also expressed their "unstinted and unqualified support for the cause of Jammu and Ladakh" (*Daily Excelsior*, September 2, 1990). The then president of the LBA was quoted as saying, "for forty-three years the people of Jammu and Ladakh have been denied their constitutional rights. We have been struggling for justice, but separately. Let us unite, for our sufferings are common" (Beek, 2004, 205).

Given the strategically sensitive nature of Ladakh, in October 1989 the central government pacified the LBA by offering an Autonomous Hill Council, along the lines of Darjeeling Gorkha Hill Council. The Council was finally established in May 1995 during the governor's rule, much to the dislike of the mainstream regional political party National Conference. The Muslims of Ladakh, who are mainly concentrated in Kargil district with a thin slice in Leh, kept themselves aloof from the separatist politics of the LBA. The reasons were obvious. They perceived the separatist politics of Ladakhi Buddhists as reflecting essentially distinct Buddhist culture which, according to them, has more affinity with Hinduism than Islam (Behera, 2000, 311–314). And the mobilization strategy they deployed was the intensification of communal polarization. As the Buddhists considered themselves different from the Muslims (moreover feeling unsafe in a Muslim-dominated state), the Ladakh Muslims also refused to be a part of any such political and administrative arrangement which would subordinate them to the Buddhist majority. In any case, for a larger political cause they preferred to be a part of the Kashmiri Muslim discourse without, however, radicalizing their politics; and in matters of day-to-day life they affiliated themselves either with the Indian National Congress or the

National Conference, while the LBA, representing the Buddhists, has been working closely with right-wing Hindu parties to further their political agenda. The RSS and the VHP have also been pressing for a trifurcation of the state that supports the LBA's demand for Union Territory status as well. The divisions within Ladkah and the close affiliation of the LBA and the Sangh Parivar at the national level have divided political discourse on religious lines.

The 'loudspeaker war', the 2006 communal clashes over the alleged desecration of the Quran in the village of Bodh Khorbu, the onslaught on Muslim minority of Zanaskar in 2012 (the conflict continued for more than three years), and the ultimatum issued by the LBA to the Muslims of Kargil to leave Leh in 2017 (because a Buddhist girl from Leh had married a Muslim boy from Kargil) further substantiate the apprehension of the Ladakh experts that the region is a tinder-box of religious radicalism. The Muslims of Kargil have been opposing Union Territory status for Ladakh tooth and nail. In October 2016 when the Leh Buddhists again raised the demand for Union Territory status for Ladakh, the Muslim religious and political leadership categorically told the then visiting home minister of India that Kargil would not accept Union Territory status for Ladakh, and Ladakh does not mean Leh district only (Sharma, 2016). The recent protests in Kargil against the government decision to have the headquarters of its Ladakh division only in Leh again brought the internal contestation with Ladakh to the forefront (Scroll.in, February 12, 2019; *The Indian Express*, February 10, 2019).

Does religious affiliation transcend regional boundaries?

As is clear from this discussion, there are clear variations on the larger issue of the political status of J&K as well as on almost all the major issues – economic, administrative and political – among and within the region. These contestations more often than not are structured around religious lines. The politics of Hindus and Buddhists of the state is diametrically opposed to the demand of the majority of Muslims of the state. The former have been vociferously demanding either the merger of the state with the Indian Union or a tripartite division of the state, with Ladakh's position as a Union Territory and Jammu as a separate state. This demand was raised by Hindu nationalist forces immediately after the accession and is repeated often, especially when the main theater of Plebiscite politics, namely the Kashmir Valley, heats up or when elections, either elsewhere in India or in the state of J&K, are around the corner.

An interesting question that emanates from this internal contestation is: Whether and how far religious identities transcend regional boundaries? Some scholars like Rekha Chowdhary argue that the Muslims of Jammu and Ladakh regions do not consider themselves as part of the larger identity politics of Kashmiri Muslims. Arguing that the Kashmiri identity politics is confined to Kashmir Valley, she maintains that:

> Even the Doda belt of Jammu region, which inhibits a large population of Kashmiri-speaking people, does not inevitably follow Kashmiri identity

politics. Though impacted in the long run by the developments in Kashmir, its politics is defined by an altogether different logic. Confronted with extreme backwardness and marginalization, development issues remain the priority of any politic over here.

(Chowdhary, 2016, 166, 169–170)

Chowdhary has built her argument on the assumption that the intensity of *azadi* sentiment found in Kashmir is not encountered in Muslim majority districts of Jammu. She further argues that "the politics of the Muslims of Doda belt of Chenab Valley of Jammu region simply revolves around developmental issues and demand for Hill Council on the pattern of Hill Councils in Ladakh" (ibid., 170). We, however, suggest that communities may be internally divided on individual or sectional issues but when they are face-to-face with a larger challenge involving the fate of their collective future, they forget their individual or sectional interests and join hands. This is exactly what happens in the religiously plural society of Jammu and Kashmir when the issue about deciding the political future of the state stares in the faces of the communities. There is an aphorism in Kashmiri often repeated by the people: *shal shal beun beun, tongi wizi quney* (though jackals live separately from one another, they howl together). This saying represents an undeniable social and political reality, a fact of real life in Kashmir.

The view that the Muslims of the state are divided on the basis of local issues, and that they have no commonality on religious-based identity politics, is not borne out by the continuous record of shared political sentiment among all the Muslims of the state cutting across the regional boundaries. This fact runs like a thread throughout the contemporary history of Kashmir right from the termination of princely order in the state till today. At no stage the Muslims of Jammu and Ladakh expressed their willingness to be part of any discourse/formation, which would run contrary to the larger political choice of Kashmiri Muslims. Interestingly, when in April 1953 Sheikh Abdullah had made up his mind to grant autonomy to different cultural units in the state, the Muslim majority of Doda raised a hue and cry against the inclusion of the district in the Hindu-dominated Jammu province. "In a convention of the Nationalist workers of the district," says P.N. Bazaz, "a curious and significant development was witnessed. While the Hindu speakers supported the official move, the Muslim leaders hotly contested and opposed it" (Bazaz, 2009, 500). The Muslims of Jammu were also actively involved in the Plebiscite Movement. Many of their prominent leaders mobilized the community around the cause. This region also provided recruits for the organizations that decided to follow a more radical path to fight against the Indian state. According to Praveen Swami, the radical organization, Students and Youth League (SYL), founded in March 1964 established its branches of SYL in most of the Kashmir Valley's main towns as well as in the district of Poonch (Swami, 2007, 57). Bashir Ahmad Kitchloo from Doda was one of the main members of the SYL-affiliated covert unit, who later became a key player of the 'Master Cell' (Swami, 2007, 57–59, 77). Similarly, another militant organization, Al-Fatah, created in the late 1960s–early 1970s, had significant support from this region. In April 1970 when this group looted the Pulwama Education Department to generate funds for the organization, three of its members had come from Doda to do the job (ibid., 93–94). Similarly, a Bhaderwah-based member, Abdul Hai, was provided money to setup a cafeteria, which could actually be used as a meeting place for Al-Fatah operatives in the remote mountain region of Doda (ibid., 94). Swami further argues that, while Al-Fatah was focusing on recruiting new cadres in the Kashmir Valley, its unit in Doda had taken up a vanguard role in covert activity. Run by Ghulam Hasan Bhat, an ethnic Kashmiri who lived in the remote Kishtiwar area, Al-Fatah's Doda unit generated much of the military intelligence (ibid.).

In 1965, Poonch and Rajouri districts witnessed a huge infiltration of armed people (locally called *razakaars*, meaning volunteers) from across the border. Quite contrary to the Kashmir Valley, the razakaars received mass support from the local populace resulting in their occupation of a vast area of the present Poonch and Rajouri districts (Choudhary, 2015, 155–156). The enormous local support for the infiltrators is not difficult to understand should we consider the large-scale massacres of Muslims in Jammu in 1947 (ibid., 95–99) and their consequent forced migrations from these districts to Pakistan-administered Kashmir. That these infiltrators comprised forced migrants was evident from their ethnicity, language and knowledge of the topography of the area (ibid., 155). The Poonch and Rajouri districts did provide recruits to militancy during the past two and a half decades, though not in the same numbers as did the Kashmir Valley.

Based on his field trips to the Jammu region during the early 1990s, Yoginder Sikand provides a vivid picture of religious polarization and rise of the militancy in Doda and other regions of Jammu:

> Communal polarization was almost complete. . . . Hindus in the region had become staunch supporters of the Hindu Right . . . after daily shakha (RSS drill) they would sing what struck me as brutally anti-Muslim songs but they believed were holy Hindu hymns . . . they unanimously believed that Hindus and Muslims could never live together in peace . . . anti-Muslimism had become in itself nothing less than a religion for them.
>
> *(Sikand, 2011, xiv)*

Arguing that the word of Muslim militants had become law in large parts of Doda, and that they were receiving mass support Sikand writes:

> right-wing Islamist groups now enjoy the support of the considerable number of Muslims in the district. A significant number of local Muslims had joined various Islamist militant outfits, and some had even crossed over to Pakistan for military training . . . majority of the Muslims of Doda, as in the Kashmir Valley, were sympathetic to the militants' demand for *azadi*.
>
> *(ibid., pp. xv–xvi)*

No doubt, the counter-insurgency response was to create the Village Defence Committees (VDCs) in 1995, strictly on communal lines and almost completely consisting of Hindus. These committees became a law unto themselves, like Ikhwan in Kashmir Valley, and were actively used by right-wing Hindu groups, thereby further exacerbating the communal divide in the region (ibid., 70–71).

Zafar Choudhary, while downplaying the participation of Jammu Muslims in the militancy, does note that, after a brief lull, the mid-1990s marked the revival of militancy in a major way across Jammu province but particularly in the Muslim majority districts of Rajouri, Poonch and Doda. "For a few years in the mid-1990s various parts of Jammu province remained the hub of the organizational and logistical activities of militant organization like Harkat-ul-Ansar and Jaish-e-Mohammad and the local youths would come and go at varying points. Doda district was an exception where the locals stayed on in the post-revival militancy for a longer while. Security agencies say that an estimated two to 30 militants are still active in Doda and Rajouri-Poonch areas" (Zafar Choudhary, 2015, 176–180).

As discussed earlier, Kargil Muslims in Ladakh generally kept aloof from the separatist politics of the LBA as well as their demand for Union Territory status for Ladakh. The Buddhist leadership recognized this sense of religious affiliation much earlier when they demanded direct rule by the maharaja or right to self-determination. In a memorandum to Nehru, while arguing for direct merger with India and to be treated distinct from Kashmir, the LBA stated:

> The right to self-determination claimed by us cannot be claimed with equal force by the people of Baltistan including Skardu and parts of Kargil tehsils predominantly populated by Muslims, as they are connected by ties of religion with the majority community in Jammu & Kashmir, nor by the people of Gilgit who came under Dogra rule through conquest after the annexation of Kashmir and whom not only identity of religion but of race as well binds to the majority community of Jammu & Kashmir.
>
> *(Beek, 1998, 38–39)*

Although the population of Kargil district has serious reservations with the Valley-based power structure and feels a sense of discrimination, however, they are also not ready to be part of the Buddhist discourse and have expressed their desire to be part of the Kashmiri Muslim discourse instead. When in the early 1950s Kushok Bakula demanded full autonomy for Ladakh, the Muslim leaders of Kargil did not support him. They preferred to be ruled by Srinagar and fiercely opposed the Buddhist monk (Bazaz, 2009, 474). They continue to maintain this position. To quote Sumantra Bose:

> In August 2002 it was reported that while "the trifurcation demand of the RSS may have sent a wave of optimism through the Ladakh Buddhist Association (LBA) which is spearheading the campaign for a union territory in Leh, opposition is gaining ground in Kargil. In response to the trifurcation

campaign, an all-party campaign was held in Kargil, and those attending the meeting unanimously opposed any division of the state [of IJK]. AsgharKarbalai, vice president of the Imam Khomeini Trust, Kargil's premier religious body, asserted: we strongly condemn the RSS and VHP move and whatever be the solution to the Kashmir dispute, we will always go with the [Muslim] majority in the state".

(Bose, 2003, 192)

Also, one of the reasons why the Kargilis did not accept the proposal of establishing an autonomous council for Kargil in 1995 was a degree of empathy of the people of Kargil for the *azadi* movement in Kashmir. In the words of Behera:

The political equation in Kargil was clearly the reverse of that in Leh. Kargil's inhabitants did not wish to antagonize the Kashmiri leadership, although they did not support the secessionist movement in the Valley. Most of the Kargil's leaders across the political spectrum supported the idea of the Hill Council in principle, but they postponed a final decision until the turmoil in the Valley was resolved.

(Behera, 2007, 118)

It was only after the government agreed to establish the Autonomous Hill Council for Kargil by rescinding the early proposal of having an inter-district council to advise the Leh Hill Council and Kargil Hill Council on matters of common interest, that the Kargil leadership gave their consent.

2008 Amarnath and subsequent agitations and the religious polarization

There is absolutely no denying the fact that regions and sub-regions do have their own respective issues, grievances and politics, but to assume that these differences do not allow the formation of collective community sentiment cutting across regions is stretching the argument too far. An analysis of some of the recent happenings is noteworthy. Our study shows that this has been the case with every religious community in the state.

The year 2008 marked the beginning of a new phase of mass protests in the Valley triggered by the transfer of 99 acres (800 kanals) of forest land to the Shri Amarnathji Shrine Board (SASB) on May 26, 2008 (Tremblay, 2009, 938–944). It was not basically the transfer of land to SASB per se which triggered the protests; it was the popular perception in Kashmir that the then Governor, General Sinha, was changing the religious demography of the valley by ultimately constructing a large township in Baltal to be named Amarnath Nagar (Sazawal, n.d.). This protest soon transformed into a full-fledged movement for self-determination, with the formation of the Action Committee against Transfer of Land (ACTL). Meanwhile, there was an equally strong reaction in Jammu when on June 21, state president of

BJP, Ashok Khajuria, threatened an economic blockade of Kashmir. Various Hindu nationalist parties – VHP, Hindustan Shiv Sena (HSS), Bajrang Dal, Akhil Bhartiya Vidhyarti Parishad (ABVP), BJP and RSS – joined together to lead the movement. Soon the BJP worked towards making the movement mass-based. Accordingly, with the RSS at its helm, the Shri Amarnath Yatra Sangharsh Samiti (SAYSS) was formed with the involvement of many groups. The SAYSS had three primary demands: restore Baltal land to the SASB; re-establish the Board; and recall the governor. However, with the replacement of Sinha with the new governor, N. N. Vohra, on June 25, 2008, the decks were cleared for reconsidering the decision.

On June 30, 2008, the BJP, Shiv Sena, VHP and Bajrang Dal enforced a blockade of the Jammu-Lakhanpur national highway. With the state government cancelling the land order on July 1, 2008, protests intensified in Jammu. While the ACTL in the Valley called off the agitation after the cabinet decision to revoke the land transfer order, in Jammu the agitation increased. SAYSS imposed a strong blockade on the national highway. The aim of the blockade was to suffocate the Kashmiris as there is only one land route for supplying essential commodities to the Kashmir Valley. It may be recalled that the first blockade was announced on June 23 (which lasted for three days) and the second on July 2. The blockade disrupted life across the region, with reports of shortfalls of food grains, medicines and other daily necessities. Horticulture too was adversely affected with fruits rotting and the traders incurring heavy losses. There was a tremendous reaction in all Muslim-dominated regions of Jammu as well as in Kargil against this move by Jammu Hindus. On August 11, traders in Kashmir staged a protest against the blockade and fruit growers gave a call for *Chalo* Muzafarabad (march to Muzafarabad), a protest march to the first town across the Line of Control in Pakistan-controlled Kashmir (ibid.). On August 12, 21 civilians were killed across Kashmir, including Kishtiwar, by the state forces (*Greater Kashmir*, August 19, 2018; Swami, 2008). While the actual number of civilians killed by forces during the 2008 uprising was more than 60, some Indian newspapers put the death toll around 15 (Pahalwan, 2008). Jammu region also witnessed communal tensions with Hindu chauvinist mobs torching houses and shops of Muslims in Kishtiwar. Eight people lost their lives in Jammu region (including suicide by a few individuals in protest against the revocation of the order) (Swami, 2008). The agitation finally ended on August 31, 2008, after members of SAYSS and representatives of the governor reached an agreement. As per the agreement, the Amarnath Shrine Board was allowed to use 40 hectares of land on a temporary basis.

Similarly, in June 2010 Kashmir Valley erupted into protests against the killing of three civilians by the Army in April 2010 and passing them off as Pakistani militants. The situation took a dangerous turn when a 17-year-old boy, Tufail Ahmad Mattoo, was killed by the forces on June 11, 2010. With his killing, a vicious circle of protests and killings started. Tufail Matoo's funeral was fired upon which resulted in more killings. This pattern went on – killings, demonstrations and more killings. By September 18, 2010 the death toll had reached 100. During the over 100 days of curfew and protests, more than 120 people, mostly teenagers, were killed in the firing by the armed forces. Though the government imposed a strict curfew, the demonstrations and killings continued unabated across Kashmiri Valley and the Muslim-dominated regions of Jammu. In September the protests and killings spread to Poonch district of Jammu (Bukhari, 2010).

Again during the long shut-down of 2016, which extended for about six months, there was renewed support for *azadi* and people living in far flung areas like Gurez, Kargil and Drass observed complete shut-downs and protests – something that had never happened in the recent history of Kashmir. The Muslims of the Chenab Valley and Pir Panchal regions demonstrated in unprecedented numbers to support the cause of the Muslims of the Valley. In all 136 persons were arrested in these two regions; charges included: raising pro-Kashmir, pro-Pakistan and anti-India slogans (Maqbool, 2017; Yusufzai, 2016). Further, in August 2016, when Kashmir was in the midst of an unprecedented popular uprising, the two prominent organizations of Kargil – Islamia School Kargil and Imam Khomeini Memorial Trust – vociferously opposed any plan to give Union Territory status to Ladakh. The president of the Imam Khomeini Memorial Trust, Kargil, Sheikh Muhammad Hussain Lutfi, while stating that Kargil would never part ways with the people of Kashmir, declared "we will support every decision taken by the people and leadership from Kashmir. We are not ready to leave people of Kashmir" (*Kashmir Reader*, August 17, 2016). Complete shut-downs were witnessed in Kargil to protest against the civilian killings in Kashmir during the 2016 uprising (*Kashmir News Portal*, July 21, 2016). It is a fact, as argued by Chowdhary, that the intensity and scope of involvement of Muslim-dominated regions outside Kashmir Valley cannot be compared to that of Kashmir; the difference in intensity cannot be attributed to the absence of strong sentiments of self-determination among the Muslims of Jammu region vis-à-vis the Muslims of Kashmir Valley. As Kashmir Valley is geographically compact and more homogeneous as compared to the geographically dispersed and heterogeneous habitations of the Pir Panchal and Chenab regions, the trajectory of their protest politics differs. Being border areas and inhabited by Muslims and non-Muslims who live together but separately, these regions are under tight surveillance as compared to Kashmir Valley. Moreover, unlike the Valley these regions are not privileged in terms of the media gaze and human rights watch. For that matter the border areas of Kashmir too, for most of the time, live in splendid isolation from the politics of the Valley and no observer/political leader took note of it for obvious reasons. What matters in these choked circumstances is the presence of identical sentiment and sympathy. Even Chowdhary acknowledges that there is "strong sense of sympathy with the people of Kashmir" (Chowdhary, 2016, 170). The demand for Hill Councils by the Muslim leadership of the Chenab Valley and Pir Panchal regions during the heyday of militancy in Kashmir was undoubtedly a weapon of the weak against the strong which is tersely summed up in a Kashmiri aphorism *hurnai pilas zangai z'las* (I will scratch his legs though I may not reach his head). Chowdhary arrives at this conclusion, though indirectly: "It was during last two and half decades that the political class in both these areas has been quite vocal about the need for the political and economic empowerment of these areas. *The demand for Chenab Valley Hill Council and Pir Panchal Hill Council has been articulated during the period of militancy only*" (emphasis ours) (ibid., 191). The Muslim districts of Jammu, as mentioned earlier, have also refused to be part of the proposed Hindu-dominated architecture of autonomy. With the rise of the BJP to power and its anti-Muslim policies, the feeling of oneness on the larger political issue deepened in the community beyond precedent. The 2016 mass uprising is clear evidence of this fact when, from Drass in Ladakh to Kishtiwar in Jammu, the whole Muslim belt rose up in protest. Insisting that the politics of Muslims of other regions revolve around issues of development and devolution of power instead of the politics that informs Kashmir Valley is stretching the argument too far as it ignores the direct and indirect demonstration of the affinity by the Muslims of other regions with the collective political conscience of Kashmiri Muslims.

The post-2014 situation

As already discussed, the politics of J&K always had shades of 'religion' over it. However, electorally speaking, the right-wing forces did not succeed in dominating the political scene till recently. The first major breakthrough came in the 2008 Assembly elections when the BJP, riding on the charged communal atmosphere as a result of the Amaranth land row, won 11 seats in Jammu compared to just one in 2002. However, the BJP emerged as a real force in state politics in the year 2014. During the 2014 parliamentary election, BJP for the first time won three parliamentary seats, two from Jammu and one from Ladakh. During the 2014 Assembly election, the BJP finished second with 25 seats, just three behind the PDP who got 28 seats, while the NC and Congress could get only 15 and 12 respectively. All 25 seats to the BJP came from the Jammu region with 19 of them coming from the Hindu-dominated areas of Jammu. The outcome clearly reflected a consolidation of the Hindu vote in the region. A significant gain for the BJP was winning six out of 13 seats in the Chenab valley and Pir-Panchal regions. However, this was fundamentally because the Muslim votes got divided between the NC, the PDP and the Congress party, while the Hindu vote consolidated in favour of the BJP (Wani, 2019b). In the Valley, on the other hand, the BJP could not win a single seat. The mobilization strategy of political parties clearly reflected a communal polarization. The BJP largely campaigned on the revocation of Articles 370 & 35A, regional disparity, a one-time rehabilitation package to three lakh refugees and citizenship rights to West Pakistan refugees in Jammu, bringing in a Hindu chief minister, granting Union Territory status to Ladakh, and so on. The idea clearly was to appeal to the Hindu vote in Jammu and Buddhists in Ladakh. This automatically generated a counter narrative in the Valley and other Muslim-dominated regions, where regional and 'secular' parties tried to mobilize Muslim voters on the plank of keeping communal and divisive forces out of Kashmir. The political parties in the Valley actually sought votes to keep the BJP out of power. Saifuddin Soz, president of the J&K unit of the Congress party, said, "Modi represents Nazi mindset, and his vision of India is suffocating; he represents a mindset prevalent in Germany where Jews were massacred and where only Christians were safe" (*Hindustan Times*, April 3, 2014, 2). Addressing the same rally Dr. Farooq Abdullah told the gathering that "the common goal of coalition is to keep Modi out of power; he accused Modi of having massacred Muslims in Gujarat" (ibid.).

On almost every crucial issue the mutually opposite stands have hardened. Today Jammu region is communally divided as never before. There have been regular cases of cow vigilantes and mobs attacking nomadic Muslims on the suspicion of cattle smuggling. The Hindutva mobs resorted to arson, burning vehicles, damaging the property of Muslims, and attacking Muslims (particularly Kashmiris) after militants carried out suicide attacks against the Central Reserve Police Force in February 2019. These incidents have further polarized the communities within the state on religious lines. An open display of communal politics was evident when in January 2018 the brutal rape and murder of Asifa, an 8-year-old girl, was carried out in Rasana village in Jammu, aimed at intimidating the Bakarwal community, who happen to be Muslims, into leaving the Hindu-dominated Kathua. The Hindu groups argued that it was a false case to deface a community (Jamwal, 2018). The charge sheet against the accused saw Hindu parties and groups up in arms. Members of political parties like the Panthers Party and the BJP openly supported the accused and demanded a CBI enquiry. BJP leaders, Chaudhary Lal Singh and Chander Prakash Ganga – both ministers in the then BJP-PDP government – openly backed the *Hindu Ekta Manch*, the group heading the agitation in support of the accused (Dutta, 2019). They were even backed by the Jammu Bar Association (ibid.; Sharma, 2018). The demand for a CBI enquiry (a national agency) was based on the argument that since the chief minister happens to be a Kashmiri Muslim and the Jammu and Kashmir Police as well as the courts are biased against a particular community, justice can only be delivered if there is an outside-the-state, national enquiry (Jamwal, 2018). When the judgement came against all but one accused, it was declared flawed. "I have not gone through the entire verdict yet," said BJP spokesperson Ashwini Kumar Chrungoo, "but from what I have come to know, it is a flawed verdict." Given the BJP's recent win in the 2019 parliamentary polls on the promise of the abolition of Articles 370 and 35A and its vision of installing a Hindu chief minister during the upcoming assembly elections, one should expect this polarization to intensify in coming times.

In conclusion, ever since the formation of the J&K state, politics has failed to divorce itself from community/religion despite the state being swept by modernization and the dominance of state politics by the 'secular' parties. The making of the princely state and the resistance against it did not only result in disturbing the social fabric of the state, dividing communities into opposite camps and following mutually opposite politics; but it also had spill-over effects which tore the state into regional/religious politics more often than not, even during the post-1947 period.

References

Abdullah, Sheikh Mohammad. 2013. *Ātash-i-Chinar*. English translation by Amarnath Land Row-chronology of Events. 2018. *Greater Kashmir*. August 19. Available from: www.greaterkashmir.com/news/gk-magazine/amarnath-land-row-chronology-of-events/ (Accessed on June 24, 2019).

Amin, Mohammad. *The Blazing Chinar.* Srinagar: Gulshan Books, (originally in Urdu under title *Ātash-i-Chinar*, 1986). Srinagar: Ali Mohammad and Sons.

Bashir, Khalid. 2017. *Kashmir: Exposing the Myth Behind the Narrative.* New Delhi: Sage.

Bates, Charles Ellison. 1873. *Central Asia Part VII Section I, a Gazetteer of Kashmir.* Calcutta: Office of the Superintendent of Government Printing.

Bazaz, Prem Nath. 1954. *The History of Struggle for Freedom in Kashmir: Cultural and Political, from the Earliest Times to the Present Day.* New Delhi: Kashmir Publishing Company.

Bazaz, Prem Nath. 1988. *Kashmir Ka Gandhi.* Vide Hassnain: 46.

Bazaz, Prem Nath. 2002. *Inside Kashmir.* Srinagar (edition): Gulshan Publishers.

Bazaz, Prem Nath. 2009. *The History of Struggle for Freedom in Kashmir.* Srinagar: Gulshan Books. (Originally published in 1954 from New Delhi: Kashmir Publishing Company).

Beek, Martijin Van. 1998. "True Patriots: Justifying Autonomy for Ladakh." *Himalayan Research Bulletin: Solukhhumba,* Vol. 18, No. 1, Article 9: 35–46.

Behera, Navnita Chadha. 2000. *State, Identity and Violence: Jammu, Kashmir and Ladakh.* New Delhi: Manohar.

Behera, Navnita Chadha. 2007. *Demystifying Kashmir.* New Delhi: Pearson/Longman.

Berger, Peter L. 1996–97. "Secularism in Retreat." *The National Interest,* No. 46: 3–12.

The Sacred Canopy: Elements of a Sociological Theory of Religion. Garden City: Doubleday.

Bose, Sumantra. 2003. *Kashmir Roots of Conflict, Paths to Peace.* New Delhi: Sage.

Brecher, Michael. 1953. *The Struggle for Kashmir.* Toronto: The Ryerson Press.

Bukhari, Shujaat. 2010. "Three Killed as Violence Spreads to Poonch." *The Hindu.* September 16. Available from: https://web.archive.org/web/20100927204659/www.hindu.com/2010/09/16/stories/2010091665151200.htm (Accessed on February 2, 2018).

Butt, Sanaullah. 1981. *Kashmir in Flames.* Srinagar: Ali Mohd and Sons.

Chowdhary, Rekha. 1998. "Muslim Identity and the Politics of Fundamentalism in Kashmir." *QEH Working Paper Series-QEHWPS19,* Paper No. 19. Queen Elizabeth House, October.

Chowdhary, Rekha. 2010. *Identity Politics in Jammu and Kashmir.* New Delhi: Vitasta Publishing.

Chowdhary, Rekha. 2016. *Jammu and Kashmir: Politics of Identity and Separatism.* New Delhi: Routledge.

Copland, Ian. 1981. "Islam and Political Mobilization in Kashmir, 1931–34." *Pacific Affairs,* Vol. 54, No. 2.

Daily Excelsior. 1990. September 2.

Dutta, Amrita Nayak. 2019. "Inside Story of How One of the Most Horrific Rape-murders or J&K Was Planned and Executed." *The Print.* June 14. Available from: https://theprint.in/india/governance/inside-story-of-how-one-of-the-most-horrific-rape-murders-of-jk-was-planned-executed/48129 (Accessed on June 20, 2019).

Glancy Commission Report. 1932. Jammu: Ranbhir Government Press.

Hassnain, F.M. 1988. *Freedom Struggle in Kashmir.* New Delhi: Rima Publishing House.

Hindustan Times. 2014. "Modi Represents Nazi Mindset." April 3.

Hussain, Malik Fazal. 1931. *Kashmir Aur Dogra Raj 1848–1931* (Urdu). Srinagar: Gulshan Publishers.

Jamwal, Anuradha Bhasin. 2018. "J&K Rape Case: Lies, False Binaries Used in Defense of Accused." *National Herald.* April 13. Available from: www.nationalheraldindia.com/india/jandk-asifa-case-lies-false-binaries-used-in-defense-of-accused (Accessed on June 24, 2019)

Jammu and Kashmir (J&K) Archives. 1922. *Order of the Maharaja of Jammu and Kashmir.* General Department, 1922, File No. 719/P-5. Jammu: Jammu and Kashmir Archives.

Kashmir News Portal. 2016. "Kargil Observes Complete Shutdown Against Civilian Killings in Kashmir." July 21. Available from: www.knskashmir.com/archives/news.aspx?news=Kargil-observes-complete-shutdown-against-civilian-killings-in-Kashmir – 9463 (Accessed on June 15, 2019).

Kashmir Reader. 2016. "Kargil's Shia Leaders Side with Kashmir, Not with Leh." August 17. Available from: http://kashmirreader.com/2016/08/17/kargils-shia-leaders-side-with-kashmir-not-with-leh/ (Accessed on October 4, 2017).

Kaul, Shridhar and H.N. Kaul. 2004. *Ladakh Through the Ages: Towards New Identity*. 3rd edition. New Delhi: Indus.

Khayal, Ghulam Nabi. 1997. *Iqbal Aur Tehreek-e-Azadi-e-Kashmir*. Srinagar: Kashmiri Writers' Conference.

Knight, E.F. 1905. *Where Three Empires Meet*. London: Longmans, Green, & Co.

Korbel, Joseph. 1954. *Danger in Kashmir*. Princeton: Princeton University Press.

Lawrence, Walter. 1895 (edition). *The Valley of Kashmir*. London: Oxford University Press.

Maqbool, Umar. 2017. "2016 Agitation: 136 Persons Booked in Chinab, Pir Panchal." *Greater Kashmir*. October 6. Available from: www.greaterkashmir.com/news/kashmir/2016-agitation-136-persons-booked-in-chenab-pir-panchal-regions/ (Accessed on June 24, 2019).

Mullik, B.N. 1971. *My Years with Nehru–Kashmir*. New Delhi: Allied Publishers.

Nehru Papers. 1940. "Proceedings of the Working Committee of the J&KNC." *Jawaharlal Nehru Papers*. Subject File 102/2, June.

Noorani, A.G. 2011. *Article 370 a Constitutional History of Jammu and Kashmir*. New Delhi: Oxford University Press.

Noorani, A.G. 2013. *The Kashmir Dispute-1947–2012*, Vol. 2. Esp. Chapter 17 'How Article 370 was Wrecked': 556–567. New Delhi: Tulika Books.

Om, Hari. 1996a. "Jammu Region-I: The Story of Neglect." *Statesman*. September, 23.

Om, Hari. 1996b. "Jammu Region-II: Not Too Late for Accession." *Statesman*. September, 24.

Pahalwan, Ashok. 2008. "Amarnath Land Issue Resolved, Protest Off." *LiveMint*. September 01. Available from: www.livemint.com/Politics/TcquQO9hAjgGZ8hNx7dIxJ/Amarnath-land-issue-resolved-protest-off.html (Accessed on June 24, 2019).

Phukon, Girin, editors. 2002. *Ethnicity and Polity in South Asia*. New Delhi: South Asian Publishers.

Puri, Balraj. 1966. *Jammu: A Clue to Kashmir Tangle*. New Delhi: Photo Flash Press.

Puri, Balraj. 1981. *Jammu and Kashmir–Triumph and Tragedy of Indian Federalism*. New Delhi: Sterling Publishers.

Puri, Balraj. 1983. *Simmering Volcano-Study of Jammu's Relations with Kashmir*. New Delhi: Sterling Publishers.

Puri, Balraj. 1999. *Jammu and Kashmir Regional Autonomy: A Report*. Jammu: Jay Kay Book House.

Puri, Balraj. 2008. *Kashmir: Insurgency and After*. New Delhi: Orient Longman.

Rai, Mirdu. 2004. *Hindu Rulers Muslim Subjects, Islam, Rights, and the History of Kashmir*. New Delhi: Permanent Black.

Saraf, Muhammad Yusuf. 2005. *Kashmiris Fight for Freedom* (1819–1946), Vols. I & II. Lahore: Feroze and Sons.

Sazawal, Vijay. n.d. "An Imperfect Storm: The Summer 2008 Uprising in Kashmir." *The Kashmir Herald*. Available from: www.kashmirherald.com/main.php?t=OP&st=D&no=386 (Accessed on January 31, 2018).

Scroll.in. 2019. "Kargil: Thousands Brave Minus 17 Degrees Celsius Temperature to Protest Creation of Ladakh Division." February 12. Available from: https://scroll.in/latest/913005/kargil-thousands-brave-minus-17-degrees-celsius-temperature-to-protest-creation-of-ladakh-division (Accessed on June 20, 2019)

Sharma, Arteev. 2016. "UT Status Demand Divides Ladakh." *Tribune India*. October 5. Available from: www.tribuneindia.com/news/jammu-kashmir/community/ut-status-demand-divides-ladakh/305091.html (Accessed on October 4, 2017).

Sharma, Ashutosh. 2018. "Mehbooba Rebukes Protesting Lawyers, Promises Justice for Kathua Rape Victim." *National Herald*. April 13. Available from: www.nationalheraldindia.com/india/jammu-and-kashmir-cm-mehbooba-mufti-rebukes-protesting-lawyers-promises-justice-in-asifa-case (Accessed on June 12, 2019).

Sikand, Yoginder. 2011. *Religion, Inter-Community Relations and the Kashmir Conflict.* New Delhi: Rupa Publications.

Sufi, G.M.D. 1996. *Kashmir: Being a History of Kashmir from the Earliest Times to Our Own,* Vol. II. New Delhi: Capital Publishing House.

Swami, Praveen. 2007. *India, Pakistan and the Secret Jihad–The Covert War in Kashmir, 1947–2004.* London: Routledge.

Swami, Praveen. 2008. "Fifteen Shot Dead in Jammu & Kashmir." *The Hindu.* August 13. Available from: www.thehindu.com/todays-paper/Fifteen-shot-dead-in-Jammu-amp-Kashmir/article15280357.ece (Accessed on February 1, 2018).

The Indian Express. 2019. "Ladakh Division: Massive Rally in Kargil for Rotational Divisional Headquarters." February 10. Available from: https://indianexpress.com/article/india/ladakh-division-massive-rally-in-kargil-for-rotational-divisional-headquarters-5577659 (Accessed on June 20, 2019).

Thorp, Robert. 1870. *Cashmere Misgovernment.* London: Longmans Green.

Torrens, Henry D'Oyley. 1862. *Travels in Ladakh, Tartary and Kashmir.* London: Saunders, Otley.

Tremblay, Reeta Chowdhari. 1992. "Jammu: Autonomy Within and Autonomous Kashmir?" Thomas, C. Raju editor. *Perspectives on Kashmir: Roots of Conflict in South Asia.* Boulder: Westview Press: 153–167.

Tremblay, Reeta Chowdhari. 2009. "Kashmir's Secessionist Movement Resurfaces: Ethnic Identity, Community Competition, and the State." *Asian Survey,* Vol. 49, No. 6: 924–950.

Verma, P.S. 1987. "Jammu and Kashmir Politics: Religion, Region and Personality Symbiosis." *The Indian Journal of Political Science,* Vol. 48, No. 4: 561–574.

Wani, Aijaz Ashraf. 2007. "The Popular Voice: Secular-Progressive Discourse in Kashmir (1932–47)." *Indian Historic Review,* ICHR/Sage, New Delhi, Vol. XXXIV, No. 1: 244–269.

Wani, Aijaz Ashraf. 2019a. *What Happened to Governance in Kashmir?* New Delhi: Oxford University Press.

Wani, Aijaz Ashraf. 2019b. "Regional Divide on Communal Lines: Lok Sabha Election 2014 in Jammu and Kashmir." Ashutosh Kumar and Yatinder Singh Sisodia, editors. *How India Votes- A State-by-State Look.* New Delhi: Orient Blackswan: 125–143.

Yusufzai, Tahir, and Nadeem Khan. 2016. "Chenab Valley Pir Panchal regions Side with Kashmir." *Greater Kashmir,* October 8. Available from: www.greaterkashmir.com/news/jammu/chenab-valley-pir-panchal-regions-side-with-kashmir (Accessed on June 24, 2019).

Zafar, Choudhary. 2015. *Kashmir Conflict and Muslims of Jammu.* Srinagar: Gulshan Books.

8
EVERYDAY COMMUNALISM AND SHIFTING FOOD PRACTICES IN JAMMU AND KASHMIR

Chakraverti Mahajan

The process of conflict leaves behind a volley of economic, political, social, cultural and emotional residues. The deep percolation of these residues into social life alters established social routines including taken-for-granted understandings of society. These residues affect not only conflict structures and situations but also people's everyday life, thus changing the ways in which they relate and communicate with the others around them. Since 1989, following the outbreak of a movement for self-determination in the Kashmir Valley, Jammu and Kashmir has been tangled in a low-intensity armed conflict resulting in the extreme militarization of the landscape (Datta, 2016). The effect of this conflict has been multifarious and is well reported in the existing literature on Kashmir. The conflict has resulted in civilian deaths (Kazi, 2010; Mathur, 2016), displacement of people (Evans, 2002; Datta, 2016), destruction of property, disrupted schooling (Parlow, 2011), normalized harassment, torture and human rights violations (Duschinski, 2009, 2010). The Kashmir conflict has influenced all spheres of life in the Valley and created vulnerability among the people.

The effect of the Kashmir conflict, however, is observed differently in Jammu than in the Valley owing to the fact that the impact of conflict and militancy in a mixed society are different from that in a homogenous one (Puri, 2008). Militancy caused a wide-scale displacement of the Valley's minority Hindu population – the Kashmiri Pandits, who settled in various towns and cities of Jammu. Tumultuous times of conflict have casted a long shadow on intercommunity relations in the region. Hindus and Muslims continue to live together, albeit separately, and have negotiated with religious and political differences on an everyday basis, at times violently.

Under the enduring strain of conflict, militancy and political divergence, religious identities have hardened and everyday communalism has come to acquire an all-pervasive presence. Everyday communalism is a type of communalism that finds itself located in the 'everydayness' of daily life. It finds expression on the roads, in the bazaars, in schools and colleges and almost in each and every public and private sphere of 'everyday'. Apart from these, everyday communalism is exhibited through cultural choices as well, for example, through choice of clothes, language, rituals and food. Among these, food serves as the central theme of this chapter to explain the shift of intercommunity relations and everyday communalism in Doda, a Kashmiri-speaking Muslim majority district in the eastern part of the Jammu region with substantial Hindu minority which speaks different western Pahari languages such as Siraji, Bhaderwahi, Kishtwari and Pogali. Both Hindus and Muslims live in mixed localities in villages as well as towns of Doda. This chapter explores Hindu–Muslim relations in Doda sub-region as affected and altered by militancy and conflict through analyzing food practices.

In the multi-religious setting of Doda, religion has always been a significant factor of identification. However, in the two decades of militancy and conflict, religion has become redefined and a more relevant force. Doda has its own peculiar history, religious demographics and a mixed way of living which sets it apart from the Kashmir Valley. Unlike the Valley, where religion and identity is clear-cut and mostly uniform, in the Doda sub-region it is intersected by regional, linguistic, cultural and multi-religious affiliations. The causes of the origin and the various stages of the growth of militancy in Jammu were different from those in Kashmir. It started much later in Jammu and by the time militancy reached Doda, it had already acquired communal overtones shedding its secular character (Kashmiri nationalism).

Doda sub-region was one of the first districts to be affected by the violent Kashmiri militant movement in Jammu division. While militancy and conflict in Doda did not cause a mass level exodus as that of Kashmiri Pandits in the Valley, it undeniably altered the way of life and caused a serious damage to the inter-community relations. With the rise of militancy, Hindutva politics and Islamism made inroads into the otherwise inaccessible region and promoted codification of religion-based identities and appropriation of various shared cultural practices.

Food, like all culturally defined material substances used in the creation and maintenance of social relationships, serves both to solidify group membership and to set groups apart. Food being so central to human existence, acts as a semiotic device (Appadurai, 1981). It bears the load of everyday social discourse and mobilizes strong emotions, both positive as well as negative. In Doda, following the militancy and hardening of religious boundaries, food practices have undergone a shift not only in the choice of what to eat but also in the choice of what not to eat, with whom to eat, with whom to share and not to share. Food has become a means of not just survival and existence but a marker of religious and political affiliations. However, the complex realities of mixed living keep challenging the orthodox positions and help in blunting the ideology thereby promoting exclusivity which defies everyday communalism. A close study of the 'everyday' and food practices brings into light cases where people have drawn new boundaries and there are cases where people also erase the boundaries set by religion and politics. In this context, the chapter argues that with the rise of everyday communalism in the shadow of severe identity politics, food practices of both the religious groups have become even more exclusive signifying disruptive potential of chronic conflict.

Region, religion and rituals: similarities and divergences

Doda[1] sub-region includes the districts of Doda, Kishtwar and Ramban. Earlier the region was administratively a single unit and comprised one single district, namely District Doda. As per 2001 census data, Muslims accounted for nearly 58 per cent of the total population of the Doda sub-region. Hindus were the second largest community and accounted for around 41 per cent of the total population. Other religious communities were Sikhs, Buddhists, Christians and Jains. Together they constituted less than 1 per cent of the total population (Census of India, 2001). However, after the reorganization of the Doda sub-region region in July 2006, there was a slight change in the demography of the region. Erstwhile Doda sub-region was trifurcated into the districts of Doda, Kishtwar and Ramban. As per the census of 2011, Muslim population in Doda district stands at about 54 per cent and Hindu population is about 46 per cent. In Kishtwar, Muslims account for 58 per cent of the total population and Hindus stand at 41 per cent. In Ramban district, Hindus are about 29 per cent while the Muslim population is 71 per cent. The sub-region as a whole shares certain commonalities, which cannot be isolated for any one of the three districts which are the part of this area – in terms of geography, terrain, people, culture and politics. The most important factor that remains common to all the three districts is their economic backwardness, if we compare it to other parts of the state. Hence it is imperative to analyze the whole sub-region in its compact form. More than 90 per cent of the Doda sub-region's population lives in the rural heartland (Economic Survey, 2010). Like Hindus, most Muslims in Doda live in rural areas. Overall, Doda's population pattern projects heterogeneity in character. The diversity is in addition to the geographical, historical and economic diversities which exist in the region.

Historically, the entire sub-region was divided into two independent principalities of Kishtwar and Bhaderwah. Kishtwar state consisted of some areas of the present District Doda, that is, Doda-Siraz excluding present Bhaderwah, Bhallessa and Thathri tehsils, Marmat Galihan, Raggi, Assar, Batote areas of Doda and Ramban districts. Imprints of the historical connection can still be found in the society and culture of the sub-region. For example, Kishtwar being topographically closer to Kashmir shares certain cultural similarities with Kashmir. Similarly, Bhaderwahi culture has certain traces of the Himachali (Himachal Pradesh in northern India borders the Jammu and Kashmir state) connection. Linguistically too, the sub-region presents a mosaic of languages and dialects. Interestingly, Muslims of the sub-region are mainly Kashmiri speakers while Hindus speak different languages in different parts; like Kishtwari in Kishtwar, Sirazi in Doda and Bhaderwahi in Bhaderwah and Padderi, Khashki, Pahari and Pogli in other parts. Despite all its diversity, the Doda sub-region shares a variety of similarities that makes it a composite unit.

A hilly terrain, shared culture, common economic interest and the conflict situation impart some homogeneity to the area. This interplay of homogeneity and heterogeneity gives it a very complex character where the former tends to generate shared regional identity and the latter generates distinct identities asserting their differences at times.

Islam reached the sub-region through the Sufis. The seventeenth century marked the prominence of Sufism in Doda, owing to the arrival of Hazrat Shah Mohammed Farid-ud-Din Baghdadi and his two sons, Hazrat Shah Asrar-ud-din and Hazrat Shah Akhyar-ud-din. It is the Sufis who provided the best and most successful missionaries of Islam. They went to the people and gave respect and regard to the people of other religions. Many Sufis like Shah Farid-u-Din, Zain-ul-Abdain and Shah Asrar-u-Din settled in the region and taught Islam to the people and brought them into the Islamic fold. The first instance of arrival of Islam in the region was in 1664 with the arrival of Shah Fariduddin Baghdadi in Kishtwar. He, along with four of his companions – Yar Mohammed, Darvaish Mohammad, Shah Abdal and Sayyed Bahauddin Samanani, travelled all the way from Baghdad to the mountains of Kishtwar. His teachings of love and devotion influenced the then Hindu ruler of the town, Raja Kirat Singh to such an extent that he became a Muslim. He adopted the uniquely syncretic name of Tegh Muhammad Singh, and gave his daughter in marriage to one of the chief disciples of Shah Fariduddin, Syed Bahauddin Simnani. Several of his subjects followed suit, yet many of those who remained Hindu held Shah Fariduddin in high respect. He married a local Rajput woman, who was later named Bibi Mai Malahat. She was the third and the last consort of Shah Saab, and became the mother of Shah Akhyarudin, the heir to the spiritual realm of his father. Even in present times, no one is permitted inside the main premises of the last resting place of Beeba Shahiba. It is only the descendants of her native family who are allowed to do the cleaning, maintenance and other such special chores inside the sanctum sanctorum of her shrine, despite the fact that they are still Hindus. After Shah Fariduddin Baghdadi, his son, Shah Asrar-ud-Din, was instrumental in the spread of Islam in the sub-region. Despite considerable success in the conversion of Hindus to Islam, the great majority of the people remained Hindus but venerate the Muslim saints equally. They visit their *ziarats* (shrines) frequently, present offerings and sacrifices and partake in their *Urs* ceremonies annually.

Along with Sufism, the Naga cult of Hinduism also enjoyed the respect of both the religions. The traditional form of Hinduism prevalent here has been the Naga cult or serpent-worship, which is associated with springs (Sharma, 2008). For Hindus these Nagas or springs have religious significance and the Nagas being the pure source of water and health-giving properties are considered sacred by the Muslims too. Many Muslims contribute in yearly Naga festivals by playing musical instruments. Wattals, a marginalized Muslim endogamous caste group, is mainly associated with the profession of playing instruments. In this manner Hindu festivities provided economic benefits to Muslims, especially the weaker sections. There are some Hindu seers who are loved and respected by the people irrespective of religious affinities.

Shaivism is a widely practiced form of worship among the Hindus. Shiva, the chief deity is worshipped and propitiated at the level of households. Two important festivals which are celebrated by the Hindus are *Khadal* and *Ghanchakkar*. Khadal is a night long ritual where in the middle of the night, a ram (*bhedu*) is sacrificed. The meat has to be consumed before dawn. *Ghanchakkar* is another tantric festival dedicated to Shiva. A sacrifice is performed early in the morning around 4 a.m. Food is cooked and several guests are invited over. Both these festivals are exclusively celebrated by Hindus with no participation from the Muslims. Since these festivals are of religious nature, the ritual meat is prepared by *jhatka* (Hindu or Sikh method of killing an animal) which is the main reason why Muslims are not invited. Thus, these festivals have historically remained exclusive to Hindus unlike the festival of Eid. In Eid, which is a Muslim festival, the meat is prepared by the *halal* method but Hindus often participate in the festival and also consume the sacrificial meat. In this context, Sufism had a big role in shaping the meat-eating practices in the region. Hindus of Doda have been fully assimilated into halal-eating Sufi ways. It is only at the time of their sacred ceremonies that Hindus go by their community rules.

The Naga deities are propitiated by sacrificing animals by the jhatka method. Muslims are not invited to such ceremonies as well. But, during life cycle ritual ceremonies such as wedding celebrations and other smaller occasions, Hindus and Muslims would invite each other. Before the advent of militancy, however, food was shared but the methodology was a bit different. While inviting guests from the other community, the host family would also request to arrange them a cook. The host family would give the invited party dried ration – a goat or sheep plus rice and other items including spices as per their requirement. Apart from that, sharing food on an almost regular basis had also become part of the social norm.

Shared socio-cultural practices

Since ancient times both the religious communities continued to co-exist peacefully and thrived alongside for centuries. Religious milieu of the village was characterized by shared sacred spaces and fluidity of beliefs. It was common for both Hindus and Muslims to visit and venerate shrines of Sufi saints and folk deities. Years of togetherness brought both the communities much closer to each other; so much so that one can find certain cultural similarities between the two which are quite distinct from their original religious tenets. Amalgamation of Hindu traditions with Muslim culture gave birth to the cultural synthesis shaping the sub-region's composite culture. Similarly, Islam too influenced Hinduism; though, the influence of Hinduism on Muslims is more manifest. In order to have a better understanding, it is pertinent to throw light on the cultural synthesis which took place on account of the coming closer of Hinduism and Islam (Rana, 2016).

The birth of a child in a family is usually followed by some rites. There is an effect of the Hindu customs and rites on the Muslims. For example, *mundan* (the first haircutting ceremony of the baby) is one of the most important Hindu ceremonies. In the same manner Muslims also celebrate a function named *zad kasim* associated with the first haircut of baby. Previously, the function was observed with fun and frolic and extended up to three days. But with the advent of modernization and education, people are becoming more aware of their original religious tenets and such practices are diminishing among Muslims. A number of customs and traditions of marriages like *mangani*, dowry, *haldi*, drum-beating, singing-dancing, *baraat*, *rukhsati*, etc. have been adopted by Muslims from the Hindus. Originally these were not part of Islamic marriages. Resemblances in social customs can be observed in death ceremonies also. In Islam, the mourning period is for three days. Thereafter a feast is held on the 40th day, and then four months, six months and nine months after death. In Hinduism, death rites generally last for 13 days. On the fourth and 10th day some important rites are performed. Officially among Muslims, there is no concept of the fourth day, or for that matter any other day except specified days for rituals. Thus a light feast ceremony (generally salt tea and *halwa*) given on the fourth and 15th day after death is something peculiar to the sub-region which seems to be influenced by local customs and practices of Hindus. *Shradh* is an important Hindu ritual performed in memory of dead ones. A little resemblance of this ritual can be seen in the Muslim ceremony of *Ruhan Darood*. In this ceremony recitation of the Quran is held and special prayers are offered for comforting the spirits of the dead. Some of the Muslims like Hindus too, share their belief in astrology and palmistry. Rana (2016) noted that Muslims frequently visit Pundits for making their *janam kundalis* (horoscope) and follow their instructions quite carefully if there is any error in the janam kundali. Ornaments are an important part of Hindu social and religious life. Though Islamic laws prohibit the use of gold for men but due to their close contact with Hindus, Muslim men adorn themselves with gold jewellery. In fact, at the time of marriage the groom is gifted gold items by his in-laws and elders from the bride's family. Nowadays, there is increasing trend of young Muslim women wearing *chooda* (red bangles) and *mangalsutra* (a necklace that the groom ties around the bride's neck), both Hindu customs, as a fashion statement (Rana, 2016).

Apart from these socio-cultural similarities, food practices of the people show a shared way of living. Food habits of Hindus of the sub-region vary from Hindus of the Jammu region and are closer to Muslims of the Doda sub-region. The meat-eating tradition of Hindus is strongly influenced by the Muslim way of life. Generally, halal meat is considered a taboo among Hindus but in Doda sub-region there are many Hindus who still consume halal meat. In fact, before the eruption of militancy there were no jhatka meat shops in Doda and Kishtwar towns. Similarly, Hindus in other parts of the state abstain from eating non-vegetarian food on specific days like Tuesdays and Sankranti, Ikadashi and Navratris (Rana, 2016). Only a few Hindus observe the rule here. Muslim locals avoid cooking meat at home when kids are suffering from small pox which is a Hindu belief. In fact, a Muslim couple had a big fight when the husband ate meat as the child was suffering from small pox. These shared practices were quite common in the sub-region. It was only the onset of militancy and the conditions it created that the sharpening of identities and consequently fast changes in food habits ensued.

Everyday communalism and hardening of religious identities

Everyday communalism is the 'grinding and routinized aspect of communalism that pervades people's daily lives' (Jeffery and Jeffery, 1998, 123). Usually located in or near people's homes, everyday communalism represents 'the trivial and non-spectacular, and is continuous in the sense that it has no beginning and no end, but simply flows by – day after day, month after month, and year after year' (Frøystad, 2005, 17). Everyday communalism is a subtle form of communalism that involves everyday stereotyping of the 'other' and the sustenance of the communal divide. It is practised through speech, acts, bodily practices and identities that make people aware of the religious and caste membership of the people they engage with (Jeffery and Jeffery, 2005, 450).

Diverse understandings of everyday communalism exist in social science literature where the concept usefully explains different contexts. Chatterji and Mehta (2007) argued that the 'intimacy of residential relationships' (Deshpande, 2000, 198) negotiated in daily life is the breeding ground of the communal mindset. Chatterji and Mehta (2007) further stated that in order 'to gauge the density of everyday communalism, it is necessary to understand its peaceful and banal incarnation, particularly at the level of the neighbourhood and the family' (p. 110). Ananya Vajpeyi (2002) explained everyday communalism as a derivative of the process of enculturation at home which is often reproduced indiscreetly and trivially. Vajpeyi used her classroom as a site to understand everyday communalism where her students would often retreat into communal positions and defensively utter phrases that she felt were not of their own making. These communal responses ranged from 'Islam is rigid' to 'Muslims are foreign' and to 'today's broken mosques pay for yesterday's broken temples'. Vajpayi (2002) further stated that such communal prejudices were often passed 'across dinner tables, in front of the television and in other sites of' the domestic sphere from where the children absorbed them (5092). Later, these children did not hesitate in spilling these phrases in a 'quasi-public' space such as a classroom even in the presence of a powerfully equipped teacher or the threat of being discredited by their more politically correct classmates. Everyday communalism becomes a part of the child's habitus and finds a home from where it operates in the society.

Apart from family and school, studies have also shown the existence of everyday communalism in state institutions which takes on the character of institutional communalism. The presence of 'community-blind institutional procedures' in a context that is enmeshed with inequalities of opportunities results in structured inequalities. Such institutional communalism is deeply embedded in the daily workings of many social institutions, including state apparatuses. Katz (2012) expanded upon the idea of institutional communalism and said that it is difficult to trace. It operates through 'established and respected forces in the society' allowing its beneficiaries to 'absolve themselves from individual blame' (Ture and Hamilton, 1967, 5). In his essay focused on 'Institutional Communalism in North Indian Classical Music', he explained how institutional structure helps in constructing communal ideologies. He achieved this by going into the historical and present-day relationship between the Lucknow *gharana* and Bhatkhande Musical College. He observed that at the time of setting up of the college and in subsequent years, the presence of hereditary musicians from the Lucknow gharana (which was predominantly Muslim) was significant. But after 1982, the college had excelled as an institute of prominence in Hindustani music yet the number of Muslim teachers and students had drastically lowered. He explained this as 'institutional communalism' and argued that the marginalization of Muslim hereditary musicians was a nearly inevitable consequence of the ideological basis on which the college was founded. This ideological basis was the liberation of the knowledge of Hindustani music from the grip of the Muslim gharanas. He concluded by saying that the undermining of the tradition of Muslim hereditary musicians was not a result of personal prejudice and specific individuals but of institutional communalism. Upon looking closely, everyday communalism in Doda can be located in almost every aspect of everyday life. It was believed that during the Dogra riyasat, Hindus were preferred over Muslims not only in the sphere of education but also in the sphere of jobs (see Zutshi, 2003; Rai, 2004). The rise of Sheikh Abdullah and his subsequent elevation to premiership in the post-partition era facilitated the entry of Muslims in government jobs. That the Sheikh favoured Muslims over Hindus was a widespread perception in the area. As Master Bhagat Ram, a local, puts it:

> If there were a hundred jobs, ninety went to Muslims. Hindus got only ten. Government service slowly and gradually slipped from the hands of the Hindus. Only Muslims were employed. Now they are the owners and we are finished (*Ab yeh malik hain aur hum khatam ho gaye*).

This narrative provides substance to the notion of a long history of institutional communalism in the region. At the time of the militancy, everyday communalism was openly practiced in the form of speech. Hindus were often heard saying that Muslims cannot be trusted. Everyday communalism as a result of socialization at home was visible in statements such as 'Muslim households are unclean and smell' or 'How can you live with a Muslim family?'. Muslims also held communal stereotypes against Hindus that involved 'Hindus do not entertain their guests (*mehmaannawazi*) with sincerity'. There was also an instance where in a school function, a Muslim teacher refused to allow cooking of food in utensils that came from a Hindu household. Such incidents of everyday communalism were often observed between people and they served to widen the gaps between the communities.

As mentioned earlier, the religious milieu of the sub-region, before the advent of militancy, was characterized by shared sacred spaces and fluidity of beliefs. But with the arrival of militancy, shared cultural practices were either appropriated in a way that they became exclusive to one religion or they were altogether abandoned. This affected the religious texture and intercommunity ties in the region, which shifted from fusion to polarization. The food habits of the people of the region were also impacted by the continuous assault of militancy and rising communalism. Another reason that brought a shift in the meat-eating tendencies was the large-scale military mobilization in the sub-region. The presence of armed forces, which were largely Hindu, introduced new demands for jhatka meat. The army men were not accustomed to the halal eating ways of the Hindus of the Doda sub-region. Thus, the army as a consumer brought a steep rise in the demand for jhatka meat which was earlier eaten by Hindus on limited occasions only. Apart from the role of the militancy and the army in the appearance of jhatka meat shops in the region, there was a general increase in the purchasing power of the people. In earlier times, buying mutton for consumption was far from an everyday practice. The village butchers would roam from one household to another asking for the amount of mutton they would like to buy before they would ritually slaughter an animal. This would ensure the sale of the meat. In the present times, albeit slowly, the economic growth in the region has enabled more people to afford meat. This fact combined with the major factor of the sharpening of religious identities and demand of jhatka meat by the army men led to the setting up of several jhatka meat shops in the region.

In the phase of active militancy, the army exercised considerable influence in the region and there was little or no outcry over the opening of these jhatka meat shops. In fact, the jhatka shops were welcomed by a lot of Hindus who felt the need to assert their religious identity during the phase of militancy. Over time, as militancy subsided and democratic institutions gained strength, the influence of military in the region weakened to a considerable extent. The revival of democratic institutions allowed people to assert religious identities with renewed vigour. The old and existing structural set up of the region had been challenged by the opening of jhatka meat shops. In retaliation, over the years, beef stalls started coming up in the region. It became another marker of religious identity and a tool of assertion of that identity. This new development in the region was a product of the hardening of religious identities and increasing communalism but it was also influenced by a larger national narrative on beef consumption.

Beef politics

In Hindu-dominant India, where the cow holds a religious significance, beef is not considered simply a food choice. Consumption of beef has an underlined legal, political and religious connotation within the Indian context. Article 48 of the Indian Constitution imposes a duty, albeit non-justiciable, on the Indian state to take steps to prohibit the slaughter of cows, calves and other milch and drought cattle (Chigateri, 2008). Following this stipulation in Article 48, laws prohibiting cow slaughter have been enacted across most states in India. The state of Jammu and Kashmir is not an exception. In fact, out of the 25 states where cow slaughter is banned and punishable under law, Muslim-majority Jammu and Kashmir is the only state where it invites the harshest penalty of 10 years of rigorous imprisonment (Gilani, 2015). Even the possession of flesh of killed or slaughtered animals is an offence punishable with imprisonment up to one year and fines.

According to some historians, the beef ban was first imposed in Jammu and Kashmir in 1819 by the Sikh rulers. According to a ruling documented under Section 298 of the Ranbir Penal Code, cow slaughter was banned during the maharaja's time in Jammu and Kashmir. The ban was strongly implemented during the Dogra regime. The law was strictly imposed especially in Srinagar, because of the Muslim majority here. According to reports, since 1947, no one from Kashmir has been punished for slaughtering a cow. But, it has also been reported that the contentious provisions of the Ranbir Penal Code are frequently used in Jammu province. Newspaper reports reveal that in the last six years, 28 FIRs (First Information Reports) were registered in Jammu province under Sections 298A and 298B of the Ranbir Penal Code that criminalizes slaughtering of bovine animals in the state. The controversial law, says the report, is being regularly used mostly in Muslim-majority districts. It revealed that since 2009, three FIRs each were lodged in Doda and Ramban under the law, two in Udhampur, four in Reasi, nine in Rajouri, three in Kishtwar, one in Jammu and five in Kathua district. Over the past 195 years, since the law has been in vogue, historians have recorded that 19 people in Srinagar were executed publicly for cow slaughter (Nabi, 2015).

In the year 2015, the Jammu and Kashmir High Court directed the state government to 'strictly implement an existing order banning sale of beef in the state' (Rashid, 2015). This resulted in an uproar in the region and, ironically, resulted in a heavy rise in the sale of beef. The order was seen as 'interference in the religion' by the state and courted heavy protests, especially in the Kashmir Valley. Different from this legal and political debate, beef consumption in Jammu and Kashmir, as already mentioned, also has a deeper significance in the religious domain. It involves a communal angle. The cow being sacred to Hindus, it is considered a sin for them to slaughter and consume its meat. There is no such religious significance of the cow for the Muslims. For a Muslim to eat cow meat, the only condition is that it should be ritually slaughtered, that is, it should be halal meat. This difference of food preference has long been a contentious issue between Hindus and Muslims across India.

In Kashmir, which is the Muslim majority region, beef is openly sold and consumed by the people. In this regard, Tremblay (2018) observed: 'Despite being illegal, beef is eaten by Kashmiri Muslims as it tends to be cheaper than other meats and useful during the winter months when every edible commodity is in short supply (although out of respect for the Hindu community, it is referred to as the "other meat").' Both Kashmiri Hindus and Muslims have known that the Kashmiri Muslim community consumes beef, but there has always existed an implicit understanding between the two communities where they have entered into '"the practice of proximity" . . . whereby differences are neither refined nor erased, but negotiated' (Tremblay, 2018, 240). According to Hanan Baba, a Quora user from Jammu and Kashmir, Kashmiris are meat eaters as beef is not hard on the poor man's pocket. It is much cheaper than mutton. So, mostly the people from the lower socio-economic group consume meat for its taste and nutrition. The elites choose mutton and lamb over beef and often look down upon the beef eaters, categorizing them as 'backward beef eaters'.[2]

However, in Jammu, beef consumption was never discussed openly. Jammu being a Hindu-dominant region, beef consumption by Muslims here was always a hush-hush affair. It involved bargaining with social and religious sentiments of their next-door, beef-conscious Hindu neighbour. An act of consuming beef in the knowledge of this Hindu neighbour would invite social stigma and strain. The following incident from Bhagwah village can be used to understand the situation regarding beef consumption in the past. Narrated by a Dalit woman during my fieldwork in Bhagwah, this 'Taraju incident' is instructive on several counts.

> Ramesh would eat from their house but not from ours. Let me tell you a story. Close to our house lives one person called Kasim. He is a Muslim, a Kashmiri; I do not know what his caste is. He may be a malik or naik. One day he borrowed my balance [taraju] to weigh ghee [clarified butter]. I too went after him after sometime to see if there was some extra ghee for me to buy. As I entered, I saw, he was weighing buffalo's meat [bhains ka] in my taraju. We had a big fight [phir meri uski bahut behes hui]. I did not take back that balance and warned him not to enter my house ever. These people sell, cook and eat cheap meat. However, Ramesh doctor would eat with them but not with us [laughs].

Referring to Doctor Ramesh, who is a high caste Hindu Rajput neighbour, Devi told me that he could eat with Muslims who eat bovine meat but not with her family. The above incident explains how beef eating is viewed by some Hindus, including those from the lower socio-economic class as well. At the inter-community level, the following analysis can be made. Devi, who identifies herself as a Hindu, was repulsed by the knowledge that her taraju was being used to weigh beef by her Muslim neighbour. Also, when I told her that I live with a Muslim family, she asserted her Hindu identity by telling me that Muslims are gande log (bad people) as they eat beef. She told me that she does not eat with Muslims.

Apart from this single incidence in which a Scheduled Caste woman told me that her Muslim neighbour used her balance to weigh bovine meat, one other Hindu claimed to have seen Muslims eating bovine meat. They (Hindus) knew that Muslims sometimes eat bovine but no one had a firsthand experience of witnessing a Muslim eating bovine meat. However, in the present times, the scenario has undergone considerable change with the opening of beef stalls in Doda. Such stalls are highly patronized by Muslim youth for whom the ability to consume beef in a public place is a task of pride. It is an act of establishment of their identity and defiance of the larger national and political discourse on beef consumption. These beef stalls serve as hangout spaces for the youth of today. Unlike the previous generation of elders who believed in co-existence and negotiation of identities in both public and private spaces, the new generation of Muslim and Hindu youth has little consideration for the sentiments of the 'other' community. The religious and structural realities in the sub-region have altered.

Another undermined reason that contributes to the development of a communal narrative in the sub-region is the proliferation of new media technologies. These media platforms have facilitated the entry of many new actors to join the religious marketplace and disseminate their religious ideology. In the process of this multiplication of diversified opinions on religion through new media platforms, there has been a veritable discursive explosion on the concept of religious identities (Hall, 2000, 15). Unlike television and radio, which were situated largely within the formal state control, new media technologies such as mobile phones, internet, audio and video CDs, cassettes and computer multimedia have created counterpublics (Warner, 2002) where the Muslim groups invent and circulate discourses that undercut the authority of media controlled by the government and the private corporate media. This indiscriminate use of uncensored information has deteriorated inter-community relations in the Valley and across the state, including the Doda sub-region.

In lieu of a conclusion

Doda sub-region includes the present-day districts of Doda, Kishtwar and Ramban. Of these three districts, Kishtwar and Ramban have Muslim majority population while the Doda district has an almost balanced population of Hindus and Muslims. Historically, the way of life in the Doda sub-region was marked by syncretism and co-existence. It was the effect of Sufism and shared socio-cultural practices that prevented religious differences from growing and promoted harmony in the everyday life of the people. It was also an impact of Sufism that, in general, Hindus of the region consumed halal meat along with the Muslims. Jhatka meat was very limited in the region, mostly used by the Hindus during religious rituals and propitiation of their deities. For other social and cultural occasions, halal meat was used. However, after the outbreak of militancy in Kashmir, the conflict slowly travelled to Doda. By the time the movement reached Doda it had acquired a communal colour and threatened the existing social fabric in the region. The experience of militancy, conflict, militarization and politics altered the established ways of life in the region, thereby challenging the intercommunity relations. Communalization of everyday life and hardening of religious identities was observed in the region and socio-cultural practices became exclusive to communities. This shift in people's lives could be seen in all aspects including food practices.

The French anthropologist Claude Lévi-Strauss (1966) finds that many items of food, and meat in particular, say much about the society where they are prepared and eaten, and that 'the cuisine of a society is a language into which that society unconsciously translates its structure' (Mennell et al., 1992, 9). This could be observed in the case of Doda sub-region. Prior to militancy and conflict, when the Hindus and Muslims of Doda believed in shared co-existence and mutual respect for the religious sentiments of each other, the way of cooking and sharing the food was harmonious, especially with respect to meat. Sufism's influence, which dictated people's everyday lives including their kitchens, also began to disappear. Jhatka meat shops emerged in the region which were later followed by the popularization of beef stalls in the region. Unlike in the past, where Hindus and Muslims negotiated their food practices to adjust to a shared way of life, militancy erased this negotiation. Food began to define communal boundaries between the people.

In this context, this recent creeping of differences into dietary practices is indicative of increasing communalization of all aspects of social life. Such differences are recognized, carefully cultivated and celebrated as part of a modern project of forging essentialized and differentiated communities. Close examination of the ethnographic material on food practices – cuisine, serving styles and hospitality – raises questions regarding typicality of 'Hindu' and 'Muslim' foods. While in the past, no food item was exclusively Hindu food or Muslim food, except beef, Muslim foods in recent times clearly and explicitly evoke Doda Muslims' links across Pir Panjals to Kashmiri culture tropes, for example, using Samovar and in some cases the import of Wazwaan style feasts. In matters of food and everyday life, these renewed attempts towards reconstructing the 'traditional' have led to everyday communalism. While the reasons behind such processes of communalization are largely on account of militancy, conflict and politicization of events, to a large extent this process of increased communalization in the present times has also been facilitated by the flow of new media practices involving the processes of digitization. The proliferation of media and means of communication have multiplied the possibilities of creating new religious communities and new networks within the Muslim population of the Valley. The access to these new media technologies has altered the ways in which religious knowledge was produced and consumed in the past (Warner, 2002). The Muslims of Doda have always looked up to the Valley for religious guidance and Islamic patronage. It shall be no surprise that the present Muslim youth in the Doda sub-region, at least a majority of them, echo the sentiments and ideologies rising from the valley. The popularization of beef stalls as public hangout spots and the pride of being a beef consumer by Muslim youth testifies the shift in their food behaviour. Similarly, in the case of Hindus, more and more jhatka shops were opened in the region and Hindus decreased the use of halal meat in their kitchens. It was an attempt by them to demarcate their Hindu identity. This explains the shift that was brought into the intercommunity relations under the influence of militancy and conflict. The shared spaces have shrunk and exclusivity has gained ground. It can be concluded that conflict, communalization and identity politics has degraded the multi-religious nature of society in the Doda sub-region. Intercommunity relations have been altered and this altered reality has manifested in the everyday life of the people.

Acknowledgements

This research was supported by University of Delhi Research and Development (DU R&D) Grant 2014–15. Indian Council of Social Science Research (ICSSR), New Delhi and Institute of Economic Growth (IEG), Delhi provided financial and infrastructural support during my doctoral fieldwork (2008–2011). Rekha

Chowdhary asked me to write this chapter and Sunaina Rana helped me with its conceptualization, I thank both of them for being constant companions in my research journey. Last but not the least, I express my gratitude to Rashmi Patel who assisted me in bringing this chapter to its present form.

Notes

1 My association with the area goes back to 2006 when I started visiting it to collect data for my doctoral dissertation (Mahajan, 2017). My PhD thesis, in classical ethnographic manner, has mapped the impact of militancy on intercommunity relations in this sub-region. The study was primarily carried out in a village called Bhagwah, located in Saraz. Most of my observations for this chapter are based on my fieldwork in Bhagwah and its adjoining villages and the towns of Doda, Bhaderwah and Kishtwar.
2 http://qr.ae/TUNE2I. Hanan Baba is a quora user from Jammu and Kashmir who provided the above information in his quora answer upon the question 'Is beef eaten in Jammu & Kashmir?' in September 2017.

References

Appadurai, Arjun. 1981. "Gastro-politics in Hindu South Asia". *American Ethnologist.* 8 (3): 494–511.

Census of India. 2001. Office of the Registrar General & Census Commissioner, India.

Chatterji, Roma, and Deepak Mehta. 2007. *Living with Violence: An Anthropology of Events and Everyday Life.* London: Routledge.

Chigateri, Shraddha. 2008. "Glory to the Cow: Cultural Difference and Social Justice in the Food Hierarchy in India". *South Asia.* 31 (1): 10–35.

Datta, Ankur. 2016. "Dealing with Dislocation: Migration, Place and Home Among Displaced Kashmiri Pandits in Jammu and Kashmir". *Contributions to Indian Sociology.* 50 (1): 52–79.

Deshpande, Satish. 2000. "Hegemonic Spatial Strategies: The Nation-Space and Hindu Communalism in Twentieth-Century India", in Partha Chatterjee and Pradeep Jeganathan (eds.), *Community, Gender and Violence.* Subaltern Studies XI, pp. 167–211. New Delhi: Permanent Black, Columbia University Press.

Duschinski, Haley. 2009. "Destiny Effects: Militarization, State Power, and Punitive Containment in Kashmir Valley". *Anthropological Quarterly.* 82 (3): 691–717.

Duschinski, Haley. 2010. "Reproducing Regimes of Impunity". *Cultural Studies.* 24 (1): 110–132.

Economic Survey, (2009–10), Chapter 24(b): 411.

Evans, Alexander. 2002. "A Departure from History: Kashmiri Pandits, 1990–2001". *Contemporary South Asia.* 11 (1): 19–37.

Frøystad, Kathinka. 2005. *Blended Boundaries: Caste, Class and Shifting Faces of 'Hinduness' in a North Indian City.* New Delhi: Oxford University Press.

Gilani, Iftikhar. 2015. "200 Years Later Beef Ban Divides Kashmir on Communal and Regional Lines". *Daily News and Analysis*, October 9.

Hall, S. 2000. "Who Needs 'Identity'?" in S. Hall and P. du Gay (eds.), *Questions of Cultural Identity.* London: SAGE Publications, 1–17.

Jeffery, Patricia, and Roger Jeffery. 1998. "Gender, Community, and the Local State in Bijnor, India", in Patricia Jeffery and Amrita Basu (eds.), *Appropriating Gender: Women's Activism and Politicized Religion in South Asia.* Hoboken: Taylor and Francis, 123–142.

Jeffery, Roger, and Patricia Jeffery. 2005. "Saffron Demography, Common Wisdom, Aspirations and Uneven Governmentalities". *Economic and Political Weekly.* 40 (5): 447–453.

Katz, Max. 2012. "Institutional Communalism in North Indian Classical Music". *Ethnomusicology.* 56 (2): 279–298.

Kazi, Seema. 2010. *Between Democracy & Nation: Gender and Militarisation in Kashmir.* Pakistan: Oxford University Press.

Khan, N. 2016. *Islam, Women, and Violence in Kashmir: Between India and Pakistan.* New York: Palgrave Macmillan.

Lévi-Strauss, Claude. 1966. "The Culinary Triangle". *Partisan Review.* 33: 586–595.

Mahajan, Chakraverti. 2017. *An Anthropological Study Exploring the Contours of Hindu-Muslim Relations in Bhagwah Village of District Doda.* Jammu and Kashmir. PhD dissertation, Panjab University, Chandigarh.

Mathur, S. 2016. *The Human Toll of the Kashmir Conflict: Grief and Courage in a South Asian Borderland.* New York: Palgrave Macmillan.

Mennell, Stephen, Anne Murcott, and Anneke H. Van Otterloo. 1992. *The Sociology of Food: Eating, Diet and Culture.* London: Sage.

Nabi, Daanish. 2015. "If BJP Cares for Kashmiris They Should Remove Beef Ban". *DailyO,* September 19.

Parlow, A. 2011. "Education and Armed Conflict: The Kashmir Insurgency in the Nineties". https://mpra.ub.uni-muenchen.de/38010/5/MPRA_paper_38010.pdf.

Puri, Luv. 2008. *Militancy in Jammu and Kashmir: The Uncovered Face.* New Delhi: Promilla & Co., Publishers in Association with Bibliophile South Asia.

Rai, Mridu. 2004. *Hindu Rules, Muslim Subjects: Islam Rights and History of Kashmir.* New Delhi: Permanent Black.

Rana, Sunaina. 2016. "Society and Culture in Doda: An Outline". *Sheeraza English: A Journal of Jammu and Kashmir Academy of Art, Culture and Languages.* January–March: 50–66.

Rashid, D. A. 2015. "Kashmir Up in Arms Over Beef Ban Order". *Greater Kashmir,* September 11.

Sharma, D. C. 2008. *Glimpses of Kishtwar History.* Kishtwar: Chander Bhaga Publishers.

Tremblay, Reeta. 2018. "Contested Governance, Competing Nationalisms and Disenchanted Publics: Kashmir Beyond Intractability?" in Chitralekha Zutshi (ed.), *Kashmir: History, Politics, Representation.* Cambridge: Cambridge University Press, 220–244.

Ture, Kwame, and Charles V. Hamilton. 1967. *Black Power: The Politics of Liberation.* New York: Vintage Books.

Vajpeyi, Ananya. 2002. "Teaching Against Communalism: Role of Social Science Pedagogy". *Economic and Political Weekly.* 37 (51): 5093–5098.

Warner, Michael. 2002. "Publics and Counterpublics". *Quarterly Journal of Speech.* 88 (4): 413–425.

Zutshi, Chitralekha. 2003. *Languages of Belonging: Islam, Regional Identity and the Making of Kashmir.* New Delhi. Permanent Black.

9

LANGUAGE, RELIGION AND IDENTITY POLITICS IN KASHMIR[1]

Sadaf Munshi

Introduction

The Kashmir conflict has been one of the many intractable conflicts of the modern world. While there are different dimensions of this long-lasting conflict, which make it very complex vis-à-vis prospects of enduring peace, the concept of identity definitions has remained central. The relationship between religious identities and community definitions in Kashmir is visibly expressed through language and literature, which can be studied in the context of different phases of its history broadly divided into: the medieval times (1320–1586), the Mughal era (1586–1752), the Afghan and Sikh rule (1753–1947), and the post-Partition era (1947 onwards). The medieval times marked the emergence of one of the greatest schools of philosophy in Kashmir – Kashmir mysticism or Kashmir *sūfism*. During this period religious identities remained secondary to the common Kashmiri identity. Kashmir was fairly peaceful though in a state of socio-political transition owing to increasing influence of Islam and large-scale conversions. Literary traditions – written and oral – which developed during this period have their origins in two strong cultural sources in terms of form and content, viz., an indigenous Indo-Aryan or 'Sanskritic' tradition, identified with the Hindu community, and a non-native Perso-Arabic tradition, associated with the Muslim community (Handu, 1988, 1295). Despite their separate origins, the two traditions existed simultaneously over a long period of time, starting from the medieval times until late nineteenth and early twentieth century, and gave rise to poetic and literary traditions that cut across communal lines.

During the era of Mughal, Sikh and Dogra rule, however, there were significant shifts in the relationship between religious identities, community definitions, and the nation. The shifts, which resulted from socio-economic and political changes, acted directly on the expression of religious identities. A conflict was generated in the public discourse, which marked the beginning of a strong religious divide in the native Kashmiri community in the post-Partition era culminating into a full-fledged struggle for freedom. Using a socio-historical perspective, this chapter explores the influence of these changes and changing identities on the Kashmiri language vis-à-vis linguistic practices and written literature.

Background

Written literature originating from Kashmir is as old as about 2,500 years, going back to the days of the Old Indo-Aryan or classical Sanskrit. Early authorships include work by the famous grammarian Patañjali (second century BC) – second only to Pāṇini. Patañjali is believed to have composed *Mahabhāṣya* ('great commentary') – a commentary on selected rules of Sanskrit grammar from Pāṇini's treatise, the *Aṣṭadhyāyī*, and the Hindu treatise known as the *Yoga Sūtra* – a collection of 196 *sūtras* (aphorisms or formulas) that constitute the foundational text of *Rāja Yoga* (lit. 'royal yoga' or 'royal union'; also known as *Classical Yoga* and *Aṣṭānga Yoga*) (see Woods, 1914).[2] The next major work originating from Kashmir was Kalhana's *Rājatarangini* 'The River of Kings' – a chronicle in verse form about the kings of the northwestern Indian subcontinent, particularly Kashmir. Based on the kingdoms mentioned in it, *Rājatarangini* is believed to have been composed during the tenth or eleventh century.[3] The work presents the heritage of Kashmir and misrule prevailing in the region during the reign of King Kalasha, the son of King Ananta Deva. Another known cosmopolitan scholar and poet of eleventh-century Kashmir is claimed to be Kṣemendra, a student of the famous Abhinavagupta; about 34 works in Sanskrit are attributed to him which include compositions that are technical, devotional and satirical in content (see Haksar, 2011).

Written traditions in the Kashmiri language itself are attested between the eleventh and thirteenth century, which is roughly the period when Kashmiri had developed as a full-fledged language alongside many other modern Indo-Aryan languages (Munshi, 2006). According to Das (2006, 193), the earliest attested work in the Kashmiri language is *Mahanayakaprakash* 'Light of the supreme lord' by Shitikantha (c. 1250). Plausible arguments can be made in terms of the origin of Kashmiri oral literature in the early Indo-Aryan literary and poetic traditions which were beautifully preserved and passed on from generation to generation without major alterations (Munshi, 2012). Most oral poetry associated with rituals and religious festivals in the case of the Hindu community has been largely unaffected by Perso-Arabic influences. However, the increasing influence of Persian and Arabic languages is observed in the oral poetry by Muslim authors. Nevertheless, both written and oral traditions flourished and existed simultaneously in Kashmir over a long period of time and were influenced and shaped by various factors.

Literary traditions of Kashmir: a historical account

This section reviews the literary traditions of Kashmir from four historically important time periods in terms of the literature that has been produced during these times (see Munshi, 2011). The medieval times or the pre-Mughal era (roughly fourteenth to sixteenth century) is generally known for the emergence of Kashmir *sufism*, with the fourteenth century as the turning point in the evolution of Kashmir's classical and literary traditions.[4] Many poets from Kashmir during this period and also afterwards were greatly influenced by this school of thought. For example, the famous poet Lalleshwari or Lalla Arifa (~1320–1378),[5] more popularly known as "Lal Ded", composed numerous verses and is popular as the first mystic poet of Kashmir. Lal Ded's compositions are celebrated for their deep and sublime nature in terms of a largely spiritual content. An advocate of the yoga philosophy and high moral truths, Lal Ded employed metaphor, riddles and other linguistic devices for her poetic expression, and her unique style of poetry became popularly known as *Lal Vākh* or 'sayings of Lal' (cf. Indo-Aryan or Sanskrit *vākya* 'sentence'). Many of these are composed in a question-answer technique (Koul, 2000, Chapter 8). In addition to *vākh*, Lal Ded also introduced another genre of classical verse in Kashmiri, that is, *vatsun*, which was later employed by Nund Rishi. *Vatsun* (from the Sanskrit *vachana* meaning 'word or speech') is a tradition of versification with varied meter and rhyme schemes, generally composed of a series of quartets in which the fourth line is a refrain (*vooj*) (Koul, 2000).

The next very popular poet after Lal Ded in this period was the famous mystic poet Sheikh Noor-ud-din (1377–1438), popularly known as "Nund Rishi" (lit. 'Nund, the saint'). Like Lal Ded, Nund Rishi's poetry was greatly influenced by Sufi mysticism. Nund also used a specific meter and style of versification representative of his poetry which was termed as *shrukh*. The word shrukh, which literally means '(a) knot' in Kashmiri, is a cognate of the Sanskrit word *shloka* which means 'wise sayings'; the term *shrukh* specifically refers to the genre of poetry introduced by Nund Rishi.

As far as we know Lal Ded and Nund Rishi are the earliest recorded poets of Kashmir whose compositions have survived till the present day, but one can very well argue that the literary tradition extant back then would have been strong enough for them to have been so fluent in their poetry. Both Lal Ded and Nund Rishi composed powerful poetry which has become representative of Kashmiri aesthetics, culture and history. Most of their compositions were orally preserved and collected by scholars much later and became part of the popular folklore. Owing to the unique styles of poetry the two have used, it was easy to identify the authorship of a number of possibly debated verses.[6] Many of their verses became part of everyday life in Kashmir in the form of conversational genres such as proverbs and idiomatic expressions.

Lal Ded and Nund Rishi, as Zutshi (2004, 19) maintains, "invariably make their appearance divorced from the historical context". The duo are often attributed with having given substance to (what later became popular as) the notion of *Kashmiriyat* through their poetry which "formed the cultural repertoire" of Kashmiris for generations (Zutshi, 2004; also see Puri, 1995; Kachru, 2003; Habibullah, 2008).[7] Lal Ded's poetry, characterized by a sense of fluidity of religious boundaries, is perceived as a manifestation of the Kashmiri ethos of religious tolerance. That she had

emerged as a secular spiritual person who did not believe in the symbolic representations of faith and ritual practice is exemplified in the following Lal *vākh*:

> (1) *diva vaṭā divur vaṭā*
> *pyeṭha bona čhuy ikavaṭā*
> *puuz kas karakh haṭha baṭā*
> *kar manas ta pavanas sangaṭhā*

> 'The idol and the temple are but stone
> The above and the below are one
> Who will you worship, O stubborn Brahmin?
> Unite your mind and your breath (spirit) into one'[8]

Like Lal Ded, Nund Rishi, who is claimed to be the founder of what is termed the
'Rishi Movement' or 'Rishi Order' in Kashmir, is said to have practiced a form of
Islam that did not observe strong religious boundaries (Koul, 2000; Zutshi, 2004).
Ironically, however, intense debate and controversy followed around the question
of the religious affiliations of both Lal Ded and Nund Rishi. For example, Hindus
claim that Lal Ded was a Shaivite member of their community but many Muslim
scholars argue that she had accepted Islam in her later years and sometimes refer to
her by the Muslim name 'Lalla Arifa'. A number of vākhs have been attributed to
Lal Ded which some critics argue to be spurious based on the linguistic and historical evidence. One such example is the following extremely very popular vākh
which some sceptics argue may not be hers:[9]

> (2) *šiv čhuy thali-thali rav zān*
> *mav zān hyond tay musalmān*
> *truk hay čhukh ta panun pān parzān*
> *ada čhey sāhibas zə̄ni zān*

> 'Shiva abides in all that is, everywhere
> Do not discriminate between a Hindu and a Muslim
> If you are wise, understand your Self
> Then, is your knowledge of the Lord true'

Notice the use of the words *Hyond* for 'Hindu' and *Sāhib* for 'Lord' in this verse.
Some critics claim that the use of both of these words became popular much later
in time (Sualeh Keen, p.c.). The word *Hyond* is a nativized Kashmiri derivation of
the Indo-Aryan *Hindu* which has a long etymological history, originating from
Sanskrit *Sindhu* that historically designated a geographical area situated by the Indus
River. Its use to designate the people of a particular religious faith (Hindus) is possibly a later development, most likely during the Mughal period.

Just like Lal Ded, both Kashmiri Hindus and Kashmiri Muslims have claimed
Nund Rishi as their spiritual guide. Thus, for Hindus, Nund Rishi is *Sahajanand*,

'one who attained ultimate truth'. However, Muslims sometimes refer to him as the *Koshur Qoran* (Kashmiri Quran) because the major theme in his poetry is Islam, Qur'anic verses and *Hadīth* (Islamic traditions). In fact, Sheikh Noor-ud-Din is perceived as the maker of what Muhammad Ishaq Khan terms "the Kashmiri Muslim identity" (Khan, 1994, 95; quoted from Zutshi, 2004, 23). Consider the following verse for illustration:

> (3) *poz dapān pan zan tshaṭakh*
> *apuz dapān lagī ras*
> *muhammad trōvith iblīs raṭakh*
> *khodōy dyutuy ta khaṭakh kas*

> 'You tremble while speaking the truth
> But take enjoyment in the falsehood
> You forsake Muhammad and follow the Satan –
> God is your Giver, who do you hide the truth from?'

Although Shaikh Noor-ud-Din has had a significant impact on Kashmiri Islamic discourse, his poetry also provided a "ready vehicle for Kashmiri nationalists" (Zutshi, 2004, 19–23). During the lifetime of Lal Ded and Nund Rishi, Kashmir witnessed a gradual cultural and religious transformation with the advent of Islam which left a great impression on their minds as reflected in their poetic compositions. Lal Ded and, in particular, Nund Rishi lived in a time period which marked what Sheldon Pollock (1998) refers to as 'vernacularization' – a period in the early centuries of the second millennium that resulted in the creation of 'new regional worlds' or regional cultures (ibid.). A significant role in the development of these regional cultures, or identities, was played by the emergence of regional or local languages, as opposed to languages of dominance, such as Persian in this context.

Although Lal Ded and Nund Rishi's poetry was in a dialect spoken by common Kashmiris, there are pronounced differences in the choice of their lexicon. Thus, there is a predominance of Sanskritized vocabulary in Lal Ded's poetry as opposed to that of Nund Rishi's verses which are rich in Persian and Arabic loanwords. Further note that although classical Persian had been introduced as the language of the court and had become the dominant literary language among the elites during this time, the use of Sanskrit was still very common among the Hindu literary class. One of the important compositions in Sanskrit during the fifteenth century was *Dvitīyā Rājataranginī* (second *Rājataranginī*) by Jonaraja, a historian and Sanskrit poet. It was a continuation of Kalhana's *Rājataranginī* down to the period of Zain-ul-Abidin (1423–1474), which, however, could not be completed owing to the death of Jonaraja. The work was later taken up as *Tritīyā Rājataranginī* (third *Rājataranginī*) by Śrīvara (Jonaraja's pupil) covering the period 1459–1486 (see Majumdar, 2006, 466).[10]

The Mughal era (1586–1758) in Kashmir was a time of great changes in the literary languages and is known for the introduction of Persian and Urdu languages.

The advent of the Mughals, which eventually resulted in the incorporation of Kashmir Valley into Mughal India after Chak rule (~1555–1586; see Hassan, 1959, 158, Bamzai, 2007, 391), marked what has been called a threat to Kashmiri nationalism (see Zutshi, 2004, 29). This period also marked the beginning of Hindu–Muslim and Shia–Sunni factionalism in Kashmir (Zutshi, 2004). On the linguistic front, Persian became the primary language of literary expression. As a result of linguistic, cultural, and religious contact many poetic and literary genres emerged, such as the *ghazal, qasida, masnavi, na'at*, and *marsiya*.[11] It was also during the Mughal period that Urdu emerged as the language of the Muslim elite throughout colonial India and it also found its way into Kashmir. The beauty of Kashmir became immortalized in the numerous *masnavis* (narrative poems). Some very significant compositions in Persian language in the field of Kashmiri historiography also came out in this period. For example, the translation of *Rājataraṅginī* which was ordered by Akbar and assigned to Mulla Ahmad Shahabadi, and the detailed histories of Kashmir by Malik Haider and Narayan Koul Aziz (Zutshi, 2004, 33). In the domain of oral traditions, a new Kashmiri poetic genre came to existence during this period, that is, *lōl*. Lōl is a short lyrical love poem, about six to 10 lines in length, expressing a single mood. The genre was introduced by the famous Habba Khatoon (or 'Zoon' in her earlier days), a sixteenth-century Muslim poet from Kashmir who became the last queen of Kashmir after marrying Yusuf Shah Chak. Lōl poetry became quite popular in Kashmir after Habba Khatoon.

The next phase in the history of Kashmir was that of the Afghans (1753–1819) followed by the Sikh and Dogra rule (1819–1947). Both Afghan and Sikh/Dogra rule were generally perceived as tyrannical and oppressive. The Afghan rule saw the re-emergence of the regional identity and the sense of belonging. Poetry became the primary means of expression of opposition to the Afghan rulers and emergence of regionalism/nationalism both among Muslims and Hindus. Interestingly, it was during the Afghan rule that Kashmiri Pandits became proficient in the Persian language. Noted among some such literary people was Dayaram Kachru (1743–1811) belonging to a family "known for its scholarship in Persian and Sanskrit" (Zutshi, 2004, 36). His most important contributions in Persian are: a translation of Bhagvadgita, and *Masnavi-e-Kashmir* (written in praise of his homeland while in Kabul). Dayaram also introduced Hindu devotional themes to Persian poetry (Zutshi, 2004, 36).

The Afghan period was followed by the Sikh rule which began in 1819. The Sikh rule established a particularly 'Hindu tone', setting the stage for the Dogra dynasty which began ruling Kashmir in 1846. As maintained by Zutshi (2004), a deep sense of regional identification 'pervaded Kashmiri discourse in this period'. Some examples of powerful nationalistic writings during this period, interestingly again in Persian, were Shahabadi's *Shahr-e-Ashoob* (city of tumult), *Babuj Nama* (story of injustice), *Na-pursan Nama* (story of anarchy/lawlessness) – stories cloaked in fictionalized characters to avoid confrontation or persecution (Zutshi, 2004, 41). Note that, in the period prior to 1850, the Muslim religious identity, though quite prominent in Kashmir, was closely enmeshed in the regional or territorial identity, as revealed by terms such as *mulk-i-Kashmir* 'the Kashmiri nation' or 'the nation of Kashmir' (Jalal, 2000; Zutshi, 2004, 43). It was during the Dogra period (1846–1947) that Kashmir witnessed the beginning of a great political transition in terms of expression of religious and regional identities; the Dogra rule in Kashmir was also the beginning of a stark socio-political divide on religious lines. Despite the political transition and the emergence of the Persian literary tradition, oral literature in Kashmiri continued to exist in the form of powerful poetic expressions by poets of the sufi cult such as Sočh Kral (1782–1854), Shamas Faqir (1843–1901), and Samad Mir (~1893–1956) which were preserved and passed on from generation to generation until the modern times.

Persian was replaced as the court language in 1889 by Urdu – which emerged as the language of the Muslim political elite of India. However, in terms of education, the indigenous tradition, firmly rooted in the community, caste and religion, was allowed to continue. Thus, basic religious and mathematical education was offered in Sanskrit and Persian/Arabic by Pandits and Molvis (Hindu and Muslim clerics, respectively) to 'local Hindu and Muslim boys in *pathshalas* and *madrasas*'[12] – institutions closely linked with temples and mosques which run through community support. Other local schools were run by Pandits in their houses where general education was still provided in Persian. By the early twentieth century, a state educational bureaucracy was in place where the school curricula were based on the model of the Punjab University. Thus, the Kashmiri language and its promotion took a backseat in the context of all educational, administrative as well as political matters (Zutshi, 2004). As a consequence, the language lost its prestige among the educated and the elite class who looked forward to Urdu as the primary language of literary and political expression.

A strong connection between education, religious affiliations and employment had already grown by the 1930s with Muslims of Kashmir seeking a separate political category vis-à-vis social and cultural factors. A plan to convert the Jammu and Kashmir state from an absolute monarchy to a constitutional democracy was put in place in the form of 'Naya Kashmir' (New Kashmir) – a memorandum submitted to Maharaja Hari Singh (the then Dogra ruler of Jammu and Kashmir) by Sheikh Muhammad Abdullah, the leader of Kashmir's leading political party the Muslim Conference (which later became the National Conference) in 1944.[13]

The Dogra rule in Kashmir ended with the partition of British India in 1947 and marked the beginning of a new political era characterized by the further consolidation of the 'Kashmiri Muslim' identity (as opposed to the 'Kashmiri' identity).

In the colonial and the post-colonial era, Urdu continued to serve as the language of the Muslim elites. After the Partition, it became the national language and *lingua franca* of Pakistan – a country with which many Kashmiri Muslims were emotionally attached. The language did extremely well in terms of attracting social prestige in Kashmir, a Muslim-dominated region. Besides the emergence of a strong language ideology where the Kashmiri language came to be perceived as less prestigious than the politically dominant Urdu, a closer look at the social and political developments in Kashmir reveals a strong influence on linguistic, ethnic, cultural, and religious identities and affiliations. Kashmiri language and literature suffered immensely at the hands of the social and political elites who were mainly from in and around Srinagar, which became the centre for all social and political activity. There were deliberate attempts even in the academia to sideline the progressive stalwarts of Kashmiri literature, such as Abdul Ahad Azad (1903–1948), Dina Nath Nadim (1916–1988), Ghulam Rasool Nazki (1910–1998), and Noor Muhammad Roshan (1919–1995). Even though many of these poets also wrote in Urdu, Kashmiri was the primary medium of expression for their satirical poetry, which was dominated by political themes while Urdu was mainly used for writing poetry for a broader audience in genres such as *ghazal* and *nazam*. Ironically, current anthologies exclude some of their classic poems, which are progressive in nature or theme. A few examples of such progressive poetry are given here for illustration:[14]

(4) Poetry by progressive modern Kashmiri poets
a. *fandbāzav bāzigārav bāz panun zyūn*
    hāvun tse thovhai kufur tai islām vanay kyah
'Conmen and tricksters have won their game,
Leaving you to fight over Kufr and Islam, what to say!'
(Abdul Ahad Azad)

b. *əmis pānas ziyāfəts jān polāvah khyon kabābah čhuy*
me dopnam māli hyas kərizi pato ākhar hisābah čhuy
rangārang khyath ta čyath pānas nasīhath jān kyah kərnam
tse čhey rahmat yi gurbat phāku rōzun bọ savābah čhuy
'For himself, he has delicacies like kebobs and pilaf
To me he says, "O friend, be afraid of the final reckoning"
Relishing on colourful dishes, he gave me a good advice:
"Blessed you are with poverty; fasting is a great virtue"'
(Ghulam Rasool Nazki)

c. *rabūdah hyuh gomut iblīs phērān ōs asmānas*
zamīn trāvith khotukh kava yōr prutshus yeli zāti rahmānan
araz kornas ilāhi čhapni ās yot kāmpanyōmut čhus
me sōruy kāri šetāni muhith nyūmut čhu insānan
'Dumbstruck, Satan was wandering in the sky aimlessly
When God asked, "Why have you come here leaving the earth?"
Satan pleaded, "I have come to seek shelter, I am terrified
Nothing is left for me as humans have robbed me off my devilry"'
(Noor Mohammad Roshan)

Kashmiri was also the primary mode of expression for a number of revolutionary poets who wrote many of their compositions using their native language. For example, following the Partition in 1947, Ghulam Ahmad Mahjoor (1885–1952) played a key role in opposing the Tribal invasions through his poetic compositions inspiring people to rise against the perpetrators in defending their land. Some of his very popular compositions include *valo hā bāgvāno* ('Come, O Gardener') and *āzōdī* ('freedom') which reflect his optimism for the future of his people in Naya Kashmir (New Kashmir) and his anguish at the state of affairs of the underprivileged and downtrodden (Sualeh Keen, p.c.). Consider these for illustration:

(5) Poetry by Ghulam Ahmad Mahjoor[15]
a. Excerpt from *Valo hā bāgvāno* 'Come, O Gardener':
valo hā bāgvāno navbahāruk šān pōdā kar
pholan gul gath karan bulbul tithī sāmān pōdā kar
Come, O gardener, create the glory of a new spring
That flowers bloom and bulbuls whirl, create such means

b. Excerpt from *āzōdi* 'freedom':
sanā sōrī pariv sānyan garan tsāyi āzōdī
syaṭha yōtskōly asi kun jalva hāvan āyi āzōdī
Let us all offer thanks for to our homes visits Freedom
After a long time, a rare glimpse towards us gives Freedom

yi āzōdī čhi trāvān magribas kun rahmatuk bārān
karān sōnis zamīnas pyaṭh tsharey gagrāyi āzōdī
This Freedom showers the rain of blessings on the West
On our soil, just empty thunderstorms are offered by Freedom

garībī muphlisī bebūj nāpursān zabān bandi
amē rutsi trāyi asi pyaṭh āyi trāvān sāyi āzōdī
'Poverty, destitution, liability, anarchy, and repression
Coming along with these blessings, a shadow on us casts Freedom'

yi āzōdī čhi sorgič hūr phēryā khāna path khānay
fakat kēntsan garan andar čhi mārān grāyi āzōdī
A *houri* from the heaven, Freedom will not visit door-to-door
Only in a select few homes does merrily dance Freedom

Besides written poetry in Kashmiri, a powerful means of social and political expression was offered by oral traditions, such as *Ladi Shah*. Ladi Shah is a particular variety of satirical ballads, or narrative songs which became a popular source of public entertainment in Kashmir until as late as the 1980s and 1990s. A characteristic feature of *ladi shah* songs is the use of a poetic formula and a fixed melody. During the performance the folk entertainer, *ladi shah*, pulls the rings on the *dehra* or *chumta* and makes witty comments in the form of poetic criticism on important social and political issues. The *dehra* or *chumta* is a tong-shaped musical instrument made of iron with copper rings in it. The topics or themes may vary and could be about current affairs, governance issues, social and political happenings, and so forth. Consider examples in (6) and (7) for illustration:

(6). Excerpt from an old Ladi Shah song with one of the most common
   refrains *Ladi-shah ladi-shah daari kin' pyav*

lại-shah lại-shah dāri kin' pyav
pyevōniy pyevōniy hāptan khyav
ōra āv drāga dyav hāvān partav
yora gayi brōr vungān kornas myav
Ladi Shah, Ladi Shah fell off the window.
And right then a grizzly bear ate him
The inflation ghost came hoisting (his) flag
He encountered the cat who meowed

(Author unknown; Dalip Langoo, p.c.)

(7). Excerpt from another old *Ladi Shah* song which became popular when
   the airplane first arrived in Kashmir

havōyi jahāz āv mulk-i-kashmīr
yimav vučh timav kor tōba-takhsīr
The airplane has come to Kashmir
Whoever saw it was flabbergasted

Jamālas Kamālas nas kǝmy vǝṭ
yimav vučh timav kor tōba-takhsīr
Who pinched Jamal and Kamal's nose?
Whoever saw it was flabbergasted

Zūni von rājas tūfan chhu yīrān
yimav vučh timav kor tōba-takhsīr
Zooni told Raja that a storm was coming
Whoever saw it was flabbergasted

gānṭi hish naba p'eth' grayi mārān
yimav vučh timav kor tōba-takhsīr
It flies in the sky like a kite
Whoever saw it was flabbergasted

shōr čhus yūtčh zan kan čīrān
yimav vučh timav kor tōba-takhsīr
Its loud noise pierces through the ears
Whoever saw it was flabbergasted

(Author unknown; Aijaz Kirmani, p.c.)

Religious identities in conflict: impact on language

Modern Kashmiri, as it is spoken today, is characterized by significant variation in terms of regional, social as well as communal divisions. There are many regional varieties and conspicuous differences between urban and rural Kashmiri in terms of accent, phonology and lexicon. According to the native speakers, rural Kashmiri has preserved many archaic forms not used in urban speech – this is the prevalent generalization but it has to be backed up with more systematic dialectal work. There are also differences between Muslim and Hindu Kashmiri (see Kachru, 1969). The differences are similar to those observed between Hindi and Urdu, which, linguistically speaking, are varieties of a single language for all purposes except for some vocabulary and use of orthography. Thus, while Kashmiri Hindus (Pandits) use more of an indigenous and Sanskrit-based vocabulary (see Kachru (n.d.), Muslim Kashmiri is characterized by the use of more Persian and Arabic loanwords. Note that these distinctions are more evident among the literate as opposed to the illiterate Kashmiris. Further, while Hindus prefer to use the Nāgri-based alphabet (which is also used for writing 'Hindi'), Muslims use a modification of the Perso-Arabic (Nastāliq) writing system. (The latter is also used for writing Urdu. More on the question of orthography in the following section.) The two varieties are often termed as 'Sanskritized' and 'Persianized' varieties of Kashmiri by some scholars (see Kachru, 2003). Consider examples in (8) illustrating some lexical difference between Hindu and Muslim varieties of Kashmiri termed as Bata Koshur (BK) and Musalman Koshur (MK) respectively:

(8) Lexical differences between 'Hindu' (Bata) and 'Muslim' Kashmiri (Koshur):

Bata Koshur	Musalman Koshur	Gloss
poyn, pa~	āb	'water'
rūn	khāndār	'husband'
Kruhun	siyah, kruhun	'black'
Wozul	wozul, sorakh	'red'
əčh	češmi, əčh	'eyes'
krūṭh	muškil	'difficult'
āsh	ummīd/womēd	'expectation'
ačhar/akšar	Haruf	'alphabet'

In any language, proper nouns and place names constitute an important part of the vocabulary. Selection of proper nouns and place names can be based on various factors – cultural, religious, historical or political. Many studies have shown that nationhood and religious affiliations are often asserted through the choice of proper names (cf. Kaul, 1982; Koul, 1995; Steedly, 1996; Chelliah, 2005). In Kashmir, Hindu and Muslim religious affiliations are expressed through the choice of personal names, especially among the socially upper and educated classes. Thus,

Muslim names as a rule are almost always either Persian-based or Arabic-based, and Hindu names are mostly Sanskrit-based, thus, asserting their 'Muslim' and 'Hindu' religious affiliations. This is also a trend generally observed in the rest of India. Consider examples in (9):

(9)   Variation in Personal Names

      a. Popular Arabic and Persian-based ("Muslim") names

      Male names: Ahmed, Akbar, Ali, Bilal, Hassan, Hyder, Mohammad, Salim, Ghulam Nabi, Ghulam Hassan

      Female names: Asma, Amina, Afreen, Khadeejeh, Bilquees, Hajirah, Maryam, Saba, Sakina, Sadaf

      b. Popular Sanskrit-based ("Hindu") names

      Male names: Avinash, Aditya, Aalok, Agni, Ajay, Bhushan, Shiva, Prateek

      Female names: Komila, Manika, Shruti, Preeti, Pushpa, Vidya, Meera, Anamika

Interestingly, such distinctions are less prevalent among the lower social classes who use more Kashmiri-based (or Kashmiri-sounding) names; this is especially true in case of female names. Consider examples in (10):

(10) Popular Kashmiri-based names

      Female names: *Zoon* 'moon', *Heemal* (name of a flower), *Anzal* (palm of hand), *Sondar* 'beauty', *Yambirzal* 'daffodil', *Arinimaal* (name of a flower), *Kong* (saffron), *Mokhta* (pearl), *Kukil* (koel/cuckoo), *Posha* (flower), *Haer* (sparrow), *Ael* (cardamom).

      Male names: *Pamposh* (lotus flower), *Gaasha* (term of endearment for males; lit. 'light'), *Jaana*

Like personal names, the choice of place names also points to the socio-political affiliations of a people. The choice of place names has often served as a point of contention and controversy between the Hindus and the Muslims of Kashmir. Thus, while Hindus generally prefer (older and) indigenous Indo-Aryan or Sanskrit-based place names, Arabic or Persian based names are generally used by the Muslims. In fact, as a general rule nowadays, most newly coined place names in Kashmir are either Arabic or Persian in origin, pointing to the role of the Muslim majority in making such decisions.[16] Consider examples in (11):

(11) Variation in Place Names

      a. Indigenous (Indo-Aryan/Kashmiri) versus Persian/Urdu/Arabic names

      Anantnag (Skt. '(place of) numerous water springs') ~ *Islamabad* 'the place of Islam/Muslims (later also the name of the Pakistani capital city)

      Shankaracharya pahaad or *Gopadri* ~ (Persian/Urdu) *Koh-i-Sulaiman* 'the mountain of Solomon' or (its Kashmiri translation) *Sulaiman Tyung*

> (*Shankaracharya* is the name of a Hindu temple situated on what is known among Hindus as the *Gopadri* hill)
>
> b. New place names asserting Muslim identity
>
> *Mominabad* ('the place of Momins/fidels'), *Daulatabad* ('the place of the riches'), *Shahr-e-Khās* ('downtown Srinagar') and so on.

While place names in (11b) are more recent in origin, those in (11a) existed prior to the era of the post-1989 conflict. A significant amount of controversy and debate revolves around some of the place names which are at times wrongly attributed to the post-1989 'Islamization efforts'. For example, the term 'Islamabad', the name given to a town within a district (Anantnag) and historically named after a certain governor of the region (Islam Shah), is often mistaken to be the result of a deliberate attempt to replace the Sanskrit-based name 'Anantnag' with the Persian/Arabic based name 'Islamabad' (which could literally mean 'the place of Islam'), a name often (wrongly) associated with the religion 'Islam' and/or with the capital of Pakistan (i.e., Islamabad) which in fact has a different history. Thus, the term 'Islamabad' (i.e. a town within a larger district, Anantnag) is often confused with 'Anantnag' and the two are sometimes used interchangeably.[17] A similar history is also shared by *Shankaracharya* versus *Takht-i-Sulaiman* (*Sulaiman Tyung*; literally 'the throne of Solomon'), names given to the site of an existing temple (i.e., the Shankaracharya temple) built on the summit of a mountain in Srinagar. The site is argued to have initially been named 'Gopadri' dating back to a much earlier period when it used to be the site for a Buddhist monument. (Note that 'Gopadri' is also a preferred term among the Hindus as opposed to 'Sulaiman Tyung' which is popular among Muslims.)

As maintained earlier, the end of Dogra rule in Kashmir coincided with the partition of British India in 1947. A new political era began in Kashmir which was marked by further consolidation of the Kashmiri Muslim identity that eventually culminated into a full-fledged armed struggle for independence from the Indian dominion in the 1990s. In the ongoing separatist movement (popularly known as the 'struggle for freedom' or the movement for 'self-determination') which started in 1989, the role of Kashmiri linguistic identity has been minimal in most of the political discourse. Urdu not only served as the main language of political expression, it was also the language of solidarity with the neighbouring Pakistan with which the Kashmiri Muslims were emotionally and to a great extent politically affiliated. Changes in the social and political scenario of Kashmir were reflected in the use of signs, slogans and terminology symbolic of the Muslim political identity. Thus, a large number of Persian-, Arabic- and Urdu-based words and phrases became a part of the political repertoire. Consider (12) for illustration:

(12) Use of Persian/Urdu/Arabic in political slogans

> Ur. *hum kyā čāhate? Azādi!*
>
> 'What do we want? *Azādi* (freedom)'

Ur. *yahān kya čalega?* Per. *nizām-e-mustafa!*
'What will prevail here? The Law of Mustafa!'
Ur. *azādi kā matlab kyaa?* Ar. *Laa-ilaha illallah!*
'What does *azādi* (freedom) mean? There is no God but Allah'

The choice of language not only contributes as a means of broader communication (with Urdu functioning as a *lingua franca* as opposed to Kashmiri) but also asserts a certain political ideology, which is Muslims as opposed to Hindus (using Urdu as opposed to Hindi). This can be compared with the use of highly Sanskritized Hindi in the larger Indian context in slogans such as *Jai Sri Ram* ('Hail Lord Rama') and *har har Mahadev* ('Everyone is Lord Shiva') by advocates of Hindutva calling for the creation of a "Hindu Rashtra" ('Hindu nation').

The question of orthography

For any language spoken by groups divided by political ideology, the question of orthography can be a highly contentious topic (see Chelliah, 2008). Historically, Kashmiri was written in the Shārada script, an ancient indigenous character set of Kashmiri based on the Brahmic family of scripts, which developed around the tenth century. Its use was, however, highly restricted to the Hindu priestly class. Nowadays only a handful of Hindu priests use it for writing *Zātuk* 'horoscope'. The officially recognized script currently in use is a modification of the Perso-Arabic or Nastālīq script. This, however, is more popular among the Muslims (note: Nastālīq was originally introduced in the pre-colonial times during the Muslim rule when literacy began to spread), while Hindus use a modified Devanāgari script

As noted earlier, the two writing systems, viz. Nastālīq and Devanāgari, were originally used for Urdu and Hindi (respectively). Urdu and Hindi, in technical linguistic terms, refer to the two standardized varieties of what is essentially one single language, sometimes referred to as 'Hindustani' (which, historically, refers to *Hindvi* or *Rekhta*) in the literature, but, which are ironically associated with the Muslim and Hindu communities (respectively). The differences between spoken Hindi and Urdu are largely ideological and perceived except for the choice of borrowed vocabulary (while Hindi is more Sanskritized, Urdu is Persianized/Arabicized) rather than linguistic or grammatical in that colloquial Hindi and Urdu are indistinguishable for all practical purposes other than the script (Nunley et al., 1999; Kachru, 2006).

Besides Nastālīq and Devanāgari, other writing systems, such as, Tākri and Roman scripts, have also been employed in the past in writing Kashmiri but these have failed to gain recognition.[18] For example, a Roman-based alphabet for Kashmiri was proposed by Raina (1972) but this has not gained much popularity.

As far as the present-day Kashmiri is concerned, the question of a common, standardized writing system continues as an ongoing debate and a great challenge in attempts towards the promotion of native language literacy among resident and non-resident Kashmiris. In the wake of the political developments along the lines of religion which also witnessed a mass migration ('exodus') of the Kashmiri Pandit community from Kashmir Valley in the early 1990s, the division has been more profoundly expressed and maintained through the continuous and simultaneous use of the two competing writing systems, Nastālīq by the Muslim majority and Devanāgari by the Hindu minority. Furthermore, any organized efforts towards the promotion and revitalization of the Kashmiri language fall into the communal trap with no broad consensus and each community pursuing these efforts separately from each other. Thus, *Adabi Markaz Kamraz* (AMK) is a Kashmir-based federation of various literary and cultural organizations predominantly (but not exclusively) led by Muslims which aims to promote Kashmiri language and culture. However, the use of terminology chosen by the organization is often heavily Persian- or Arabic-based. For example, the term *shahr-i-khās* 'the city centre' was proposed for what has been popularly known as 'Downtown (Srinagar)'.[19] The title of the confederation itself as well as its constituent organizations contain heavy use of Perso-Arabic words (Per. *adabi* 'literary' and *markaz* 'center'). This use of new terminology in Kashmiri seems to follow the same borrowing pattern as that in Urdu, the state official language of Jammu and Kashmir.[20] Like AMK, there is a United States-based organization led by expatriate Kashmiri Pandits (Hindus), the *Kashmir Overseas Association*, which, among other things, aims to protect, preserve and promote Kashmiri (Pandit) ethnic and socio-cultural heritage.

Recently, a number of people from the displaced Hindu community have proposed attempts to revive the practically dead Shāradā script, invoking 'stronger links' and therefore, stronger claims to the homeland or *māj Kashir* (mother Kashmir) by referring back to a period prior to the Islamic era in Kashmir. The advocacy for the revival of Shāradā, nowadays being propagated through different media including the social networking site Facebook, primarily comes from the members of a politically oriented group, *Panun Kashmir*, known for its objective to fight for a separate homeland (*Panun Kashmir* or 'our' [own] Kashmir) within Kashmir for the displaced Kashmiri Pandit community.[21]

Conclusion

In an essay published in Wright (1998, 2), Dan Smith argues that "conflict brings us inexorably to nationalism, then to identity and thus to language". As maintained by Paul Chilton in another essay of the same publication, social scientists, and especially peace researchers, are often hesitant in investigating the role of language in conflict (Wright, 1998, 2). While language is unlikely to play a central role in situations of political conflict, forms of language and communication not only inform but also constitute political institutions and ideologies. Since the 1930s the so-called notion of *Kashmiriyat* had come to be perceived as an outcome of a continued tradition of regional identity and nationalism, which, according to Rai (2004), was beyond the purview of religious divide. It was founded on "the historical survival of what is perceived as a more salient legacy of cultural harmony" (Rai, 2004, 224). To this cultural harmony, let me emphasize, language is the central and unifying factor.

Language serves both as a reflection of social change and strife as well as a catalyst towards peace and harmony. In the wake of any reconciliation efforts between the estranged Kashmiri Hindu and Muslim communities, it seems to me the concept of Kashmiriyat, which had been more or less dormant for a long period of time, is often resurrected by Kashmiris across community lines. A number of efforts – both systematic and/or organizational as well as sporadic or individual – are, at various fronts, being propagated by a new generation of young and progressive Kashmiris, which aim at the reconciliation of the two communities, many of which are currently living away from the homeland. The internet, especially the social networking site Facebook, has offered a very powerful medium in the past few years to express shared cultural values and practices and also to bridge distances through the common thread of language between Kashmiris living in and outside of Kashmir.

A number of Facebook groups with memberships in the thousands have emerged which provide a platform for an increasing and renewed interest in the Kashmiri culture and the ethnic Kashmiri identity expressed through the use of the Kashmiri language which is reinforced by a strong advocacy for the promotion of the Kashmiri language, literature and conversational genres. One of the many challenges facing the young reformist Kashmiris wanting to connect (or reconnect) with their homeland and with other fellow ethnic Kashmiris across the world, and advocating the use and promotion of Kashmiri language, again, is the question of orthography. Because the Devanāgari and the Arabic-based writing systems are largely associated with communal divisions, and also because a majority of these youths are not literate in either of these (i.e., modified Devanāgari and Perso-Arabic writing systems), there is a strongly increasing and renewed demand for a Roman-based writing system, especially among the youth and more so among the Kashmiri diaspora. It will be interesting to see what direction these efforts take and how effective they will be; in other words, what will be the future of the Kashmiri language and its literary traditions in the larger political context of the divided identities and ideologies.

Recall that similar ideological divides, as observed in Kashmiri vis-à-vis language and linguistic practices, are also observed in some other cases, such as the larger context of the Hindu–Muslim linguistic divide in the Indian subcontinent and the subsequent controversies over Hindi and Urdu. It will be interesting to compare and analyze the similarities and the differences in these situations in order to better understand the influence of various identical factors in different contexts – a topic for future investigation. It will also be interesting to see how the language factor will play into the notion of (primarily) religion-based nationalism vis-à-vis efforts towards reconciliation.

Notes

1 I am grateful to Shobhana Chelliah and Sualeh Keen for providing useful input on this chapter.
2 According to Woods, the identity of Patañjali, the author of the *Sūtras*, and Patanjali, the author of the *Mahabhāshya* is yet to be proved. The opinion in India and in the West about the two being the same person has not been traced to a definite period (see Woods, 1914, xiii).

3　See 'Rājatarangini'. *Encyclopædia Britannica*. Encyclopædia Britannica Online. Encyclopædia Britannica Inc., 2011. Web. 17 December 2011.
4　An important composition of the medieval times was *Baharistan-e-Shahi* – a chronicle of medieval Kashmir written in the Persian language by an anonymous author (see Pandita, 1988).
5　Note that some critics have disputed the authenticity of the dates for Lal Ded's birth or death.
6　Some Lal *vākhs* are found in Shāradā script in old manuscripts (cf. Parimoo, 1978, 1)
7　Kachru (2003, 4) describes *Kashmiriyat* (Kashmiriness) as "an elusive term evoking a rich pluralistic literary, cultural and aesthetic tradition of the Pandits and Muslims of the Valley". The term is actually claimed to have been coined quite recently by a writer and political activist, Prem Nath Bazaz "to project a common cultural heritage among Kashmiri Muslims and Hindus" (Habibullah, 2008, 24). It was arguably coined in analogy with another similar term, *Punjabiyat* (Punjabiness), which was first used by Kuldip Nayyar in the 1980s with reference to "some presumed essentials of the Punjabi character that overrode sectarian hatred". The term *Kashmiriyat* is claimed to have emanated from the same sources in Delhi with a similar scope of meaning and presumed to describe "some essential characteristics of Kashmiris that overrode communal separatism to bind Muslims and Pandits" (Birinder R Singh, p.c.). Its use became popular in the post-1989 era.
8　All translations by the author, unless stated otherwise.
9　Another example cited in this context by Zutshi (2004, 22, quoted from Inayatullah [n.d.]) is the following translation of a similar verse likely attributed to Lal Ded in error:

> I said la *ilaha ilallah*
> I destroyed my Self in it
> I left my own entity and caught Him who is all-encompassing
> ... Lalla then found God
> I went to look for Shiva
> I saw Shiva and Shaitan together
> Then I saw the devil on the stage
> I was surprised at that moment
> I adore Shiva and Shiva's house
> When I die, what then?

10　Koul (2000, Chapter 8) talks about the introduction of a new genre to the literary traditions of Kashmir, that is, narrative verse, and cites two compositions – *bhānasurkatha* (mid-fifteenth century) and *such-dukha carit* (c. 1476), which are apparently also in the Sanskrit language.
11　*Ghazal, Masnavi* and *Marsiya* are poetic genres which originated in the Persian literary tradition and were later adopted in Urdu and other languages. *Ghazal* is a love poem consisting of a fixed metrical pattern, rhyming couplets and a refrain. *Masnavi* consists of a long narrative poem with rhyming couplets of profound spiritual meaning. The tradition is claimed to have started with the great *masnavi* of Jalal-ud-Din Rumi which consisted of 25,000 rhyming couplets. *Marsiya* is an elegiac poem commemorating the martyrdom of Imam Hussein (the third of the 12 Imams – divine spiritual leaders) and his companions in Karbala. *Qasīda* (a lyrical poem) and Na'at (written in praise of Prophet Muhammed) are Arabic in origin (See Bailey, 1979).
12　*Pathshala* and *madrasa* mean 'school' in Sanskrit and Persian respectively.
13　See https://en.wikipedia.org/wiki/Naya_Kashmir (last date of access: February 6, 2020); also see Taseer (1973) which gives an account of events in Kashmir from 1932 to 1946 as seen by a local journalist.
14　*Progressive Writers' Movement* was a progressive literary movement, originally in the Urdu language, in the pre-partition British India, consisting of a number of writers around the world (see Jafri, n.d.).

15 See Raina (1989) for poetry by Mehjoor.
16 Note that there are only a small number of Kashmiri Pandits left in the Kashmir Valley after the 1990 mass exodus of the minority community (see Habibullah, 2008).
17 Note that the town was referred to as 'Islamabad' by Sister Nivedita in 1898. See *The Complete Works of Swami Vivekananda*, Volume 9: Excerpts from Sister Nivedita's Book, Chapter X "The Shrine of Amarnath".
    Source: http://en.wikisource.org/wiki/The_Complete_Works_of_Swami_Vivekan anda/Volume_9/Excerpts_from_Sister_Nivedita's_Book/X_The_Shrine_Of_Amar nath, accessed 6 February 2020.
18 Takri is a Brahmi-based script derived from Shāradā, closely related to Gurmukhi, which was used to write Punjabi. It has also been used for writing Kashtwāri and some dialects of the adjoining areas.
19 www.risingkashmir.com/news/renzu-hails-amks-efforts-8037.aspx (An article by Sumeer Shaukeen titled 'Renzu Hails AMK's Efforts' published in the Srinagar-based daily *Rising Kashmir*, Monday April 4, 2011).
20 Note that despite Urdu being the official language of the state of Jammu and Kashmir, it is not a second language of the all the literate people in the state. While Muslims are generally proficient and literate in Urdu, Hindus prefer Hindi as their second language (written and spoken). This difference is representative of the Hindu–Muslim linguistic differences at the national level in India.
21 Links for 'Groups' on social networking site FACEBOOK advocating the revival of Shāradā: www.facebook.com/#!/groups/shardalippi/ www.facebook.com/#!/group s/208759249144375/.

References

Bailey, G. (1979). *History of Urdu Literature*. New Delhi: Sumit Publications.
Bamzai, P. N. K. (2007). *Cultural and Political History of Kashmir*, Vol. 2. Srinagar: Gulshan Books: 80–84.
Chelliah, S. (2005). 'Asserting Nationhood Through Personal Name Choice: The Case of the Methei of the Northeast India'. *Anthropological Linguistics*, 47.2: 169–216.
Chelliah, S. (2008). 'Competing Ideologies, Competing Scripts: The Politics of Orthographic Choice in North East India', paper presented at *InField*, Santa Barbara.
Das, S. K. (2006). *A History of Indian Literature, AD.500–1399: From Courtly to the Popular*. New Delhi: Sahitya Akademi.
Habibullah, W. (2008). *My Kashmir: Conflict and the Prospects of Enduring Peace*. Washington, DC: United States Institute of Peace Press.
Haksar, A. N. D. (2011). *Khemendra: Three Satires from Ancient Kashmir*. New Delhi: Penguin Classics.
Handu, J. (1988). 'Folk Literature–Kashmiri'. In Amaresh Datta (ed.) *The Encyclopedia of Indian Literature*, Vol. 2. New Delhi: Wellwish Printers: 1293–1297 (First edition 1988; reprinted in 1995, 1996, 2001, and 2006).
Hassan, M. (1959). *Kashmir Under the Sultans*. New Delhi: Aakar Books (reprinted in 2005). Available at URL: http://books.google.co.in/books?id=EUlwmXjE9DQC&pg=PA158 &source=gbs_toc_r&cad=4#v=onepage&q&f=false; retrieved on February 6, 2020.
Inayatullah, Hafiz Mohammad. (n.d). *Lalla Arif barzhbane Kashmir*. Lahore: Din Mohammad Electric Press.
Jafri, A. S. (n.d.). 'Progressive Movement and Urdu Poetry'. Available at URL: www.urdupo etry.com/articles/art9.html; retrieved on February 6, 2020.
Jalal, Ayesha. (2000). *Self and Sovereignty: Individual and Community in South Asian Islam since 1850*. London and New York: Routledge.

Kachru, B. B. (1969). *A Reference Grammer of Kashmiri*. Urbana: University of Illinois.

Kachru, B. B. (2003). 'The Dying Linguistic Heritage of the Kashmiris: Kashmiri Literary Culture and Language'. Available at URL: http://koshur.org/pdf/DyingLinguistic.pdf; retrieved on February 6, 2020.

Kachru, B. B. (n.d.). 'Naming of the Kashmiri Pandit Community: Sociolinguistics and Anthropology'. Available at URL: www.ikashmir.net/names/kpnames.html; retrieved on February 6, 2020.

Kachru, Y. (2006). *Hindi*. Amsterdam: John Benjamins.

Kaul, R. K. (1982). *Sociology of Names and Nicknames of India with Special Reference to Kashmir*. Motiyar, Rainawari, Srinagar and Kashmir: Utpal Publications.

Khan, Mohammad Ishaq. (1994). *Kashmir's Transition to Islam: The Role of Muslim Rishis*. Delhi: Manohar Publications.

Koul, O. N. (1995). 'Personal Names in Kashmiri'. In Omkar N. Koul (ed.) *Sociolinguistics: South Asian Perspectives*. New Delhi: Creative Books.

Koul, O. N. (2000). *Kashmiri Language, Linguistics and Culture: An Annotated Bibliography*. Mysore: Central Institute of Indian Languages.

Majumdar, R. C. (ed.). (2006). *The Delhi Sultanate*. Mumbai: Bharatiya Vidya Bhavan.

Munshi, S. (2006). 'Kashmiri'. In Keith Brown (ed.) *Encyclopedia of Language and Linguistics*. Second Edition, Vol. 6: 156–158. Oxford: Elsevier Limited.

Munshi, S. (2011). 'Kashmiri Poetic Traditions: A Socio-historical and Linguistic Perspective', paper presented at *Kashmir: Beyond Security Paradigms*, a one-day workshop at the University of Texas at Austin, April 9.

Munshi, S. (2012). 'Metrical Structure of Kashmiri Vanvun'. *Ars Metrica, Journal of Metric and Metrical Systems*: 1–36.

Nunley, R. E., Severin, M. R., George, W. W., and Daniel, L. R. (1999). *The Cultural Landscape an Introduction to Human Geography*. Upper Saddle River, NJ: Prentice Hall.

Pandita, K. N. (trans.) (1988). *Baharistan-i-Shahi: A Chronicle of Medieval Kashmir*. Calcutta: Firma KLM Private Limited. (Originally a Persian manuscript by anonymous author).

Parimoo, B. N. (1978) (translation and commentary). *The Ascent of Self: A reinterpretation of the Mythical poetry of Lal Ded*. New Delhi, Varanasi and Patna: Motilal Banarasidas.

Pollock, S. (1998). 'India in the Vernacular Millennium: Literary Culture and Polity, 1000–1500'. *Daedalus*, 127.2: 41–74.

Puri, B. (1995). 'Kashmiriyat: The Vitality of Kashmiri Identity'. *Contemporary South Asia*, 4.1.

Rai, M. (2004). *Hindu Rulers, Muslim Subjects: Islam, Rights & the History of Kashmir*. New Jersey: Princeton University Press.

Raina, T. N. (1972). *An Anthology of Modern Kashmiri Verse (1930–1960)*. Poona: Suresh Raina.

Raina, T. N. (trans.). (1989). *The Best of Mahjoor: Selections from Mahjoor's Kashmiri Poems*. Srinagar: J&K Academy of Art, Culture and Languages.

Steedly, M. M. (1996). 'The Importance of Proper Names: Language and "National" Identity in Colonial Karoland'. *American Ethnologist*, 23: 447–475.

Taseer, R. (1973). *Tehreek e Hurriyat e Kashmir (URDU)*, Vol. 2. Srinagar: Muhafiz Publications.

Woods, J. H. (trans.). (1914). *The Yoga System of Patanjali*. Cambridge, MA: The Harvard University Press. (Translated from the original).

Wright, S. (ed.). (1998). *Language and Conflict: A Neglected Relationship*. Clevedon: Multilingual Matters.

Zutshi, C. (2004). *Languages of Belonging: Islam, Regional Identity and the Making of Kashmir*. New York: Oxford University Press.

10

'FOR THE CONVERSION OF KASHMIR'

The massacre at St Joseph's mission hospital in Baramulla

Andrew Whitehead

The Sisters were, at first, not sure how – or whether – to mark the 70th anniversary of the massacre. The death of a young Spanish nun, Sister Teresalina, and five others at St Joseph's hospital on October 27, 1947 was a defining moment in the history of the mission. It was the time that the community's faith was most keenly tested. When the survivors were evacuated almost two weeks after the attack, the ransacked mission lay abandoned – but two years later, the nuns returned. The memory of the fellow nun they regarded as a martyr was part of the imperative to resume the work of the mission. In more recent years, when the nuns' order, the Franciscan Missionaries of Mary, has gently suggested that the security situation merits a rethink about the future of the convent and hospital, the example of Sister Teresalina has been an important factor in the nuns' resolve to remain at Baramulla. But the contested claims to Kashmir which lay behind the killings in October 1947 remain unresolved, and the town of Baramulla and the surrounding district has been at the sharp end of the conflict. Staging memorial events offered not simply logistical but also security and political challenges – not least because October 27, regarded by the Sisters as martyrs' day, is marked in Kashmir as a 'black day'. On the same day in 1947 that the Baramulla mission was overrun by tribal fighters from Pakistan, the first Indian troops were airlifted into the Kashmir Valley commencing a military presence that has persisted ever since.

Just as the attack on the mission in October 1947 arose from India and Pakistan's competing claims to Kashmir so too the 70th anniversary was embroiled in the continuing conflict. The Indian army – which at moments of tension has gone out of its way to protect the convent and hospital – advised that any memorial events should be small and restricted to those known to the nuns. The army has its own stake in the killings and their memorialising. Among the dead was Lt-Col Tom Dykes, a British officer in the Sikh Regiment who had agreed to stay on for a short while after independence in mid-August 1947 to help with the handover. He is buried in the only Commonwealth War Grave in Kashmir; his wife, Biddy, was also killed and is buried in the same plot at the back of the hospital. Colonel Dykes was serving in the Indian army at the time of his death, and the army continues to tend his grave. On the anniversary, the most senior Indian general in the Baramulla district was among those to lay a wreath at the graves. This brought along with it an array of security measures: armed soldiers keeping watch in the orchard surrounding the burial site; an army jeep with mounted machine gun in the hospital grounds; camouflage sheets curtaining the burial plot, perhaps to foil snipers; and the extraordinary sight, and sound, of a surveillance drone overhead.

The memorial services on October 27, 2017 had begun on a more solemn note. At seven in the morning, a mass of remembrance was held in the mission church. It was celebrated by Bishop Ivan Pereira, based in Jammu, and attended by the provincial head of the Franciscan Missionaries of Mary, Sister Taurina Vaz, who had travelled from Delhi. Among the congregation were the two surviving sons of Tom and Biddy Dykes (both of whom had been at the mission when their parents were killed) and members of the small local Catholic community, some from families that had suffered grievously during the turmoil seven decades earlier. After the service, the congregation formed a procession bearing candles to the spot amid apple and walnut trees where five of those killed in the attack lie buried. From there, the worshippers moved on to a small graveyard on the other side of the church where women in holy orders are interred. Sister Teresalina's grave had been covered in petals. During the ceremonies, Sister Josephine, the superior at the convent, twice reminded those assembled of what the church records as Sister Teresalina's dying words: 'I offer myself as a victim for the conversion of Kashmir.'

This chapter will explore how the Baramulla mission came to be established; what happened there on October 27, 1947; the manner in which those events have been memorialised by the church and by others; the reworking of the concept of 'conversion' as envisaged by the woman who remains the Catholic church's only martyr in Kashmir; and the interlocking of clerical and geopolitical narratives in a region which has become painfully familiar with the concept of martyrdom.[1]

The Kashmir Valley is, in religious terms, one of the less diverse regions of India. It has for centuries been overwhelmingly Muslim, and the exodus in 1990 during the early stages of a separatist insurgency of almost all Kashmiri-speaking Hindus further accentuated that dominance. Currently – if one excludes the Indian armed forces and others not permanently resident in the region – the Kashmir Valley is about 97 per cent Muslim. Among non-Muslims, Sikhs and Hindus comfortably outnumber Christians. Kashmir was never promising territory for missionaries seeking new audiences for the Christian gospel. 'Your work is not easy, your lives have an element of peculiar loneliness not found in other missions,' the head of a missionary order counselled his priests during a visit to Kashmir. 'You have not the consolation of seeing the Church thrive and expand as a result of your labours. You are not cheered and encouraged by a great influx of converts into the Church. You sow in hard, stony arid soil so that in God's own time, others may reap.'[2] Most of the very small number of Catholics in Kashmir are from families whose roots lie outside the region and who were Christians before they came to the Valley. The usual Sunday congregation at the mission church in Baramulla is about 30, of whom more than half are in holy orders. The Holy Family church in Srinagar sometimes attracts a slightly greater number of worshippers; the city is also home to another Christian place of worship, the Anglican-foundation All Saints church, now part of the Church of North India.

The influence of Christian medical and educational pioneers in Kashmir has been out of all proportion to the size of the community. From the 1860s, a series of notable Protestant medical missionaries from Britain – particularly William Elmslie, described as 'the founder of modern medicine in Kashmir' (Mufti, 2013, 51), Irene Petrie and the brothers Arthur and Ernest Neve – brought allopathic medicine to Srinagar, and established hospitals and dispensaries. Among Protestant educational missionaries, Cecil Tyndale-Biscoe arrived in Kashmir in 1890, taking under his wing a Church Mission Society school established a decade earlier. The school that continues to take his name has claim to being Kashmir's most prestigious educational institute and retains a link to the Church of North India. These distinctly colonialist and unbending Christian zealots also produced a copious stream of missionary memoirs and travel journals, sometimes more revealing about their authors than the region in which they laboured. These missionaries were not alone, in the sense that from the 1890s until independence in 1947, Srinagar was home to a significant European and Christian population attracted by the temperate summers and majestic landscape. During the Second World War in particular, thousands of soldiers, administrators and others made their way to Kashmir to seek respite from the burning summer heat of the plains. Indeed, it was 'white mischief' territory, where some of the colonisers came to have a 'good time' and generally misbehave.

The contribution of Catholic educational missionaries has been quite as pronounced – and the well-regarded Burn Hall and Presentation Convent schools in Srinagar and St Joseph's school in Baramulla, on a large site adjoining the convent and hospital, remain church-run and over-subscribed. The Baramulla hospital has been the most conspicuous achievement of Catholic medical missionaries.

The Mill Hill Missionaries – or more formally, the St Joseph's Missionary Society, for many years based in the Mill Hill district of north London – was given the task in 1887 by the Sacred Congregation for the Propagation of the Faith of evangelising Kashmir and what was then termed Kafiristan (the latter now being part of Pakistan and Afghanistan). Four years later, a Catholic mission school was opened in Baramulla – a key staging post on the recently constructed road entering the Kashmir Valley from the west – and from this St Joseph's school was established in 1909. The Mill Hill Missionaries, mainly British and Dutch, maintained their presence until recent years, when the increasingly onerous restrictions placed by the Indian government on foreign missionaries occasioned the handing over of responsibility to Capuchin Fathers from South India.

Once established in Baramulla, these pioneering male missionaries appealed for help from the Franciscan Missionaries of Mary (FMM) to reach the women of Kashmir, who were particularly in need of medical and primary health services.

The FMM is the only Catholic missionary order of women religious founded on Indian soil. It was established in South India in 1877 by a French-born nun, Helene de Chappotin de Neuville, better known as Blessed Mary of the Passion. The order is now the fifth biggest institute for women in the Catholic church, with a presence in more than 70 countries. It retains a particular strength in South India and of the 50 or so provincial heads, five are based in India. In 1916, two nuns based in Rawalpindi, Mother St Michel and a colleague, made an exploratory journey to Baramulla, a journey mainly by horse-drawn tonga and taking several days. 'Your daughters are the first women religious who have ever set foot in Kashmir', they reported to their superior-general. 'What a mission here in Kashmir − not a single indigenous Christian! . . . I pray that we can make this foundation, for this is utterly virgin soil which has never been evangelised nor even visited by missionaries until barely twelve to fifteen years ago. I would be happy if we could bring exposition of the Blessed Sacrament here that would be the sun which would render fruitful a land arid up to now.'[3]

Five years later, by which time Mother St Michel had been elevated from a provincial head of the FMM to the order's superior-general, the nuns established a small convent in Baramulla. It was in part funded by a Scottish man whose daughter was an FMM nun in India (in 1926, she became the superior at Baramulla). The initial task of the nuns was to visit women in their villages and provide medical care. The order's archives include an account of the work of the nuns based on the journal kept in their initial months at Baramulla:

> In their visits, made on horseback or *shikara* (a small boat. . .) they sometimes tended 20 or 30 patients a day. Soon a poor Sikh who had become a Catholic brought his six children whom he could no longer feed asking the Sisters to take them and baptise them as Catholics; this was the beginning of a small orphanage which continued to grow slowly until it was transferred to Rawalpindi. At Christmas the Sisters were able to give this report on the Christians of Baramulla, where a few years earlier there had been none but the missionary priest: six boys, four girls and one old man were Catholics, while a Protestant and a Muslim were preparing for baptism. The dispensary, handed over to the FMM by the Mill Hill Missionary, treated an average of 60 patients a day. . . . The baptism of the little girls was the first religious ceremony in Baramulla, and the first Christmas there was a joyful feast. By 15 August 1922, the numbers had risen to 518 child baptisms and two baptisms of adults; eight conversions at the point of death; 16,500 patients treated in the dispensary; 17 children in the orphanage.[4]

The mission was not simply about saving souls and winning converts, but the number of Kashmiris being baptised and seeking conversion was clearly an important measure of the nuns' success.

In the mid-1920s, the convent's chapel room was no longer sufficient for those who came to worship and a purpose-built chapel was constructed. The hospital opened in 1929, initially with 15 beds, on occasions being served by an FMM doctor and sometimes by a woman lay doctor. It developed a reputation as a good maternity hospital but this was not an easy posting. In 1943, the resident doctor died during a virulent typhus epidemic; two of the sisters who nursed her also contracted the illness and died. The order's Baramulla roll call for 1947 lists 16 nuns: a Belgian superior, and Sisters from Spain, France, Italy, Ireland, Scotland, Portugal, Germany, the Netherlands and England along with just one Indian nun. Most had specialist roles as nurses and pharmacists. Only four of the sisters were under 40.

When India and Pakistan gained independence in mid-August 1947, the maharajah of Kashmir had still not decided to which new dominion he would accede. The territories under his rule extended well beyond the Kashmir Valley, which constituted by population under half and by area less than a tenth of the princely state. The working assumption of the British appears to have been that Kashmir would go to Pakistan. The maharajah, however, was a Hindu, though more than three-quarters of his citizens were Muslims, and when it became apparent that his preferred goal of independence was unachievable, he edged towards signing up to India. In this he had the support of his nemesis, the radical Kashmiri nationalist leader Sheikh Abdullah, who was released from the maharajah's jail in late September 1947. He was a Muslim and on occasions used Islam to mobilise political support, but he was more inclined towards secular and socialist India rather than the more clerical and feudal-minded Pakistan.

In an attempt to forestall Kashmir's accession to India, tribal fighters from Pakistan staged an invasion (Whitehead, 2007, passim). In the early hours of October 22, 1947, armed contingents from the North West Frontier and adjoining tribal agencies, many of them Mahsuds and Afridis, crossed into the princely state, seized control of the town of Muzaffarabad and advanced east along the Jhelum valley road towards Baramulla and Srinagar. They had been encouraged by some of their religious leaders, notably the Pir of Wana and the Pir of Manki Sharif; sections of Pakistan's government and armed forces provided more tangible support in the form of trucks, fuel and rifles and a few key personnel. The attackers' motives were mixed: they were conducting jihad, looking for loot, avenging anti-Muslim violence in Jammu and Punjab, seeking the overthrow of a non-Muslim princely ruler and claiming Kashmir for Pakistan. They rapidly overcame the maharajah's army and on October 26, the fifth day of their military campaign, the tribal fighters entered Baramulla, then the second biggest town in the Kashmir Valley. Many of the invaders turned to gathering booty and abducting non-Muslim women, and the discipline of the attacking force ruptured.[5] By then, the maharajah had fled the Kashmir Valley to the safety of his palace in Jammu to the south, where he signed the document by which his princely state became part of India. At first light on October 27, India's armed forces began an airlift to the rudimentary landing strip outside Srinagar to protect the Kashmiri capital and repel the invading force. Some of the first troops to land, from the Sikh Regiment, headed towards Baramulla, but finding themselves outnumbered took up a position a couple of miles to the east of the town. They could hear the tumult and gunfire but were unable to intervene.

As the tribal fighters approached, and word got out about their looting aimed particularly at non-Muslims, many Hindus and Sikhs living in Baramulla fled – among them several patients in the mission hospital. The Sisters and the two British missionary priests at St Joseph's school made no attempt to evacuate as they didn't expect to be targeted. Late in the morning of October 27, the first groups of attackers reached the hospital, and began smashing doors and seizing any items of value. Their violence seems to have been restricted to those who sought to impede their progress. Within a matter of minutes, six people had either been killed or suffered fatal injuries. Besides Sister Teresalina and Tom and Biddy Dykes, these were a nurse or nursing assistant, Philomena, the husband of the hospital doctor, Jose Barretto, and Mrs Motia Devi Kapoor, a patient and the only non-Christian among those killed at St Joseph's. The superior, Mother Aldetrude, suffered a bullet wound but survived. The initial wave of violence seems to have ended when a Pakistani army officer in civilian clothes arrived at the mission by motorbike and ordered the attackers to stop.

The survivors of the attack, joined by some local families who had sought refuge at the mission – about 80 people in total – then endured 10 days in captivity in the hospital's Baby Ward. They were joined by a British war correspondent, Sydney Smith of the *Daily Express*, who happened to be in Kashmir, arranged a lift with the Indian army towards the frontline, and then was captured by the tribesmen. Father George Shanks, the senior priest at the school, emerged as the leader of the beleaguered group. While tribal fighters abducted and raped women and girls in and around Baramulla, those confined to a single room at the mission hospital appear – though the evidence is contradictory – to have been spared sexual violence.[6] The ordeal ended when those held captive at the mission were evacuated by the Pakistan army, reaching Abbottabad on November 7; once there, Sydney Smith reported the attack on the mission and the battle for Kashmir in breathless style for his newspaper.[7] By then, the Indian army – supported by strafing and bombing from the air – was gaining the upper hand. Indian troops took Baramulla without a fight on November 8, 1947 and it has been under Indian control ever since. Journalists and news photographers who followed in the army's wake recorded the extent of the devastation at the mission, which included the desecration of the chapel.

The killings at St Joseph's were not the bloodiest episode of the tribesmen's invasion. In all, several hundred people – perhaps as many as a few thousand – were killed during the three weeks that the Pakistani irregulars were present in the Kashmir Valley. But the attack on a hospital, the desecration of a place of worship and the killing of foreigners all contributed to make the Baramulla massacre the most notorious aspect of these opening salvos in the Kashmir conflict. The British government was concerned both to investigate the deaths of two of its nationals and to safeguard the 400 or so British residents of Srinagar. The British high commissioner in Karachi wrote to Pakistan's prime minister, Liaquat Ali Khan, urging that those responsible for the killings at the mission be found and punished. The prime minister replied that 'the incidents took place in non-Pakistan territory and the Pakistan Government cannot assume any responsibility in respect of them.'[8]

A British official, Major W.P. Cranston, reached the mission just a few days after Indian troops took control of Baramulla. 'The Convent buildings and hospital and chapel had been completely wrecked inside,' he reported. 'All the furniture was pulled about, books had been pulled out of their racks and largely torn up, including a very good library in the Convent itself. All articles of value had been looted.'

In the Church the destruction and desecration of the altar, statues, crucifixes, books and furniture, was most deliberate. It was obvious that this had not been done merely in the first hurried search for loot but was a deliberate policy carried out over a period of time and the thoroughness with which this desecration had been done and the deliberate maltreatment of holy emblems and statues showed that the action taken must have been done under the instructions of persons who knew exactly what they were doing.[9]

To add to the sense of Christian disquiet, Major Cranston noted that while a section of Baramulla had been burnt down, 'by far the greater part of it was left untouched. It was a strange contrast that many Hindu temples and buildings should have been left completely untouched by the raiders, whilst the Catholic Convent and hospital and Church should have been deliberately destroyed and desecrated in a most thorough manner.'

In the established clerical narrative of the attack on St Joseph's, the victims died in particularly valorous circumstances. Motia Devi Kapoor was stabbed through the heart in her hospital bed; Philomena was shot while seeking to protect the patients; Colonel Tom Dykes, who had come to the hospital to collect his family, sought to stop the attackers assaulting the nuns and was shot; his wife, Biddy Dykes – who had given birth in the hospital two weeks earlier – ran out on seeing her husband fall down, and was herself shot; Jose Baretto rushed to stop nuns being molested in the hospital grounds, was led to a tree – some accounts say he spread his arms as if being crucified – and shot; Sister Teresalina, the 29-year-old assistant to the superior who had arrived in Baramulla just a few weeks earlier, leapt out in front of Mother Aldetrude, taking bullets intended for the older woman. It's very difficult to distinguish hard fact from accounts intended to offer solace to relatives and provide the seeds of religious fable.

The initial memorialising of the Baramulla massacre, and adapting of its narrative, was to meet a secular rather than religious purpose. In the immediate aftermath of the attack, the bare facts of what happened at the hospital and across the town were difficult to ascertain: all those at the mission had been evacuated; many residents of the town had fled to escape the violence and looting; the destruction was evident, but the extent of casualties much less so. Reporters had to rely on eye witness accounts, hearsay and the version passed on by the Indian soldiers who accompanied them. The tone of much of the coverage was set by Robert Trumbull of the *New York Times* who reported from Baramulla on November 10:

> This quiet city in the beautiful Kashmir Valley was left smoking, desolate and full of horrible memories by invading frontier tribesmen who held a thirteen-day saturnalia of looting, raping and killing here.

The city had been stripped of its wealth and young women before the tribesmen fled in terror at midnight Friday before the advancing Indian Army.

Surviving residents estimate that 3,000 of their fellow townsmen, including four European nuns and a retired British Army officer known only as Colonel Dykes and his pregnant wife, were slain.

Thirteen other foreigners, mostly priests and nuns and two of Colonel Dykes' three children – the third child is missing – were taken under the protection of the raiders' commander, said to be a Pakistan Army officer, and evacuated to Rawalpindi, in the West Punjab Province of Pakistan. . .

Today, twenty-four hours after the Indian Army entered Baramula [sic], only 1,000 were left of a normal population of about 14,000.[10]

Trumbull was not asserting that all but a thousand of Baramulla's residents had been slaughtered (and the casualty estimate he recited of 3,000 dead in the town is unreliable and almost certainly a considerable exaggeration) but that's often how his report is cited. His account of the attack on the mission assumed that all the dead there apart from the British couple were nuns when only one of them was in holy orders. The tribal invasion led eventually to war between India and Pakistan and the delineation of a ceasefire line partitioning the former princely state, though the Kashmir Valley was on India's side of the line. As the tussle for Kashmir moved away from the battlefield towards the United Nations and international opinion, Trumbull's account and similar reportage were eagerly circulated by the Indian government and excerpts were included in an Indian government 'white paper' in support of its claim to Kashmir.

Some of the news reports included in the white paper again featured in another propaganda piece published half-a-century later. In 1997, on the 50th anniversary of both India's independence and Kashmir's accession to India, a well-produced 32-page pamphlet entitled 'The Horror of Baramulla 1947' once again threw the spotlight on the attack on St Joseph's. Alongside the snippets of reportage from 1947, it published lengthy excerpts of interviews which All India Radio had recorded in Baramulla in 1958 with Father Shanks and several of the sisters recalling the attack. The introduction made an overt political link between the invasion by Pakistani tribesmen in 1947 and subsequent Pakistan-backed militant activity in the Kashmir Valley. 'For Pakistan, incursions into Kashmir have become a habit. The operation "Gulmarg" of 1947 was replaced by Operation "Gibraltar" of 1965, when raiders were sent into Kashmir by Ayub Khan, self-styled Field Marshal of Pakistan. Now we have to deal with blood-thirsty outfits like the Harkat-ul-Ansar, which has just been declared a terrorist set-up by the US Government. . . . But over the decades, it is worthwhile to recall the statements of Father Shanks and the Nuns at the Franciscan Convent of St Joseph's.' The attack on the convent and hospital attracted the notoriety which made it potent propaganda.

Neither Trumbull nor the other Indian and foreign journalists who reached Baramulla once India had taken control of the town suggested that nuns had been raped. But the desecration of the convent and the undoubted prevalence of sexual violence elsewhere in Baramulla were soon conflated to support India's narrative of Pakistani barbarism. Even before Indian troops took the town, India's deputy prime minister, Sardar Patel, issued a statement on Kashmir drawing from the confused and conflicting reports from areas under the invaders' control. 'The grim tragedy which overtook the British members of a religious order at Baramula [sic], the details of which are too heart rending to state, and the murder in cold blood of European families there are sufficient to reveal the true character of the so-called missionaries of liberation and emancipation.'[11] This hints at sexual violence at the mission. Over the years, Indian diplomats and politicians made repeated references to the fate of the nuns at St Joseph's and 'the rape of Baramulla' when making their case on Kashmir. Sheikh Abdullah, speaking as prime minister of Indian Kashmir at the opening of the Jammu and Kashmir Constituent Assembly in 1951, recalled: 'Even the nuns and nurses of a Catholic Mission were either killed or brutally mistreated' (Abdullah, 1951, 17). The starkest version, curiously, appears in a work of history which lacks any obvious partisan purpose. In *Freedom at Midnight*, Larry Collins and Dominique Lapierre recounted – with more than a touch of hyperbole – how in Baramulla 'the Pathans . . . were giving vent to their ancient appetites for rape and pillage. They violated the nuns, massacred the patients in their little clinic, looted the convent chapel down to its last brass door-knob' (Collins and Lapierre, 1957, 357).

Alongside Trumbull's reporting, another American, the renowned photo-journalist Margaret Bourke-While, also helped to establish the totemic significance of the attack on St Joseph's. She was in Pakistan when the invasion of Kashmir began. 'The stories that began leaking out about the violating and shooting of the nuns of the Order of St. Francis,' she aptly commented, 'sounded like old-fashioned atrocity tales.' In spite of the best endeavours of the Pakistani authorities to keep her away, she managed to reach the town of Abbottabad, the key staging post for the invasion, and spoke to armed tribesmen who were heading towards Kashmir. She also chanced across some of the nuns from Baramulla just as they reached Abbottabad.

The Mother Superior had been seriously wounded and was rushed to the hospital. The grave-faced sister from whom I got the details had been in the babies' ward on the convent grounds when the tribesmen began smashing up X-ray equipment, throwing medicine bottles to the ground, ripping the statuettes of saints out of the chapel, and shooting up the place generally. Two patients were killed; an Englishman and his wife who were vacationing at the mission were murdered; and two nuns were shot. 'They didn't hurt my babies,' added the sister triumphantly.

For nine days there was a reign of terror in the convent. The nuns, their hospital patients, and a few stray townspeople who had taken refuge at the mission were herded into a single dormitory and kept under rifle guard. On one of these days, after an air attack from the Indian Army had left the tribesmen in a particularly excited and nervous mood, six of the nuns were brought out and lined up to be shot. It was the accident that one of them had a conspicuous gold tooth that saved the sisters. One of the riflemen wanted to get that tooth, before his colleagues had a chance at it. In the scuffle that followed, one of their chiefs arrived; he had enough vision to realise that shooting nuns was not the thing to do, even in an invasion, and the nuns were saved[12] (Bourke-White, 1949, 206–207).

A few weeks later, in December 1947, Margaret Bourke-White managed to get to the other side of the front-line, and travelled from the Kashmiri capital, Srinagar, to see what was left of the Baramulla convent. She was accompanied by a Punjabi communist, B.P.L. Bedi, who had taken the lead in drafting the notably radical *Naya Kashmir* manifesto adopted by Sheikh Abdullah's Kashmiri nationalists. After Partition, Bedi and his family had moved from Lahore to Srinagar to work with Sheikh Abdullah. He had a particular responsibility for counter-propaganda, making the case for a secular and progressive (and Indian-ruled) Kashmir in preference to either the religious intolerance associated with Pakistan or autocratic princely rule.

'Bedi and I walked up the hill to the deserted convent,' Bourke-White wrote. 'It was badly defaced and littered, and a delegation of students from Srinagar was coming next day to clean it up and salvage what remained of the library.'

The group had been carefully selected to include Hindus, Sikhs and Muslims, and would be escorted by members of the Kashmiri Home Guard, both men and women – these too chosen symbolically from the three religions. They would put the Christian mission in as good order as they could in time for Christmas Day.

> We made our way into the ravaged chapel, wading through the mass of torn hymnbooks and broken sacred statuary. The altar was deep in rubble. Bedi stooped down over it and picked up one fragment, turning it over carefully in his big hands. It was the broken head of Jesus, with just one eye remaining.
>
> 'How beautiful it is,' said Bedi, 'this single eye of Christ looking out so calmly on the world. We shall preserve it always in Kashmir as a permanent reminder of the unity between Indians of all religions which we are trying to achieve.'
>
> *(Bourke-White, 1949, 211)*

This was a propaganda triumph for both Indian and Kashmiri nationalism. Bedi's English wife, Freda Bedi, was among those who sought to make good the damage to the chapel: 'how happy we were on Christmas Eve to see the chapel looking its old self again (if only a war battered self!)', she wrote to Bourke-White. 'By some miracle, we managed to piece the altar together from panels scattered over the floor + even mounted the reredos again in its old place. It at least had the illusion of completeness, even if the images were battered + pathetic on their pedestals' (Whitehead, 2019, 178).

Once the nuns returned to Baramulla, a string of journalists visited the mission and sought to retrieve their memories. Frank Moraes, the first Indian editor of the *Times of India*, had been an intimate friend of Margaret Bourke-White and knew the Bedis too. In 1957, he visited St Joseph's and spoke to three nuns who had lived through the attack. '"As they looted and attacked us, the raiders kept shouting 'Pakistan has come'", said the Italian nun. "I only knew that the devil had come."'[13]

There was, however, an attempt to challenge this pro-India narrative. Ian Stephens, who had been editor of another leading newspaper, the *Statesman*, and was sympathetic to Pakistan, came to Baramulla in 1952, visited the convent and spoke to some of the nuns who had survived what 'had certainly been a very shameful affair' (Stephens, 1953, 216–218). But some years later he dismissed the attack on the mission as 'a bad but secondary episode, soon inflated out of all proportion by Indian propaganda aimed at countries of the Christian West. And the time lost over these misdeeds, we can now see, also lost them the campaign – it was of no avail that later waves of invading tribesmen behaved much better, sometimes fighting superbly' (Stephens, 1963, 202–203). Novelists too were attracted to the story – H.E. Bates never travelled to Kashmir, but borrowing liberally from Sydney Smith's journalism in the *Daily Express*, he wrote *The Scarlet Sword*, published in 1950 and (as with his earlier novels, *The Purple Plain* and *The Jacaranda Tree*, both set in Burma) primarily concerned about the response of an isolated group of Europeans to extreme adversity.

The initial priority of the sisters evacuated at Baramulla was to decide on their future, and above all whether they would return to Kashmir, and once they had resolved to re-establish the convent and hospital to see through that goal. They returned in March 1949 and the patients' admissions book, still kept at Baramulla, records that the hospital was up-and-running again from August. The Franciscan Missionaries of Mary were well aware of the value of martyrs in strengthening a sense of mission. In China in 1900, seven of the order's sisters – all European and in their 20s and 30s – were killed during the anti-colonial Boxer Rebellion. The founder of the order, Blessed Mary of the Passion, is reputed to have said when she heard of the killings: 'I can say with St. Francis: now, I have seven true Franciscan Missionaries of Mary.' They are known within the order as the seven martyrs of China, and highly stylised paintings of the group are on display at St Joseph's, Baramulla, and every other FMM convent. One of the nuns at Baramulla told me: 'we pray through their intercession to have such a daring attitude for each one of us if such situations come to any one of us that we may give our lives for the sake of Jesus whom we love.' The seven martyrs were beatified in November 1946 – an event which would have been fresh in the minds of the nuns at St Joseph's as they came under attack the following year; they were canonised in 2000.

From 1949, a cascade of clerical publications appeared proclaiming the valour of Sister Teresalina and the FMM sisters at Baramulla. Among the first was *Una Victima Perfecta* (A Perfect Victim), an account of Sister Teresalina's life and death by a Franciscan friar, Father Ignacio Omaechevarria who, like his subject, was from northern Spain (Omaechevarria, 1949).[14] It included an account of her dying words: 'Ya termino. . . . Ofrezco mi vida por la conversion de Cachemira' (I'm already finished. . . . I offer my life for the conversion of Kashmir), and related how her 'fertile blood' has already delivered converts in Kashmir and in Pakistan. This became the hallowed account of a martyr's last words: 'Je vais mourir. . . . J'offre ma vie pour la conversion du Cachemire' (I'm about to die. . . . I offer my life for the conversion of Kashmir), according to an FMM publication in French, which was the sisters' common language at Baramulla in 1947 (*Jusqu'a La Mort*, 1956, 112–113). The following year, an account of the martyrdom was published in English:

> Night fell and darkness filled the ward. The continual murmur of prayer was interrupted only by an occasional cry from a baby or a terrified shriek from the women over the least incident. Near nine or ten o'clock – all the watches had been stolen–Mother Teresalina called to the nurse: 'I am dying.' She was unable to move and did not even realise that the Sister had joined her hands on her breast. She accepted a few drops of water and softly murmured:
> 'It is finished. I offer myself for the conversion of Kashmir.'
> Father Shanks gave her a last absolution and suggested some invocations in her familiar Spanish. She renewed her Vows, and again repeated words at the end:
> 'I offer myself as a victim for the conversion of Kashmir.'
> A willing victim, bathed in her own blood, with a smile of peace on her lips, she closed her eyes and died.
> A deep hush fell upon the crowded ward . . . all the more profound, filled as it was with more than 90 people. Father Shanks softly started the *De Profundis*. Later he wrote:
> 'Seeing her die like this before my eyes, and hearing her pray for the murderers, I felt as though I were assisting at the death of a saint . . . she suffered as a martyr. She had the happiest and most beautiful death.'
> One of the Sisters affirmed later: 'I can assure you that she died in an ecstasy of joy in the midst of atrocious suffering.'
> Mother Teresalina had always yearned to be a saint. Her soul had instinctively turned towards martyrdom.
>
> (*I Will be the First*, 1957, 28–29)[15]

This clerical pamphlet *I Will be the First*, the title derived from the nun's light-hearted comment to an uncle who remarked that there was no Saint Teresalina, was for many years given to visitors to the Baramulla mission. It takes the reverential tone common to popular hagiography. The conversion on Sister Teresalina's lips was clearly the winning of Kashmir to Catholicism. Indeed, even as she was dying the two British priests in that same hospital ward were receiving non-Christians into the church as long as they promised that 'if they ever get out alive they will complete the instruction and live as catholics'.

There is strong reason to doubt that Sister Teresalina uttered the words attributed to her. The most detailed account of the attack on the mission by one of those present was written a few years after the event by Father George Shanks. The unpublished account he set down in a desk diary appears to have been prompted by H.E. Bates's novel, and the less than flattering account in it of a priest very loosely based on Shanks. It offers a detailed account of the Spanish nun's last hours, lying alongside the injured superior and being tended by the doctor, Greta Baretto, whose husband had been killed by the attackers just hours earlier. 'I knelt on the floor by the side of Mother Teresalina,' Shanks recorded. 'She was conscious, but her eyes were closed, and only the frequent contraction of her limbs and the contortion of her face told of the spasms of pain which racked her. Sister Celeste, who had come out from Spain with her only two months before, knelt at the other side … re-arranging the sheet over her torn abdomen, whispering prayers into her ear.'

> 'Ma Mere, Father has come.' I took her hand in mine: it was icy cold. Her eyes flickered and opened a little. She tried to smile.
>
> 'Mon père – est-ce que – je – je – mourrai?' [Father, am I going to die?]
>
> 'Oui, ma mère: le bon Dieu vous appelle. Y'a-t-il quelque chose?' [Yes mother, the good Lord is calling you. Is there anything?]
>
> Haltingly, breathlessly, pausing every little while to struggle against a new surge of pain which tightened the grip on my hand, but brought no cry from her clenched teeth, she made her last Confession.
>
> I gave her Absolution, the last blessing; whispered a few words of encouragement to her, and left her to the watchful care of Sister Celeste who had not stirred from her side since she entered the ward.
>
> 'She is in terrible pain, Father', said Mother Gertrude as I passed her 'we had a little morphine left, but she refused it – told me to give it to the others. She says she would rather offer up her sufferings for the poor Kashmiris, and for those awful men who shot her.'

A few hours later, her last moment came – Father Shanks recorded the scene in lyrical fashion:

> Mother Teresalina died at about 10 that night – a death that must live long in the memories of those who assisted at it. The prayers of the dying nun, gradually fading away as she slowly sank into unconsciousness: the tear-stricken faces, the bloodstained, torn habits of the Sisters kneeling around: the wailing of the babies, ready for food again: the floor with its jumble of refugees: the pallid face of the Rev. Mother, just visible in the outer circle of the light of the hurricane lamp, watching the last moments of her heroic subordinate: the murmur of voices, the frequent ribald chuckle, from the circle of guards: the distant sounds of brawling from the raiders' camps all round: The occasional silhouette of a raider against the moonlit lawn: the red glow of the burning village lighting up the wall behind the dying nun. 'Greater love hath no man than this that a man give up his life for his friend'. We took her body immediately and put it in the private room outside.[16]

It is difficult to imagine Father Shanks hearing or being aware of Sister Teresalina's dying words and not mentioning them in this account. So it seems that while the words ascribed to her may well have been an accurate reflection of the dying nun's sentiment, she didn't give it expression.

Nevertheless, the dying words of a religious martyr do not lose strength because they may not be accurate. They are designed to give force to an existing narrative – and the order's repeated use of Sister Teresalina's story through the 1950s, with at least six tracts or books in English, French and Spanish, was intended not so much to bolster the mission in Kashmir, where mass conversion was never in prospect, as to reinforce the FMM's missionary credentials in taking the gospel to difficult corners of the world in the European countries which provided many of its recruits and much of its finance. This left St Joseph's in Baramulla in a difficult situation – the order, and the wider church, proclaimed the valour and sanctity of its martyr, but given that Kashmir was not easy to reach and never a focus of church activity, few came to the grave and there was no sustained attempt to make a case for the beatification of the Spanish nun.

Among many of those in holy orders in Kashmir, there was a fervent desire to see Sister Teresalina recognised in the same way as the China martyrs. Father Hormise Nirmal Raj, in his account of the Catholic Church in Kashmir written when he served therein the 1970s, said he had been told that when the sisters returned to Baramulla in 1949, they disinterred Sister Teresalina's hastily buried remains so that she could be laid to rest in the plot reserved for women religious. He states that her body was found to be intact, and the carpenter had to make a coffin rather than a small casket to rebury her. Father Nirmal Raj argued that the nun should be 'canonised as the first Martyred saint of the Valley by the Catholic Church. Let us pray to her, that through her mediation the work of beatification may be taken up and [that] it become an occasion of rejoicing for all of us, to see one of our great heroes be honoured by the Church and people in a fitting manner.'[17] Another missionary priest who served in Kashmir for much of the 1990s, the most turbulent period in the separatist insurgency and brutal response to it of the Indian security forces, also harboured hopes that Sister Teresalina would be recognised as a saint. He recounted that in 1992, a number of elderly Muslims in Baramulla reported regularly seeing Sister Teresalina in their dreams. A petition was made to the bishop 'to exhume her body for veneration, in their hope that a devotion to her might deliver them from the scourge of terrorism and violence in the Valley. The Bishop and the local clergy at that time . . . though receptive to the petition, mindful of the repercussion it might lead to from the militant muslims against the Church with an agenda for proselytising, decided to keep quiet over it.' But he reported continuing instances of people in Baramulla receiving favours asked through the intercession of Sister Teresalina in their prayers. 'You must forgive me for having this Catholic outlook to say that God in His Providence and the fulness of time will bring about such a circumstance/situation for her case to be taken up for the cause of beatification and canonisation.'[18] The Jammu–Srinagar diocese appears never to have failed to put its weight behind the beatification of its martyr, but it did in 2004 commission an artist, Felix Thenganakunel Chembery, to undertake a series of paintings reflecting the progress of the church. The most dramatic, with the title 'The Battle Field', is a somewhat naive representation of the tribesmen's attack on St Joseph's and the death of Sister Teresalina.

The sensitivity about seeking converts in an area so overwhelmingly Muslim, and where religion had been an important aspect of the increasing tide of separatism, has been a persistent concern of the church. Father Shanks insisted that, when he was head of St Joseph's school, 'in no cases have these young men . . . emerged from our care as Christians: we have made no attempt to push religion down their throats'. Much more recently a South Indian priest serving in the Kashmir Valley told me that he refused to give out copies of the New Testament, even when specifically requested, to avoid any taint of seeking converts. 'The day we do that,' he said, 'is our last day here.' Allegations of proselytising have dogged the church in Kashmir and the last Mill Hill missionary in Kashmir, Father Jim Borst – who has served there since the early 1960s – has faced repeated threats of expulsion, the most recent in 2011.

Given this sensitivity, the dying words of Sister Teresalina have been both an inspiration and a liability. Both priests and sisters have insisted that the 'conversion' for which the nun sacrificed her life was not from one faith to another, but a conversion of hearts and minds. At one point, the church got around this awkwardness by printing over the account of Sister Teresalina's death in the most widely circulated of its tracts, *I Will be the First*. I have copies in which her dying words have been amended. One word has been printed over, carefully but in a slightly different typeface, making 'I offer myself for the conversion of Kashmir' read as 'I offer myself for the People of Kashmir'. It is startling that the dying words can be subject to modification in this manner, though in the volatile political climate of Kashmir it's easy to understand why the church might regard this as circumspect. What's perhaps as surprising is that the church wished to continue to proclaim Sister Teresalina rather than simply withdraw altogether a pamphlet in which her dying words might imperil its continuing mission in Kashmir. The remarks by Sister Josephine at the memorial services 70 years on – albeit to a small audience – indicate that the church is clear in its belief that their martyr sought the conversion of Kashmir.

At the 70th anniversary, 13 FMM sisters served at Baramulla, all Indian (the last European nun, Sister Emilia, died in 2004 and is buried next to Sister Teresalina); four Carmelite nuns and two priests, again all Indian, were based at the adjoining school. None of the nuns were from Kashmir and they are not aware of any Kashmiri who has become a woman religious. Two of the sisters at St Joseph's are doctors and several others have nursing and pharmacist qualifications. The hospital remains open, and the baby ward where the survivors of the 1947 attack were held captive has a marble slab inset into the floor inscribed: 'Sr Teresalina was martyred at this spot in 1947.' The mission has raised money for new buildings but feels denuded of patients, partly as a consequence of competition from a nearby government hospital. The main focus of the mission is its training institute for nurses. In October 2017, 67 young women were in training – three of them Catholics, the overwhelming majority from local Muslim families.

Among those attending the memorial events, Sister Taurina Vaz, the provincial head of the FMM, recalled how at the Catholic school she attended in Mumbai the head teacher, an Irish nun, encouraged her to read *I Will be the First*. She was 12 or 13 at the time and devoured the tract eagerly – she regards learning about the example of Sister Teresalina as the first step on her religious vocation. 'That's where the inspiration began that I too wanted to be a missionary. That's how God worked in my life.' The nuns at Baramulla continue to hope that Sister Teresalina will be beatified, though they admit it seems unlikely and complain that they haven't the resources to make the detailed and documented case which the church would require. They also seek her intercession. 'A few of our sisters and myself personally pray through her for protection,' one told me, 'and her prayers are answered.' In this version of the Baramulla story, Sister Teresalina's martyrdom serves to guard the mission of which she was part against succumbing once more to the geopolitical battle for Kashmir. There have been occasions when the nuns have feared for their safety, and spent the entire night in prayer seeking to forestall any repeat attack on the mission.

For more than 70 years, Sister Teresalina's fate and the wider tragedy that befell St Joseph's has fed into multiple narratives, religious, political and literary. A foreign life lost has attracted more attention than the tens of thousands of Kashmiris who have been killed in decades of conflict. Among that casualty toll are many who would be described or regarded as martyrs: those who were shot down by the maharajah's forces in the early stages of Kashmir's political awakening; those who were killed 70 years ago by the invading tribesmen; those who have lost their lives in the fight against Indian rule; those in India's security forces who have died combating the separatist insurgency or while guarding the line of control. The concept of martyrdom has become so universal that it has lost some of its force. For the Catholic church, Sister Teresalina is exceptional – for Kashmiris, she is anything but unique. The spiritual example that she offers is complicated by the geopolitical conflict in which her death, and her memorialisation, are entwined and the political parable is made less compelling because she is one among so many martyrs.

Notes

1 I would like to record my appreciation to the nuns of St Joseph's for their warm and generous hospitality during my stay in Baramulla in October 2017. An account of the memorial services is available online: www.bbc.co.uk/news/stories-41996612, accessed February 5, 2020. In earlier visits to the mission, I met and interviewed Sister Emilia, an Italian nun who was the last survivor at the convent of the 1947 attack. This chapter has been informed by conversations with several of the sisters at Baramulla and with other members of the Franciscan Missionaries of Mary.
2 The words of Father Thomas McLaughlin, superior general of the Mill Hill Missionaries, while visiting Kashmir in 1960, cited in Father Hormise Nirmal Raj's unpublished work written in 1976, 'Unknown Churches, Unknown Martyrs' f.96. Father Nirmal Raj went on to comment on the paucity of conversions: 'One may say nil in Kashmir, and few in Jammu.' A copy of this typescript is held in the archives of the Mill Hill Missionaries.
3 This extract from the records of the Franciscan Missionaries of Mary was made available to me by Sister Sheila O'Neill, who at the time was researching the history of the order in South Asia.
4 From documents made available to me by Sister Sheila O'Neill, FMM.

5 In a remarkable confirmation of the flow of loot and abducted women back to the tribal regions, a BBC journalist, M. Ilyas Khan, gathered testimony 70 years later of some of those in Pakistan with memories of the invasion: www.bbc.co.uk/news/world-asia-41662588, accessed February 5, 2020. Powerful Kashmiri testimony of the invasion is contained in Asad (2010, passim).

6 Father Shanks reported privately in a letter to the Very Rev T. McLaughlin on November 14, 1947, held in the archives of the Mill Hill Missionaries: 'there was always the constant fear that they [the attackers] would run true to type and interfere with the womenfolk. That was attempted only on one occasion, thank God, and was interrupted quite providentially.' It is possible, however, that Father Shanks was referring simply to the days spent captive in the hospital ward rather than the initial attack.

7 Sydney Smith's news reports appeared in the *Daily Express* on November 10 and 11, 1947, headlined 'Captive Reporter Sees Bus Invasion' and 'Ten Days of Terror'.

8 India Office Records (IOR), LP&S/13/1850, ff20, 76, British Library.

9 'Note on St Joseph's Convent and Hospital at Baramulla', November 27, 1947 – IOR, LP&S/13/1850, f.36. Major Cranston visited the Baramulla mission, in the company of another army officer and two medical missionaries, on November 13 and 16.

10 *New York Times*, November 11, 1947. All three children of Tom and Biddy Dykes, then aged five, two and two weeks, survived the attack. Two of them were present at the services at St Joseph's 70 years after their parents' deaths.

11 *Statesman*, November 7, 1947.

12 Tom and Biddy Dykes were not on holiday at Baramulla – she had gone to the mission hospital to give birth to her third child.

13 *Times of India*, April 13, 1957.

14 Sister Teresalina was born Joaquina Zubiri. Although now known within the order and described on her gravestone as Sister Teresalina, in earlier clerical publications she is often described as Mother Mary Teresalina. She was sent to Baramulla as assistant superior and would have had some authority over the other sisters.

15 An earlier and broadly similar account of Sister Teresalina's death had been published in English by the FMM as 'Even Unto Death'.

16 Father George Shanks's manuscript account of the raids in Baramulla in October 1947, written in 1953 and held in the archives of the Mill Hill Missionaries. In the extracts quoted, punctuation and abbreviations have been standardised. With the archivist's permission, this account has been transcribed and posted online here: www.andrewwhitehead.net/father-shankss-kashmir-diary.html, accessed February 5, 2020.

17 Nirmal Raj, 'Unknown Churches, Unknown Martyrs', f.92.

18 Personal communication, November 2001.

References

Abdullah, Sheikh Mohammed. 1951. *Jammu and Kashmir Constituent Assembly: Opening Address*, Srinagar: Constituent Assembly Secretariat.

Asad, Mohammad Saeed (editor). 2010. *Wounded Memories of the Tribal Attack on Kashmir*, Mirpur: National Institute of Kashmir Studies.

Bates, H.E. 1950. *The Scarlet Sword*, London: Cassell.

Bourke-White, Margaret. 1949. *Halfway to Freedom: A Report on the New India*, New York: Simon and Schuster.

Collins, Larry and Lapierre, Dominique. 1957. *Freedom at Midnight*, London: Collins.

Franciscan Missionaries of Mary, 1957. *I will Be the First: The Story of Mother Mary Teresalina*. London: Franciscan Missionaries of Mary.

Franciscan Missionaries of Mary, 1956. *Jusqu'a la Mor.* London: Franciscan Missionaries of Mary.

Mufti, Gulza. 2013. *Kashmir in Sickness and in Health*, New Delhi: Partridge.

Omaechevarria, Father Ignacio. 1949. *Una Victima Perfecta*, Vitoria: Editorials Catolica.

Stephens, Ian. 1953. *Horned Moon: An Account of a Journey Through Pakistan, Kashmir, and Afghanistan*, London: Chatto & Windus.

Stephens, Ian. 1963. *Pakistan*, New York: Ernest Benn.

White Paper on Jammu & Kashmir. 1948. New Delhi: Government of India.

Whitehead, Andrew. 2007. *A Mission in Kashmir*, New Delhi: Viking Penguin.

Whitehead, Andrew. 2019. *The Lives of Freda: The Political, Spiritual and Personal Journeys of Freda Bedi*, New Delhi: Speaking Tiger.

11

DISPERSED RESISTANCE

When art is the weapon

Zehra Abrar and Namitha George

Amarnath land row in 2008 'breathed new life into the Valley's demands for Azadi' (Tremblay, 2009, 924) and consequently, Kashmir saw a massive uprising and a shutdown for several months. You couldn't go to schools, colleges, workplaces and let alone to places you like. It felt like you were incarcerated inside your homes. I remember of a time when the situation was improving, one could just go out very early in the mornings before the curfew even started. I used to take coaching classes for my medical course. One day while coming back home, I had to walk for 5 kms because of unavailability of public transport and otherwise too, authorities did not let people use their vehicles. The fear of walking home alone was so overwhelming that I didn't want to step out of the classroom. Outside the class, the roads were desolate, screaming that I am born in conflict and this is what I should get used to. Nevertheless, with fear comes the strength to resist the oppression. I began my walk of resistance, defying the rules of curfew with strength, which I believe came from the conflict itself. Barbed wires and men in uniform at every 500 meters is frightening but I was determined to confront them. They did obstruct me at almost every blockade with questions as to why I am on the street regardless of their directions. My answers were direct and determined: to acquire knowledge.

Zehra[1] recalls

Every person who lives in Kashmir expresses resistance every single day; be it spoken, silent or violent. As Malik says, 'the target attacks by militants, reprisal by the government and security forces, search operations, disappearances, and call for strikes, fake encounters have become a part of the daily life of a Kashmiri' (Malik, 2015, 409). With the killing of Burhan Wani, the localized 'poster boy' of militancy in Kashmir, 'modes of resistance by common people against the human right violations, in turn, have acquired different forms' (Malik, 2015, 409). One mode was where the youth of Kashmir, be it marginalized, educated or other, joined the militant outfits (while alive, Burhan Wani was able to recruit almost 30 youths from South Kashmir).

Another faction who acknowledge, as Malik says, 'futility and brutality associated with overt resistance' resorted to 'subtle' ways of resistance (Malik, 2015, 413). These subtle forms of resistance are mostly inspired by some form of art. The youth of Kashmir is increasingly using art to protest oppression – in music, poetry, graffiti, paintings, or photography (Dhar, 2018). In addition, the experiences of people in the face of conflict are vividly explained by the earlier writings of Mirza Waheed (novelist and the author of *The Collaborator*), Basharat Peer (journalist), the late Agha Shahid Ali (Kashmiri-American poet whose renowned collections include *A Walk Through the Yellow Pages, The Half-Inch Himalayas, A Nostalgist's Map of America, The Country Without a Post Office, Rooms Are Never Finished*).

Art provides Kashmiris 'a sense of solidarity in terms of the shared experiences they have had and binds them in a community of the suffered and deprived' (Malik, 2015, 413) and acts as 'collective effervescence'. While for Durkheim, collective effervescence 'refers to moments in societal life when the group of individuals that makes up a society comes together in order to perform a religious ritual' (Carls, 1995), we use this concept to imply rituals of any form which make individuals come together, not limited to poetry but to all forms of artistic expression.

This chapter looks at photography as an art giving voice to everyday resistance. Focusing on four pictures, we speak to the use of photography as a weapon of resistance. We attempt to unravel the discourses in which Kashmiris are breaking the boundaries within themselves to stand against a much bigger threat, a threat to their freedom. The idea behind utilizing four photographs from four different people is to unpack, step by step, the components of class, gender, demographics and finally some boundaries that cannot be broken. Although individual photographers, whether they are students in government schools or private schools, or among those already in universities, living in the up-market, residential areas of the capital city Srinagar, or growing up in its older areas or remote rural districts, may be divided in their aspirations, it is their eventual prayer for peace in their homeland which unites them. Even though the photographers chosen in this study come from varied backgrounds – different age groups, social classes, and localities – their contribution towards the resistance makes them kin. The multiple intersections of class, locality and gender make them portray the resistance in their photography in different ways, yet they all maintain the political impetus of resistance – *azadi*.

Photography as dispersed resistance

Resistance can be defined as an act challenging dominant representations of a social reality and artistically articulating counter-discourses. It is a 'social and individual phenomenon, a constructive process that articulates continuity and change and as an act oriented towards an imagined future of different communities' (Awad et al., 2017, 161). It is also an expansive concept that encompasses activities that are organized, violent and visible as well as unorganized, non-violent and latent. Addressing resistance practices that fall between the two extremes of the resistance spectrum, Lilja and Vinthagen propose the concept of dispersed resistance. It constitutes unorganized practices of resistance performed by one or few individuals which might be 'every day and subtle or loud and extraordinary' (2018, 212). For them, it 'could either be of a subtle and everyday character or have a more glaring appearance' (Lilja and Vinthagen, 2018, 216).

Practices of dispersed resistance are positioned between the categories of social movements and 'everyday resistance' (Scott, 1985, 1989, 1990). Those engaging in dispersed resistance do not belong to an organized group but act in a scattered manner. Their acts of resistance, however, can motivate similar acts, which can escalate to large-scale organized resistance. Freelance resistance photography aptly fits into the category of dispersed resistance: it can be both subtle and extraordinary in nature.

The concept of resistance is closely intertwined with the concept of power. It is 'a response to power from below' (Lilja and Vinthagen, 2018, 215). Dispersed resistance may thus take two different forms, depending on the kind of power being resisted. First, it may act as counter-repressive resistance against repressive power in Foucault's sense of 'legal sovereign power', which is closely related to 'bio-power' that uses legality to legitimize coercion (Foucault, 1978). In Kashmir, resistance photography can be understood as a practice of counter-repressive resistance against the state-imposed Armed Forces Special Powers Act (AFSPA) in the region – an emergency measure which grants armed forces special powers and impunity to combat security issues like militancy and insurgency in the imposed regions. Second, the productive practice of resistance can be performed against discursive power. It engages in meaning-making against the prevalent hegemonic discourses. Here, power is conceptualized in terms of its ability to create subjectivities, narratives and identities. In the case of Kashmir, the coercive framework of AFSPA is justified by the state as a necessity to combat security issues such as insurgency and cross-border terrorism and as a means to establish peace in the region. The resistance photography displays AFSPA as a security apparatus of the state but throws light on the injustice and fear perpetrated by AFSPA in the lives of the people of Kashmir. It breaks the meaning attached to the state's discourse of its actions as 'just' to a counter reality of injustice perpetrated by the state. Therefore, it attaches a different meaning to the discourse established by the state. Thus, resistance photography can be understood in the light of both counter-repressive resistance and productive or discursive resistance.

Photographs not only depict the resistance of the subject but also of the photographer (Dean, 2015, 194). Miller Bianucci notes, 'the power of photography endures . . . it continues to have a unique capacity to reinforce or subvert power' as the pictures used in the chapter validate (Bianucci and Cole, 2004). Similarly, as Suvir Kaul points out eloquently in his book, *Of Gardens and Graves: Kashmir, Poetry, Politics*, pictures convey stories.

> The tone of the photograph is uncannily like the tone of the stories: the roar of the blast is muted into the visual whoosh of debris flying high, with the quiet, understated certainty of death. Pictures and poetry, stories and songs – who could have known that two decades of violence could have made these

the weapons of the weak? And then there are other pictures that are as inspiring: masses of men, and of women, mobilized into processions, surging forward, arms in the air and mouths open with slogans, storming into a future that holds few promises except for the certainty of more pain (Kaul, 2015, 47).

The boundless articulation of resistance through various forms of art is increasingly being addressed today (LeVine, 2015; Awad and Wagoner, 2017; Sue, 1989; Jonson and Erofeev, 2018). However, in the scholarship on 'resistance art', photography remains underexplored as a relevant resistance art. In this chapter, we explore 'resistance photography' as a practice of resistance in terms of its both self-reflexivity and its expression of the collective trauma of the repressed society. Thus, we suggest that photographs are to be interpreted as a representation of the photographer's 'self' – the personal experiences and perspectives. These are also to be examined as a representation of the collective climate of resistance, resonating with individuals who share similar narratives and perspectives. Within this context, resistance photography is a form of 'dispersed resistance' (Lilja and Vinthagen, 2018, 211). Dispersed resistance refers to practices of resistance that can be both subtle and clamorous. A small sample of photographers we have selected for this chapter is a solid example of the dispersed resistance. In the first place, they are not explicitly a part of any organized resistance. Second, they capture both everyday lives and organized resistance. Third, they use different platforms to disseminate their photographs such as social media, online news portals, and private communities (among friends and family). Finally, they identify themselves as part of the broader cause of resistance by using photography as a powerful medium of resistance.

In the digital era where digital transformation has become global, photography has emerged as a powerful means of communication with a universal reach cutting across cultural barriers. Conceptualizing photographs, Barthes argues that photographs can be distinguished from other forms of pictorial arts as they capture the closest representation of the object (Goran, 1989, 40). He further highlights three distinct characteristics of photography: 1) it is not dictated by any rules or artistic conventions; 2) it cannot alter the details of the object it captures; and 3) it can be engaged in by anyone irrespective of any formal training. These three qualities show the ease with which ordinary citizens can express their everyday resistance through photography, allowing its global circulation through the internet and social media. Drawing from Barthes, Bate distinguishes between the notion of 'denotation' and 'connotation' represented in an image[2] (Mitchell, 1984, 505). He points out, 'a denotation is what we see, what can be described as simply there in the picture. Connotation is the immediate cultural meaning derived from what is seen but is not actually in the picture' (Bate, 2009, 17).

As mentioned earlier, resistance photography can embody connotation at an individual level and a collective level. Though primarily the photograph is a representation of the photographer's individual experiences and perspective on the object, it can connote a different meaning from individual to individual with respect to their own experiences and perspectives. On a collective level, resistance photographs can inspire a 'collective meaning' within a group of individuals who share similar experiences and perspectives. When resistance photographs get circulated, it can create a virtual network of resistance consisting of individuals who identify with a similar cultural connotation of the image. Thus, resistance photography can influence a climate of resistance within a social and cultural context. In the same vein, Awad and Wagoner, who primarily focus on 'graffiti art' as a form of resistance, argue, 'the interpretation of images is part of a social process' (2017, 6) which can motivate collective action. They also characterize images in terms of their symbolic, dialogical, contextual and transformative character.

Though photographs are produced through automation, the agency of the photographer is paramount in the meaning-making and discourse attached to the photograph. Agency shows how the subject perceives herself or himself from within through a process of self-reflection and it displays the 'possibility of resistance towards the pressure of hegemonic discourses' (Lilja and Vinthagen, 2018, 214). It can also be viewed in the context of power relations, in terms of how the subject positions herself/himself and how it translates through her or his photographs. The representation of an individual's subjectivities through resistance photography can also be understood in terms of Foucault's perspective of creating subjectivity through 'technologies of the self' (Foucault, 1988), that is, personal practices such as diaries, confessions, etc. These are practices that contain an extension of one's own subjectivities. We argue that resistance photography can be categorized as a 'technology of the self', as the practice of photography engages in the manifestation of the photographer's subjective positioning and representation of personal experiences and narratives.

The photograph is primarily the articulation of the photographer's narratives and perspectives. However, the process of meaning-making in resistance photographs is not restricted to the agency of the photographer. In this regard, Awad and Wagoner introduce a tripartite framework explaining the exercise of agency by three social actors in the social life of images – producers, audience and the authority (Awad and Wagoner, 2017, 7). Producers are the creators of an image, such as photographers, graffiti artists, caricaturists, etc. The audience are those who come in contact with the image. The circulation of the image exercises its own agency. What is significant here is the interpretation of the image by the observer/s and their choices in destroying or continuing its circulation. For instance, an audience can both contain the circulation of a photograph and continue its circulation by passing it on to others. The 'authority' refers to the government and local authorities that can control the social life of an image, restricting its circulation through censorship. The audience can also exert authority in both the choice they make to contain or continue the circulation of the image and in the meaning they attach to the photograph while forwarding it on. The photographs can also be used by the authority to project a false reality against the original meaning attached to it by the photographer. Thus, manipulation of the meaning attached to resistance photographs by both the authority and the audience is a serious issue, which can control the social life and effectiveness of resistance photographs.

This brings us to another fundamental feature of resistance photography, namely 'indexicality'[3] that refers to the dependency of 'meaning' to the 'context' (Indexicals,

2001). The meaning attached to the photograph depends profoundly on various contextual factors. It includes socio-political, cultural and historical contexts which influence the production, circulation and effectiveness of the photograph. For example, the time (or circumstance) in which the photograph was taken, the identity of the photographer, the photographer's perspectives and experiences related to the circumstance, socio-political conditions, etc. Art especially, emerges as an important tool for ventilation in social contexts wherein the scope for organized resistance is limited by the presence of a powerful repressive power. In such repressed social and cultural setting, as LeVine asserts, 'art serves as both a vehicle and creates space for subcultures to become countercultures-how groups of (usually) marginalized young people, drawn together by common cultural tastes and performances, gradually articulate a powerful oppositional political vision that challenge authorities state power' (Levine, 2015, 1277). In a broader sense, photography contributes towards the process of culture-making through the discourse it creates. As Raphael argues from a visual sociology perspective, 'photography is a means through which a given truth about a given culture is made intelligible' (Raphael, 2018, 296).

Resistance photography captures moments and narratives that challenge dominant discourses, displaying counter realities. Upon circulation, it contributes towards creating a connection between individuals who undergo similar experiences and trauma. Resistance art mobilizes the marginalized through effectively emoting sentiments of oppression and injustice. By the virtue of a globalized world, its circulation can extend beyond the targeted audience to a global audience, particularly aided by the internet and social media. It can potentially increase the momentum of resistance and can escalate to organized resistance. The intensification of resistance can be profoundly attributed to the 'affectiveness' of resistance forms of art. It passively unites individuals engaging in similar practices of resistance. For instance, an attack against an artist often leads to the mobilization of fellow artists which eventually can escalate the resistance and be identified with an organized resistance movement. It is facilitated through 'passive networks' (Lilja and Vinthagen, 2018, 218) of individuals who are dispersed but remain passively connected by the virtue of the similar ways of resistance. So, these passive networks can emerge into a collective effort to demand justice and rights against an authority (mostly the state). In addition, 'affects' translated in resistance photographs are intensified through circulation in networks, in turn intensifying the climate of resistance.

Barbed aspirations

> The mourning has lost its value. We all want to end it, we all want to be free. We just don't know how to.
>
> *Harris Zargar*

Not many people want to leave their comfort zone and capture the everyday tales of visible, overt tyranny. Therefore, they discover oppression in seemingly small things such as barbed wires. In Kashmir, privilege means keeping your loved ones out of the mainstream resistance. Coming from the family of businesspersons, Harris Zargar, an engineering student identifies himself as someone who uses photography to feel tranquility. His interest in photography had developed at a very early age and it is synonymous to 'escape' for him. An escape from the persisting conflict and a way to feel free. He deliberates that, 'the conflict has been there for such a long time that people have adapted themselves to live with it'.[4]

He considers people like him and his friends as fortunate. They have never been through any of the confrontations as have those who take up arms or resort to stone pelting, yet he feels part of the movement and finds art as a medium to display his resistance. According to him, those who pick up arms 'do not want to do it' but instead 'they are forced to by circumstances'. They take up arms as a last resort as they have either been tortured, or lost their loved ones in the conflict, or the surroundings make them resilient to the fear of losing their own lives. His perspective from very close to the sidelines paints an authentic true picture of resistance.

From capturing beautiful daffodils to portraying serene Dal Lake, his interests mainly lie in landscapes; he has an eye for beautiful things and he ensnares them creatively into his photographic device. Resistance has various meanings and for Harris, it is, 'something that saved this city from being completely destroyed . . . If it wouldn't have been for these individual practices from everyone, I don't know how much worse would have happened.' The picture (Figure 11.1), unlike his other

FIGURE 11.1 Barbed wires depicting the conflict in the beautiful valley of Kashmir.

Source: Image courtesy Harris Zargar[5]

photographs, is unique, as it not only signifies the beauty of mountains and the lakes but also the barbaric shadow of oppression. The picture reconstructs the notion of exquisiteness as entangled with conflict. Even though Kashmir is conflicted and always consumed in clashes, still the beauty of its landscapes reminds the people how peaceful it can be.

This picture plays in the politics of solidarity where the author through his photograph wants to contribute to the resistance of those protesting blatantly, even if it is not much. The photograph acts as a perfect medium to depict how subaltern demonstrates resistance by exercising power over space. One click and a picture uploaded on the internet occupies space without borders. It becomes a symbol of resistance internationally; as Johansson and Vinthagen say, 'the international community is constructed as a target as well, relative to whose interpretative horizon all acts of resistance should be scripted' (Johansson and Vinthagen, 2015, 119). That is what most Kashmiris want – their voices to be heard.

Veiled – coming out of the veil

> No picture is worth your life.
>
> *Faisal Khan*

Faisal Khan was born before the era of extreme militancy in Kashmir. Photography for him started as a hobby and transformed into a career on which his livelihood rests. Currently, he works with a local run newspaper and has a contract with the government-owned Turkish agency for which he is a photographer. He believes journalism in Kashmir is a struggle due to the conflict as well as the very limited earnings it provides. Therefore, most of his friends and colleagues changed their professions and found employment in banks, and other government institutions. However, there remains a large number of youth who pursue journalism because they doubt the mainstream national media's portrayal of Kashmir conflict, and the international journalists fail to be adequately effective.

Many of the photographers seek press affiliation because it has two benefits. It helps them to cover all forms of overt resistance practices and gives security to the individual. Despite these privileges, one is still not allowed to cover each and every aspect of the conflict because of the unjustified, often arbitrary will of the security forces. Faisal recalls that he wasn't allowed to cover some incidents because of his appearance: 'my beard always makes me susceptible to security forces, and they question me more even after I show them my press ID (identification card).'[6]

Gradually, the conditions are getting worse for those in this field. One of his colleagues is on trial facing a charge of harbouring militants, following the story he wrote on Burhan Wani in 2016 (Naseem 2018).[7] On another occasion, a friend who is also a photojournalist partially lost his eyesight as police forces fired well-aimed pellets at him and other journalists.[8] Incidents like these, as Faisal educes, compel you to think thrice before one publishes stories or broadcasts the photographs as 'no picture is worth your life'. Moreover, he feels 'there is continuous monitoring by the Indian agencies on some people and I am among them' considering that his pictures have been blocked on social networking sites time and again. This fear of continuous surveillance is used as a tool of counter-resistance by the authorities to deter people from reporting the happenings in Kashmir. Faisal persists, believing that even if his pictures don't get published when he clicks, they will be there in the archives and surface whenever the time is right: they will be part of history, someday. He understands the pros and cons of working as a journalist in Kashmir, but he has invested so much in it that no amount of uncertainty can lead him to abandon his profession.

In April of 2017, there were protests by students of a degree college in Pulwama. As a result, many students were injured and almost 15 students were rushed to the nearby hospital. This one incident sparked mass protests all around the Kashmir Valley and for the first time since 1989, women were on the streets throwing stones along with their male counterparts. Women have always contributed to the resistance in the form of singing songs lauding militants but not of this nature. This time resistance was used by women to emerge from the gender specialization imposed on them by culture and religion (Johansson and Vinthagen, 2016, 425, 426). Figure 11.2 not only expresses resistance to the power of the oppressor but also from the shackles of culture and religion, which provides for separate spaces for men and women. These girls were on the streets protesting in the space of the other gender,

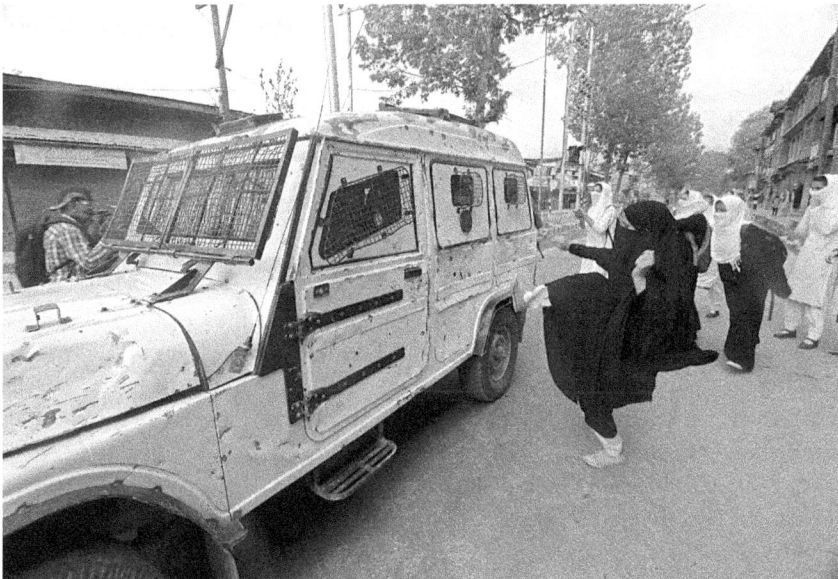

FIGURE 11.2 An angry girl protesting in Srinagar in solidarity with other students who were harmed by security forces in Pulwama.

Source: Image courtesy Faisal Khan[9]

resisting the religious practices to the degree it allows them to participate in outside space designated for them. Here the resistance was against the political, religious and cultural power.

Azaadi and Azadari[10]

> Even the policeman by day becomes a civilian by night who will be frisked by security forces . . . occupation is for everyone.
>
> *Syed Shahriyar*

An independent photojournalist, Syed Shahriyar belongs to a Shia-populated area of Srinagar. His pro-freedom ideology is reflected through the legacy of his grandfather, Akbar Jaipuri. Jaipuri was a revolutionary Urdu poet whose timeless poetry 'Maaro ya Marjao' (kill or get killed) is chanted at the funerals of militants and at pro-freedom protests alike. Inspired by his grandfather, he was initially entranced by the idea of writing. The uprising of 2008 (Amarnath land row) compelled him to keep a scrapbook but unlike other children, his scrapbook was filled with pictures of people killed in that uprising. He named it 'Kashmiri Intifada' bringing an analogy between the struggle in Kashmir and Palestine, reviving the solidarity which Kashmiris feel towards oppressed Palestinians. The killing of a childhood friend, Tufail Mattoo (in 2010, 17-year-old Tufail Mattoo died after being hit on the head by a tear gas cannister), finally led him to follow journalism as his choice of career so that he could voice what was happening in the valley. He used to take part in the stone pelting but after he joined his journalism course, he was more inclined towards taking pictures of protests. He thinks, 'if you want your struggle to reach a bigger audience, you need to do things differently'. He has been freelancing since then and his pictures have been featured in *VICE*, *TIME*, Le Monde, Radio France International, *The Quint*, and Catch News. With all this fame, he believes comes the responsibility to portray the things as they are and not change the narrative according to the whims of those who publish your work.

On the professional front, Syed Shahriyar reveals that common people, as well as the army, have issues with journalists. People mistrust them especially if they have been talking to the police and will sometimes end up abusing, hurting and threatening the photographers or journalists. They see them as agents of the other side. On the other hand, security forces clearly dislike them, and are suspicious of them simply because they are Kashmiris. As a journalist, Syed Shahriyar has had to hide his profession from security forces as he can be subjected to violence for just doing his job. He has encountered incidents such as when army personnel have destroyed his equipment while he was going to cover a funeral procession.

Moreover, even if the intention behind the resistance is the same, belonging to a particular community can make a difference. The perception among the new generation has changed regarding the Shia community's aspirations as somewhat separate from the rest of the Muslim population. Being associated with the Shia community of Kashmir, Shahriyar contemplates 'there are times when you feel intimidated in your professional community'.[11] He manages to highlight through his photography that the purpose of Kashmiri resistance is the same for dissimilar groups regardless of their diverse beliefs and affiliations. He finds it his responsibility, as a member of the Shia community, to illustrate solidarity in belief for *azaadi through azadari* and to counter the state-backed narrative.

The narrative of the state is being changed by the new generation of Shia and they are using the battle of Karbala (in which Husayn, whom the Shia consider the legitimate heir to the Prophet Muhammad, was killed, precipitating the Sunni–Shia chism) as a model to understand the resistance in Kashmir. The processions of (the month of) Muharram, memorializing Karbala, are used as a medium to voice the resistance movement and put forward the notion that an oppressed Kashmiri and a Shia is the same person. Figure 11.3 demonstrates how the minority religious sect (i.e., Shia Muslims) are often perceived to be on the other side (those who do not support the resistance movement) of the resistance movement and show their allegiance to their fellow Kashmiris. The religious identity is used to supplement the political narrative which in turn helps them establish an equal position in the struggle. 'In the same way as there are a multiplicity of power relations played out on the grounds of ethnicity, class, age, sexuality as well as functionality and religion, there is a multiplicity of resistance relations as well' (Johansson and Vinthagen, 2015, 112) as faced by the minority religion in the valley. The quote on the banner followed by the picture of a pellet victim opens the discourse that religion acts as an agent in resistance in the everyday life of people in Kashmir. Furthermore, Shahriyar's photograph aptly represents how the youth are bridging the disparity between the Sunni and Shia community thereby demonstrating their collective resistance.

Lifeless memories

> Our work is jihad (struggle). What you do through publishing one picture is far greater than emptying a magazine full of bullets.
>
> *Vikar Syed*

Vikar Syed, a multimedia editor at a digital magazine and freelance journalist for national and international agencies, hails from a village 20 km away from the district of Pulwama. His parents being government employees wanted him to be a medical professional. However, he had entirely different interests. The age-old black and white camera of his grandfather used to fascinate him. Like many village boys, his dream was to do something great and receive recognition. His idea of great achievement was getting his love for photography acknowledged. Since then he has adopted photography as his profession, his passion and a way to remain sane in the conflict and oppression around him. Moreover, his profession and his affiliation to an agency make him take risks which would deter an ordinary civilian.

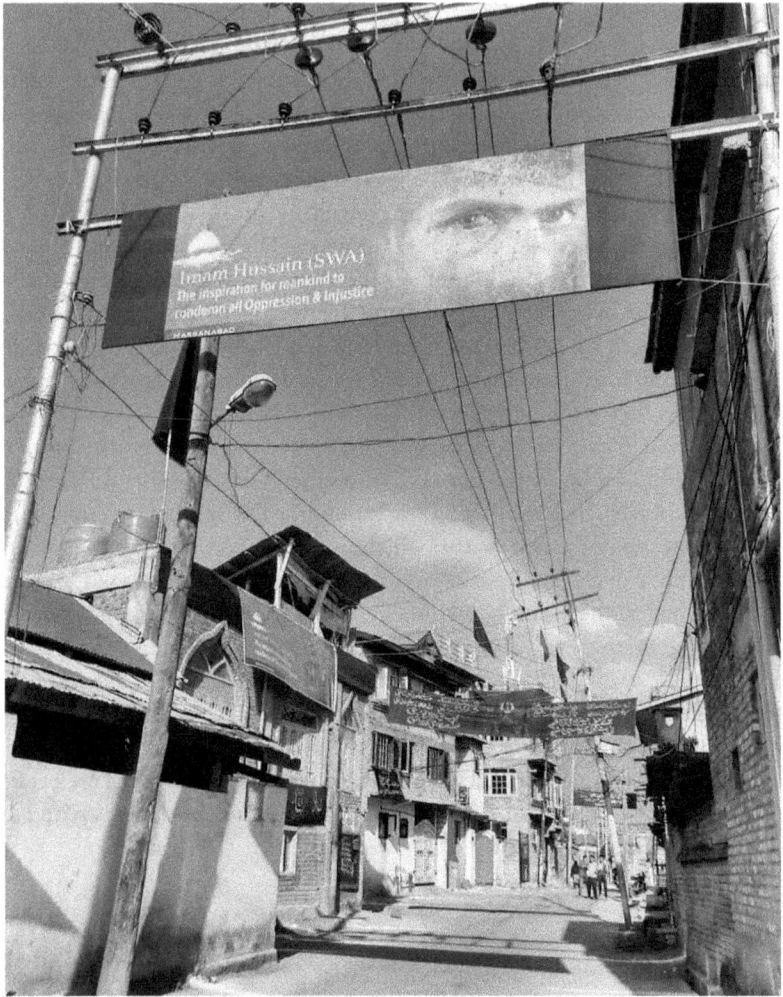

FIGURE 11.3 A Muharram banner hoisted at the entrance of a Shia locality which reads 'Imam Hussain (as), the inspiration to mankind to condemn all oppression and injustice' and besides it is a picture of a pellet victim.

Source: Image courtesy Syed Shahriyar[12]

In South Kashmir, where most of the youth are enticed by the idea of joining the militancy, Vikar believes 'publishing one picture is much more significant than emptying the whole gun magazine'.[13] A picture influences more than violence. He did not deny that the thought of picking up the arms had crossed his mind because he comes from a place where the comfort and peace of his home has been disturbed almost every day. Nevertheless, he keeps reminding himself that the power of photography is profound, and his photography can give voice to many more. He thinks youth in the outskirts of Kashmir are more inclined to militancy, 'they all seem to be militants but without guns'. In contrast, whenever he visits the city of Srinagar itself with its culture that is a world apart from that of other parts of the valley, he realizes why people in his hometown are so ready to take up arms. For their part, the youth in Srinagar have a café culture, they can get out of their houses whenever they want and are not subjected to curfews and shut-downs as much as in the outskirts.

Locality influences the tactics of resistance one uses. For the people of South Kashmir, the day-to-day killings and the more limited options for channelling their frustration make them vulnerable to overt forms of resistance. To guide them better, he has started pro bono photography workshops in his village and many young people, who used to participate in stone pelting, are now channeling their anger into the positive art of photography.

Vikar's work is mostly conflict-based. His photography is a narrative of every person who is a victim and has suffered at the hands of tyranny. At the beginning of his career, he mostly covered funerals of militants but now thinks that funerals do not reveal the emotions as closely as picturing the belongings of the dead. Therefore, he visits the households of victims of oppression, be it students, militants, or those disabled by the conflict. During the 2017 parliamentary by-elections, the usual clashes in Kashmir took the life of a 13-year-old. A cricket enthusiast, Faizan was killed while coming back from his tuition centre. What is left behind are his

FIGURE 11.4 Folded uniform of 13-year-old school-going Faizaan who was killed in cross fire while coming back from his study center.

Source: Image courtesy Vikar Syed[14]

memories that make his parents question those who say only protesters or militants get killed. Picturing the memories of the victims is not a simple act but a whole process; as he states, 'you have to gain the trust of the family to click a picture of the belongings of their now lost, loved ones'. He goes on to describe the process, 'until and unless they repose have faith in you, no one will let you take the pictures ... it is 20 minutes of meaningful conversation before you take out your camera'.

The folded uniform in Figure 11.4 was an expression of everyday life for the boy who according to Vikar, 'has left, never to come back'. The picture depicts lifelessness. The absence of colour signifies oppression, sadness and most importantly, emptiness. Moreover, photographing the belongings of a dead person voices the narrative of several actors who are somehow related to the subject: The father who wants the world to know the subjugation faced by him and the community likewise and nevertheless wants the people to continue their resistance; the mother who has lost herself in the process of grieving her son and still believes that she will get justice. The resistance may signify different things for them, but it is exerted against the same power.

Notes

1 Zehra Abrar is a post-insurgency female youth and has grown up in Srinagar.
2 See Mitchell (1984): 'Image' is an umbrella concept which consists of various categories of imagery. Mitchell's classification of images consists of graphic, optical, perceptual, mental and verbal images. According to this classification, photographs are classified as optical images.
3 An indexical is an expression with an unvarying character but may vary in content from context to context. Though broadly 'indexicals' refer to linguistic expressions, the concept is used from a visual sociology point of view wherein the meaning-context dependency in the content of an image (in this case photographs) is emphasised | *Stanford Encyclopedia of Philosophy, Indexicals* (2001).
4 Zargar, Harris. Interview with Zehra Abrar. Personal Interview. May 3, 2019.
5 Sent directly to Zehra Abrar via email with permission to use.
6 Khan, Faisal. Interview with Zehra Abrar. Personal Interview. May 8, 2019.
7 Naseem, I. 'Jailed reporter Asif Sultan gets support from Kashmir's journalist community; father questions conduct of forces 2018, Firstpost', online: www.firstpost.com/india/ jailed-reporter-asif-sultan-gets-support-from-kashmirs-journalist-community-father-questions-conduct-of-forces-5166021.html, accessed February 5, 2020.
8 Kashmir Scenario Desk, 'Zuhaib, PhotoJournalist Narrates Story When He Was Hit by Pellet', online: http://thekashmirscenario.com/zuhaib-photojournalist-narrates-story-when-he-was-hit-by-pellet/.
9 Sent directly to Zehra Abrar via email with permission to use.
10 Azadari means commemorating the dead. For a detailed study, check 'AZĀDĀRĪ – Encyclopaedia Iranica', online: www.iranicaonline.org/articles/azadari, accessed February 5, 2020.
11 Shahriyar, Syed. Interview with Zehra Abrar. Personal Interview. May 1, 2019.
12 Sent directly to Zehra Abrar via email with permission to use.
13 Syed, Vikar. Interview with Zehra Abrar. Personal Interview. May 5, 2019.
14 Sent directly to Zehra Abrar via email with permission to use.

References

Awad, S. H., and Wagoner, B. 2017. *Street Art of Resistance*. Cham, Switzerland: Springer International Publishing.

Awad, S. H., Wagoner, B., and Glaveanu, V. 2017. "The (street) Art of Resistance". In: N. Chaudhary, P. Hviid, G. Marsico, and J. Villadsen, eds. *Resistance in Everyday Life: Constructing Cultural Experiences*. New York: Springer: 161–180.

Bate, D. 2009. *Photography: The Key Concepts*. Oxford: Berg.

Bianucci, M., and Cole, E. 2004. "Looking at Power: The Relevance of Apartheid Photography Today". *Lensculture*. Available at: www.lensculture.com/articles/ernest-cole-looking-at-power-the-relevance-of-apartheid-photography-today [Accessed 29 June 2019].

Calmard, J. 1987. "Azadari". In: *Encyclopaedia Iranica. Iran: Encyclopædia Iranica Foundation*, Vol. III, Fasc. 2. New York: 174–177.

Carls, P. 1995. "Émile Durkheim". *Internet Encyclopedia of Philosophy* (IEP) (ISSN 2161–0002). Available at: www.iep.utm.edu/durkheim/ [Accessed 27 May 2019].

Dean, A. V. 2015. *Framing the Photographer: Discourse and Performance in Portrait Photography* (Doctoral dissertation, Arts & Social Sciences: English).

Desk, K. 2016. "Bandipora Police Vandalize Editor Kashmir Scenario House". *The kashmirscenario.com*. Available at: http://thekashmirscenario.com/bandipora-police-vandalize-editor-kashmir-scenario-house/ [Accessed 7 June 2019].

Dhar, A. 2018. "How the Kashmiris Are Dropping Guns and Using Art, Music, Poetry to Protest". *ED Times | The Youth Blog*. Available at: https://edtimes.in/how-the-kashmiris-are-dropping-guns-and-using-art-music-poetry-to-protest/ [Accessed 4 June 2019].

Foucault, M. 1978. *The History of Sexuality: An Introduction*, Vol. I. New York: Pantheon Books.

Foucault, M., et al. 1988. "Technologies of the Self". In: L. H. Martin, ed. *Technologies of the Self: A Seminar with Michel Foucault*. Amherst: The University of Massachusetts Press: 16–49.

Johansson, A., and Vinthagen, S. 2015. "Dimensions of Everyday Resistance: The Palestinian Sumūd". *Journal of Political Power*, 8(1), 109–139.

Johansson, A., and Vinthagen, S. 2016. "Dimensions of Everyday Resistance: An Analytical Framework". *Critical Sociology*, 42(3), 417–435.

Jonson, Lena, and Erofeev, A. 2018. *Russia: Art Resistance and the Conservative-authoritarian Zeitgeist*. Abingdon, Oxon and New York: Routledge.

Kaul, S. 2015. *Of Gardens and Graves: Essays on Kashmir, Poems in Translation*. Gurgaon: Three Essays Collective.

LeVine, Mark. 2015. "When Art Is the Weapon: Culture and Resistance Confronting Violence in the Post-Uprisings Arab World". *Religions*, 6(4), 1277–1313. Available at: https://doi.org/10.3390/rel6041277.

Lilja, M., and Vinthagen, S. 2018. "Dispersed Resistance: Unpacking the Spectrum and Properties of Glaring and Everyday Resistance". *Journal of Political Power*, 11(2), 211–229.

Malik, A. 2015. "Negotiating Everyday Via the Act of Reading Resistance Poetry: A Study Based on the Analysis of Readership of Poetry by Agha Shahid Ali on Kashmir". *Journal of South Asian Studies*, 3(3), 407–415.

Michael, W. Raphael. 2018. "The Politics of Twilights: Notes on the Semiotics of Horizon Photography". *Visual Studies*, 33(4), 295–312.

Mitchell, W. J. T. 1984. "What Is an Image?" *New Literary History*, 15(3), 503–537.

Naseem, I. 2018. "Jailed Reporter Asif Sultan Gets Support from Kashmir's Journalist Community: Father Questions Conduct of Forces". *Firstpost*. Available at: www.firstpost.com/india/jailed-reporter-asif-sultan-gets-support-from-kashmirs-journalist-community-father-questions-conduct-of-forces-5166021.html [Accessed 17 May 2019].

Scott, J. C. 1985. *Weapons of the Weak: Everyday Forms of Peasant Resistance*. New Haven, CT: Yale University Press.

Scott, J. C. 1989. "Everyday Forms of Resistance". *Copenhagen Papers*, 4, 33–62. doi:10.22439/cjas.v4i1.1765.

Scott, J. C. 1990. *Domination and the Arts of Resistance: Hidden Transcripts*. New Haven, CT: Yale University Press.

Sonesson, Goran. 1989. *Semiotics of Photography- On Tracing the Index*, Part III, Report 4 from the project 'Pictorial meanings in the society of information'. Lund: Department of art History. Available at: http://faculty.georgetown.edu/irvinem/theory/Sonesson-semiot ics_of_Photography.pdf.

Tremblay, Reeta Chowdhari. 2009. "Kashmir's Secessionist Movement Resurfaces: Ethnic Identity, Community Competition, and the State". *Asian Survey*, 49(6), 924–950.

Williamson, Sue. 1989. *Resistance Art in South Africa*. New York: St. Martin's Press.

INDEX

For Product Safety Concerns and Information please contact our EU
representative GPSR@taylorandfrancis.com
Taylor & Francis Verlag GmbH, Kaufingerstraße 24, 80331 München, Germany